War Refugees and the Labour Market

This book addresses the complex socio-economic situation in the Polish-Ukrainian borderland, in the context of the labour market, following Russia's invasion of Ukraine.

War Refugees and the Labour Market: Crisis-Driven Mobility in the Polish-Ukrainian Borderland analyses and assesses the measures which influence the process of Ukrainian war refugee adaptation to the Polish labour market, surveying the engagement of local actors, such as employers, labour market institutions, and non-governmental organisations. It examines the impact of the refugee crisis on this market, as well as the mobilisation of various groups of actors in order to support this specific group of migrants in adapting to life in Poland. The authors argue that this phenomenon of the migration of war refugees confirms the thesis that political instability can be a factor in pushing people abroad as equally important as inequalities in prosperity.

The book identifies the characteristic features of the stream of war refugees from Ukraine as a category of cross-border flows. Before the Russian attack, the influx of Ukrainians to Poland was due mainly to economic pressures, whereas, after the outbreak of war, Ukrainian motivation to cross the border with Poland, as well as the structure of this migration stream, have radically changed. The book offers in-depth insight into the development of borderland regions, especially the cross-border labour market as a specific element of the borderland economic ecosystem. It highlights the positive outcomes of the migration crisis, which will serve as examples of best practices for other regions in Europe.

This book will be of interest to scholars, researchers, and policymakers concerned with regional development, including contact regions, as well as cross-border flows, the labour market, and migration.

Ewa Łaźniewska is Professor in the Department of Business Cycles and Economic Policy, at Poznań University of Economics and Business, Poland.

Joanna Kurowska-Pysz is Professor in the Department of Management at WSB University in Dąbrowa Górnicza, Poland.

Tomasz Górecki is Professor in the Department of Mathematical Statistics and Data Analysis, Faculty of Mathematics and Computer Science at Adam Mickiewicz University, Poznań, Poland.

Khrystyna Prytula is Associate Professor, Dr.Sci. (Econ.), Head of Cross-Border Cooperation Sector, Dolishniy Institute of Regional Research of National Academy of Sciences of Ukraine, Lviv, Ukraine.

Klaudia Plac is Assistant Professor in the Department of Strategic and Regional Studies, University of Economics, Katowice, Poland.

Routledge Studies in Labour Economics

The Digital Economy and the European Labour Market
Edited by Maria Urbaniec

Digital Labour Markets in Central and Eastern European Countries
COVID-19 and the Future of Work
Edited by Beata Woźniak-Jęchorek and Kamilla Marchewka-Bartkowiak

Trade Union Finance
How Labor Organizations Raise and Spend Money
Marick F. Masters and Raymond Gibney

India's Informal Economy
Contractual Labour in the Formal Manufacturing Sector
Bir Singh

The Political Economy of Immigration in The Netherlands
Population, Land and Welfare
Joop Hartog

Social Transformation and the Global Economy
Labour, Latin America and the Lefts
Ronaldo Munck

War Refugees and the Labour Market
Crisis-Driven Mobility in the Polish-Ukrainian Borderland
Ewa Łaźniewska, Joanna Kurowska-Pysz, Tomasz Górecki, Khrystyna Prytula, and Klaudia Plac

For a full list of titles in this series, please visit: www.routledge.com/Routledge-Studies-in-Labour-Economics/book-series/RSLE

War Refugees and the Labour Market

Crisis-Driven Mobility in the Polish-Ukrainian Borderland

Ewa Łaźniewska, Joanna Kurowska-Pysz, Tomasz Górecki, Khrystyna Prytula, and Klaudia Plac

Routledge
Taylor & Francis Group
LONDON AND NEW YORK

First published 2025
by Routledge
4 Park Square, Milton Park, Abingdon, Oxon OX14 4RN

and by Routledge
605 Third Avenue, New York, NY 10158

Routledge is an imprint of the Taylor & Francis Group, an informa business

British Library Cataloguing-in-Publication Data
A catalogue record for this book is available from the British Library

Library of Congress Cataloging-in-Publication Data
Names: Nowińska-Łaźniewska, Ewa, author. | Kurowska-Pysz, Joanna, author. | Górecki, Tomasz, author. | Prytula, Khrystyna, author. | Plac, Klaudia, author.
Title: War refugees and the labour market : crisis-driven mobility in the Polish-Ukrainian borderland / Ewa Łaźniewska, Joanna Kurowska-Pysz, Tomasz Górecki, Khrystyna Prytula, and Klaudia Plac.
Description: Abingdon, Oxon ; New York, NY : Routledge, 2025. | Series: Routledge studies in labour economics | Includes bibliographical references and index.
Identifiers: LCCN 2024018318 (print) | LCCN 2024018319 (ebook) | ISBN 9781032749440 (hardback) | ISBN 9781032749457 (paperback) | ISBN 9781003471646 (ebook)
Subjects: LCSH: Labor market--Poland--History--21st century. | Ukrainians--Employment--Poland--History--21st century. | Ukrainians--Poland--Social conditions--21st century. | Russo-Ukrainian War, 2014---Refugees--Employment--Poland. | Ukraine--Boundaries. | Poland--Boundaries.
Classification: LCC HD5797.7.A6 N73 2025 (print) | LCC HD5797.7.A6 (ebook) | DDC 331.1209438--dc23/eng/20240613
LC record available at https://lccn.loc.gov/2024018318
LC ebook record available at https://lccn.loc.gov/2024018319

ISBN: 978-1-032-74944-0 (hbk)
ISBN: 978-1-032-74945-7 (pbk)
ISBN: 978-1-003-47164-6 (ebk)

DOI: 10.4324/9781003471646

Typeset in Sabon
by KnowledgeWorks Global Ltd.

Contents

Figures and Tables

Figures

Tables

Acknowledgements

Portions of this document include the intellectual property of Esri and its licensors and are used under license. Copyright © various. Esri and its licensors. All rights reserved. Some data was developed using ArcGIS software from the producer Esri, Inc.

Spatial data sources: OpenStreetMap (CC BY-SA 2.0; https://www.openstreetmap.org/copyright) and National Register of Boundaries (PRG open datasets): https://www.geoportal.gov.pl/en/data/national-register-of-boundaries/. OpenStreetMap® prepared by OpenStreetMap Foundation (OSMF) and National Register of Boundaries (PRG open datasets), Head Office of Geodesy and Cartography, Service www.geoportal.gov.pl is a central node of the Spatial Information Infrastructure.

1 Introduction

1.1 Main Objective, Research Questions, and Framework of Analysis

Escalation of the armed conflict in Ukraine in 2022 has had an impact on the economies of neighbouring countries within their border regions, due mainly to war refugees accepted by Ukraine's nearest neighbours. Until January 2023, Poland accepted 9.49 million people escaping the war, of which 7,639 million returned to Ukraine. This produced the following socio-economic consequences: an increase in supply on the labour market in the host countries, growing needs in the scope of housing, educational infrastructure, healthcare, security, and others. In the work, we analyse the region of the Polish-Ukrainian borderland, which on the Polish side of the border includes two voivodeships (level NUTS-2): Subcarpathian and Lublin (see Figure 1.1). On the Ukrainian side, the point of reference is the borderland region of Western Ukraine.

The war in Ukraine has had a dichotomous impact on socio-economic phenomena on the Polish-Ukrainian borderland. On the one hand, it manifests itself in the influx of refugees and, on the other hand, in the erosion of labour in Ukraine and an increase in unemployment caused by the weakening of the Ukrainian economy. However, it should be noticed that the analysed part of the Polish-Ukrainian borderland is a target region for Ukrainians who would wish to stay close to their own country. The Polish-Ukrainian borderland is, however, to a lesser extent, a region to which refugees have bound themselves for the long term. Since February 2022, the region has seen the arrival mainly of people from Western Ukraine, but far fewer people from regions where heavy fighting has taken place. The Ukrainian labour market is unbalanced; the structure of the supply and demand of labour has changed dramatically both in terms of quantity and quality. On the one hand, the drop in GDP is predicted at the level of 35–40%; on the other hand, the number of internally displaced persons and those who went abroad has reached a third of the population, approximately 12–15 million. These processes have yet to cease. According to various estimates, more than five million Ukrainians lost their jobs, and the unemployment rate reached 35%. There are 13 applicants

DOI: 10.4324/9781003471646-1

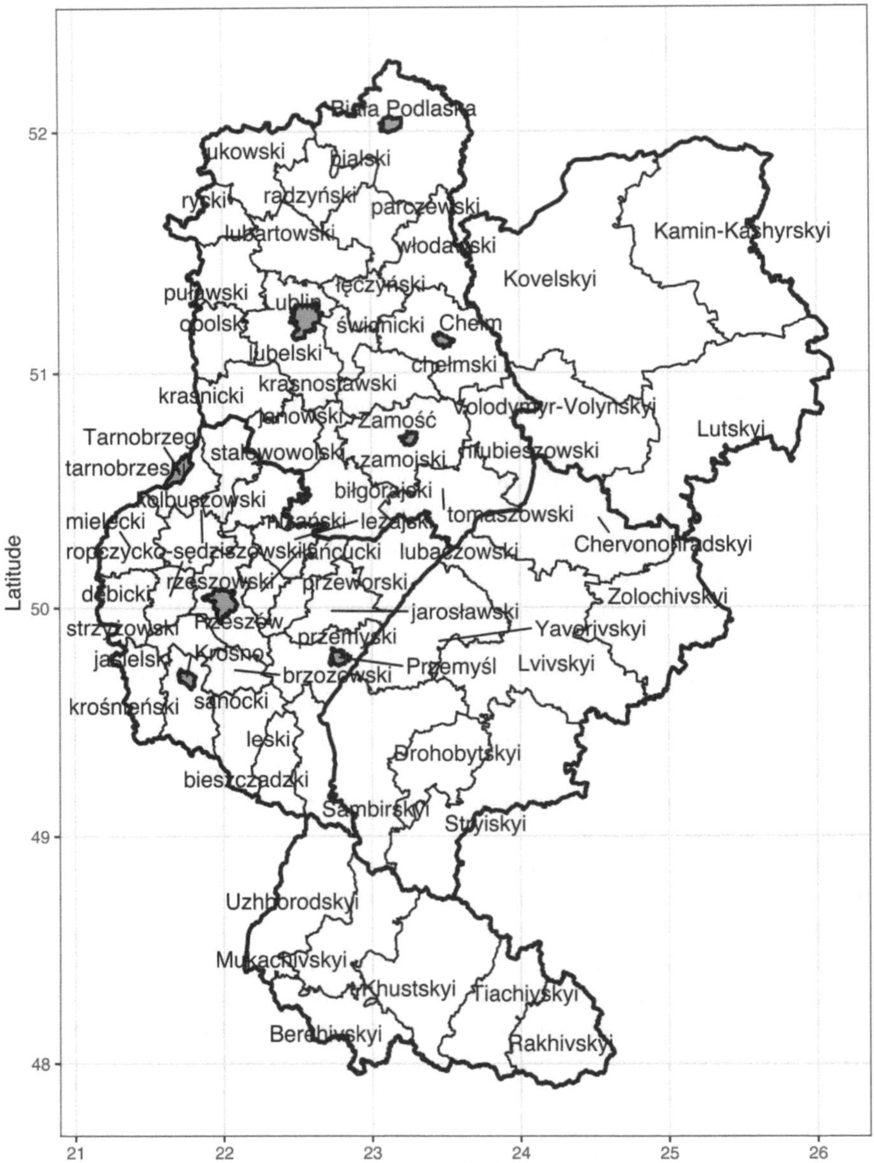

Figure 1.1 Polish-Ukrainian borderland.

Source: Own study.

for every job in Ukraine. It should also be mentioned that the refugee crisis began after the COVID-19 pandemic, which has had a negative impact on the economic condition of all regions, especially the peripheral regions with a weaker economic structure.

The main objective of this work is to analyse the impact of war refugees from Ukraine on the labour market in the Polish-Ukrainian borderland in 2022. Attention was focused on the area of the Polish-Ukrainian borderland, which is a particularly interesting case for analysis due to its physical proximity to Ukraine and the fact that this region now faces challenges related to the assumption of new socio-economic functions. This book consists of the following ten chapters:

- Introduction (Chapter 1) – The objective of the book is discussed, research questions are presented, and the correlations of particular elements of the book are illustrated with a diagram. Determinants that have an impact on the current situation on the labour market in the Polish-Ukrainian borderland are divided into external and internal ones. As one of the crucial factors influencing the labour market, the settlement network with its border infrastructure that had an impact on the directions of refugees' flows, is indicated. At the end, the data and methodology of research applied in the study on the impact of war refugees from Ukraine on the labour market are presented.
- Migration as a Factor for Regional Development in Border Regions (Chapter 2) – Considering regional development, border regions tend to be differentiated in terms of economic backwardness and often significant asymmetries in economic development (Jakubowski, 2018; 2020), which has an impact on increased cross-border flows (Castells, 1999), e.g., related to the labour market (Borsekova & Korony, 2022; Duszczyk & Kaczmarczyk, 2022a; 2022b; Wang et al., 2020). Russia's aggression towards Ukraine has exacerbated this problem (Shubalyi & Gordiichuk, 2022). There is no general consensus on what should be considered good management of cross-border cooperation in order to counteract crises and strengthen the inclusive direction of problem-solving through the participation of various local and regional actors (Wang et al., 2020). The authors took a better look at the phenomenon of the migration of war refugees. This research problem was analysed in the context of the unprecedented influx of war refugees from Ukraine to Poland after Russia's attack on Ukraine in February 2022. This phenomenon confirms the thesis that political instability can be a factor in pushing people abroad as equally important as inequalities in prosperity (Arango, 2000). The aim of the chapter is to identify characteristic features of the stream of war refugees from Ukraine as a category of cross-border flows. Previous literature reviews (Duszczyk & Kaczmarczyk, 2022a; Szpakowska et al., 2016) prove that before the Russian attack, the influx of Ukrainians to Poland was due mainly to economic pressures, whereas, after the outbreak

of war, Ukrainians' motivation to cross the border with Poland as well as the structure of this migration stream have radically changed. Referring to the mobility transition theory (Zelinsky, 1971), in compliance with which circumstances causing migration to determine its process, the authors in the last part of the work assessed changes in the stream of migrants from Ukraine to Poland.

- Research Methodology (Chapter 3) – The chapter presents the methodology of the study conducted within the project titled "Challenges for the labour market in counties in the Polish-Ukrainian borderland about the influx of war refugees from Ukraine" undertaken in 2022–2023 with the financial support of the Polish National Agency for Academic Exchange. The research area was the Polish and Ukrainian border regions. In both parts of the borderland, the secondary data were analysed. Additionally, in the Polish border regions, the groups targeted by the qualitative and quantitative research were the representatives of self-government units, public employment services, and non-governmental organisations, as well as Ukrainian refugees employed in Poland and managers who had employed them in the Polish border regions. A mixed approach was taken, including secondary and primary research (qualitative and quantitative). Data sources, methods, and research techniques were triangulated.
- Features of Socio-Economic Development and Competitiveness of the Ukrainian Border Regions (Chapter 4) – This chapter explores the socio-economic characteristics of the studied regions and describes the processes determining how regional labour markets operate in eastern Poland (Lublin and Subcarpathian Voivodeships), along with selected western border regions of Ukraine (Volhynia, Lviv, and Zakarpattia oblasts). The regions of analysis constitute the border area of countries involved in bilateral relations (including regional) and the external border of the European Union (EU) (eastern border). Moreover, the increase in the flow of people and goods and in the significance of border areas has resulted from the Eastern Partnership agreement between Ukraine and the EU. The examined border area is also a sensitive place for population flows due to its geographical location, as well as the principled role played by Poland in terms of the number of EU residence permits issued to Ukrainian citizens in the period immediately preceding Russia's attack on this country (83% of all work permits issued to citizens of Ukraine in the EU in 2021 were issued in Poland). The scale of the supply of workers from Ukraine for EU labour markets is demonstrated by the fact that in the years 2014–2021, nearly five million citizens from this country received residence permits for the first time in the EU-28, including 84% of permits issued for work.
- The Socio-Economic Situation of the Polish-Ukrainian Borderland with Particular Emphasis on the Cross-Border Labour Market (Chapter 5) – The chapter is devoted to the issue of economic development of the studied regions of Eastern Poland (the Lublin and Subcarpathian Voivodeships) compared to other regions of the EU and the eastern part of this grouping.

A detailed analysis shows a higher level of development in these regions than in other eastern regions of the EU. It may be an attractive factor related to these regions of Poland despite their lower level of development measured by macroeconomic indicators compared to other Polish regions. The labour market research shows a relatively higher level of unemployment in these regions than the average in Poland, a lower share of people of working age in the Subcarpathian Voivodeship, and a much lower level of professional activity of the population in both border regions, as well as different trajectories of processes in this market (e.g., delay in the decline in unemployment compared to other regions). The chapter comparatively analyses the issues of poverty among people on both sides of the border, which, in the authors' opinion, may have a key impact on the decisions made by people, including those regarding looking for employment outside Ukraine. In this context, historical data on population migration from Ukraine after 2011 were analysed, which allowed for the identification of key time intervals during which bilateral labour market relations were dependent on various factors flowing from the environment, also taking into account the supply of workers from Ukraine in sectoral and spatial (regional) terms.

- Activities of Polish Self-Governments Mitigating the Refugee Crisis (Chapter 6) – The chapter describes the actions undertaken by Polish local governments in border regions to assist refugees from Ukraine, particularly towards boosting their activeness on the labour market. It presents the obligatory duties and tasks of the Polish self-governments addressed to migrants, including war refugees, analysed in the context of the outbreak of the war in Ukraine and its consequences for the Polish self-governments on the local, poviat, and voivodeship levels, particularly in the regions bordering Ukraine. These consequences cover the conditions of existence of the Ukrainian refugees in Poland and their assimilation into Polish society, and the organisational changes in the self-governments responsible for the social support for the war migrants. This analysis was supported by qualitative research conducted in the Polish border regions: the Subcarpathian and Lublin Voivodeships.
- Labour Market Institutions in a Situation of Inflow of War Refugees from Ukraine to Polish Border Regions (Chapter 7) – This chapter answers the question about the procedures, actions, and tools used by public employment services to adapt refugees in the labour market in the Polish regions neighbouring Ukraine. It analyses changes in the institutional environment of the Polish labour market after the outbreak of the war in Ukraine from legal, administrative, social, and economic perspectives. The chapter presents the response of the Polish labour market institutions to the influx of refugees to Poland, as well as selected projects and good practices addressing this issue. The results of this research also reveal the types and range of support provided by Polish labour market institutions for war migrants, as well as areas of cooperation with other local partners to create

appropriate conditions for Ukrainian refugees to enter the labour market in Poland. The figures result from qualitative research conducted in two regions: the Subcarpathian and Lublin Voivodeships.

- Non-Governmental Organisations' Support for Ukrainian War Refugees on the Polish Labour Market (Chapter 8) – This chapter addresses the support of Polish non-governmental organisations for Ukrainian refugees in their accommodation in the Polish border regions and entering the labour market. It illustrates the changes in legal regulations concerning the social economy after the outbreak of war in Ukraine and focuses on the social economy-related activities of non-governmental organisations addressing Ukrainian war refugees in adapting to temporary or permanent life, learning, and working in Poland. The authors analyse the social services, projects, and other undertakings in which the third sector can supplement or replace public institutions and labour market institutions. They are analysed as examples of bottom-up deinstitutionalisation changing relations between the state and the third sector regarding refugees' support. These analyses are based on qualitative research conducted in two regions: the Subcarpathian and Lublin Voivodeships.
- Local Labour Market Actors: Refugees and Employers on the Polish-Ukrainian Border during the Migration Crisis in 2022 Caused by the War in Ukraine (Chapter 9) – This chapter describes the reaction of main actors involved in development in the border area immediately after Russia's attack on Ukraine and in the first year of armed conflict in this country. Actors actively engaged in development include refugees from Ukraine and employers on the Polish side of the Polish-Ukrainian border due to their activity and direct involvement in the aid process in the first weeks after the attack. The main objective of this chapter is to discover the extent of the impact of forced mass migration on the region and the situation facing local units (LAU) on the Polish-Ukrainian border (the actors' perception of the situation). For this purpose, a questionnaire was given to all study groups. The results are presented in terms of subgroups of local actors, respectively, as follows: point 9.1. Migrants from Ukraine and point 9.2. Employers on the Labour Market in the Polish-Ukrainian border area.
- Summary (Chapter 10) – We believe that the changing political situation consequent to the war in Ukraine has a significant impact on establishing a new development path for the Polish-Ukrainian borderland. These regions are open to new challenges related to performing logistics functions and the function of a military hub. Furthermore, these regions are open to new investment as well as provide infrastructure for future rebuilding of Ukraine. We based these challenges in the context of the discussion regarding development of universities in the borderland, vocational education, housing needs, and openness to the development of housing. A lot of these challenges have been covered with current measures developed by economic policy. Future research is related to the

observation of various socio-economic phenomena of a cross-border nature. The research covered processes of cross-border cooperation of enterprises and self-governments. A separate issue would be the assessment of the attractiveness of investment locations in the borderland region, and the process of relocation of Ukrainian enterprises. An important direction of research would be to extend research on new development paths for Polish borderland regions due to new functions taken over by these regions.

All chapters in the book are treated as studies on the theme, but they can also function as independent works from various thematic categories. Analysis of the research results is conducted in a regional dimension and, in certain aspects, in a cross-border dimension through a comparative analysis. However, it should be underlined that in both cases we have other factors influencing these phenomena.

1.2 Potential Barriers and Trends on the Labour Market in the Polish-Ukrainian Borderland

In order to illustrate the described processes, factors influencing the potential of the Polish-Ukrainian borderland region, barriers hindering development, and current trends have been synthetically described. Figure 1.2 outlines factors determining changes on the labour market in the Polish-Ukrainian borderland region.

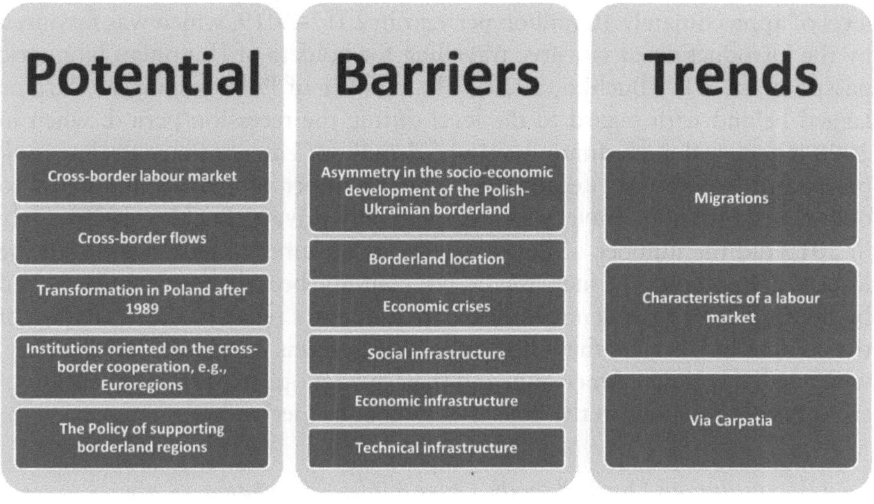

Figure 1.2 Potential, barriers, and trends on the labour market in the Polish-Ukrainian borderland.

Source: Own study.

1.2.1 *Potential of the Polish-Ukrainian Borderland Region*

1.2.1.1 *Cross-Border Labour Market*

Cross-border labour market developed by labour markets of neighbouring states covers the entirety of subject matters related to shaping the demand for work and supply of work on both sides of the border and is realised by cross-border workforce migration. It rests on two pillars: partnership and exchange. Cross-border partnership comprises various forms of cooperation of labour market institutions and other entities concerning employment in borderland areas. Exchange covers possibilities to apply for jobs in and accepting work in neighbouring states, creating systems of cooperation, and the exchange of experiences and information and promoting educational and social-professional integration.

1.2.1.2 *Cross-Border Flows*

Cross-border flows consist in crossing the state border by persons as well as goods, services, capital, investment, means of transportation, elements of natural environment, including, among others, surface waters and ground waters, pollution, and animals, as well as intangible elements such as energy, gas, information, and data. A crucial element of the analysis of cross-border flows is the movement of tourists between Poland and Ukraine until 2022. Persons arriving in Poland mostly come from Ukraine, Belarus, Russia, European Union Member States, Great Britain, and Germany. The number of people arriving in Poland from Ukraine underwent constant growth from a low during the recession of 2008 (2.2 million) to 10.1 million in 2016 and remained at a stable level of approximately 10 million per year in 2017–2019, which was favoured by the introduction of visa-free travelling for holders of Ukrainian biometric passports in 2017 (Buchko, 2020). The number of Poles staying in Ukraine lagged behind with regard to the level during the recession period, when in 2008 it achieved a maximum level of 5.2 million. Later, a sharp decline took place, and for the next decade, the annual number of arrivals amounted to only 1.1–1.2 million. Travel was predominantly private (Buchko, 2020). Only in 2019 did the number of Poles arriving in Ukraine increase again – to the level of 2.4 million. The increase did not continue because tourism was halted by the COVID-19 pandemic in 2020. In 2022, as a result of the escalation of the conflict in Ukraine, these flows changed in terms of quality and quantity, which had a regional dimension, and their impact opened a new dimension of cross-border relations in the Polish-Ukrainian borderland.

1.2.1.3 *Institutions Oriented on the Cross-Border Cooperation*

Institutions oriented on the cross-border cooperation, e.g., Euroregions – the willingness to reinforce cross-border cooperation at a local level, since Euroregions are situated at all borders, and not only where differences in development occur, which provided the opportunity to bring regions closer in various important socio-economic aspects. The willingness to gradually consolidate conditions for the functioning of the borderland region in the strategic perspective of cooperation of both countries underlined the initiative of the Cross-border Association Euroregion of the BUG and Carpathians, a systemic initiative brought to life in 1995 inspired by self-government and public administration authorities. The following are among the most important initiatives: a common Polish-Ukrainian cross-border cooperation strategy for 2005–2015 and several dozens of pro-development cross-border projects undertaken in the Euroregion area implemented with European funds, including the Small Project Fund within the National Programme PHARE – Polish Eastern Border (1998–2005) and the Neighbourhood Programme Poland – Belarus – Ukraine INTERREG III/TACIS CBC5 (Skowron et al., 2015). Experiences in the scope of cross-border cooperation and implementation of projects come across many significant barriers and do not generate a measurable effect of economies' integration.

1.2.1.4 *Transformation in Poland after 1989*

It is assessed in the category of a successful systemic transformation; it produced a high speed of economic development at 4–5% each year since the '90s of the 20th century. Average income per citizen upon separation from the former Eastern Bloc amounted to 38% of the EU average. Currently, with regard to the average of all EU Member States by the current population of the grouping, it amounts to 76%. The International Labour Organisation (ILO), actively supporting and counselling in the scope of systemic transformation in Poland as of the beginning of the '90s of the 20th century, currently emphasises one of the lowest unemployment rates in Poland (approx. 3%) and an employment rate higher than average in the EU (74% in comparison to 72%).

1.2.1.5 *The Policy of Supporting Borderland Regions*

It is a crucial element of Poland's regional policy. Western Poland regions (voivodeships: Lublin and Subcarpathian, and voivodeships not covered with the research: Podlaskie, Świętokrzyskie, and Warmian-Masurian) from the moment of Poland's accession to the European Union received strong support under the cohesion policy in order to catch up with development lagging in comparison with other regions of the Community and Poland. As a result of this activity, in 2020, a gap by the level of GDP per capita in PPS of Eastern Poland (currently covering five regions) amounted to 53.6% of the GDP per capita of EU-27, which meant diminishing development disproportion by 12.6 pp in the period between 2004 and 2020 (the Ministry of Development Funds and Regional Policy, 2022). Support under the instrument, that is, Eastern Poland Programme 2014–2020, was focused on socio-economic development, especially the development of innovativeness, entrepreneurship, and investments in communication infrastructure (including road and railway) in order to increase access throughout the area.

1.2.2 *Barriers Hindering Cross-Border Labour Market*

1.2.2.1 *Asymmetry in the Socio-Economic Development of the Polish-Ukrainian Borderland*

It is a combination of various natural, historical, geopolitical, and even civilisational conditions, as well as different dynamics and directions of socio-economic and political processes that sometimes lead to create significant disproportions and differences in the developmental level of the borderlands and other areas (Jakubowski, 2020; Krätke, 1999; Miszczuk & Jakubowski, 2019). Socio-economic asymmetries arise from the diversity of regions on both sides of the border and, in extreme cases, can be a hindrance to cooperation (Jakubowski, 2018; 2020). The Polish-Ukrainian borderland on a scale of the entire European Union is characterised with the highest asymmetry measured with GDP per capita (Bronisz et al., 2017). With it come specific economic, social, and political consequences, including labour migration, intensified border traffic, creating fragmented commercial informal economic networks, and borderland commerce in the form of a marketplace, intensifying traffic and diminishing the capacity of border crossings (Peciakowski & Gizicki, 2021). Border crossings constitute a barrier to mobility, which undoubtedly does not favour cross-border contracts and, during war, does not facilitate the provision of aid.

1.2.2.2 *Borderland Location*

It is an important development determinant that can promote or hinder development. The borderland region is an area constituting a part of geographic space distinguished by features and relations that distinguish it from its surroundings (Miszczuk, 2013). On this basis, the cross-border region can be defined as an area that covers territory on both sides of the border, delimited on the grounds of integrated studies on travelling or administrative division. Cross-border areas can concern smaller spatial units (Cierpiał-Wolan, 2017). Due to the abundance of processes characteristic of these regions, the regions have for a long time been a subject of interest for many researchers from various fields (Chandra et al., 2022; Ferreira et al., 2019; Klatt & Herrmann, 2011; Korhonen et al., 2021). Both sides of the border are characterised by high diversity. Asymmetry is expressed in differing levels of socio-economic, cultural, and natural development, legal provisions, demographic, political, and other conditions. In many cases, areas located on both sides of the state border show certain common characteristics due to geographical proximity, common historical experiences, economic cooperation, and social contacts

(Krätke, 1999). On the basis of these similarities, due to local and regional initiatives as well as initiatives of the regions' inhabitants, cross-border cooperation is initiated, which, due to open borders, is reinforced by the freedom of workforce, capital, and foreign investment flows. Research concerning migration shows that, contrary to expectations, reinforced borders lead to an increase in immigration flows (Schon & Leblang, 2021). Bigger economic or political differences of neighbouring states are related to bigger differences in population or settlement accumulation in borderland regions, and strong fortifications separating states with big economic or political differences cause settlement and accumulation of population on the side which is weaker in terms of economic structure or the side more liberal in terms of economy (Taubenböck et al., 2023). The authors of the work underline that general trends based on medians are only partially statistically significant; thus, they are not as strong and univocal as assumed. Borderland regions have higher poverty rates in comparison to regions centrally located in the country, fewer education offers less attractive offers of incentives for investors, etc. This situation is especially visible in the described region of the Polish-Ukrainian borderland. Economic and macroeconomic issues should also be taken into consideration in assessing the borderland region. War does not favour assessment of this situation by investors, and the cross-border location may be even debatable. Factors that can have a positive impact on the development of peripheral areas are the activities of business environment institutions (funds, foundations, business incubators, clusters, commercial chambers, Euroregions, etc.).

1.2.2.3 Economic Crises

The research shows that Poland (Bristow & Healy, 2017) underwent the period of crisis in 2008 and the period of COVID-19 pandemic relatively mildly, reacting to the improvement thereafter with a strong recovery and an increase in the GDP. The ILO cites the main challenges on the labour market in Poland: an ageing society, emigration, the low rate of women's employment (the main obstacle for growth), low participation in the labour market of the elderly and persons with disabilities, the high uncertainty of employment (popularisation of flexible, short-term forms of employment), and the low availability of care for children affecting women's employment. The described challenges result in the influx of migrants (predominantly from Ukraine) underway even before the outbreak of armed conflict in Ukraine, having been an important component of the economic development in the country.

1.2.2.4 Social Infrastructure

The R&D as well as scientific-educational base of the Lublin Voivodeship consists of 16 universities (including seven private universities of a vocational nature) and seven scientific institutes with profiles in chemical synthesis, agrophysics and development, agriculture, and rural medicine. The Central Europe Institute has also been operating since 2018 in Lublin, which focuses on social, political, economic, and cultural processes in Central and Eastern Europe (Institute of Central Europe, 2023). The scientific-educational base of Subcarpathian Voivodeship consists of 18 universities (including seven private universities of a vocational nature) (Ministry of Education and Science, 2023). In the Subcarpathian Voivodeship, there are no institutes conducting scientific activity. The educational offer at the higher level in the academic year 2022/2023 in both regions comprised over 570 accredited faculties (Ministry of Education and Science, National Information Processing Institute, 2023). None of the regions' universities were included in the years 2015–2022 in 1,000 of the most influential world universities in the Academic Ranking of World Universities (ARWU) (Shanghai Ranking, 2022).

1.2.2.5 Economic Infrastructure

In Lublin Voivodeship, there are approximately 150 business environment institutions and organisations that reinforce entrepreneurship, innovations, and technology transfer (in the form of: industrial and science-technology parks, clusters, chambers, local development agencies, local action groups, and craft guilds), including (Biznes Lublin, 2022) the Lublin Science – Technology Park, Puławy Science – Technology Park, the Regional Industrial Park in Świdnik, "Starachowice" Special Economic Zone, the Euro-Park Mielec Special Economic Zone, and the Tarnobrzeg Euro-Park WISŁOSAN Special Economic Zone. In the Subcarpathian Voivodeship, there are four industrial and science-technology parks (Polish Investment and Trade Agency, 2023): Mielec Industrial Park, Leżajsk Commune Industrial Park, Subcarpathian Science – Technology Park AEROPOLIS, Tarnobrzeg Industrial and Technology Park, and two special economic zones, Euro-Park Mielec Special Economic Zone and Euro-Park Wisłosan Tarnobrzeg Special Economic Zone. Since 2018, selected groups of industrial entities in the regions have been granted preferential conditions within the Polish Investment Zone (The Act of 10 May 2018 on support…, 2018). In the case of four voivodeships of Eastern Poland, including the Lublin and Subcarphatian Voivodeships, the highest CIT and PIT exemptions were cited at 50% for large enterprises, 60% for medium enterprises, and 70% for micro and small enterprises (Biznes Lubelskie, 2022).

1.2.2.6 Infrastructure

Infrastructure allowing the establishment of bilateral relations in the research region consists of:

- Nine border crossings: Dorohusk – Jagodzin, Zosin – Ustyluh, Dołhobyczów – Uhryniv, Hrebenne – Rava Ruska, Budomierz – Hruszew, Korczowa – Krakovets, Medyka – Shehyni, Malhowice – Niżankowice,

Krościenko – Smolnica, including two railway border crossings: Dorohusk – Jagodzin and Przemyśl – Mostyska.
- Two airport border crossings: Świdnik near Lublin and Rzeszów – Jasionka.
- Border crossing: Medyka – Shehyni.

Similarly, as in the case of a settlement network, the linear transport infrastructure (road and railway) has a light traffic density. In the case of roads, in recent years, consecutive sections of high-grade roads have been handed over – motorways and expressways (motorways: A4 and A2, fragments of expressways: S12, S17, and S19).

1.3 Trends Influencing the Development of the Labour Market and Economy

1.3.1 Migrations

Migrations from Ukraine to Poland since 2008 have been of an economic, political, and social nature. Both countries (predominantly Ukraine) feel their impact in all domains, on micro and macro levels. Searching for a job abroad was influenced by the level of unemployment and remuneration. Among the primarily enumerated economic factors that were attracting migrants to Poland were the relatively high remunerations and tight domestic labour. The liberalisation of provisions concerning work performed by migrants from Ukraine (political factor) and cultural proximity (social stimulus) are also of importance (Paszkowicz & Hrynenko, 2019). The war in Ukraine presents mortal threats to citizens, which prompted masses of people to flee abroad (Baszczak et al., 2022; Chmielewska-Kalińska et al., 2022; Duszczyk & Kaczmarczyk, 2022a; Firlit-Fesnak et al., 2022; Polakowski & Szelewa, 2016; Zymin et al., 2022). The armed conflict in Ukraine caused an unexpected and sudden flight of war refugees to various countries. Experiences from the past indicate that migration compelled by war is completely different from economic migration (Igielski & Sowa, 2019; Jaroszewicz & Małynowska, 2018). After the Russian attack against Ukraine in 2014, the immigrants coming to Poland were motivated mainly by economic pressures, whose stated reasons for their removal to Poland were the economic situation and high unemployment in Ukraine. The time since February 2022 has seen the arrival of refugees from the Ukrainian borderland and the areas witnessing active hostilities. Families who live at a relatively short distance from the border, often at a risk of unemployment, have also been arriving in borderland regions. Therefore, this qualifies as forced migration. Due mainly to the scale of the phenomenon and the fact that the refugees are mostly women and children, the presence of the refugees is a factor that is changing the functioning of labour markets in the host countries. International migrations constitute a subject of interest for geographers, historians, sociologists, and economists. The scientific analysis of the theory of migration obliges us to take an interdisciplinary approach. The review of literature in terms of the theory and the possibility of explaining contemporary phenomena is broad. One of the theories is the gravitational theory, which explains that the size of a city means, in fact, the density of an entire series of potential migration determinants (Nijkamp & Ratajczak, 2021) strongly correlates to the size of the city centre (Cymanow, 2010). A city's population is therefore a kind of substitute variable, representing a group of features that determine the city's allure for emigrants. The size of the city centre in this construct gains, therefore, the name of a legitimate migration determinant. Taking the form of one variable, it has a multidimensional nature resulting from the fact that it represents many determinants, which can be treated as a functional advantage. Another theory that is inscribed in asked research questions is the mobility transition theory (Upham & Gathen, 2021). Information flows in tandem with emigration, which over time supplants the flow of people. The migration systems theory (Echeverría, 2020) assumes that after some time, as of the occurrence of the first emigrations, regularities are formed between specific locations that govern further flows (Janicki, 2015). Each group of states can be of a different nature, evolve differently, and be based on other grounds, yet they connect states by giving and accepting migrants in a relatively permanent manner. Each group of such states creates a migration system, composed of one or sometimes several immigration states and the group of emigration states. A relatively intensive flow of people, capital, and goods occurs among states of the group, much more intensive than between any of these states and states belonging to other systems (Janicki, 2015). Another group of sociological theories, which can provide grounds for explaining the irregularities is the migration networks theory (van Meeteren & Pereira, 2018), which assumes that interpersonal relations between former emigrants and future emigrants have the biggest impact on making a decision on migration. For those contemplating emigration, emigrants are the best source of information on the benefits of emigration and advice on how to circumvent the problems they might encounter. Slightly similar in its assumptions to the theory of migration networks is the institutional theory (Wickramasinghe & Wimalaratana, 2016), which assumes that each consecutive emigration is generated by institutional relations. Another is the cumulative causation theory, which assumes that the existence of consecutive waves of migration results directly from the existence of previous ones, whereas the intervening opportunities theory (Birnbaum et al., 2022) assumes that, in spite of frequent opinions, there is no direct correlation between distance and size of migration. It results from the existence of so-called indirect opportunities, that is, alternative destinations competing to attract migrants. The more such opportunities occur between two analysed destinations, the smaller the flow of people between them. The new economics of migration is helpful for explaining a crisis situation on the labour market in Ukraine, which results from both the war situation and the previous assessment of the labour market and its parameters (Hunter & Simon, 2022). One of the basic manners of achieving this objective is the diversification of family incomes. To this end, some family members can work at a great distance from their place of residence so that, in the event of economic issues in the region, the family has a guaranteed source of permanent income. Another explanatory theory is the theory of the dual labour market (Arango, 2000). It is concluded that immigrants are necessary for the labour market. Thus, employing them does not result in the increase of the unemployment rate but has a stabilising effect on the economy of the host country. The problem of the shortage of workers for jobs associated with low-life cannot, in fact, be solved by increasing the level of wages, since it leads straight to a structural inflation (Massey, 1998).

1.3.2 Characteristics of a Labour Market

In the borderland region results from complex economic and social conditions, where a significant role is played by local employers and employees of each of the neighbouring countries. The barometer of these trends can comprise demographic and political conditions. Compared to other regions of Ukraine, the Ukrainian borderlands enjoy a favourable demographic situation distinguished by a relatively high birth rate and a lower demographic burden, with a population of pre- and post-production age (Matkovs′kyĭatkovs′ky, 2017). Regions with lower socio-economic development are usually outflow regions in terms of population. Almost two million Ukrainians relocated to Poland by 2022. Accorded the freedom to work, they supplemented the Polish labour market and were a valuable transfer of human capital to the market. Apart from work, citizens of Ukraine contribute the value of their own experiences and the gift of their individual predispositions (Szast, 2019).

1.3.3 Via Carpatia

The Polish transport system is characterised by lack of access to and inadequate communications within the north-eastern and eastern parts of the country, as well as the hitherto intensive development of latitudinal systems. In consequence, over 50% of voivodeships of Eastern Poland are at risk of permanent marginalisation, and the majority of urban centres (apart from capital cities of regions) are cities losing their functions (*Sustainable Transport Development Strategy*, 2019, pp. 16, 161). The key investment to improve the logistics and international exchange, national and interregional access to and within Eastern Poland, other countries, and regions of Central and Eastern Europe, from north to south, is Via Carpatia integrating transport systems and seaports of the Baltic States (Lithuania, Poland), Ukraine, Belarus, Slovakia, and Hungary with seaports of the Black Sea and distribution-logistics centres in Romania, Bulgaria, Turkey, the Aegean Sea in Greece, and more broadly, national systems, with seaports of the Adriatic Sea in Croatia and Greece (the Three Seas Initiative) (General Directorate for National Roads and Motorways, 2022). Furthermore, Via Carpatia has the perspective of being extended to other countries, among others, the Western Balkans and the Eastern Partnership. It is supposed to be a part of the Trans-European Transport Networks TEN-T with a length of almost 9,000 km joining territory inhabited by 125 million people (*Sustainable Transport Development Strategy*, 2019, pp. 51, 90). In Poland, it proposes to cover sections of expressways S61, S16, and S19 with a total length of 730 km with a perspective completion date of 2025. The route is planned to run between the following locations: Budzisko (state border PL/LT), Suwałki, Ełk, Białystok, Lublin, Rzeszów, Barwinek (state border PL/SK) (The General Directorate for National Roads and Motorways (GDDKiA) [2]; Ministry of Infrastructure and Construction, 2023). It is a strategic investment in infrastructure, the improvement of transportation and communication, the stimulation of social and economic development, and in eastern Poland generally. The EUR 326 million allocated to it will come from the funds of the CEF (the EU instrument). The total length of the route in the Subcarpathian Voivodeship will be 168.6 km and 227.3 km in the Lublin and Masovian Voivodeships (The General Directorate for National Roads and Motorways, 2022, 2023). In voivodeship strategic documents Via Carpatia was included in key directions of intervention – Lublin Voivodeship (Lublin Voivodeship Development Strategy), key opportunities for development of the roles of metropolitan voivodeship cities and their functional areas – Subcarpathian Voivodeship (Subcarpathian Voivodeship Development Strategy 2030). The first results of the implemented measures are already visible in the newly established economic zones and workplaces (e.g., in Nisko, a town in the Subcarpathian Voivodeship).

References

Arango, J. (2000). Explaining Migration: A Critical view, (Vol. 165). Blackwell Publishers/UNESCO.

Baszczak, Ł., Kiełczewska, A., Kukołowicz, P., Wincewicz, A., & Zyzik, R. (2022). *Pomoc polskiego społeczeństwa dla uchodźców z Ukrainy*. Polski Instytut Ekonomiczny.

Birnbaum, L., Sonnert, G., Chen, C., Sadler, P. M., & Kröner, S. (2022). Intervening opportunities between home and college: Students' geographic mobility by college type. Community *College Journal of Research and Practice*, 1–16. https://doi.org/10.1080/10668926.2022.2064372

Biznes Lubelskie. (2022). *Self-government of the Lubelskie Voivodeship*. https://gospodarka.lubelskie.pl/pl/sse-473

Bronisz, A., Miszczuk, U., & Jakubowski, A. (2017). Polityka spójności oraz europejski instrument sąsiedztwa i partnerstwa jako narzędzia wsparcia współpracy transgranicznej na wewnętrznych i zewnętrznych granicach Unii Europejskiej. *Roczniki Nauk Społecznych*, *45*(3), 73–89.

Borsekova, K., & Korony, S. (2022). Resilience and Vulnerability of Regional Labour Markets: Principal Component Analysis of Labour Market Efficiency in the EU. *Regional Studies*. https://doi.org/10.1080/00343404.2022.2042507

Bristow, G., & Healy, A. (2017). Innovation and Regional Economic Resilience: An Exploratory Analysis. *The Annals of Regional Science*. https://doi.org/10.1007/s00168-017-0841-6

Buchko, Z. (2020). Cross-border Ukrainian–Polish Cooperation in the sphere of tourism. *Economic and Regional Studies/Studia Ekonomiczne i Regionalne*, *13*(3), 271–283. https://doi.org/10.2478/ers-2020-0020

Castells, M. (1999). Grassrooting the space of flows. *Urban Geography*, *20*(4), 294–302. https://doi.org/10.2747/0272-3638.20.4.294

Chandra, K., Wang, J., Luo, N., & Wu, X. (2022). Asymmetry in the Distribution of Benefits of Cross-Border Regional Innovation Systems: The Case of the Hong Kong–Shenzhen Innovation System. *Regional Studies*. https://doi.org/10.1080/00343404.2022.2126450

Chmielewska-Kalińska, I., Dudek, B., & Strzelecki, P. (2022). *Sytuacja życiowa i ekonomiczna uchodźców z Ukrainy w Polsce. Raport z badania ankietowego zrealizowanego przez OO NBP*.

Cierpiał-Wolan, M. (2017). Wpływ dynamicznych przemieszczeń ludności na rozwój społeczno-gospodarczy polsko-ukraińskich obszarów transgranicznych. In *Wyzwania rozwojowe pogranicza polsko-ukraińskiego*. Norberinum.

Cymanow, P. (2010). Przegląd teorii migracji w świetle współczesnych wyjazdów zarobkowych. Krakowskie Studia Małopolskie, 14.

Duszczyk, M., & Kaczmarczyk, P. (2022a). *Poland and war refugees from Ukraine – Beyond pure aid*. In *Cesifo forum*. München: Ifo Institut-Leibniz-Institut Für Wirtschaftsforschung An Der Universität München.

Duszczyk, M., & Kaczmarczyk, P. (2022b). *The war in Ukraine and migration to Poland: Outlook and challenges. Intereconomics*, *57*(3), 164–170.

Echeverría, G. (2020). *Towards a systemic theory of irregular migration*. Springer International Publishing. https://doi.org/10.1007/978-3-030-40903-6

Ferreira, R., Verschelde, N., & Cenacchi, V. (2019). Debating European Commission's Support to Cross-Border Cooperation: Time to Move beyond Funding. *Regions*. https://doi.org/10.1080/13673882.2018.00001033

Firlit-Fesnak, G., Jaroszewska, E., Łotocki, Ł., Łukaszewska-Bezulska, J., Ołdak, M., Zawadzki, P., Żołędowski, C., & Żukowski, T. (Eds.). (2022). *Inwazja Rosji na Ukrainę. Społeczeństwo i polityka wobec kryzysu uchodźczego w pierwszym miesiącu wojny. Raport roboczy – Working paper*. Uniwersytet Warszawski. https://wnpism.uw.edu.pl/wp-content/uploads/2022/04/Kryzys-uchodzczy-2022-raport-KPS.pdf

The General Directorate for National Roads and Motorways. (2023). *Porozumienie dla transgranicznego odcinka szlaku Via Carpatia – stan realizacji*. https://www.gov.pl/web/gddkia/porozumienie-dla-transgranicznego-odcinka-szlaku-via-carpatia (access: 27.04.2023)

Hunter, L. M., & Simon, D. H. (2022). Time to mainstream the environment into migration theory? *International Migration Review*, 019791832210743. https://doi.org/10.1177/01979183221074343

Igielski, K., & Sowa, B. (2019). Migracja obywateli Ukrainy do Polski i jej konsekwencje dla rynku pracy. *Rynek – Społeczeństwo – Kultura*, *2*(33), 44–47

Institute of Central Europe. *O nas*. https://ies.lublin.pl/instytut/misja

Jakubowski, A. (2018). Asymmetry of economic development of cross-border areas in the context of perception of near-border location. *Barometr Regionalny. Analizy i Prognozy*, *16*(2), 123–131.

Jakubowski, A. (2020). Asymmetry of the economic development of cross-border areas in the European Union: Assessment and typology. *Europa XXI*, *39*(December 2020), 45–62. https://doi.org/10.7163/eu21.2020.39.6

Janicki, W. (2015). *Migracje kompensacyjne jako czynnik wzrostu obszarów peryferyjnych. Rola ukrytego kapitału ludzkiego*. Wydawnictwo UMCS.

Jaroszewicz, M., & Małynowska, O. (2018). Najnowsza migracja z Ukrainy do Polski: (nie)stały fenomen? Fundacja Batorego. https://udsc.gov.pl/statystyki/rapor-

Klatt, M., & Herrmann, H. (2011). Half empty or half full? Over 30 years of regional cross-border cooperation within the EU: Experiences at the Dutch–German and

Danish–German border. *Journal of Borderlands Studies*, *26*(1), 65–87. https://doi.org/10.1080/08865655.2011.590289

Korhonen, J. E., Koskivaara, A., Makkonen, T., Yakusheva, N., & Malkamäki, A. (2021). Resilient cross-border regional innovation systems for sustainability? A systematic review of drivers and constraints. *Innovation: The European Journal of Social Science Research*, *34*(2), 202–221. https://doi.org/10.1080/13511610.2020.1867518

Krätke, S. (1999). Regional integration or fragmentation? The German-Polish border region in a New Europe. *Regional Studies*, *33*(7), 631–641. https://doi.org/10.1080/00343409950078675

Massey, D. S., A. G., H. A., Kouaouci, A., Pellegrino, A., Taylor, J. E. (1998). Worlds in Motion. Understanding International Migration at the End of the Millenium. Clarendon Press, Oxford.

Matkovs′kyĭ, S., Miszczuk, A., & Матковський, C. (2017). *Wyzwania rozwojowe pogranicza polsko-ukraińskiego*. Vol. 1.

Ministry of Education and Science. Republic of Poland. 2023 https://dane.gov.pl/pl

Ministry of Education and Science, National Information Processing Institute. (2023). *The integrated system of information on science and higher education POL-on, RAD-on system*. National Research Institute (OPI PIB), Higher education provided in a given field of study. https://radon.nauka.gov.pl/dane/studia-prowadzone-na-okreslonym-kierunku?&pageNumber=1&

Ministry of Infrastructure and Construction. (2023). *Issues Related to the Road Route Via Carpatia in Poland*. https://www.gov.pl/static/mi_arch/files/0/1796967/viaCarpatiaprezentacjaminJSzmit.pdf

Miszczuk, A. (2013). *Uwarunkowania peryferyjności regionu przygranicznego*. Norbertinum.

Miszczuk, A., & Jakubowski, A. (2019). Borders and border cities in transition: Towards a typology. *Barometr Regionalny. Analizy i Prognozy*, *17*(1), 7–14. https://doi.org/10.35480/braip-2019.17.1-720

Nijkamp, P., & Ratajczak, W. (2021). Gravitational analysis in regional science and spatial economics: A vector gradient approach to trade. *International Regional Science Review*, *44*(3–4), 400–431. https://doi.org/10.1177/0160017620980519

Paszkowicz, M. A., & Hrynenko, A. (2019). Przyczyny i Skutki Migracji Zarobkowych z Ukrainy Do Polski. *Studia Oeconomica Posnaniensia*, 7(4), 7–26.

Peciakowski, T., & Gizicki, W. (2021). Identity dimension of cross-border cooperation between Poland and Ukraine. Studies on the collective awareness of borderland areas' citizens. *Athenaeum. Polskie Studia Politologiczne*, *70*, 175–195.

Polakowski, M., & Szelewa, D. (2016). *Kryzys uchodźczy – Czy jesteśmy gotowi?* Warszawa.

Polish Investment and Trade Agency (2023), https://www.paih.gov.pl/strefa_inwestora/parki_przemyslowe_i_technologiczne (access: 13.04.2023).

Schon, J., & Leblang, D. (2021). Why physical barriers backfire: How immigration enforcement deters return and increases asylum applications. *Comparative Political Studies*, *54*(14), 2611–2652. https://doi.org/10.1177/00104140211024282

Shanghai Ranking. (2022). *Academic Ranking of World Universities*. http://www.shanghairanking.com/rankings/arwu/2022

Shubalyi, O., & Gordiichuk, A. (2022). The socio-economic consequences of the war in Ukraine: The national, regional, and global dimensions. *Barometr Regionalny. Analizy i Prognozy*, *18*(1), 19–37. https://doi.org/10.56583/br.721

Skowron, Ł., Skowron, S., & Gąsior, M. (2015). Atrakcyjność rynku sąsiada w opinii środowisk biznesowych Polski i Ukrainy. *Ekonomista*, *3*, 351–368.

Sustainable Transport Development Strategy 2030. (2019). Ministry of Infrastructure and Construction. https://www.gov.pl/web/infrastruktura/projekt-strategii-zrownowazonego-rozwoju-transportu-do-2030-roku2 (access: 27.04.2023).

Szast, M. (2019). Transfer kapitału ludzkiego pomiędzy Ukrainą a Polską – Wyzwanie czy zagrożenie dla bezpieczeństwa społecznego obu krajów? *Athenaeum. Polskie Studia Politologiczne*, *62*(1), 9–17. https://doi.org/10.15804/athena.2019.62.06

Szpakowska, J., Buchwald, T., & Romanowski, R. (2016). Atrakcyjność polskiego rynku pracy dla obywateli Ukrainy – przyczyny, mechanizmy, konsekwencje migracji zarobkowych. Optimum. *Studia Ekonomiczne*, *2*(80), 163–184. https://doi.org/10.15290/ose.2016.02.80.12

Taubenböck, H., Otto, C., Gülzau, F., & Mau, S. (2023). Border regions across the globe: Analyzing border typologies, economic and political disparities, and development dynamics. *Applied Geography*, *151*. https://doi.org/10.1016/j.apgeog.2022.102866

The Act of 10 May 2018 on support for new investments (Journal of Laws of 2020, item 1752). https://isap.sejm.gov.pl/isap.nsf/download.xsp/WDU20180001162/T/D20181162L.pdf

The Central Europe Institute 2023, https://ies.lublin.pl/instytut/misja/ (access: 17.01.2023).

The General Directorate for National Roads and Motorways (GDDKiA), https://www.gov.pl/web/gddkia/via-carpatia---stan-realizacji (access: 27.04.2023).

Upham, P., & Gathen, L. (2021). Actors in transitions: narratives of roles and change in the German e-mobility transition. *Environmental Innovation and Societal Transitions*, *40*, 450–460. https://doi.org/10.1016/j.eist.2021.09.009

van Meeteren, M., & Pereira, S. (2018). Beyond the 'Migrant Network'? exploring assistance received in the migration of Brazilians to Portugal and the Netherlands. *Journal of International Migration and Integration*, *19*(4), 925–944. https://doi.org/10.1007/s12134-018-0578-9

Wang, Y., Jia, F., Schoenherr, T., Gong, Y., & Chen, L. (2020). Cross-border e-commerce firms as supply chain integrators: The management of three flows. *Industrial Marketing Management*, *89*, 72–88. https://doi.org/10.1016/j.indmarman.2019.09.004

Wickramasinghe, A. A. I. N., & Wimalaratana, W. (2016). International migration and migration theories. *Social Affairs*, *1*(5), 15–32. www.socialaffairsjournal.com

Zelinsky, W. (1971). The hypothesis of the mobility transition. *Geographical Review*,. 61(2), 219–249

Zymin, A., Kowalski, M., Karasińska, A., Lytvynenko, O., Dąbrowska, E., Bryzek, S., Gliński, P., & Koszykowska, D. (2022). *Special Report. Refugees from Ukraine in Poland*. Platforma Migracyjna EWL, Fundacja na Rzecz Wspierania Migrantów na Rynku Pracy "EWL" i Studium Europy Wschodniej Uniwersytetu Warszawskiego. https://ec.europa.eu/migrant-integration/system/files/2022-04/Raport%20Specjalny%20Uchod%C5%BAcy%20z%20Ukrainy%20w%20Polsce.pdf

2 Migration as a Factor for Regional Development in Border Regions

2.1 Introduction

In our current socio-economic reality, there is a growing need for a debate on migration as it evolves and affects economies in various ways. Dynamic cross-border processes force us to take a fresh look at previous theoretical generalisations, which assume that ongoing processes will follow a linear path (Ciok, 2004; Martinez, 1994). The intensity of spatial interactions, including cross-border flows, has turned out to be dependent on many political, economic, social, and infrastructural factors. The universal interpretation of migration lies at the intersection of geographical, economic, and social sciences (Komornicki et al., 2023). To illustrate the heterogeneity of cross-border phenomena, we present a regional approach (characterised by tremendous diversity in terms of the scale of the phenomenon and its impact) as well as an interdisciplinary approach (from the perspective of social and management science). The study considers two unprecedented events that significantly changed the significance of the issue. The first was the COVID-19 pandemic, which caused an unprecedented restriction of international population flows. In many cases, it led to the complete closure of state borders. The second event was the Russian attack on Ukraine in February 2022, which has resulted in huge population movements, both nationally (within Ukraine) and internationally, which is the subject of considerations in Chapters 3 and 6 of this monograph. The scale of the migration problem in four contexts is presented in Figure 2.1. In terms of quantity of refugees from Ukraine accepted, Poland and Germany are among the leading European countries.

Increasingly, since the last financial crisis in 2008, other crises have occurred that have forced us to take action to counteract the damage caused and to anticipate the consequences of inappropriate political decisions. The ongoing armed conflict in Ukraine since 2022 has brought numerous and unprecedented challenges for the countries of Central and Eastern Europe. The consequences of "forced" migration have become one of the main areas of interest in social discourse. The considerations also reveal the issue's growing role in the literature and point to gaps that need to be addressed.

DOI: 10.4324/9781003471646-2

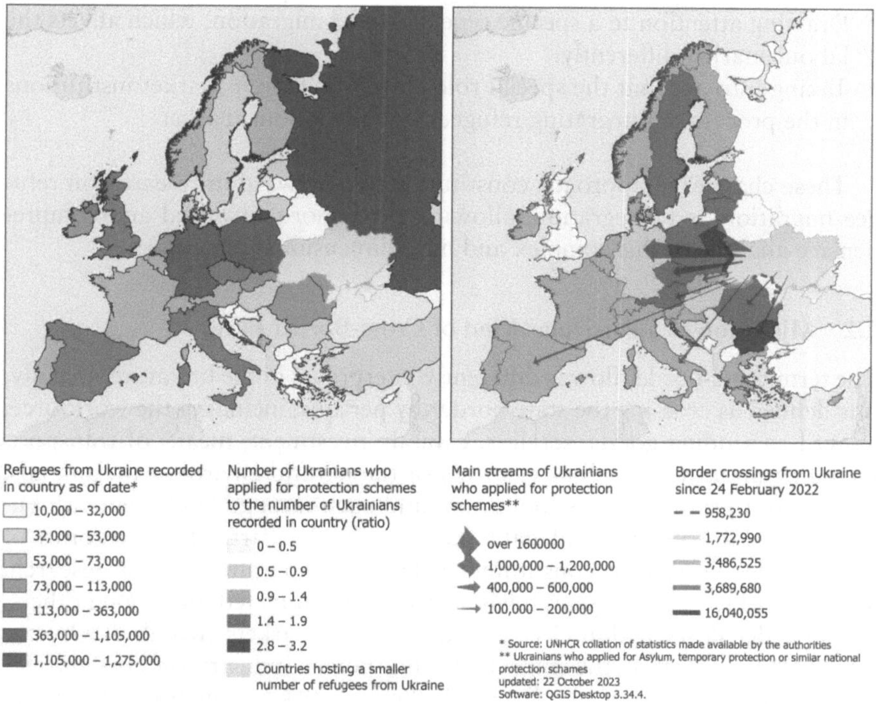

Figure 2.1 Migration from Ukraine.

Due to the wide spectrum of possible issues that might provide a basis for the considerations in this monograph, it was necessary to narrow the focus to just some selected processes. Ultimately, the authors decided to examine issues connected with the following key concepts: migration as a special type of cross-border flow and as a factor of regional development, the borderland as a region, war refugees, and the labour market. Conclusions from quantitative and qualitative research conducted in the border region are the main axis of these considerations.

The authors introduce a new approach to the literature on the integration of refugees within the labour market. They present a comprehensive and theoretically grounded framework that explains differences between countries in terms of integrating refugees into the labour market that arise from institutional circumstances, presenting the problem in a regional context referring to macroeconomic aspects. Features that distinguish literary discourse from what is presented here are as follows:

- Migration as a special type of cross-border flow.
- Integrating the phenomenon of migration with the regional context.
- Taking into account the specificity of border regions.

- Drawing attention to a specific type of forced migration, which affects the labour market differently.
- Taking into account the special role played by labour market institutions in the process of integrating refugees into the labour market.

These changes in approach constitute a step forward in research on refugee migration and integration, allowing for a more advanced and comprehensive analysis of this complex and multidimensional phenomenon.

2.2 Migration as a Particular Kind of Cross-Border Flow

The term cross-border flow is differently interpreted in the literature. Usually, it is defined as crossing the state border by persons, including the workforce, as well as sending goods, services, capital, investment, means of transport, including aircraft, as well as elements of the natural environment: animals, surface and ground waters, pollution, and such intangible elements as: energy, gas, information, and data (Ładysz, 2022). Particular categories of cross-border flows also constitute a subject of separate scientific research. With regard to goods, research has so far been conducted on, among others, cross-border flows within electricity and power markets (Korab & Owczarek, 2016), as well as the impact of wind power industry on cross-border energy flows (Zugno et al., 2013). As far as cross-border flow of services is concerned, so far, the following issues have been analysed: supply chains (Wang et al., 2020), transport systems (Barattieri et al., 2014), traditional services (Sirotić et al., 2021), and e-services (Medeiros et al., 2021). The research concerning cross-border capital flows concentrated on, among others, issues concerning mergers and acquisitions (Julio & Yook, 2016), flows on the monetary (Correa et al., 2021), capital, and currency markets (Choi & Furceri, 2019), as well as venture capital investments (Moore et al., 2015).

Due to the changing technological reality related to the digitalisation of the contemporary world, the intangible sphere is becoming a new area of interest for cross-border flow researchers. In this scope, research is currently conducted regarding flows of data (Meltzer, 2015), information (Di Iorio et al., 2013), media activity (Kumar & Semetko, 2018), knowledge (Miörner et al., 2018), interpersonal interactions (Andersen & Dalgaard, 2011), new technologies (Cooper & Perkins, 2012; Dechezleprêtre et al., 2015), intangibles (Neubig, 2017), diseases (Dean et al., 2013), crime in various dimensions (Van Schendel & Abraham, 2005), and terrorism (Sumpter, 2018). At least several of the aforementioned categories of flow are also related to the phenomenon of war migration. This stream of research also includes more and more numerous works concerning cross-border hybrid warfare between Russia and Belarus, the Baltic States, and Poland (Muradov, 2022), in which the object of attacks and disinformation are, among others, migrants (Gasztold & Gasztold, 2022), as well as societies of neighbouring countries providing them with shelter (Ochmann & Wojas, 2018).

As far as cross-border movements of people are concerned, some studies have focused on the cross-border mobility of workforces (Heinz & Ward-Warmedinger, 2006), as well as the mobility of entrepreneurs (Abdeljaber et al., 2021), students (Li & Bray, 2007), patients, and healthcare employees (Runnels, 2009), as well as persons engaged in business, shopping, health, religious tourism, etc. (Więckowski, 2019). More and more research has also been conducted on interpersonal cross-border relations (Kurowska-Pysz et al., 2022), which are developing within cross-border projects (Kanwal et al., 2020), clusters, and networks (Reznikova et al., 2020).

In the scientific discourse concerning personal cross-border movements, a separate area of research concerning migration issues has become ever-more distinct. More and more publications discussing, among others, cross-border asymmetries in the social and economic development that trigger legal and illegal labour migration (Ford & Lyons, 2010) are published. The subject matter of the rights of migrants (Piper & Withers, 2018), cross-border employment policy in the context of labour migration (Tunon, 2013), as well as the professional re-orientation of migrants are discussed (Desiderio & Urso, 2013). A separate area of the analysis of cross-border movements comprises migrant smuggling and human trafficking. In recent years, this issue has concerned, among others, the Polish-Belarusian and Polish-Ukrainian borders, where the phenomenon of illegal migration from Africa and Asia has intensified (Młynek et al., 2022). Migrant smuggling was predominantly carried out outside border crossings through the so-called green border (paths through areas not easily accessible for border guard patrols and forested areas) (Kozłowski, 2020) and was perceived by persons organising this shady business as a source of earnings based on the lack of border tightness due to, for example, natural geographic barriers (mountains, rivers, etc.), as well as the imperfect border monitoring system.

In post-war Central-Eastern Europe, the issue of migration was analysed predominantly from an economic perspective. The subject matter of migration due to political reasons was analysed significantly less often due to the fact that this group of countries remained under the political influence of the Soviet Union, which limited the freedom to conduct research. Simultaneously, in the sphere of Soviet impact, the phenomenon of political migration from one communist country to another did not occur, while both the politically and the economically motivated migration to Western European countries was not officially written about. However, in recent years, a problem of historic circumstances and tensions in Polish-Ukrainian relations has occurred in the scientific discourse. This area of research predominantly focused on social or cultural consequences of mutual negative perception of Poles and Ukrainians (Olech & Dobrowolska, 2022), which until 2022 was clearly visible also in the borderland (Stępka et al., 2019). When the war migration influx started in February 2022, previous negative attitudes or hostility against Ukrainians arriving in Poland were not in evidence.

Cross-border flows are related to, among others, selected concepts explaining the causes and effects thereof presented below. Nowadays, an explicit departure from perceiving cross-border flows only in tangible categories is evident. More and more often, cross-border transfers also cover intangibles such as information, knowledge, cultural, social or economic phenomena, and even specific ventures such as cross-border projects. Cross-border flows can be characterised by advanced networking. Various types of cross-border relations, which, just as with flows, can be of a one-way or two-way nature, are more and more often developing on the basis of cross-border flows. In the initial phase, usually, one-way or two-way cross-border relations between two entities prevail. However, along with the increase in the number and dynamics of cross-border flows, these relations more and more often gain a multilateral and multidirectional nature. Furthermore, in the post-pandemic reality, virtualisation of cross-border flows (e.g., cross-border e-services), as well as cross-border relations (e.g., cross-border online meetings of cooperating institutions), became apparent, which in turn favoured networking.

With reference to the theory of network (Castells, 2011), Błaszczak (2016) perceives cross-border flows as tools enabling the study of the dynamics of structures and processes grounded in a specific time and spatial framework, which function in the world of fluid connections and are subject to continuous change. According to this author, construction of network interstate initiatives reinforces development of "cross-borderism". In this aspect, the stream of war migration can be assessed as a phenomenon occurring in swiftly changing conditions and circumstances, subject to changes dependent on external factors, i.e., cross-border cooperation (or a lack of cooperation) of institutions responsible for internal affairs in the country from which this stream originates and the neighbouring country to which this stream is directed. An important criterion for selecting a country in which war migrants decide to search for a shelter is its social and economic situation (e.g., social conditions, the standard of living, and the possibility of starting gainful employment), as well as cultural and linguistic similarity or the society's attitude towards migrants.

An interesting depiction of the issue of cross-border flows, with regard to the deliberations concerning the so-called network society (Castells, 2004), is presented by, among others, the concept of "space of flows" by M. Castells. On a basic level, it concerns the relations between social actors, which can be considered in the cross-border context. Although originally such relations were understood as interactions in real time between social actors who had to be present in the same physical space, this approach has changed. Currently, such flows also refer to the same information space that functions within international networks of varied themes (e.g., network of information on the possibility of gaining employment in other countries, i.e., EURES, etc.). Moreover, there are a lot of networks of a cross-border nature, which provide their users on each side of the border with the same access to information regarding the entire borderland. The functioning of territorial networks is currently of fundamental significance for the transformation of social processes, including those occurring in borderlands. The "space of flows" defined by M. Castells includes the following components: the technological infrastructure of IT systems; junctions and hubs structuring connections and key measures in a given location or locations; social actors servicing networks; the electronic environment, such as websites and interaction spaces, as well as (interactive/non-interactive) communication spaces – IT systems (Castells, 1999). In the context of the Polish-Ukrainian borderland, the network of information regarding vacancies provided by Polish poviat labour offices that have established cooperation with their Ukrainian counterparts may be mentioned, for example. The information available in this network was used before the outbreak of war by economic migrants from Ukraine, and after the Russian aggression, it has also become an important forum of information on the terms and conditions of war refugee employment in Poland. It is worth emphasising that in compliance with the aforementioned approach, the condition for the occurrence of cross-border flows (providing, among others, the workforce and information on the possibilities of employment in the neighbour's country) consists of the deployment of the aforementioned components on both sides of the border.

Another approach to cross-border flows is proposed by Sohn (2014). He connects the category of cross-border flows with cross-border integration processes, thereby also referring to the aforementioned phenomenon of forming cross-border relations. According to C. Sohn, the cross-border exchange and relations established on these grounds, connecting social spaces that used to be separate, can be acknowledged as a part of the above-described "space of flows" by Castells. Thus understood, integration is also understood as cross-border penetration of certain values (e.g., perception of professional work in the hierarchy of social values on the sides of the border), models of living and acting (e.g., personal entrepreneurship of citizens of both parts of the borderland), as well as the cross-border flow of information concerning, for example, terms and conditions of employment on the other side of the border, which constitute an inevitable consequence of opening state borders to the movement of, among others, people. In this aspect, the integration is related to the process of evolution based on the increase in interactions in borderland regions and the process of the progressive elimination of barriers. C. Sohn also underlines the role played by motivation in the development of cross-border integration. Due to the fact that not all entities can be interested in flows or other cross-border interactions underlining integration, a strong asymmetry of flows can occur, resulting in the emergence of resentment and political tensions between communities on both sides of the border (Sohn, 2014). In the context of the difficult social situation in Ukraine after the outbreak of war, on the one hand, one can discuss various types of tensions in relations between Ukrainian refugees who have left the country and arrived in neighbouring countries and Ukrainians, who, in the face of a threat to the independence of their state, decided to actively defend it against the Russian invader. Another category of tensions concerns historical circumstances, among others, Polish-Ukrainian that have remained the source of mutual resentment in certain social and political circles on both sides of the border. Further tensions can be triggered by, among others, the attitude of neighbouring countries to the high level of social support for Ukrainian refugees, whose rights in host countries are often equal to the rights of the citizens of the host countries. For example, for the first time in the history, Ukrainian refugees who have crossed the border of the European Union (EU) and Moldova after February 24, 2023, have been covered by the Directive on Temporary Protection granting them numerous rights (European Council, 2001). In practice, the professional status of war refugees from Ukraine is currently very similar to the status of citizens of the EU in the scope of the right to free movement of persons.

In the context of deliberations concerning movements in the cross-border labour market, it is also worth citing the opinion of V. Houtum (2010), who researched the issue of cross-border interactions. He indicated the flow approach as one of the theoretical approaches for the purposes of analysing such interactions. In this author's understanding, a border constitutes an artificial barrier, and the limitations resulting therefrom should be perceived as an economic loss (Paudel et al., 2018). This concept has been confirmed by recent global events, caused by the periodical closures of borders during the pandemic that resulted in large losses in incomes, primarily for the citizens of the borderland, including cross-border employees. In this aspect, the stream of war refugees from Ukraine, who have a status given under the aforementioned Directive on Temporary Protection, can be perceived in the neighbouring country as an element reinforcing the labour market, resulting in an increase in the competition among employees in this market and, in some cases, also solving the problem of a shortage of workers.

2.3 Migration as a Factor of Regional Development

Basic migration theories include Zelinsky's (1971) concept of spatial mobility transition, which describes all population movements, and the neoclassical theory of migration based on Lee's (1966) "push-pull framework". Other theoretical approaches concern transnational migration, networked social spaces, incomplete migration – i.e., within the country of origin – and fluid migration, all of which reflect complex migration systems associated with broad sociocultural changes (Komornicki et al., 2023). It should also be emphasised that mobility increases along with technological progress and widespread access to fast transport. The growth in mobility is also a consequence of rising affluence. The basic push factor in international migration is still income disparity (Komornicki et al., 2023). Migration then generates circular traffic, not only for the migrants themselves but also for their visiting families. Small-scale trade and procurement are also associated with low levels of income (Powęska, 2016).

International migration describes a range of population movements, regardless of their duration, course, and causes. The perpetrators of migration movements understood in this way are refugees, displaced people, and economic migrants, as well as those moving for other reasons, including family reunification. The movement of people that involves leaving their country of origin or permanent residence to settle permanently or temporarily in another country by crossing an international border, is called "international migration" (Jaskułowski & Pawlak, 2016; Kacperska et al., 2019). One particular type of migration is "forced migration" and this term is also used in relation to war refugees, treated as a separate category.

Migration theories are various scientific approaches that try to explain the causes, processes, and effects of population movements. Several of the main migration theories (Jaskułowski & Pawlak, 2016; Kacperska et al., 2019) are presented here:

- Classical migration theory provides the basis for many other migration theories. It assumes that migration is the result of inequalities and differences between regions, such as variations in resources, demography, climate, and other factors. According to this theory, migration is a natural reaction to these inequalities and the pursuit of balance.
- Neoclassical migration theory focuses on the economic motivations for migration, such as differences in wages and employment opportunities between countries. According to this theory, migrants make their decisions based on costs and benefits, trying to maximise their income and improve their living conditions.
- Migration system theory assumes that migration is part of a broader socio-economic system that includes both the countries of origin and destination. According to this theory, migration is the result of mutual dependencies and interactions between both countries, and their impact can have both positive and negative effects on either side.
- Migration conflict theory assumes that migration is the result of social, political, and economic conflict that forces people to leave their places of residence. According to this theory, migration can lead to tension and conflict between social and ethnic groups, and their impact may be negative for society and the economy.
- Migration network theory assumes that migration is the result of social networks that connect people in different countries. Therefore, migration is often influenced by family, friends, and other members of migration networks who assist in finding work and adapting to the new country.
- Transnational migration theory assumes that migration is the result of globalisation and the increase in international mobility. Migration is increasingly transnational, which means that people living in different countries maintain constant contact with each other and connect their lives in different countries.

The cited migration theories differ in their approach to explaining the causes and effects of population movements. Some theories focus on the economic aspects of migration, while others take into account the broader sociopolitical and cultural context.

Taking into account the wide spectrum of issues related to migration, it is impossible to ignore internal migration, which may also involve foreign migrants. From this perspective, the authors have analysed the impact of internal migration on population redistribution from a regional perspective (Rowe et al., 2019). Other authors have written about its effect on the demographic dynamics of cities (Dauth et al., 2016; López-Gay et al., 2020) and rural areas (Collantes & Pinilla, 2019). To provide a more precise analysis of interregional migratory movements, and due to the territorial heterogeneity within each region, we combine both perspectives: regional and urban–rural (González-Leonardo et al., 2022). There is evidence that highlights a growing polarisation not only between regions (González-Leonardo et al., 2022) but also between cities (Martinez, 1994), which was exacerbated after the economic crisis of 2008 (Audirac et al., 2012).

Analysis of the broad and complex implications of migration for regional development covers economic, demographic, and sociocultural dimensions, incorporating both the positive and negative aspects of this phenomenon (Heffner & Opolska, 2016). Table 2.1 presents various effects of migration, both regionally and locally.

From the point of view of the research conducted by the authors of this monograph, the impact of migration on the local labour market is an interesting topic. Migration can have a significant influence on the regional and local labour market:

- Migration can help fill labour shortages in certain sectors, while also increasing competition for jobs in other sectors (Ministerstwo Rodziny i Polityki Społecznej, 2022).
- Migrants can bring new skills and experience to the labour market, which can contribute to economic growth and development.
- Migrants can also face challenges in the labour market, such as discrimination, social exclusion, and language barriers, which can hinder their integration into the local community.
- The structure of migration, including age and gender, can also affect the labour market. For example, an influx of young migrants can lead to an increase in the working-age population, which can have a positive impact on the labour market and the economy.
- Policies and programmes that support the integration of migrants into the labour market can help maximise the benefits of migration and minimise the challenges.
- A larger workforce implies growth for the entire economy, including regionally. The scale of adjustment depends on the employment and productivity rates of refugees from Ukraine (Jaumotte et al., 2016).

Table 2.1 The impact of migration on regional development

The impact of migration on regional development	*Possible changes caused by migration*
Demographic changes	Migration can lead to changes in the demographic structure of a region. For example, an influx of young migrants can lead to an increase in the working-age population, which can have a positive impact on the labour market and the economy.
Labour market	Migration can also affect the labour market in a region. An influx of migrants can help fill labour shortages in certain sectors while also increasing competition for jobs in other sectors.
Economic growth	Migration can contribute to economic growth in a region. Migrants can start new businesses, invest in the local economy, and contribute to the tax base.
Social and cultural changes	Migration can also lead to social and cultural changes in a region. Migrants can bring new customs, traditions, and languages, which can enrich the cultural diversity of a region.
Challenges	While migration can have positive effects on regional development, it can also pose challenges. For example, migrants may face discrimination, social exclusion, and language barriers, which can hinder their integration into the local community. Additionally, migration can put pressure on public services, such as healthcare and education, which may not be equipped to handle the needs of a growing population.

Source: Own elaboration based on Heffner and Opolska (2016) and Solga (2017; 2023).

- The positive impact can be stronger. Research shows that in the long run, an increase in the share of immigrants in the labour force by 1% increases not only the size of the economy but also labour productivity by 2% (Jaumotte et al., 2016).
- Overall, the literature suggests that migration can have both positive and negative effects on the regional and local labour markets. It is important for policymakers to consider the potential impacts of migration and to develop strategies to maximise the benefits and minimise the challenges.

The migration crisis is increasing the burden on many sectors of the economy, such as transport, education, healthcare, and water supply. Providing the necessary resources for a larger number of residents resulting from the influx of refugees creates additional challenges for local authorities and requires adequate support from the international community (Shubalyi & Gordiichuk, 2022). Migration may lead to a loss of labour force, especially if migrants decide to extend their stay in another country, adapt to their new living conditions, and find new employment. Another negative effect of migration is the increase in social tensions, especially in the context of increased populism and opposition to immigrants.

Another approach to migration is to take a place (e.g., a city) as an entry point to studying population flow, which facilitates analysis of the "migrant" category and its meaning in specific territories (Wyss et al., 2023). Using place as an entry point to study human movements helps to avoid an ethnic or national perspective and instead examine the very processes that lead to the ethnicisation or migratory description of certain groups of people. Place-specific research methods enable the study of different forms of mobility associated with specific areas, even if they are not traditionally considered migration. The study identifies three important themes that shape how mobility becomes unequally embedded in places: mobility regimes, temporality, and imagination. Research on these topics can provide new insights into the relationship between mobility and territory.

Migration is often associated with a negative impact related to low regional resilience (Galgóczi et al., 2016; Prytula & Łaźniewska, 2023; Szaban, 2022). Migration, as an external factor, affects the regional labour market. The extent to which the impact will be noticeable depends largely on regional resilience, which is a multidimensional phenomenon (Sutton et al., 2023). Features of regional resilience can be divided into several categories:

- Regional resilience is multidimensional and includes reorientation, vulnerability, resistance, and recoverability (Martin & Sunley, 2020; Masik, 2017; Pendall et al., 2010; Sánchez-Zamora & Gallardo-Cobos, 2019).
- Four main types of regional resilience can be distinguished in the literature (Martin & Sunley, 2020). Engineering resilience: the ability of the regional economy to return to its pre-shock equilibrium. Ecological resilience: the ability of the regional economy to absorb shocks and maintain the current equilibrium through minimal structural and/or functional change. Evolutionary resilience: the ability of the regional economy to adapt parts of its structures and functions in response to shocks. Transformational resilience: the ability of a regional economy to create new reconfigurations of structures and functions in response to shocks.
- Another feature of regional resilience is that research conducted on this topic so far has often been context-free (Guan et al., 2020). Regions are treated as homogeneous, regardless of their size, economic performance, and industrial structure. In reality, regions differ in terms of capacities, resources, and constraints, so it is necessary to focus on different types of regions and take into account the regional context when it comes to studying resilience.
- In addition, regional resilience is also related to the concept of adaptive capacity and adaptability of regions (Hu & Hassink, 2017). Adaptation refers to the ability of regions to accommodate the current growth pattern in the short term, while adaptability refers to the ability of regions to

create a new growth path in the long term. There is some controversy in the literature as to whether adaptation and adaptability share a common goal or are opposites. These concepts are often used interchangeably, or some are omitted, leading to confusion and a need for greater conceptual clarity (Pike et al., 2010).

Urban centres are more flexible to changes (Wodzicki et al., 2022). Looking at the prospects for refugees from Ukraine in practical economic terms, 53% of vacancies in 2022 were for jobs in the seven largest Polish cities, and four out of ten poviats with the highest salaries are the capitals of voivodeships in Poland (Wodzicki et al., 2022). This means that larger cities in Poland have greater employment opportunities and a more flexible labour market. The report provides information on the number of regulated professions in selected EU countries and the UK, which suggests that there are regional differences in the range of professions requiring qualifications in individual countries.

Analysis of resilience in border regions may help identify significant differences affecting the asymmetry of the cross-border region, which in turn influences workforce migration (Prytula & Łaźniewska, 2023). One of these factors is the misallocation and misuse of local budgets. Uneven development and increasingly difficult access to services also present significant challenges and risks for local communities. Other problems include lack of investment attractiveness, problems with waste treatment and disposal, degraded sewage systems, risk of accidents, low demand for local products, and limited access to good-quality drinking water. Additionally, the lack of information for potential entrepreneurs on how to start and run a business in a foreign market, the shortage of qualified management staff, and problems with preserving items of cultural heritage also contribute to local communities' lack of resilience in the cross-border area.

Poland's eastern border, which acts as a spatial barrier, has a significant impact on shaping the regional development of neighbouring areas (Komornicki et al., 2023). Literature analysis indicates that this border has both a negative (Gorzym-Wilkowski, 2014) and partially positive (Bański et al., 2010) impact. Negative aspects result from the peripheral location of border areas, manifested in a slower pace of economic development, especially in terms of road infrastructure, which then translates into more difficult accessibility and poorer investment attractiveness. There is a risk of migration outflow, which in turn weakens human and social capital (Gorzym-Wilkowski, 2014). The positive impact of the border, in turn, seems to be spatially specific, concentrating mainly around border crossings and main communication routes as areas of increased economic activity (Bański et al., 2010). The peripheral geographical location therefore translates into socio-economic peripherality, as confirmed by research conducted by Jakubowski and Bronisz (2015). It is worth noting that border control agreements with neighbouring countries, such as Ukraine, Belarus, and Russia, introduce additional elements to this context, which may cause further shifts in this area (a border control agreement was signed with Ukraine in 2009, with Belarus in 2010, and with Russia in 2012) (suspended in 2016).

2.4 Border Regions in Terms of Migration Processes

The multi-faceted topic of cross-border cooperation and border development is an important and extensive subject of interdisciplinary research (Popescu, 2011). It should be noted that the literature contains no generally accepted definition of cooperation and stability. Related research has been conducted in many scientific disciplines (including economics and management) via extremely different quantitative and qualitative methods. A very extensive line of research has studied human behaviour and the inclination towards interpersonal cooperation (Számadó et al., 2016), cooperation between scientists (Cainelli et al., 2010; Celińska-Janowicz et al., 2013; Płoszaj, 2013), and cooperation in the context of public goods (Fischbacher & Gächter, 2010). Many publications have analysed the stability of cooperation between companies, including the following areas: strategic company alliances, transnational corporations, joint ventures, supply chains, clusters (Chrupała-Pniak et al., 2016; Cohendet et al., 1998), and cooperation in the field of R&D (Zeng et al., 2017). Research on the stability of cooperation between states in terms of international organisations and treaties also plays an important role (Langlois & Langlois, 2001) – including on the repeatability of various stability issues that have a significant impact on shaping cross-border cooperation, such as:

- Preferences/motivations for cooperation.
- The subject of cooperation (e.g., thematic scope).
- Partners (including project consortiums).
- Responsibilities arising from cooperation (e.g., division of responsibilities between partners within joint ventures).
- Spatial structures of cooperation (e.g., locations of organisations involved in cooperation and places where the projects are run).
- Relationship between the above features (e.g., stability of the structures as well as the subject of cooperation).

The stability of cooperation in a cross-border context is closely related to the impact of the crisis on flows in the labour market, disrupted by war or other crises. It should be noted that in the context of the existing literature, the stability of cross-border cooperation should not be treated as a clearly positive (or unequivocally negative) phenomenon, but, above all, should offer a better understanding of how it works (Dołzbłasz & Raczyk, 2022).

A consequence of asymmetry, instability, and crisis is migration, which has tangible outcomes on many economic and social levels. While there is extensive literature on the impact of inward migration on the labour market in countries of destination (Dustmann et al., 2015) and on the consequences of emigration for countries of origin (Butikofer et al., 2019), there is a lack of literature on how local development is affected. One study in this area reveals the consequences of opening the labour market to Czech citizens on the Czech-German border (Illing, 2023). Location, rather than the economic situation in a given German municipality, influenced Czech workers' decisions to move. On the German side of the border, the labour supply of semi-skilled workers (i.e., workers with vocational education) increased as a result of the inflow of Czech workers, which is consistent with the findings of previous studies that migrants from Eastern Europe are relatively highly skilled (Kahanec & Pytliková, 2017).

The urbanisation process in eastern Poland has implications for regional development, land use, infrastructure, and the quality of life in urban and rural areas. Understanding the dynamics of urbanisation in the eastern regions of Poland is essential for informed decision-making, sustainable development, and effective urban and regional planning. Small and medium-sized cities in sending peripheral regions have been negatively affected by the increase in interregional migration. These cities are currently experiencing an intense negative net migration of young adults, contributing to processes of urban shrinkage. Industries in these regions have low technological capacity and are unable to employ the increasing number of university graduates, resulting in high levels of unemployment and over-education among this population. The emigration of qualified individuals, especially among the highly educated, has led to a loss of human capital in these cities. This trend has been strengthened since the 2008 economic crisis and has resulted in educational decapitalisation and urban shrinkage in depopulated peripheral regions (González-Leonardo et al., 2022).

The characteristics of borders largely determine how local development is affected. A border acts as a filter for flows and migration, which is manifested in a selective approach to the movement of people between countries, based on the fulfilment of the conditions that apply to migration to and from a given country. The literature distinguishes three basic types of borders that influence cross-border movement (Kolosov & Więckowski, 2018; Więckowski, 2019):

- A closed border with no cross-border flow.
- Border – filter – partially open, where there is selected cross-border movement of a unidirectional or bidirectional nature, characterised by variable intensity, speed, and direction, which – especially in the long run – may contribute to the emergence of asymmetry in the transfer of what is associated directly with this flow.
- A fully open border, where there is full freedom to shape cross-border movement depending on needs arising from, for example, the flow approach, and, as in the case of a partially open border, the movement might be unidirectional or bidirectional, characterised by variable intensity, speed, and direction, but free from the restrictions imposed by the second type of border.

Practice shows that there are many intermediate stages between the degrees of border openness outlined by Więckowski (2019). The Polish-Ukrainian border may serve as an illustration of this issue. From a long-term perspective, it can be assumed that the Polish eastern border has changed in character from local to global and vice versa several times over the last 30 years. It is possible to distinguish the following phases in this respect (Komornicki et al., 2023):

- During the period until 1991, the border was difficult to cross and at the same time local in nature (mainly transversed by citizens of Poland and the Soviet Union), but there was some licensed transit (e.g., from Romania through the Ukrainian SSR to Poland).
- Between 1991 and 2001, the border rapidly grew more open. Border traffic soared. The ethnic diversity of people crossing the border increased rapidly and then gradually decreased. The border became more global and registered crossings of people from many countries, including non-Europeans.
- In 2001–2013, the border tightened again as a result of Poland's accession to the EU and the Schengen area. The movement of citizens from "third" countries was minimal. The structure of traffic on sections of the border with individual eastern neighbours varied, but it was prevailingly local.
- From 2014 to 2019, the border began to be affected by conflicts both in its immediate vicinity (Ukraine) and in more distant countries (Syria). This impact was selective and expressed differently for different groups of travellers. The border began to manifest the characteristics of a "global" border once again.
- In 2020–2021, the volume and structure of border traffic began to shift rapidly again, the final outcome of which cannot yet be predicted. On the one hand, traffic fell due to the COVID-19 pandemic. On the other hand, there was a politically provoked migration crisis, drastically increasing the scale of refugees and the number of illegal border crossings.

According to excerpts from certain documents (Smętkowski et al., 2023), there are several barriers to Polish-Ukrainian cooperation, which can be categorised into different groups:

1 Financial, including the lack of funds for local cultural projects in the centralised state budget in Ukraine. In addition, there is a lack of experience in applying for external funds in Ukraine.
2 Administrative-Legal, including the obsolescence of some agreements due to administrative reforms in Ukraine. There is also the incompatibility of competencies of authorities in cross-border cooperation. Furthermore, the frequency of changing territorial authorities can pose a barrier. Moreover, unstable political situations can affect cooperation.

3 Institutional, including the non-existence of cooperation between NGOs and national bodies in Ukraine, as well as the lack of systemic solutions and long-term planning in Ukraine. Additionally, there is a lack of adequate educational programmes in Ukraine.
4 Sociocultural, including dissimilar mentalities of Polish-Ukrainian border region residents and complex historical relations, leading to misunderstandings and tensions.
5 Physical, such as natural barriers, including mountains and ecological problems like biogenic water pollution, can impede cross-border cooperation with Ukraine.
6 Language and knowledge, specifically related to lack of knowledge and experience in establishing international relations and language differences.

These barriers hinder the cooperation between Poland and Ukraine, and they need to be addressed to enhance and promote effective cooperation between the two countries.

Asymmetries on the border are a common and acceptable phenomenon from a social point of view. In the case of regions with similar socio-economic development, they are imperceptible to borderland residents. The literature also contains analyses of shifts in economic development asymmetries between neighbouring border regions in the context of European integration (Jakubowski & Wójcik, 2023). The relative asymmetry index is used to compare the GDP per capita of these border regions and apply the concepts of σ-convergence and absolute β-convergence. The findings indicate convergence in border areas, although it is usually slower than convergence internationally. The authors emphasise the importance of borders as barriers to socio-economic interaction and highlight the potential of European integration and territorial integration in reducing inequalities and promoting economic integration in border regions. Another document notes that regions on the EU's external borders, such as agricultural regions in Bulgaria, Poland, and Romania, show low overall growth potential and low levels of preparation for digital and green transition, although they have recorded the fastest growth rates in recent years (Maucorps et al., 2023). This regularity is emphasised as a result of the structure of the economy and the specialisation of individual regions.

Analysis of the impact of unemployment on the socio-economic development of Poland and Ukraine indicates wide asymmetry. Unemployment in Poland and Ukraine has a significant impact on the socio-economic development of these countries. The authors examine indicators such as economic growth and the unemployment rate to prove the validity of the Okun effect, which states that economic growth leads to a decrease in unemployment, while economic recession leads to an increase in unemployment (Biloshkurska et al., 2023). A comparative analysis of these factors conducted for Poland, Ukraine, the EU, and the world concluded that Poland is the least prone to changes in unemployment and real GDP, while Ukraine is the most. Unemployment in Ukraine has had the following consequences (Biloshkurska et al., 2023):

- In 2020, unemployment grew by 186,400 people, which represents an increase of 12.5%. Compared to 2009, unemployment has risen by 532,600 people – an increase of 37.4%.
- The Government of Ukraine allocated UAH 1.4 billion for one-off material assistance to businesses and employees affected by quarantine restrictions.
- In 2020, nominal per capita income increased by 6.1% and real income by 2.6%.
- The Great Construction infrastructure programme provided approximately 200,000 new jobs.
- The dynamics of the COVID-19 pandemic in Poland and Ukraine were very similar. In both countries, unemployment and socio-economic development were priority issues.

The authors of this article conclude that state anti-crisis management in the social sphere should focus on financial support for employers and employees as well as infrastructure projects aimed at creating new jobs.

Cross-border cooperation between enterprises is related to the regional development of border regions. The attractiveness of the border region market from the perspective of a specific company is influenced by several factors: (a) the company's ability to compete in the neighbouring market, this includes knowledge of the company's brand and its products on this market as well as experience in running a business there, (b) the importance of this market for the company's development strategy, and (c) the "halo" effect generated by the image of the neighbouring country (Skowron et al., 2015). The latter is especially relevant for consumers' perceptions of product value and for noticing and valuing differences in conducting business in this market compared to the domestic market. According to this theory, how the neighbouring country is imagined on the other side of the border may generate a coherent stereotype of ideas not only about products but also about the entire infrastructure of its market (DiCarlo, 2022). DiCarlo (2022) studied a Swiss commuting policy and showed that worker outflows resulted in decreased productivity for Italian firms. Butikofer et al. (2019) found positive wage and employment effects for stayers as a result of out-migration in relatively wealthy European border regions. Studies on out-migration, such as Dustmann et al. (2015), noticed more generally that stayers benefit from worker outflows in terms of wage increases.

Modern technologies also helped to conduct global research describing and quantifying border typologies, documenting changes over a period of 15 years from 2000 to 2015 for all 315 land borders around the world (Taubenböck et al., 2023). This research was based on a completely new set of empirical data. Greater political or economic differences translate into stronger border fortifications. Stronger economic or political differences between neighbouring nation-states are associated with stronger differences in population density in border regions. Strong fortifications separating nation-states with distinct economic or political differences have greater population densities on the less developed side of the border or the less free side of the border.

An additional element related to cross-border movement is the concept of "space of flows" (Castells, 1999). Basically, this concerns the relationships between social actors, which can also be considered in a cross-border context. Although such relationships were originally understood as real-time interactions between social actors who had to be in the same physical space, this approach has changed over time. Currently, such flows also refer to the same information space that operates within international networks on various topics (e.g., networks of information about employment opportunities in other countries, i.e., EURES, etc.). There are also many cross-border networks that provide users on each side of the border with equal access to information regarding the entire border area. The functioning of such networks is now fundamental to the transformation of all social processes, including those occurring on the border. The spaces of flows include the following components: IT system infrastructure, the hubs that structure connections and key activities in a given location or locations, the social actors operating the networks, the digital environment such as websites, interaction spaces, communication spaces (interactive/non-interactive) – IT systems. In the context of the Polish-Ukrainian border, one example is the information network regarding job vacancies provided by district labour offices on the Polish side, which have also established cooperation with their Ukrainian counterparts. The information available from this network was used by economic migrants from Ukraine before the outbreak of the war, and after the Russian aggression, it also became an important forum regarding employment conditions in Poland for war refugees. It is worth noting here that, in accordance with the approach described above, the condition for cross-border movement to occur (involving, inter alia, labour force and information about employment opportunities in a neighbouring country) is the deployment of the components described above on both sides of the border.

The development of border regions is largely related to the complementarity of the territories throughout the entire border region and does not always develop in the same way as regions located centrally in different countries. The literature mentions specific features attributed to border regions (Miszczuk & Jakubowski, 2019; Sohn, 2014). The combination of various natural, historical, geopolitical, and even civilisational circumstances, as well as different dynamics and directions of socio-economic and political processes, leads to significant disproportions in border regions in terms of development as well as other areas (Jakubowski, 2018).

The literature contains ongoing discussions about borders and border regions in the context of challenge and change (Lechevalier & Wielgohs, 2013). For a long time, the study of borders focused on national borders as static ontological entities with dominant physical features, but the last two decades have witnessed a diametric shift in border studies. The new perspective moved the focus towards the socially constructed features of borders. In this way, the traditional view of borders as static structures has made way for a new theoretical understanding of borders as "historically contingent processes" (Newman & Paasi, 1998), which, by definition, implies their potential for change. Borders are understood through dynamic cultural processes (Paasi et al., 2003). Borders are always (potentially) "subject to political contestation and change". They "do not exist prior to political action but acquire their societal relevance only as a result of [...] political processes and the accompanying legitimisation strategies that produce these borders". Consequently, from this point of view, borders must be considered as "historically and politically contingent"; they "are continuously remade on the basis of concrete political, cultural, and economic practices". The conventional view of borders has been criticised due to the significant increase in the diversity of transnational cross-border activities – for example, in the EU. A completely different situation occurs on the borders of Central and Eastern Europe. This example can also be used to develop discussion about the diversity of borders within this group of countries – for instance, in terms of political stability. "Consequently, the EU/Polish-Ukrainian border must be viewed as a fluid social construct and as a result of ongoing communications at different functional and symbolic levels, communications that do not necessarily have to be congruent with the territorial border on the map that separates the EU and Poland from Ukraine" (Lechevalier & Wielgohs, 2013).

Asymmetries disclosed in the variation of features characterising territories of neighbouring countries can lead to an intensification of related cross-border flows, usually one-way and visible mostly in the borderlands. This issue has been addressed in borderland research (Heyman, 2010; Laine, 2012; Scott & Collins, 1997; Xianghui, 2020). Usually, borderlands deal with asymmetric movements of people to a neighbouring country, for example, for work or tourist purposes, or in order to obtain various types of goods at lower prices. In the case of this type of flow, a key role is played by the so-called location rent, resulting from the proximity of the border. Asymmetries occurring between neighbouring territories do not have to further deepen differences, but they can favour reinforcement of cross-border transfers and drive competition in a given area, which ultimately generates mutual benefits in relationships. Such a situation occurred in the labour market at the Polish-Ukrainian borderland before the outbreak of war in February 2022, where due to the shortage of workers in Poland, employees from Ukraine were eagerly employed, who, in turn, transferred a great part of their remunerations to their country, thus reinforcing the internal demand in Ukraine. Furthermore, it is worth underlining that the presence of Ukrainian employees in the

Polish labour market allowed them to develop professional knowledge and skills, as well as gain know-how. Together with the return of those persons to the labour market in Ukraine, the cross-border flow of knowledge and social capital occurred.

However, there are asymmetries, such as, for example, differences in legal provisions or administrative or customs barriers, which hinder cross-border transfers and thus do not allow the full use of the aforementioned differences in potentials and economic-social features of neighbouring territories. It can be assumed that in some situations asymmetries between neighbouring territories can additionally contribute to deepening development differences primarily in borderland regions, which are often recognised as peripheral areas at risk of marginalisation. In the long term, asymmetries resulting from differences in cross-border flows and consequences thereof that occur on both sides of the border contribute to creating irregularities concerning production, social affairs, military power, geographical range, population, political impacts, administrative systems, etc. In the cross-border context, at the level below the national, these types of asymmetries are also demonstrated as differences in competencies, central-local relations, budgetary cycles, or administration hierarchy (Laine, 2012). Authors also indicate in the literature various other types of asymmetry related to cross-border flows concerning, among others: flows of information and capital (Portes & Rey, 2005); cross-border commutes (Mathä & Wintr, 2009); movements of citizens in the borderland (Fujimura, 2004), using cross-border transportation infrastructure, flows of knowledge between enterprises (Singh, 2007), distribution of cross-border benefits within regional systems of innovation (Chandra et al., 2022); cross-border openness of service providers with regard to cities divided by a border (Dołzbłasz & Raczyk, 2012), pollution flows, currents, and voltages in the electricity network of international connections (Wasilewski & Robak, 2012), and the impact of cross-border tourist mobility (Mikhaylova et al., 2022) on the activity of local economies (Stepanova, 2019). As shown in practice, in the event of asymmetric relations between states, a weaker partner can choose two strategies: closure (in order to secure himself) or openness (in order to use the partner's potential). Furthermore, the stronger party can try to dominate or ignore the weaker partner (Jańczak, 2018). Application of each strategy is limited by many conditions. Whereas, in the case of the European internal market, which was established under the Single European Act, there is freedom of flow with regard to all of the enumerated components (Moravcsik, 1991), from a global perspective, these conditions are developing in a varied manner, which also results in various consequences, primarily for borderland regions. Such negative consequences include, among others, the phenomenon of the workforce backwash effect (Veneri & Ruiz, 2013), traditionally attributed in the literature to peripheral regions, where work and living conditions are much worse than in growth centres such as, for example, metropolitan areas. The backwash effect was introduced to the theory of regional development by Gunnar Myrdal in 1957 as a phenomenon resulting in unfavourable changes in trade, migration, and capital flow that act centrically and trigger recession processes in less developed regions, as well as increasing the distance thereof with regard to the growth poles (Zimnoch, 2013). In the aspect of the subject matter hereof, the phenomenon of the backwash effect in the borderland can also be justified by factors such as, for example, proximity of a military conflict, worsening of conditions for cross-border development of tourism, trade, and services, as well as worsening of moods of the borderland citizens experiencing a threat resulting from the risk of Russian aggression spreading to other countries. These factors, apart from traditional determinants of the labour market, should be taken into consideration while deliberating on the impact of war migration on the labour market of the borderland. Motivations of war refugees from Ukraine, who after February 24, 2022 found themselves on the Polish side, not by choice but by coercion resulting from the fear for their lives and health, currently shed another light on their situation in the Polish labour market. In order to assess this stream of migrants in the category of cross-border flow, it is necessary to take a closer look at the motivations of refugees to stay in Poland and at the demographic, social, and professional profiles of this group of migrants.

2.5 Migration of Refugees as a Distinct Economic Group

Refugee migration may be caused by armed conflict, political persecution, human rights violations, or other situations that force people to leave their homeland. Refugee migration can impact political and social stability both in the country of origin and the country of destination. Displaced people are forced to migrate from their place of residence due to natural disasters, armed conflicts, changes in the natural environment, or other factors. Due to the specific nature of refugee migration, its effects are still the subject of scientific debate (Colic-Peisker & Tilbury, 2007). The differences between refugees and other migrants through the prism of a different perspective include (Ortlieb & Knappert, 2023):

- Lack of clear definition and legal protection. The article highlights the importance of terminology and legal definitions in distinguishing refugees from other migrants. Refugees are protected by special regulations and have certain rights and obligations that distinguish them from other migrants.
- Greater difficulties for refugees to integrate into the labour market, caused by lack of language skills and recognised qualifications, than for other migrants.
- The need to conduct research to identify and understand the macroeconomic factors that influence the effective integration of refugees into the labour market. Comparative trials can help to better understand the different contexts and factors that affect the integration process.

- Host country institutions can play a key role in either helping or hindering the integration of refugees into the labour market. The activities of these institutions are important for the integration process and may affect refugees' chances of finding employment and equal coexistence in the workplace.

The terminology used to describe refugees can be ambiguous, so there is a need for clear and recognised definitions that ensure protection and rights for refugees (Ortlieb & Knappert, 2023). Economic migration is related to seeking better living conditions, work, education, or other material benefits and may provide a foundation for assimilation and attracting refugees in times of crisis. The impact of economic migration may have an impact on economic development both in the country of origin and destination. Different types of migration are accompanied by family reunification and involve the movement of people to join their loved ones who have already migrated or settled abroad. The impact of family reunification migration may have an impact on the social and demographic structure both in the country of origin and destination.

Migration forced by military conflict is highly topical in the context of the war in Ukraine (2022) and the escalation of unrest in the Middle East (2023), where Islamic State is subjugating increasingly large areas (Nickel & Nowak, 2017). The migration crisis caused by Russian aggression against Ukraine has recently been emerged in the literature. Several studies have been conducted in Poland so far, based mainly on qualitative methods, which often treat this issue briefly or fragmentarily (Duszczyk & Kaczmarczyk, 2022; Gluszak & Trojanek, 2023). Almost immediately after the outbreak of the war in Ukraine – from March 23 to April 3, 2022 – research was conducted on a group of war refugees from Ukraine who arrived in Poland after February 24, 2022 (Gylfason et al., 2022; Zymin et al., 2022). The elements of the analysis included family and origin, education, and knowledge of foreign languages, stay in Poland and abroad, employment in Poland, fears, and plans. These studies were conducted throughout Poland, in locations where migrants were staying.

In the context of the war in Ukraine, it is also reported that refugee migration is characterised by specific features as follows (Dodds et al., 2023):

1 The feminisation of forced migration: As a result of the war, the proportion of women among migrants has increased, and they now constitute about three-quarters of migrants in Europe. Women face challenges related to systemic violence and the need to combine work with child care.
2 The largest wave of migration in Europe: The forced displacement of Ukrainians constitutes one of the largest waves of migration in Europe since World War II. Some Ukrainian refugees do not apply for temporary protection in order to maintain the possibility of regular travel to Ukraine.
3 Disruption of movement and associated political implications: The invasion and population displacement have disrupted the flow of people, goods, and ideas within countries and internationally.

4 Impact on labour markets: The conflict has transformed labour markets both domestically and abroad, leading to a loss of economic output in Ukraine and lower wages for workers in all sectors.
5 Trauma and reconstruction: The post-war reconstruction process can help improve the sustainability and resilience of Ukraine's already struggling labour market.

The overall migration caused by Russia's invasion of Ukraine has had far-reaching consequences for affected people, host countries, labour markets, and the need for post-war reconstruction and investment.

The term "refugee" is not appropriate to describe the situation of Ukrainian forced migrants for several reasons (Trzeszczyńska et al., 2023):

- The term "refugee" conveys an impression of passivity and dependence on institutional actors and humanitarian aid. It does not take into account the possibility that forced migrants may have agency and be able to take action since they often plan and organise their lives in a new place according to their needs, ambitions, and capabilities.
- Ukrainian forced migrants do not fit the stereotypical image of a refugee, who is often perceived as a person deprived of various forms of capital, such as economic, cultural, or social.
- Thirdly, "refugee" is an abused term because in practice only a small number of forced migrants from Ukraine have availed themselves of the refugee procedure and applied for international protection. Most are temporary city residents planning to return to Ukraine.

To summarise, the term "refugee" does not reflect the specificity and diversity of the situation facing Ukrainian forced migrants. The term "forced/war migrant" is more precise and less stigmatising, taking into account the aspirations, agency, and future plans of these people (Trzeszczyńska et al., 2023).

2.6 The Role of Labour Market Institutions in the Process of Integrating Refugees into the Labour Market

Institutional theory has many implications that can be used in various areas of research and practice. One of them is the integration of refugees into the labour market. Analysing labour market institutions can help understand the institutional factors that influence the process of integrating refugees into the labour market and can help develop effective policies and practices. Kostova (1999) suggests that the Country Institutional Profile (CIP) consists of three elements that vary more between countries than within countries: regulatory (i.e., laws and regulations), cognitive (i.e., shared knowledge and cognitive frameworks), and normative (i.e., values and norms) (Kostova, 1999). All three elements influence the way individuals think and act. For example, managers' decisions to adopt specific anti-discrimination policies are shaped by national anti-discrimination laws, managers' common knowledge of anti-discrimination policies in a given country, and their shared values and social norms regarding minorities and anti-discrimination. Differences in how countries shape the institutional environment on a microscale may be reflected in entrepreneurship (Busenitz et al., 2000) and managerial attitudes (Parboteeah et al., 2008).

The arrival of refugees involves various institutions (Gericke et al., 2018). At the stage of arrival in the country and the asylum procedure, political decision-makers, employees of institutions responsible for integration, public services related to employment, and volunteers and advisors providing assistance to refugees are involved. During the phase of finding employment and inclusion in the workplace, employers, recruiters, managers, and fellow refugees play a key role. It is important that these actors are aware of the importance of integrating refugees within the workplace and that they strive to create a supportive working environment for the refugees. Refugee support organisations, such as career advisors and volunteers, play an important role in helping refugees find work and integrate into the workplace. Building awareness and knowledge among employees of these institutions about integrating refugees may be key to effectively helping refugees find jobs and join the local labour market. Interinstitutional cooperation and coordinating the actions of various actors also play an important role in the process of integrating refugees into the labour market.

To summarise, the integration of refugees into the labour market is down to many different actors, such as policymakers, employees of institutions responsible for integration, employers, recruiters, the refugees' managers, and co-workers, as well as refugee support organisations and public employment services. Each of these groups of actors plays different roles and takes different actions at different stages of the integration process, such as during arrival, the asylum procedure, finding employment, and inclusion in the workplace. The integration of refugees into the labour market requires cooperation between these actors and coordinated action. Practical experience of integrating refugees from Ukraine has been thoroughly described in reports (Duszczyk & Kaczmarczyk, 2022; IOM, 2023; UNHCR, 2022; Zymin et al., 2022).

Institutional theory suggests that institutions are of key significance in terms of decision-making and agency. In the context of refugee labour market integration, institutions play a role in creating conditions and policies that affect refugees' employment opportunities and success (Kostova, 1999). For example, the law on discrimination and equal rights, followed by regulatory institutions, may influence employers' decisions to employ refugees. Shared values and cognitive frameworks in society can influence employers' attitudes and behaviour towards refugees. Social and cultural norms may influence society's and workers' acceptance of refugees (Ortlieb & Knappert, 2023).

Institutional theory suggests that institutions are created and maintained by individuals who operate in a specific institutional context. In terms of integrating refugees into the labour market, employees and employers, government institutions, non-governmental organisations, and the local community play a role in creating institutions related to employing refugees. Employees and employers, for example, may have certain beliefs, expectations, and attitudes regarding refugee employment that are embedded in their institutional environment. Institutions related to the refugee labour market may influence how employers perceive and treat refugees.

Institutionally oriented research can offer a deeper insight into the factors related to the role played by regional and local institutions that affect the integration of refugees into the labour market and the differences between countries in this regard. By analysing regulatory, cultural, and social norms, it is possible to identify factors that may contribute to the successful integration of refugees into the labour market. Such research may have practical implications for developing policies and practices that help integrate refugees into the labour market, for example, by creating anti-discrimination laws, training workers, and educating the public to accept and include refugees. Refugees often have difficulty mastering the language and obtaining recognised qualifications, and institutions in the host country may either help or hinder their efforts to integrate (IOM, 2023; Wodzicki et al., 2022). An important factor that affects integration is the macroeconomic environment. Countries offer different macroeconomic conditions that are responsible for successful integration in the labour market.

Market institutions are also perceived to play a role in the context of migrant entrepreneurship. The literature describes the challenges and opportunities that migrant entrepreneurs encounter when running their own companies (Vershinina & Rodgers, 2023). Labour market institutions affect the uncertainty and complexity that migrants experience, as well as their ability to cope with challenges. Entrepreneurs undertake various actions such as developing resources and capabilities, building legitimacy, and creating networks to improve their ability to survive and grow in a competitive environment (Pio & Essers, 2014). Migrant entrepreneurs not only work but also actively build their place in communities. It is not only a matter of gaining recognition among their compatriots or the local community, but also the ability to establish relationships and build networks in ethnic as well as business circles (Lassalle & Scott, 2018). It is emphasised that migrants face numerous institutional and external constraints that pose challenges for their companies and require appropriate action (Vershinina & Rodgers, 2023).

Labour market institutions are characterised by varying degrees of resistance to external factors. Crisis situations can significantly affect them. Literature studies arrive at the conclusion that institutions directly influence local economic growth by affecting the capacity of economic actors to attract or repel investment and high-growth industries within different regions. In the context of the UK, the regional institutional framework is described as fragmented, suffering from poor coordination between different levels of government, and subject to instability and short-termism (Sensier et al., 2023). The document suggests that strong and effective labour market institutions are crucial for promoting economic resilience, mitigating the impact of economic shocks, and aiding in recovery from crises. Resilience is related to convergence, which in the context of border regions may lead to some interesting outcomes (Hippe et al., 2023).

The labour market in the EU is characterised by strong heterogeneity between countries and within individual regions in these countries (Elhorst, 2003). Strong interregional impact arises from the mobility of production factors (Baltagi et al., 2012; Molho, 1995). Interactions between different actors in this market are studied within the framework of spatial econometrics. Research on the EU labour market often takes into account socio-economic and institutional factors such as population density, education level, labour market activation programmes, employment protection, unemployment benefits, and early retirement (Elhorst, 2003). This type of research uses spatial regression models and dynamic panel models while taking into account the endogeneity of explanatory variables (Halleck Vega & Elhorst, 2017). In the case of the EU, neighbouring regions play an important role in determining labour force participation rates. The authors use a spatiotemporal modelling approach, taking into account previous work participation rates in nearby regions, to examine the relationship between these rates. Proximity to regions with higher participation rates can help bolster participation rates in nearby regions. The study findings underline the importance of various socio-economic factors and the need to take endogeneity into account in spatial econometric models. Research shows that labour market characteristics are strongly correlated with the characteristics of labour markets in neighbouring regions (Halleck Vega & Elhorst, 2017). Controlling the endogeneity of variables is crucial because failing to do so may lead to serious errors in interpretation and policy outcomes (Halleck Vega & Elhorst, 2017). Additionally, the authors analyse the impact of political variables related to EU employment strategy on labour force participation rates. They discovered that the variables are statistically significant in many cases and that unemployment activation programmes have a positive impact on participation rates, while the level of unemployment benefits and rate of early retirement have a negative impact. Job protection legislation also has a negative relationship with employment participation rates. The study also highlights the importance of controlling the endogeneity of these variables.

The literature contains some key discussions on the Local Active Labour Market Policy – LALMP (Campbell, 2000), which focuses on long-term unemployment. The phenomenon of unemployment is spatially diverse, which means that action should be adapted to the specific needs and challenges facing different regions. The LALMP should focus on improving employability by developing jobseekers' skills, motivating them, and solving related problems such as addictions, health problems, and relationship issues. It is important to involve the local community, employers, and employees in the process of designing and implementing local labour market policies. Research on action taken locally can offer guidance on effective practices, and analysing the outcomes of labour market projects and programmes can be as enlightening as quantitative evaluation. Implementing the LALMP regionally requires multi-agency collaboration and partnerships nationally, regionally, and locally, including partnerships between the private, public, and social sectors. It is also crucial to have solid data on the labour market that may help tailor action to the local needs of individuals, businesses, and communities. It is also emphasised that drawing conclusions for specific regions requires a detailed analysis of their situation and context, and these conclusions are general and refer to a general need for local labour market policies. The success of active policies depends on regional labour market circumstances, so politicians should adapt labour market policy strategies to regional economic structures. The effectiveness of ALMPs varies depending on the type of programme, with wage subsidies and assistance for job seekers being the most relevant (Altavilla & Caroleo, 2013). Training programmes, although the most common type of active policy, do not have a major impact on labour market participation (Altavilla & Caroleo, 2013).

2.7 Conclusions

Rapidly changing socio-economic circumstances generate concerns about how well theories match reality. A good theory adequately describes and explains reality and, as such, potentially creates opportunities for practical application (Gorynia, 2023). This is why it is so important to learn the mechanisms that actually govern regional development, as a starting point for making recommendations on how to shape reality. Regional development is determined by new factors, meaning that not all regularities are sufficiently described and explored. Literature studies clearly reveal a schism between the changes taking place in regions with an established market economy background and those in areas that have embarked upon this path relatively recently. Regions also vary in terms of their susceptibility to changing their development path. The need to build greater regional resilience to the impact of negative external factors is widely discussed. Emerging economic crises also have a regional dimension. "Black swans" do happen, and it is only a matter of time before more occur. The issue of building regional security in various dimensions – for example, migration, energy, and infrastructure – poses a challenge for contemporary regional development. The ability to anticipate crises may be crucial for regional competitiveness.

The four issues addressed in this chapter exemplify the most important problems to be resolved in the context of refugee migration, the role of labour market institutions, regional development, and the specificity of border regions caused by the Russian-Ukrainian war. Of course, this is not an exhaustive list of all the issues involved but rather a conventional catalogue that could be included in the empirical research presented in subsequent stages of this monograph. The theoretical issues discussed form a basis for establishing the research topics for subsequent chapters of this volume. Literature review proved to be an indispensable stage of the research process, enabling precise determination of directions for further empirical research. The analysis of available literature sources served as a foundation on which subsequent sequences of empirical scientific investigations could be based. The findings of this review not only offered insight into existing knowledge gaps but also created solid grounds for further conclusions and implications for local governments, labour market institutions, and other relevant research areas. In this way, the literature review played a key role in shaping the research structure, contributing to the development of a deeper understanding of the topic and identifying perspectives that require additional investigation.

References

Abdeljaber, O., Al-masaeed, S., Azam, S., Ab Yajid, M., AlSoud, A., & Johar, M. (2021). The role of trade integration and cross-border entrepreneurship in international relations: A moderating role of IT infrastructure. *Croatian International Relations Review*, *27*(87), 63–94.

Altavilla, C., & Caroleo, F. E. (2013). Les Effets Asymétriques Des Politiques Actives En Faveur Du Marché Du Travail Au Niveau National. *Regional Studies*, *47*(9), 1482–1506. https://doi.org/10.1080/00343404.2011.635139

Andersen, T. B., & Dalgaard, C.-J. (2011). Flows of people, flows of ideas, and the inequality of nations. *Journal of Economic Growth*, *16*(1), 1–32. https://doi.org/10.1007/s10887-011-9060-7

Audirac, I., Cunningham-Sabot, E., Fol, S., & Moraes, S. T. (2012). Declining suburbs in Europe and Latin America. *International Journal of Urban and Regional Research*, *36*(2), 226–244. https://doi.org/10.1111/j.1468-2427.2011.01093.x

Baltagi, B. H., Blien, U., & Wolf, K. (2012). A dynamic spatial panel data approach to the German wage curve. *Economic Modelling*, *29*(1), 12–21.

Bański, J., Dobrowolski, J., Flaga, M., Janicki, W., & Wesołowska, M. (2010). *Wpływ granicy państwowej na kierunki rozwoju społeczno-gospodarczego wschodniej części województwa lubuskiego*. Studia Obszarów Wiejskich.

Barattieri, A., Borchert, I., & Mattoo, A. (2014). *Cross-border mergers and acquisitions in services: The role of policy and industrial structure*. The World Bank.

Biloshkurska, N., Biloshkurskyi, M., Popadynets, N., Plets, I., & Karpyak, M. (2023). Impact of unemployment on socio-economic development of Poland and Ukraine: Governance aspects. *Zeszyty Naukowe Politechniki Częstochowskiej. Zarządzanie*, *50*(1), 31–45. https://doi.org/10.17512/znpcz.2023.2.03

Błaszczak, D. (2016). Sieć uniwersytetów pogranicza – Konfiguracja społeczeństwa sieciowego na wschodnim pograniczu Polski. *Pogranicze. Studia Społeczne*, *27*(1), 199–219. https://doi.org/10.15290/pss.2016.27.01.14

Busenitz, L. W., Gomez, C., & Spencer, J. W. (2000). Country institutional profiles: Unlocking entrepreneurial phenomena. *Academy of Management Journal*, *43*(5), 994–1003. https://doi.org/10.2307/1556423

Butikofer, A., Løken, K. V., & Will, A. (2019). Building bridges and widening gaps: Efficiency gains and equity concerns of labour market expansions. *SSRN Electronic Journal*. https://doi.org/10.2139/ssrn.3472984.

Cainelli, G., Maggioni, M. A., Uberti, T. E., & De Felice, A. (2010). The strength of strong ties: Coauthorship and productivity among Italian economists. *Marco Fanno*, *125*, 1–32.

Campbell, M. (2000). Reconnecting the long term unemployed to labour market opportunity: The case for a local active labour market policy. *Regional Studies*, *34*(7), 655–668. https://doi.org/10.1080/00343400050178447

Castells, M. (1999). Grassrooting the space of flows. *Urban Geography*, *20*(4), 294–302. https://doi.org/10.2747/0272-3638.20.4.294

Castells, M. (2004). *The Network Society*.

Castells, M. (2011). Network theory. A network theory of power. *International Journal of Communication*, *5*(15).

Celińska-Janowicz, D., Zawalińska, K., & Widła-Domaradzki, Ł. (2013). *Structural equation model of successful territorial cooperation*. Wydawnictwo Naukowe Scholar.

Chandra, K., Wang, J., Luo, N., & Wu, X. (2022). Asymmetry in the Distribution of Benefits of Cross-Border Regional Innovation Systems: The Case of the Hong Kong–Shenzhen Innovation System. *Regional Studies*. https://doi.org/10.1080/00343404.2022.2126450

Choi, S., & Furceri, D. (2019). Uncertainty and cross-border banking flows. *Journal of International Money and Finance*, *93*, 260–274. https://doi.org/10.1016/j.jimonfin.2019.01.012

Chrupała-Pniak, M., Grabowski, D., & Sulimowska-Formowicz, M. (2016). The value of trust in inter-organizational relations. *Economics and Business Review*, *16*(2), 127–143. https://doi.org/10.18559/ebr.2016.2.8

Ciok, S. (2004). *Pogranicze polsko-niemieckie. Problemy współpracy transgranicznej*. WUW.

Cohendet, P., Llerena, P., Stahn, H., & Umbhauer, G. (1998). *The economics of networks: Interaction and behaviours*. Springer.

Colic-Peisker, V., & Tilbury, F. (2007). Integration into the Australian labour market: The experience of three 'visibly different' groups of recently arrived refugees. *International Migration*, *45*(1), 59–85. https://doi.org/10.1111/j.1468-2435.2007.00396.x

Collantes, F., & Pinilla, V. (2019). *¿Lugares Que No Importan? La Despoblación de La España Ruraldesde 1900 Hasta El Presente*. Prensas de la Universidad de Zaragoza.

Cooper, A., & Perkins, C. (2012). Borders and status-functions: An institutional approach to the study of borders. *European Journal of Social Theory*, *15*(1), 55–71. https://doi.org/10.1177/1368431011423578

Correa, R., Paligorova, T., Sapriza, H., & Zlate, A. (2021). Cross-border bank flows and monetary policy. *The Review of Financial Studies*, *35*(1), 438–481. https://doi.org/10.1093/rfs/hhab019

Dauth, W., Hujer, R., & Wolf, K. (2016). Do regions benefit from active labour market policies? A macroeconometric evaluation using spatial panel methods. *Regional Studies*, *50*(4), 692–708. https://doi.org/10.1080/00343404.2014.931571

Dean, A. S., Fournié, G., Kulo, A. E., Boukaya, G. A., Schelling, E., & Bonfoh, B. (2013). Potential risk of regional disease spread in West Africa through cross-border cattle trade. *PLoS ONE*, *8*(10), e75570. https://doi.org/10.1371/journal.pone.0075570

Dechezleprêtre, A., Neumayer, E., & Perkins, R. (2015). Environmental regulation and the cross-border diffusion of new technology: Evidence from automobile patents. *Research Policy*, *44*(1), 244–257. https://doi.org/10.1016/j.respol.2014.07.017

Desiderio, M., & Urso, G. (2013). *Recognition of Qualifications and Competences of Migrants*.

Di Iorio, C. T., Carinci, F., & Brillante, M., et al. (2013). Cross-border flow of health information: Is 'privacy by design' enough? Privacy performance assessment in EUBIROD. *The European Journal of Public Health*, *23*(2), 247–253. https://doi.org/10.1093/eurpub/cks043

DiCarlo, E. (2022). *How Do Firms Adjust to Negative Labour Supply Shocks? Evidence from Migration Outflows*.

Dodds, K., Taylor, Z., Akbari, A., Broto, V. C., Detterbeck, K., Inverardi-Ferri, C., Ok Lee, K., Mamadouh, V., Ramutsindela, M., & Woon, C. Y. (2023). The Russian Invasion of Ukraine: Implications for Politics, Territory and Governance. *Territory, Politics, Governance.*

Dołzbłasz, S., & Raczyk, A. (2012). Transborder openness of companies in a divided City: Zgorzelec/Görlitz case study. *Tijdschrift Voor Economische En Sociale Geografie, 103*(3), 347–361. https://doi.org/10.1111/j.1467-9663.2011.00688.x

Dołzbłasz, S., & Raczyk, A. (2022). Stability of cross-border cooperation in Poland in thematic and spatial dimensions. *Studia Regionalne i Lokalne, 2022*(4), 64–75. https://doi.org/10.7366/1509499549006

Dustmann, C., Frattini, T., & Rosso, A. (2015). The effect of emigration from Poland on Polish wages. *The Scandinavian Journal of Economics, 117*(2), 522–564. https://doi.org/10.1111/sjoe.12102

Duszczyk, M., & Kaczmarczyk, P. (2022). Poland and war refugees from Ukraine – Beyond pure aid. In *Cesifo forum.* München: Ifo Institut-Leibniz-Institut Für Wirtschaftsforschung An Der Universität München.

Elhorst, J. P. (2003). The mystery of regional unemployment differentials: Theoretical and empirical explanations. *Journal of Economic Surveys, 17*, 709–748.

European Council. (2001). *Dyrektywa Rady 2001/55/WE.*

Fischbacher, U., & Gächter, S. (2010). Social preferences, beliefs, and the dynamics of free riding in public goods experiments. *American Economic Review, 100*(1), 541–556. https://doi.org/10.1257/aer.100.1.541

Ford, M., & Lyons, L. (2010). Travelling the aspal route: Grey labour migration through an Indonesian border town. In *The state and illegality in Indonesia* (pp. 107–122). BRILL.

Fujimura, M. (2004). Cross-Border Transport Infrastructure, Regional Integration and Development. *ADBI Discussion Paper.*

Galgóczi, B., Leschke, J., & Watt, A. (2016). *EU labour migration and labour markets in troubled times.* Routledge.

Gasztold, A., & Gasztold, P. (2022). The Polish counterterrorism system and hybrid warfare threats. *Terrorism and Political Violence, 34*(6), 1259–1276.

Gericke, D., Burmeister, A., Löwe, J., Deller, J., & Pundt, L. (2018). How do refugees use their social capital for successful labour market integration? An exploratory analysis in Germany. *Journal of Vocational Behavior, 105*, 46–61. https://doi.org/10.1016/j.jvb.2017.12.002

Gluszak, M., & Trojanek, R. (2023). *War in Ukraine, Refugee Crisis, and Housing Market in Poland.*

González-Leonardo, M., López-Gay, A., & Esteve, A. (2022). Interregional migration of human capital in Spain. *Regional Studies, Regional Science, 9*(1), 324–342. https://doi.org/10.1080/21681376.2022.2060131

Gorynia, M. (Ed.). (2023). *Pandemia, wojna, globalne przesilenie.* Wydawnictwo Uniwersytetu Ekonomicznego w Poznaniu.

Gorzym-Wilkowski, W. A. (2014). Wpływ granicy wschodniej na przestrzeń społeczno-ekonomiczną lubelszczyzny. *Zeszyty Naukowe WSEI: Ekonomia, 9*(2), 29–43.

Guan, D., Wang, D., & Hallegatte, S., et al. (2020). Global supply-chain effects of COVID-19 control measures. *Nature Human Behaviour, 4*, 577–587. https://doi.org/10.1038/s41562-020-0896-8

Gylfason, U. T., Hochreiter, E., & Kowalski, T. (2022). *Different Choices, Divergent Paths: Poland and Ukraine.*

Halleck Vega, S., & Elhorst, J. P. (2017). Regional labour force participation across the European Union: A Time–Space recursive modelling approach with endogenous regressors. *Spatial Economic Analysis, 12*(2–3), 138–160. https://doi.org/10.1080/17421772.2016.1224374

Heffner, K., & Opolska, P. (2016). Studia Migracyjne-Przegląd Polonijny, z. 3 (161)/2016, ss. 149–164.
Heinz, F. F., & Ward-Warmedinger, M. E. (2006). Cross-border labour mobility within an enlarged EU. *SSRN Electronic Journal*. https://doi.org/10.2139/ssrn.923371.
Heyman, J. (2010). US-Mexico Border Cultures and the Challenge of Asymmetrical Interpenetration. *Borderlands: Ethnographic Approaches to Security, Power, and Identity*, 21–34.
Hippe, S., Bertram, D., & Chilla, T. (2023). Convergence and Resilience in Border Regions. *European Planning Studies*. https://doi.org/10.1080/09654313.2023.2170214
Hu, X., & Hassink, R. (2017). Exploring adaptation and adaptability in uneven economic resilience: A tale of two Chinese mining regions. *Cambridge Journal of Regions, Economy and Society*, *10*(3), 527–541. https://doi.org/10.1093/cjres/rsx012
Illing, H. (2023). *Crossing Borders: Labour Market Effects of European Integration*.
IOM. (2023). *Access to Labour Markets and Employment in Europe for Refugees from Ukraine*.
Jakubowski, A. (2018). Asymmetry of economic development of cross-border areas in the context of perception of near-border location. *Barometr Regionalny. Analizy i Prognozy*, *16*(2), 123–131.
Jakubowski, A., & Bronisz, U. (2015). Granica Unii Europejskiej jako czynnik (dez) aktywujący rozwój i konkurencyjność obszarów przygranicznych. *Wybrane Aspekty Rozwoju i Konkurencyjności Nowych Krajów Członkowskich Unii Europejskiej*, 627–639.
Jakubowski, A., & Wójcik, P. (2023). Towards Cohesion at the Interface between the European Union States? Cross-Border Asymmetry and Convergence. *Regional Studies*. https://doi.org/10.1080/00343404.2023.2187767
Jańczak, J. (2018). Symmetries, asymmetries and cross-border cooperation on the German–Polish border. Towards a new model of (de)Bordering. *Documents d'Anàlisi Geogràfica*, *64*(3), 509. https://doi.org/10.5565/rev/dag.518
Jaskułowski, K., & Pawlak, M. (2016). Główne teorie migracji międzynarodowych: przegląd, krytyka, perspektywy. *Sprawy Narodowościowe. Seria Nowa*, (48), 128–146. https://doi.org/10.11649/sn.2016.008
Jaumotte, F., Koloskova, K., & Saxena, S. C. (2016). Impact of migration on income levels in advanced economies. In *Spillover notes*, *8*, *International Monetary Fund*.
Julio, B., & Yook, Y. (2016). Policy uncertainty, irreversibility, and cross-border flows of capital. *Journal of International Economics*, 103, 13–26. https://doi.org/10.1016/j.jinteco.2016.08.004.
Kacperska, E., Kacprzak, M., Kmieć, D., Król, A., & Łukasiewicz, K. (2019). *Migracje międzynarodowe w Europie: Trendy, problemy, wyzwania*. Wydawnictwo SGGW.
Kahanec, M., & Pytliková, M. (2017). The economic impact of East–West migration on the European Union. *Empirica*, *44*(3), 407–434. https://doi.org/10.1007/s10663-017-9370-x
Kanwal, S., Pitafi, A. H., Ahmad, M., Khan, N. A., Ali, S. M., & Surahio, M. K. (2020). Cross-border analysis of China – Pakistan Economic corridor development project and local residence quality of life. *Journal of Public Affairs*, *20*(2). https://doi.org/10.1002/pa.2022
Kolosov, V., & Więckowski, M. (2018). Border changes in Central and Eastern Europe: An introduction. *Geographia Polonica*, *91*(1), 5–16. https://doi.org/10.7163/GPol.0106
Komornicki, T., Wiśniewski, R., Szejgiec-Kolenda, B., & Ciołek, D. (2023). *Ekonomiczne, społeczne i geopolityczne uwarunkowania ruchu granicznego (Economic, Social and Geopolitical Conditioning of the Cross-Border Traffic)* Vol. 280. Instytut Geografii i Przestrzennego Zagospodarowania im. Stanisława Leszczyckiego, Polska Akademia Nauk.

Korab, R., & Owczarek, R. (2016). Impact of phase shifting transformers on cross-border power flows in the Central and Eastern Europe region. *Bulletin of the Polish Academy of Sciences*, *64*, 127–133.

Kostova, T. (1999). Transnational transfer of strategic organizational practices: A contextual perspective. *Academy of Management Review*, *24*(2), 308–324.

Kozłowski, P. (2020). Przestępczość transgraniczna w latach 2015–2017 zagrożeniem dla bezpieczeństwa wewnętrznego państwa w świetle danych statystycznych Bieszczadzkiego Oddziału Straży Granicznej w Przemyślu. *Współczesne Problemy Zarządzania*, *8*(1(16), 83–95. https://doi.org/10.52934/wpz.86

Kumar, A., & Semetko, H. A. (2018). Peace communication in cross-border media flows. *Journal of Communication*, *68*(3), 612–635. https://doi.org/10.1093/joc/jqy018

Kurowska-Pysz, J., Łaźniewska, E., Böhm, H., & Boháč, A. (2022). Cross-border cooperation in the shadow of crisis – The Turów Coalmine Case. *Journal of International Studies*, *15*(4), 43–63. https://doi.org/10.14254/2071-8330.2022/15-4/3 Kanwal

Ładysz, J. (2022). *Delimitacja transgranicznych obszarów funkcjonalnych*. Wydawnictwo Uniwersytetu Ekonomicznego we Wrocławiu.

Laine, J. (2012). Border paradox: Striking a balance between access and control in asymme-trical border settings. *Eurasia Border Review*, *3*, 51–79.

Langlois, C. C., & Langlois, J. P. (2001). Engineering cooperation: A game theoretic analysis of phased international agreements. *American Journal of Political Science*, *45*(3), 599. https://doi.org/10.2307/2669241

Lassalle, P., & Scott, M. (2018). Breaking-out? A reconceptualisation of the business development process through diversification: The case of Polish new migrant entrepreneurs in Glasgow. *Journal of Ethnic & Migration Studies*, *44*(15), 25224–25243.

Łaźniewska, E., Prytula, K., & Trojszczak, D. (2023). Migracje z Ukrainy do państw członkowskich UE w latach 2014–2023. *Rocznik Integracji Europejskiej*, *17*, 221–242.

Lechevalier, A., & Wielgohs, J. (2013). *Borders and Border Regions in Europe – Changes, Challenges and Chances*.

Lee, E.S. (1966). A theory of migration. *Demography*, *3*(1), 47–57. https://doi.org/10.2307/2060063

Li, M., & Bray, M. (2007). Cross-border flows of students for higher education: Push–Pull factors and motivations of mainland Chinese students in Hong Kong and Macau. *Higher Education*, *53*(6), 791–818. https://doi.org/10.1007/s10734-005-5423-3

López-Gay, A. (2020). Canvis residencials i moviments migratoris en la renovació poblacional de Barcelona.

Martin, R., & Sunley, P. (2010). The place of path dependence in an evolutionary perspective. *The Handbook of Evolutionary Economic Geography*, *438*(4), 62–93. https://doi.org/10.1093/jeg/lbl012

Martin, R., & Sunley, P. (2020). Regional economic resilience: Evolution and evaluation. In *Handbook on regional economic resilience* (pp. 10–35). Edward Elgar Publishing.

Martinez, O. J. (1994). The dynamic of border interaction. New approaches to border analysis. In C. H. Schofield (Ed.), *Global boundaries. World boundaries*. Vol. 1 (pp. 1–15). Routledge.

Masik, G. (2017). Concepts and research of economic resilience of regions. *Prace Naukowe Uniwersytetu Ekonomicznego we Wrocławiu*, *477*, 154–162. https://doi.org/10.15611/pn.2017.477.15

Mathä, T., & Wintr, L. (2009). Commuting flows across bordering regions: A note. *Applied Economics Letters*, *16*(7), 735–738. https://doi.org/10.1080/13504850701221857

Maucorps, A., Römisch, R., Schwab, T., Vujanović, N., & Stiftung, B. (2023). *The Future of EU Cohesion – Effects of the Twin Transition on Disparities across European Regions*.

Medeiros, E., Ferreira, R., & Boijmans, P., et al. (2021). Boosting cross-border regions through better cross-border transport services. The European case. *Case Studies on Transport Policy*, *9*(1), 291–301. https://doi.org/10.1016/j.cstp.2021.01.006

Meltzer, J. P. (2015). The internet, cross-border data flows and international trade. *Asia & the Pacific Policy Studies*, *2*(1), 90–102. https://doi.org/10.1002/app5.60

Mikhaylova, A. A., Wendt, J. A., Hvaley, D. V., Bógdał-Brzezińska, A., & Mikhaylov, A. S. (2022). Impact of cross-border tourism on the sustainable development of rural areas in the Russian–Polish and Russian–Kazakh borderlands. *Sustainability*, *14*(4), 2409. https://doi.org/10.3390/su14042409

Ministerstwo Rodziny i Polityki Społecznej. (2022). *Uchodźcy na rynku pracy w Polsce*. Warszawa.

Miörner, J., Zukauskaite, E., Trippl, M., & Moodysson, J. (2018). Creating institutional preconditions for knowledge flows in cross-border regions. *Environment and Planning C: Politics and Space*, *36*(2), 201–218. https://doi.org/10.1177/2399654417704664

Miszczuk, A., & Jakubowski, A. (2019). Borders and border cities in transition: Towards a typology. *Barometr Regionalny. Analizy i Prognozy*, *17*(1), 7–14. https://doi.org/10.35480/braip-2019.17.1-720

Młynek, W., Pasternak, K., & Komenda, A. (2022). Nielegalna migracja w Polsce w latach 2015–2021. *Zeszyty Naukowe Pro Publico Bono*, *1*(1), 369–382. https://doi.org/10.5604/01.3001.0016.1992

Molho, I. (1995). Spatial autocorrelation in British unemployment. *Journal of Regional Science*, *35*(4), 641–658.

Moore, C. B., Payne, G. T., Bell, R. G., & Davis, J. L. (2015). Institutional distance and cross-border venture capital investment flows. *Journal of Small Business Management*, *53*(2), 482–500. https://doi.org/10.1111/jsbm.12079

Moravcsik, A. (1991). Negotiating the single European act: National interests and conventional statecraft in the European community. *International Organization*, *45*(1), 19–56.

Muradov, I. (2022). The Russian hybrid warfare: The cases of Ukraine and Georgia. *Defence Studies*, *22*(2), 168–191. https://doi.org/10.1080/14702436.2022.2030714

Neubig, T. (2017). *A Missing Link in the Analysis of Global Value Chains: Cross-Border Flows of Intangible Assets, Taxation and Related Measurement Implications*.

Newman, D., & Paasi, A. (1998). Fences and neighbours in the postmodern world: Boundary narratives in political geography. *Progress in Human Geography*, *22*(2), 186–207.

Nickel, A., & Nowak, M. (2017). Trendy migracyjne w XXI wieku. *Roczniki Studenckie Akademii Wojskowej*.

Ochmann, P., & Wojas, J. (2018). Prawne aspekty konfliktu zbrojnego na ukrainie jako przykład wojny hybrydowej. *Sprawy Międzynarodowe*, *71*(1), 283–302. https://doi.org/10.35757/SM.2018.71.1.20

Olech, A., & Dobrowolska, J. (2022). Polish-Ukrainian Relations and Russian disinformation activities. *National Security Studies*, *26*(4), 63–72. https://doi.org/10.37055/sbn/156978

Ortlieb, R., & Knappert, L. (2023). Labour market integration of refugees: An institutional country-comparative perspective. *Journal of International Management*, *29*(2). https://doi.org/10.1016/j.intman.2023.101016

Paasi, A., Anderson, K., Domosh, M., & Thrift, N. (2003). *Boundaries in a Globalizing World*.

Parboteeah, K. P., Hoegl, M., & Cullen, J. B. (2008). Managers' gender role attitudes: A country institutional profile approach. *Journal of International Business Studies*, *39*(5), 795–813. https://doi.org/10.1057/palgrave.jibs.8400384

Paudel, U. R., Devkota, N., & Bhandari, U. (2018). Socio-cultural and economic factors in cross-border purchase: A study of customers' perspective in Sunauli-Nepal/

India border. *Modern Economy*, *09*(06), 1089–1102. https://doi.org/10.4236/me.2018.96070
Pendall, R., Foster, K. A., & Cowell, M. (2010). Resilience and regions: Building understanding of the metaphor. *Cambridge Journal of Regions, Economy and Society*, *3*(1), 71–84. https://doi.org/10.1093/cjres/rsp028
Pike, A., Dawley, S., & Tomaney, J. (2010). Resilience, adaptation and adaptability. *Cambridge Journal of Regions, Economy and Society*, *3*(1), 59–70. https://doi.org/10.1093/cjres/rsq001
Pio, E., & Essers, C. (2014). Professional migrant women decentring otherness: A transnational perspective. *British Journal of Management*, *25*(2), 252–265.
Piper, N., & Withers, M. (2018). Forced transnationalism and temporary labour migration: Implications for understanding migrant rights. *Identities*, *25*(5), 558–575. https://doi.org/10.1080/1070289X.2018.1507957
Płoszaj, A. (2013). *Sieci instytucji otoczenia biznesu*. Wydawnictwo Naukowe Scholar.
Popescu, G. (2011). *Bordering and ordering in the twenty-first century*. Rowman & Littlefield.
Portes, R., & Rey, H. (2005). The determinants of cross-border equity flows. *Journal of International Economics*, *65*(2), 269–296. https://doi.org/10.1016/j.jinteco.2004.05.002
Powęska, H. (2016). *Handel przygraniczny w warunkach zmian przenikalności granicy*. Wydawnictwo SGGW.
Prytula, K., & Łaźniewska, E. (2023). Modern trends and challenges of the development of adjacent border regions of Ukraine and Poland. *Efektivna Ekonomika*, (5). https://doi.org/10.32702/2307-2105.2023.5.8
Runnels, V. (2009). *Globalization and the cross-border flow of health workers*. Routledge.
Reznikova, N., Rubtsova, M., & Yatsenko, O. (2020). The role of innovation clusters in building up investment and innovation strategies in the crossborder cooperation context. *Actual Problems of International Relations*, *142*, 85–98. https://doi.org/10.17721/apmv.2020.142.1.85-98
Rowe, F., Bell, M., Bernard, A., Charles-Edwards, E., & Ueffing, P. (2019). Impact of internal migration on population redistribution in Europe: Urbanisation, counterurbanisation or spatial equilibrium? *Comparative Population Studies*, *44*. https://doi.org/10.12765/CPoS-2019-18
Sánchez-Zamora, P., & Gallardo-Cobos, R. (2019). Diversity, disparity and territorial resilience in the context of the economic crisis: An analysis of rural areas in Southern Spain. *Sustainability*, *11*(6). https://doi.org/10.3390/su11061743
Scott, J. W., & Collins, K. (1997). Inducing transboundary regionalism in asymmetric situations: The case of the German-Polish border. *Journal of Borderlands Studies*, *12*(1–2), 97–121. https://doi.org/10.1080/08865655.1997.9695500
Sensier, M., Rafferty, A., & Devine, F. (2023). The Economic Resilience Scorecard: Regional Policy Responses for Crises Recovery. *Regional Studies*. https://doi.org/10.1080/00343404.2023.2234950
Shubalyi, O., & Gordiichuk, A. (2022). The socio-economic consequences of the war in Ukraine: The national, regional, and global dimensions. *Barometr Regionalny. Analizy i Prognozy*, *18*(1), 19–37. https://doi.org/10.56583/br.721
Singh, J. (2007). Asymmetry of knowledge spillovers between MNCs and host country firms. *Journal of International Business Studies*, *38*, 764–786.
Sirotić, M., Žuškin, S., Rudan, I., & Stocchetti, A. (2021). Methodology for the sustainable development of the Italy-Croatia cross-border area: Sustainable and Multimodal/Cross-border passenger services. *Sustainability*, *13*(21), 11895. https://doi.org/10.3390/su132111895
Skowron, Ł., Skowron, S., & Gąsior, M. (2015). Atrakcyjność rynku sąsiada w opinii środowisk biznesowych Polski i Ukrainy. *Ekonomista*, *3*, 351–368.

Smętkowski, M., Kniazevych, A., Olechnicka, A., Orchowska, J., & Przekop-Wiszniewska, E. (2023). *Cooperation between EU Cities and Regions with Their Ukrainian Partners Policy Department for Structural and Cohesion Policies Directorate-General for Internal Policies PE*. https://policycommons.net/artifacts/3524200/research-for-regi-committeecooperation-between-eu-cities-and-regions-with-their-ukrainian-partners/4324843

Sohn, C. (2014). Modelling cross-border integration: The role of borders as a resource. *Geopolitics*, *19*(3), 587–608. https://doi.org/10.1080/14650045.2014.913029

Solga, B. (2017). Znaczenie migracji zagranicznych w rozwoju regionalnym w polsce. *Studia Ekonomiczne*, *309*, 122–130.

Solga, B. (2023). *Migracje i rozwoju regionu: Materiały z III Kongresu Demograficznego. Part 7*. Zakład Wydawnictw Statystycznych.

Stepanova, S. V. (2019). Czynniki rozwoju turystyki przygranicznej na rosyjsko-fińskim pograniczu (factors underpinning the development of tourism in Russian-Finnish borderland areas). *Przegląd Geograficzny*, *91*(4), 573–587. https://doi.org/10.7163/PrzG.2019.4.7

Stępka, M., Mazurkiewicz, A., & Zubek, M. (2019). Local spoilers and pathways to reconciliation: The Polish perspective on the Polish-Ukrainian relations in the borderlands. *Politické Vedy*, *22*(4), 8–32. https://doi.org/10.24040/politickevedy.2019.22.4.8-32

Sumpter, C. (2018). Transnational crime and terrorism: Exploring the nexus in Europe and Southeast Asia. *Perspectives on Terrorism*, *12*(5), 36–50.

Sutton, J., Arcidiacono, A., Torrisi, G., & Arku, R. N. (2023). Regional economic resilience: A scoping review. *Progress in Human Geography*, *47*(4), 500–532. https://doi.org/10.1177/03091325231174183

Szaban, D. (2022). Ukrainian Migrants in the Polish Labour Market: HRM Selected Issues.

Számadó, S., Szalai, F., & Scheuring, I. (2016). Deception undermines the stability of cooperation in games of indirect reciprocity. *PLOS ONE*, *11*(1), e0147623. https://doi.org/10.1371/journal.pone.0147623

Taubenböck, H., Otto, C., Gülzau, F., & Mau, S. (2023). Border regions across the globe: Analyzing border typologies, economic and political disparities, and development dynamics. *Applied Geography*, 151, 102866. https://doi.org/10.1016/j.apgeog.2022.102866

Trzeszczyńska, P., Luchik-Musiyezdova, S., & Dymanus, J. (2023). *Migranci i migrantki przymusowe z Ukrainy w Krakowie w świetle badań jakościowych*. https://owim.uek.krakow.pl/index.php/2022/12/12/migranci-i-migrantki-przymusowe-z-ukrainy-w-krakowie-w-swietle-badan-jakosciowych-seminarium-owim

Tunon, M. (2013). *Cross-border labour migration in Cambodia: Considerations for the national employment policy*. ILO.

UNHCR. (2022). *Uchodźcy z Ukrainy w Polsce. Profilowanie, Czerwiec 2022*. https://data.unhcr.org/en/documents/details/96508

van Houtum, H. (2010). Human blacklisting: The global apartheid of the EU's external border regime. *Environment and Planning D: Society and Space*, *28*(6), 957–976. https://doi.org/10.1068/d1909

Van Schendel, W., & Abraham, I. (2005). *Illicit flows and criminal things: States, Borders, and the other Side of globalization*. Indiana University Press.

Veneri, P., & Ruiz, V. (2013). *Urban-to-rural Population Growth Linkages: Evidence from OECD TL3 Regions*.

Vershinina, N., & Rodgers, P. (2023). Self-regulation, micro-foundations and migrant entrepreneurs' capacities for resilience. *Entrepreneurship and Regional Development*, *35*(7–8), 644–665. https://doi.org/10.1080/08985626.2023.2216174

Wang, Y., Jia, F., Schoenherr, T., Gong, Y., & Chen, L. (2020). Cross-border e-commerce firms as supply chain integrators: The management of three flows. *Industrial Marketing Management*, *89*, 72–88. https://doi.org/10.1016/j.indmarman.2019.09.004

Wasilewski, J., & Robak, S. (2012). *Analiza asymetrii napięć i prądów w układzie sieci elektroenergetycznego połączenia Polska–Litwa*. Energetyka.

Więckowski, M. (2019). Od barier i izolacji do sieci i przestrzeni transgranicznej – Konceptualizacja cyklu funkcjonowania granic państwowych (from barriers and isolation to transboundary space and networks – Conceptualising ways in which state borders function). *Przegląd Geograficzny*, *91*(4), 443–466. https://doi.org/10.7163/PrzG.2019.4.1

Wodzicki, M., Herbik-Piszczako, E., Pichola, I., Patorska, J., Tomera, E., Laszek, A., Komada, O., & Trzeciakowski, R. (2022). *Refugees from Ukraine in Poland Challenges and Potential for Integration*.

Wyss, A., Zittoun, T., Pedersen, O. C., Dahinden, J., & Charmillot, E. (2023). Places and mobilities: Studying human movements using place as an entry point. *Mobilities*, *18*(4), 567–581. https://doi.org/10.1080/17450101.2023.2235904

Xianghui, Z. (2020). Book review: Asymmetrical neighbors: Borderland state building between China and Southeast Asia, by Enze Han. *Contemporary Southeast Asia*, *42*(1), 126–128. https://doi.org/10.1355/cs42-1g

Zelinsky. (1971). The hypothesis of the mobility transition. Geographical review. *Geographical Review*, *61*(2), 219–249.

Zeng, D., Xu, L., & Bi, X. (2017). Effects of asymmetric knowledge spillovers on the stability of horizontal and vertical R&D cooperation. *Computational and Mathematical Organization Theory*, *23*(1), 32–60. https://doi.org/10.1007/s10588-016-9216-2

Zimnoch, K. (2013). Wymywanie zasobów ludzkich barierą rozwoju regionów peryferyjnych (na przykładzie województwa podlaskiego). *Ekonomia i Zarządzanie*, *5*(3), 206–220.

Zugno, M., Pinson, P., & Madsen, H. (2013). Impact of wind power generation on European cross-border power flows. *IEEE Transactions on Power Systems*, *28*(4), 3566–3575.

Zymin, A., Kowalski, M., Karasińska, A., Lytvynenko, O., Dąbrowska, E., Bryzek, Sz., Gliński, P., & Koszykowska, D. (2022). *Special Report. Refugees from Ukraine in Poland*. Platforma Migracyjna EWL, Fundacja na Rzecz Wspierania Migrantów na Rynku Pracy „EWL" i Studium Europy Wschodniej Uniwersytetu Warszawskiego. https://ec.europa.eu/migrant-integration/system/files/2022-04/Raport%20Specjalny%20Uchod%C5%BAcy%20z%20Ukrainy%20w%20Polsce.pdf

3 Research Methodology

3.1 Research Approach and Concept

The study was conducted within the project titled "Challenges for the labour market in counties in the Polish-Ukrainian borderland with regard to the influx of war refugees from Ukraine" in the period 2022–2023 with the financial support of the Polish National Agency for Academic Exchange. The subject matter of the study is part of the academic considerations concerning the development of border regions, in particular the cross-border labour market, in the wake of the refugee crisis caused by the outbreak of war in Ukraine. Given the research gap outlined in Chapter 2, a research problem was defined, which boils down to the question of the situation of war refugees on the labour market in the Polish border regions after the 2022 Russian invasion of Ukraine, as well as the impact it has on the cross-border labour market, along with its institutional and social environment. The study's objective is a multidimensional assessment of the situation of war refugees in the Polish labour market after the Russian attack on Ukraine in 2022, including recommendations for changes in the long-term labour market policy considering the expected migration increase.

To solve these research problems and achieve the objective of the study, quantitative and qualitative studies and empirical research were carried out in the Polish border regions and neighbouring Ukraine, including Lublin and Subcarpathian Voivodeships, in the period from July 2022 to March 2023.

The following exploratory questions were posed:

- Question 1: What are the specifics of the Polish-Ukrainian borderland, with particular emphasis on the economy and cross-border flows, including the labour market?
- Question 2: Were the Polish border regions prepared to perform new roles regarding war migration after the Russian aggression on Ukraine?
- Question 3: What actions have been undertaken by Polish local governments in border regions to assist refugees from Ukraine, particularly towards boosting their activeness on the labour market?

DOI: 10.4324/9781003471646-3

- Question 4: What procedures, actions, and tools have been used by public employment services to adapt refugees in the labour market in the Polish border regions?
- Question 5: How have Polish non-governmental organisations supported refugees in their accommodation in the Polish border regions and their adaptation to the labour market?
- Question 6: How did migration forced by the war in Ukraine in 2022 affect the labour market on the Polish-Ukrainian border?
- Question 7: How do refugees assess the living and working conditions on the Polish side of Polish-Ukrainian border area?
- Question 8: To what extent has the migration crisis, caused by the influx of refugees from Ukraine, had a positive impact on the development of entrepreneurship on the Polish-Ukrainian border, and how do entrepreneurs assess the situation?

The study was divided into three thematic areas. The research concept, which takes into the main subject areas and the relationship between them, is presented in Figure 3.1. The first thematic area of study was the socio-economic analysis of the situation in the Polish-Ukrainian borderland, particularly concerning the labour market (1), taking into account the pre-war perspective (1a, 1b), selected categories of cross-border flows between Poland and Ukraine (1c), and the phenomenon of Ukrainian migration abroad (1d). The second area of study concerned the evaluation of measures taken by the institutional and social actors of the labour market in Polish border regions in the face of the influx of refugees (2). In this regard, the activities of local governments (2a), labour market institutions (2b), and NGOs (2c) were analysed. The third area of study concerned the analysis of attitudes and behaviour of key labour market institutions in Polish border regions in the context of the wartime migration crisis (3), including refugees (3a) and the employers who hire them (3b). The partial results of all three areas of study, which take into account the theoretical aspects of the academic considerations (outlined in Chapter 2) enabled a comprehensive assessment of the situation of war refugees in the Polish labour market after Russia attacked Ukraine in 2022 and formulating recommendations for changes in long-term labour market policy due to the expected increase in migration.

3.2 Research Methods and Procedure

The authors conducted an interpretative empirical study (Sułkowski, 2009, pp. 127–149). This stems directly from the assumptions made by the authors of the study that in solving the defined research problem, assigning social meanings to the formulated conclusions plays a critical role (Sandberg, 2005, pp. 41–68). This means that the studied phenomenon can be interpreted in different ways, depending on the context, while the conclusions resulting from the claims are analytical in nature and require carrying out a

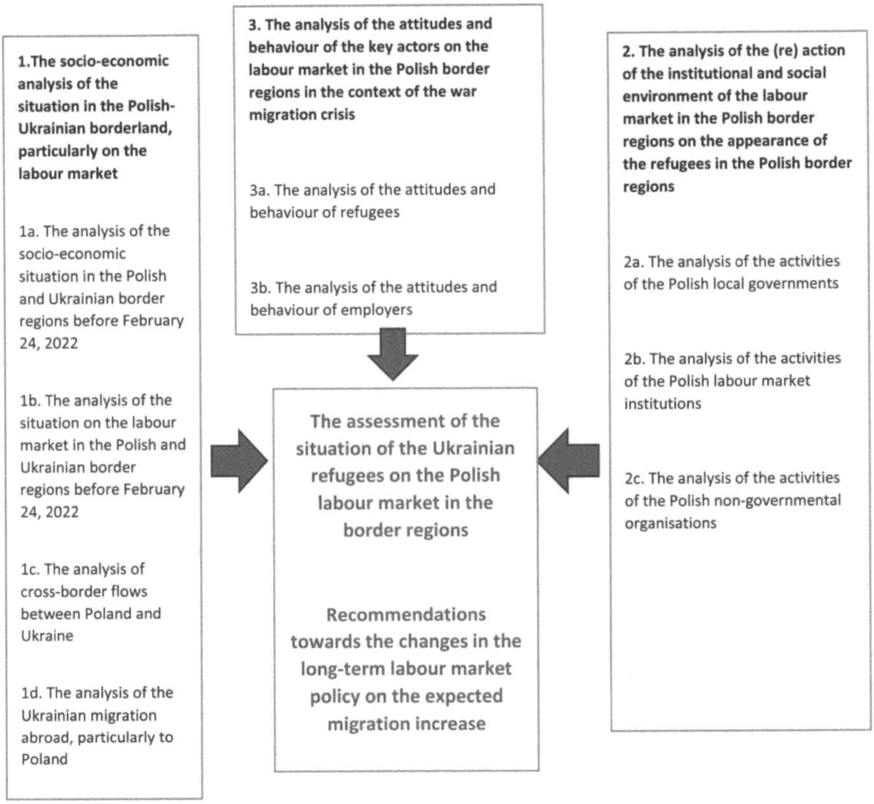

Figure 3.1 Research concept.

Source: Own elaboration.

research process in line with the relevant procedure (Elbardan et al., 2017, pp. 111–165). The authors assumed that the study concerns the impact of war migration on the labour market in Polish regions bordering Ukraine. In particular, they analyse the situation of war refugees on the cross-border labour market in the wake of Russia's attack on Ukraine in 2022, as well as the response of the institutional and social actors to this refugee crisis. In line with the interpretive paradigm, the authors did not suggest any research hypotheses. This was justified by the inability to conduct the survey in a fully representative manner (Groeneveld et al., 2015, pp. 61–86).

The method of incomplete numerical induction was chosen as the general study methodology. This method enables inferring a general rule based on a limited data set, following the principle of observation followed by generalisation (Basri, 2014, pp. 831–838). It involves moving from specific empirical phenomena and processes, gleaned from observation, through the justification and establishment of a theory to the determination of its validity.

The authors selected the following specific research methods:

- Desk research analysis of documents, reports, and secondary data on the issues raised in the study, including the socio-economic situation in the Polish-Ukrainian borderland areas, in particular the situation in the labour market, as well as the outbreak of the refugee crisis in Poland and its course in 2022 and 2023.
- Questionnaire study using the Computer-Assisted Web Interview (CAWI) method.
- Questionnaire study using the Paper & Pen Personal Interview (PAPI) method.
- Individual In-depth Interview (IDI Interview).
- Case study.

The authors of the study also used triangulation:

- Of data sources, by using primary data obtained through surveys conducted among several target groups, as well as secondary data.
- Of research methods and techniques, by using a mixed approach (Trumbull & Watson, 2010, pp. 62–78) comprising both qualitative and quantitative research.

Using triangulation made it possible to include different perspectives concerning data and information collection. The knowledge gained from the triangulation effect proved more comprehensive than compared to that obtained from just a single research method and data source. This ensured a holistic view of the issue at hand and provided a better, more consistent empirical basis for inference (Tashakkori & Teddlie, 2010, pp. 271–277).

The mapping of research questions to target groups and research methods is shown below, along with an indication of the sections of the study containing the answers to the research questions (see Table 3.1). The target groups and how they were selected are detailed in Section 3.3.

The process of carrying out all research listed above is shown in the chart below (see Figure 3.2). The research process was divided into two phases. In the first phase, a critical analysis of the literature covering publications up to 2022 was conducted, providing an overview of theories, concepts, and models on the issue of the study. The list of analysed issues included migration as a particular kind of cross-border flow of people, the specific nature of borderland as a region, migration as a factor in regional development, the specificity of the labour market in border regions, and the character of war refugees on the labour market of the border regions. As part of the first phase of the study, a desk research analysis of available secondary data, results of previous studies, analytical reports, and other printed and online materials for the years 2010–2022 was carried out. This was helpful in outlining the socio-economic characteristics of the Polish and Ukrainian neighbouring

Table 3.1 Mapping research questions to target groups and research methods, along with sections of the study that contain the answers to the questions posed

Research question	*Target group*	*Research methods used*	*Section of the study containing answers to the research question*
1 2	study based on secondary data concerning Poland and Ukraine, including border regions and specifics of labour market	- desk research analysis	Chapter 4 Chapter 5
3	local government units from the Lublin and Subcarpathian Voivodeships	- questionnaire study using the CAWI method	Chapter 6
4	public employment services from the Lublin and Subcarpathian Voivodeships	- questionnaire study using the CAWI method - IDI interviews - case study	Chapter 7
5	non-governmental organisations operating, among others, in the Lublin and Subcarpathian Voivodeships,	- IDI interviews - case study	Chapter 8
6	Ukrainian refugees employed in the Lublin and Subcarpathian Voivodeships	- questionnaire study using the PAPI method	Chapter 9, Section 9.1.
	Polish enterprises employing Ukrainian refugees in the Lublin and Subcarpathian Voivodeships	- questionnaire study using the CAWI method	Chapter 9, Section 9.2.
7	Ukrainian refugees employed in the Lublin and Subcarpathian Voivodeships	- questionnaire study using the PAPI method	Chapter 9, Section 9.1.
8	Polish enterprises employing Ukrainian refugees in the Lublin and Subcarpathian Voivodeships	- questionnaire study using the CAWI method	Chapter 9, Section 9.2.

Source: Own elaboration.

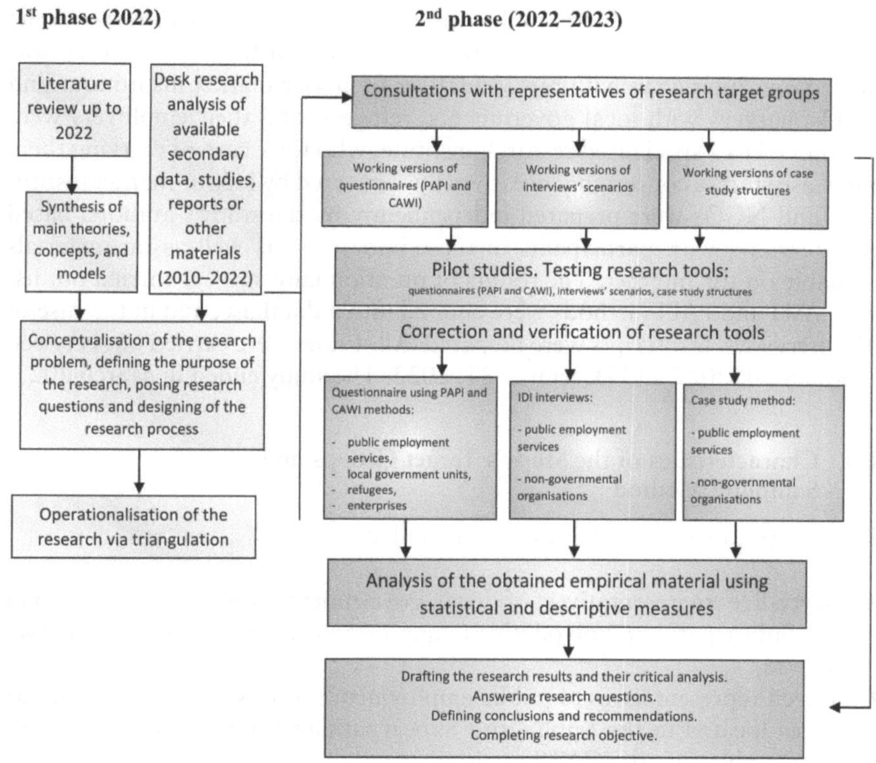

Figure 3.2 Research procedure.

Source: Own elaboration.

regions, with a particular focus on the labour market situation in both countries and cross-border flows in terms of economic migration from Ukraine to Poland, as well as other factors. This enabled the conceptualisation of the research scope and problem, as well as the definition of the research objective and design. The first phase of the study concluded with the operationalisation of the process, taking into account the triangulation of data sources and research methods described above.

In July 2022, the second phase of the study began. The research team consulted with representatives of the project's target groups to verify whether it would be possible to conduct research with the direct participation of respondents representing refugees employed in enterprises and their employers, as well as representatives of local governments, labour market institutions, and NGOs involved in assisting war migrants in the circumstances of the refugee crisis developing in Polish border regions. Once the study was deemed feasible, the work on outlining the framework of the survey began, alongside the development of the research tool templates – the CAWI and PAPI interview questionnaires, the IDI interview questionnaires, and the assumptions for the case studies. After conducting pilot surveys on small groups of respondents (two–three each), the survey tools were adjusted and the actual survey was carried out. Interviews with representatives of labour market institutions and NGOs, surveys with local governments, refugees, and their employers were outsourced to a specialised research institute, who took care of carrying them out. Case studies concerning initiatives implemented by labour market institutions and NGOs were prepared independently by the study's authors, based on interviews with participants in these initiatives, as well as on materials available on the Internet. The results of questionnaire surveys carried out using CAWI and PAPI methods were entered into a database, and in the case of IDI interviews, transcripts were prepared. All studies were carried out between February 24, 2022 and December 31, 2022. The study ended in March 2023.

3.3 Characteristics of the Study's Target Groups and Sampling Method

The groups targeted by the research included:

- Thirty-five representatives of local government units from the Lublin and Subcarpathian Voivodeships (questionnaire study using the CAWI method).
- Sixteen representatives of public employment services, e.g., district labour offices located in the Lublin and Subcarpathian Voivodeships (questionnaire study using the CAWI method).
- Six representatives of public employment services, e.g., district and voivodeship labour offices located in the Lublin and Subcarpathian Voivodeships (IDI interview).
- Five representatives of non-governmental organisations operating, among others, in the Lublin and Subcarpathian Voivodeships (IDI interview).
- Five hundred and one Ukrainian refugees employed in Poland after the outbreak of the war in Ukraine (questionnaire study using the PAPI method).
- Fifty-five enterprises operating in the Lublin and Subcarpathian Voivodeships and employing refugees (questionnaire study using the CAWI method).

The non-random selection of the sample in the conducted research was justified by their specific circumstances (Rahman et al., 2022), e.g.:

- The proximity to military operations.
- the dynamically changing geopolitical situation and refugee migrations in particular parts of the Lublin and Subcarpathian Voivodeships.
- The need to demonstrate empathy towards the difficult personal situation of the refugees, as well as towards representatives of local governments, employers, labour market institutions, and non-governmental organisations operating under tremendous pressure.

Taking into account the above-described circumstances, the most appropriate method of selecting respondents was considered to be:

- Regarding representatives of local government units – location and scale of involvement in the process of offering assistance to refugees.
- Regarding representatives of public employment services – documented action related to introducing systemic changes in the labour market and helping Ukrainian refugees find employment in Poland, the distance from the border crossing point is no longer than 100 km.
- Regarding representatives of public employment services – involvement in the direct activities on boosting the activities of refugees in the labour market and helping Ukrainian refugees find employment in Poland.
- Regarding representatives of non-governmental organisations – documented action and projects assisting Ukrainian refugees entering the Polish labour market.
- Regarding refugees and enterprises – the snowball method, i.e., initially small groups of respondents, recommended other units that should be subjected to further research. In this way, it was possible to reach respondents more organically.

The characterisation of survey respondents was outlined using basic descriptive statistics methods.

When it comes to local governments, a total of 35 representatives of local governments, representing municipalities with a total population of 552,417 residents (as of the end of 2022), took part in the study. According to declarations, 3,203 registered refugees resided in the municipalities in question in December 2022. Among the local government representatives taking part in the study were: 11 representatives of urban municipalities, four representatives of urban-rural municipalities, and 20 representatives of rural municipalities.

The list of respondents included mayors of towns and heads of municipalities, secretaries of towns and municipalities, as well as directors (heads) of departments responsible for assisting refugees in town or municipal offices. In the case of municipalities, such as Hrubieszów, Jarosław, Leżajsk, Łańcut, Przemyśl, Przeworsk, Radymno, and Sanok, the survey covered two representatives of local government bodies (separately for representatives of urban and rural municipalities) (see Figure 3.3). All local governments participating in the study were involved in supporting refugees. The location of the local governments participating in the study is presented in Figure 3.4.

One should note that the Polish regions bordering Ukraine are characterised by mainly extensive development and mostly rural character. The study included representatives of various types of municipalities. The sample included local governments in towns, which (as of December 2022) were taking in as many as 65.28% of all refugees residing in the region in question during that period. At the same time, 30.35% of refugees resided in rural

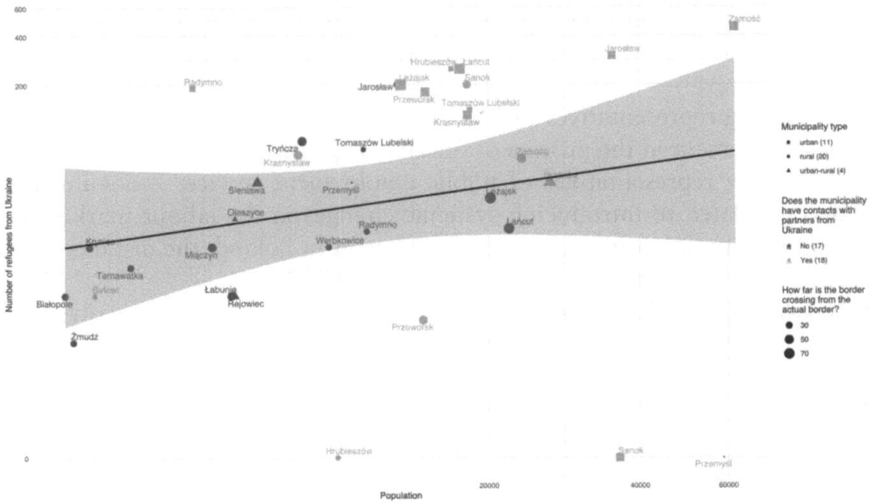

Figure 3.3 General characteristics of the local governments participating in the survey.

Source: Own elaboration based on the results of the study.

areas in the region, with 4.37% of war migrants living in urban-rural areas. All of the urban municipalities participating in the study maintained partnerships with towns on the Ukrainian side before the invasion of Ukraine. This was also true for some urban-rural and rural municipalities (see Table 3.2).

As far as the poviat labour offices operating in the Lublin and Subcarpathian Voivodeships are concerned, 16 of them participated in the CAWI survey. The surveyed labour offices cover an area of up to 100 km from the nearest border crossing, and some of them saw real interest among migrants in support of joining the Polish labour market (see Table 3.3). The heads of these labour offices filled out the survey.

The research using the IDI interview method was conducted in six labour market institutions, including five poviat labour offices (Przemyśl, Tomaszów Lubelski, Zamość, Chełm, and Stalowa Wola) and the Voivodeship Labour Office in Lublin. The respondents included employees who were directly involved in activities supporting the professional activation of refugees in the labour market.

IDI interviews were also conducted in five NGOs operating in the Lublin and Subcarpathian Voivodeships. For this study, their names and data have been anonymised.

The respondents were employees and volunteers of these organisations, directly involved in helping refugees and carrying out projects supporting the professional activation of refugees in the labour market.

A total of 501 refugees participated in the survey of employees of companies in the Lublin and Subcarpathian Voivodeships, 74.7% (374) of whom were women, and 25.4% (127 people) were men. The main group (266 people) was

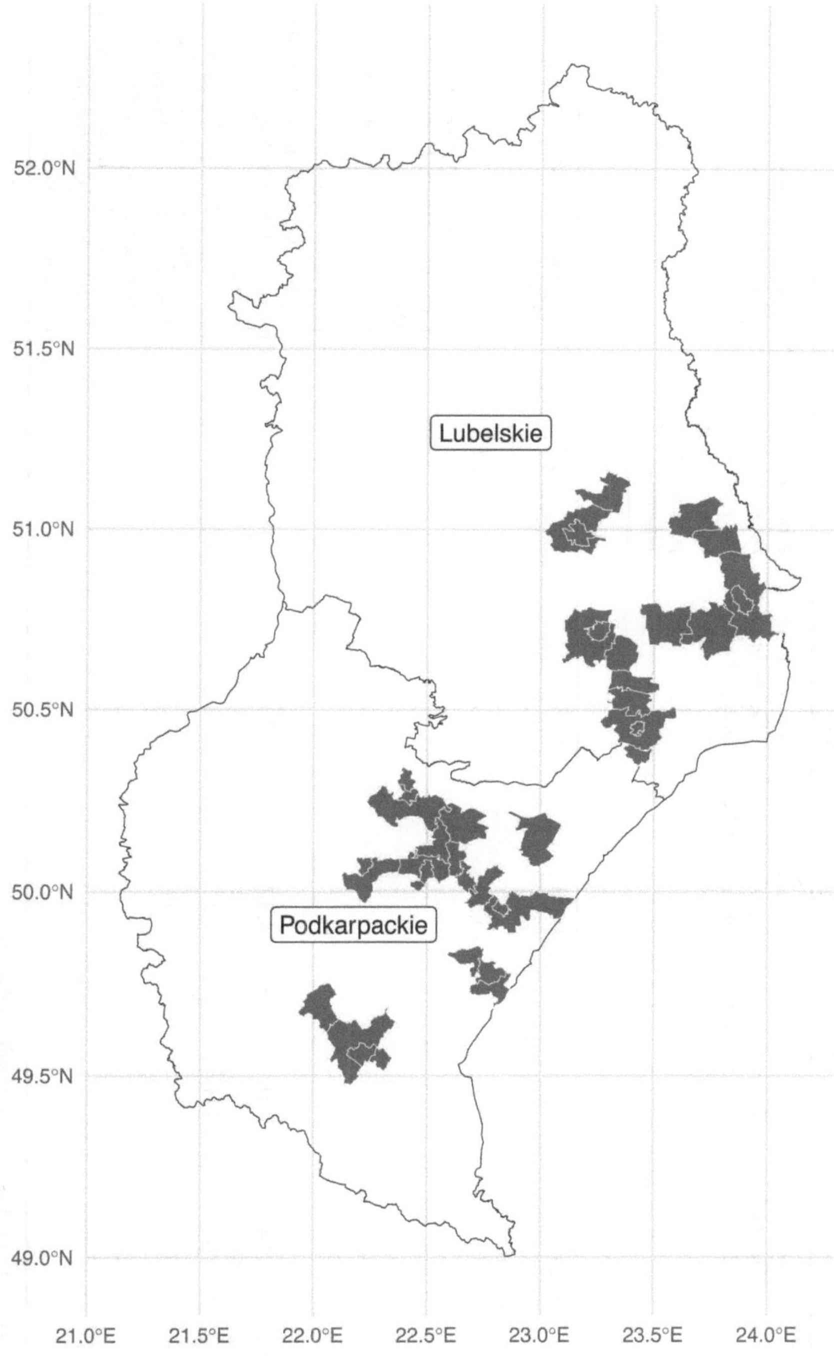

Figure 3.4 Location of local governments participating in the survey.

Source: Own elaboration based on the results of the study.

Table 3.2 Detailed characteristics of the local governments participating in the survey

	Population (as of December 2022)	*Number of refugees (as of December 2022)*	*Percentage of refugees admitted in municipalities in question*	*Percentage of refugees in the total population*	*Does the municipality have partnership relations with partners from Ukraine?*		*Names of participating municipalities (in alphabetical order)*
					Yes	No	
Total	552417	3203	100.00	0.58	18	17	According to the classification below
by municipality type:							
rural	209343	972	30.35	0.46	6	14	Bełżec, Białopole, Hrubieszów, Jarosław, Krasnystaw, Krynice, Leżajsk, Łańcut, Łubunie, Miączyn, Przemyśl, Przeworsk, Radymno, Sanok, Tarnawatka, Tomaszów Lubelski, Tryńcza, Werbkowice, Zamość, Żmudź
urban-rural	45914	140	4.37	0.30	1	3	Brzozów, Oleszyce, Rejowiec, Sieniawa
urban	297160	2091	65.2	0.70	11	0	Hrubieszów (2 people), Jarosław (2 people), Krasnystaw, Leżajsk (2 people), Łańcut (2 people), Przemyśl (2 people), Przeworsk (2 people), Radymno (2 people), Sanok (2 people), Tomaszów Lubelski, Zamość

Source: Own elaboration based on the results of the study.

Table 3.3 Sampling in the CATI/CAWI surveys in poviat labour offices

No.	*Labour office location*	*Poviat population*	*Distance from the border crossing (in km)*	*Services offered in Ukrainian or Russian languages (Yes/No)*	*Employment of refugees at the labour office (Yes/No)*
1	Przemyśl	73556	14	Yes	No
2	Jarosław	118906	44	Yes	No
3	Sanok	92900	50	Yes	No
4	Brzozów	64991	72	Yes	No
5	Rzeszów	170285	97	Yes	No
6	Przeworsk	77593	58	No	No
7	Leżajsk	68529	87	Yes	Yes
8	Łańcut	80993	80	Yes	No
9	Lubaczów	54172	14	No	No
10	Chełm	76872	34	No	No
11	Tomaszów	80828	24	No	No
12	Hrubieszów	62473	24	No	No
13	Zamość	104327	60	Yes	No
14	Krasnystaw	62125	55	Yes	Yes
15	Łęczna	56925	60	No	No
16	Lubartów	87034	80	Yes	No

Source: Survey results.

aged 25–44, while 112 people were aged 45–67. Education-wise, the most had higher education (264 people), followed by secondary education (214 people). In the Polish border regions, these people were employed mainly in the service sector (286 people) and trade and sales (146 people), with the majority classified as ordinary trade and service workers (360 people). Thirty-four and four people were employed as specialists and managers, respectively (7.6% of total respondents).

Regarding the 2021 National Census (NSP2021) results, the average percentage of the Polish population with higher education is 23.2%, and secondary education is 32.4% (in towns 27.4% and 33.6%, respectively). In Lublin Voivodeship, 18.4% of the population has higher education, and 33.1% have secondary education (in towns, 21.2% and 34.7%, respectively), while in Subcarpathian Voivodeship, 21% of the population has higher education and 33.5% of the population has secondary education (in towns, 28.1% and 35.4%, respectively). These statistics allow us to conclude that migrants arriving in the border areas have, on average, much higher education than the native population – 95.4% of the population in this group has secondary or higher education in comparison with only 51.5% in the Lublin Voivodeship, 54.4% in the Subcarpathian Voivodeship, and 55.5% in Poland as a whole (see Table 3.4).

War migration from Ukraine mainly involved women and children, so it is important to consider the internal characteristics of the group of working female refugees. Among this group, there is a clear tendency, compared to

Table 3.4 Characteristics of the respondent sample – refugees (n=501)

	Number of refugees			*Proportion by sex [%]*	
	Female	*Male*	*Total*	*Female*	*Male*
TOTAL	374	127	501	74.65	25.35
according to age					
a. 18–24	34	10	44	9.09	7.87
b. 25-44	224	42	266	59.89	33.07
c. 45–54	77	35	112	20.59	27.56
d. 55–67	34	38	72	9.09	29.92
e. Older	5	2	7	1.34	1.57
according to education					
a. primary	14	9	23	3.74	7.09
b. secondary	160	54	214	42.78	42.52
c. higher	200	64	264	53.48	50.39
d. additional courses	28	7	35	7.49	5.51
according to employment sector in Poland					
a. Trade and sales	134	12	146	35.83	9.45
b. Services	201	85	286	53.74	66.93
c. Manufacture	30	29	59	8.02	22.83
d. Public sector	9	1	10	2.41	0.79
according to position employed in Poland (group classifications)					
a. Managerial	2	2	4	0.53	1.57
b. Specialist	21	13	34	5.61	10.24
c. Trade, sales and service employee	306	54	360	81.82	42.52
d. Skilled labourer	9	48	57	2.41	37.80
e. Unskilled labourer	36	10	46	9.63	7.87

Source: Own elaboration based on research results.

the group of surveyed men, towards younger age groups – nearly 60% of the female respondents are aged 25–44, while another 20% are in the 45–54 age group. In the case of men, younger age groups (under 45) are clearly underrepresented, probably due to the eligible age for military mobilisation. Regarding education, there are no significant differences between men and women – most of the surveyed refugee women (53.5%) have higher education, and 42.8% have secondary education (96.3%). Women tended to be employed in trade and sales (35.8%), with a smaller percentage than the men employed in services (53.7% compared to 66.9%) and in the manufacturing sector (8% compared to 22.8%). Among the women, a smaller percentage held specialist or managerial positions in Poland (5.6% and 0.5%, respectively, compared to 10.2% and 1.6% of the men), and the skilled labourer percentage was smaller (2.4% vs. 37.8%). As many as 81.8% of the employed women worked regularly in trade or services. The described disproportions require a deeper analysis of how well the women's qualifications and education match the work performed in the border regions studied here and their aspirations.

There were 51 surveyed enterprises employing 1,503 workers, including 10% from Ukraine (151 people in total, which means an average of 2.75 refugees per enterprise). These enterprises mainly represented the following sectors: services (65.5%, 36 enterprises), trade and sales (23.6%, 13 enterprises), and, to a lesser extent, manufacturing and public sector (5.5% each, three enterprises). 98.2% are from the SME sector (which reflects the structure of the Polish economy), including 61.8% (34) micro-enterprises, 30.9% small businesses (16 from the private sector, one from the public sector), and 5.5% medium-sized enterprises (three, including one from the private sector, two from the public sector). The study also included one large enterprise operating in the manufacturing sector, employing 522 workers, including 21 Ukrainians (see Figure 3.5).

Among the surveyed enterprises, 30 (54.5%), declared equity as the origin of capital, while the remaining 25 (45.5%) reported mixed forms of financing (including bank loans or leasing). Before the systemic transformation at the turn of the 1990s, four enterprises were already up and running, including three public sector enterprises and one large manufacturing enterprise. The location criterion shows that the examined group included ten enterprises from the Rzeszów area, eight from Przemyśl, seven from Zamość, five from Chełm, three from Biała Podlaska and Jarosław, two from Lubaczów, Sanok, and Świdnik, and the remainder from other towns. At the same time, out of the 151 employees from Ukraine, the largest spatial concentrations were in Jarosław (26 people, 17.2%), Rzeszów (25 people, 16.6%), Przemyśl (22 people, 14.6%), Zamość (17 people, 11.3%), and smaller ones in Hrubieszów

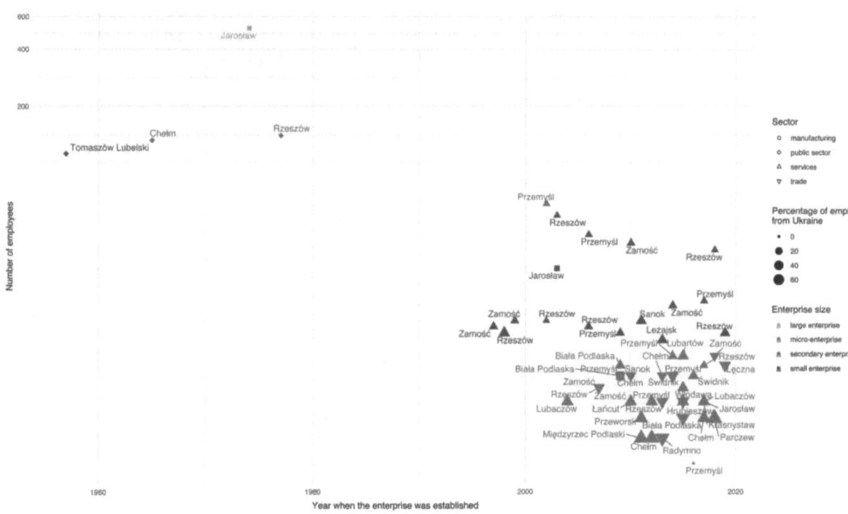

Figure 3.5 The year when the enterprise was established and the size of the company versus employment level and percentage of employees from Ukraine.

Source: Own elaboration.

(11 people, 7.3%), Sanok (seven people, 4.6%), and Biała Podlaska (six people, 4.0%). Regarding the surveyed enterprises from other towns, the total number of employees did not exceed five. For medium and large enterprises (employing 50 or more employees), the percentage of employees from Ukraine ranged from 2.1 to 8.3%. More refugees were employed in small enterprises and micro-enterprises – in 24 out of 51 enterprises; they exceeded 30%, and even 50% in the case of six companies. In contrast, one construction company employed four Ukrainians (75% of its staff).

References

Basri, H. (2014). Using qualitative research in accounting and management studies: Not a new agenda. *Journal of US-China Public Administration*, *11*(10), 831–838.

Elbardan, H., Kholeif, A. O., Elbardan, H., & Kholeif, A. O. R. (2017). An interpretive approach for data collection and analysis. In *Enterprise resource planning, corporate governance and internal auditing: An institutional perspective*.

Groeneveld, S., Tummers, L., Bronkhorst, B., Ashikali, T., & Van Thiel, S. (2015). Quantitative methods in public administration: Their use and development through time. *International Public Management Journal*, *18*(1), 61–86.

Rahman, M. M., Tabash, M. I., Salamzadeh, A., Abduli, S., & Rahaman, M. S. (2022). Sampling techniques (probability) for quantitative social science researchers: a conceptual guidelines with examples. *Seeu Review*, *17*(1), 42–51.

Sandberg, J. (2005). How do we justify knowledge produced within interpretive approaches? *Organizational Research Methods*, *8*(1), 41–68.

Sułkowski, Ł. (2009). Interpretative approach in management sciences. *Argumenta Oeconomica*, 2(23), 127–149.

Tashakkori, A., & Teddlie, C. (2010). Putting the human back in "human research methodology": The researcher in mixed methods research. *Journal of Mixed Methods Research*, 4(4), 271–277.

Trumbull, M., & Watson, K. (2010). *Qualitative research methods. Integrating quantitative and qualitative methods in research*. University Press of America.

4 Features of Socio-Economic Development and Competitiveness of the Ukrainian Border Regions

4.1 Introduction

The development of the Ukrainian labour market in 2012–2021 was characterised by the presence of complex problems, including a reduction in the supply of labour and an increase in its demand, low wages, a lack of highly productive workplaces, a mismatch of the professional and general competencies of employees with the needs of employers, irregular employment of the population, etc. (Decree of the Cabinet of Ministers of Ukraine, 2019). The crisis in the national economy in 2014 and 2015, caused by the temporary occupation of part of the territories of Ukraine as a result of the armed aggression of the Russian Federation, led to the decline of the economy and the curtailment of production, which led to the emergence of negative trends in the labour market, in particular the increase in the number of the unemployed population. During these two years, the GDP of the country decreased by 15%. The exchange rate of the national currency collapsed more than three times. The real income of households decreased by 30%. In 2014, the annual level of consumer inflation in Ukraine was 24.9%, and in 2015, it rose to 43.3%.

Three border regions of Ukraine adjoin Poland: Volynska, Lvivska, and Zakarpatska Oblasts. The length of the common Ukrainian-Polish section of the state border is ≈ 535 km (including ≈ 228 km in the territory of Volynska Oblast, ≈ 278 km of Lvivska Oblast, and ≈ 33 km of Zakarpatska Oblast). A peculiarity of the development of border regions is, on the one hand, their proximity to the regions of neighbouring countries and, on the other hand, their distance from the central regions of the country, which are usually areas of concentration of investment and economic activity. The increasing transparency of borders and the attractiveness of foreign labour markets and educational services create the risk of losing part of the human capital of border regions and Ukraine in general. At the same time, they have additional competitive advantages related to the development of cross-border cooperation.

In the wake of a full-scale war with Russia, which began on February 24, 2022, the border regions have become humanitarian hubs, a refuge for hundreds of thousands of internally displaced persons (IDPs), and a destination for business relocation from regions where active hostilities are taking place.

DOI: 10.4324/9781003471646-4

4.2 The Development of Border Regions of Ukraine: Socio-Economic Trends

The development of the Ukrainian western border regions, as well as that of many other border regions (Hansen, 1976), is largely determined by their proximity to the border – a favourable geographical location at the intersection of the main European and global transport arteries. The high density of roads and railways and the development of a network of educational institutions and scientific centres offer significant logistical, transport, and scientific and educational potential for the development of border regions. At the same time, the proximity to the border facilitates the outflow of qualified labour and young people to the border regions of neighbouring countries. In 2019, the number of migrants amounted to 2.7 million people, of which more than 50% were residents of the Western regions (Verkhovna Rada of Ukraine, 2021). Monitoring the GRP per capita for 2011–2021 shows that the economic development of the border regions of Ukraine is lagging behind the rest of the country (Kyiv City State Administration, 2022). This, accordingly, means lower levels of total income for the residents of these regions. In the border regions, the ICT sector is actively developing. The proximity to European markets of goods and services and the establishment of production on the terms of raw materials made Zakarpatska Oblast one of the most open economies among the regions.

Ukrainian border regions are characterised by developed social, transport and engineering infrastructure, landscape diversity, rich natural and recreational resources, and developed human potential. A favourable geographical position and developed foreign economic relations have contributed to the integration of regions into the world economy and the involvement of various forms of international cooperation. The general characteristics of the regions are given in Table 4.1.

Among the three border regions of Ukraine, the Lvivska Oblast is the largest in terms of area. As of January 1, 2022, twice as many people lived there as in the Volynska and Zakarpatska Oblasts. It is characterised by a high population density (113.5 people/km^2). According to this indicator, it is also ahead of the average indicator for Ukraine. In the Lvivska and Volynska Oblasts, most of the population lives in urban settlements, while in Zakarpatska Oblast, 63% of the population lives in rural areas.

During 2022–2023, the demographic situation in the regions of Ukraine underwent drastic changes. Since 2014, Ukraine has been in a state of undeclared war. Part of the country's territory was illegally annexed and temporarily occupied by the Russian Federation, and hostilities are taking place in part of it. The start of active hostilities after February 24, 2022, and the introduction of martial law in Ukraine caused mass displacement – citizens left their homes in search of safety and protection. Some citizens left for abroad (about eight million Ukrainians) (IOM, 2023); some moved to safer regions. Currently, the number of officially registered IDPs in the country has reached

Table 4.1 General characteristic of the border regions of Ukraine

Indicators	*Ukraine*		*Volynska Oblast*		*Lvivska Oblast*		*Zakarpatska Oblast*	
Area*	thousand ha	% to the total area	thousand ha	% to the total area	thousand ha	% to the total area	thousand ha	% to the total area
	60,354.9	**100.0**	**2014.4**	**3.3**	**2,183.1**	**3.6**	**1,275.3**	**2.1**
Population**	thousand persons	% to the total population	thousand persons	% to the total population	thousand persons	% to the total population	thousand persons	% to the total population
	41,167.3	**100.0**	**1021.3**	**2.48**	**2,478.1**	**6.02**	**1,244.5**	**3.02**
incl. the urban population	**28,693.7 (69.7%)**	**100.0**	**533.5 (52.2%)**	**1.9**	**1,516.4 (61.2%)**	**5.3**	**463.4 (37.2%)**	**1.6**
Population density**, persons per km²	**68.2**		**51.7**		**113.5**		**97.6**	
Gross Regional Product (GRP)***	mln.UAH	Share of GRP in general total, %	mln.UAH	Share of GRP in general total, %	mln.UAH	Share of GRP in general total, %	mln.UAH	Share of GRP in general total, %
	5,450,849	100.0	92,535	1.7	296,182	5.4	75,626	1.4
Gross Regional Product per capita***	UAH	% to the average for the country	UAH	% to the average for the country	UAH	% to the average for the country	UAH	% to the average for the country
	131,734	**100.0**	**90,331**	**68.6**	**119,049**	**90.4**	**60,632**	**46**

Source: State Statistics Service of Ukraine (accessed: 12.02.2023).

* as of January 1, 2021
** as of January 1, 2022
*** as of 2021

4.9 million people (Ministry of Social Policy of Ukraine, 2023). At the same time, according to unofficial data of the Ministry of Reintegration of the Temporarily Occupied Territories of Ukraine, the real number of IDPs, as of 2023, is about seven million people. Therefore, the main task of the Ministry and local authorities is to integrate IDPs into the new social environment in new hromadas. Last year, 55 billion hryvnias of living allowance were paid from the budget. IDPs receive humanitarian aid, food packages, clothing, and basic necessities from the state (Word and deed, 2023).

As of May 1, 2023, the Volynska Oblast sheltered 77,462 people who, due to the large-scale invasion of the Russian Federation into Ukraine, were forced to evacuate from the areas of hostilities (Volyn Regional State Administration, 2023). A total of 245,000 people registered as IDPs in the Lvivska Oblast. However, resettled people often do not register in a new place and rent housing on their own; therefore, Lvivska Oblast sheltered twice as many people as registered with state authorities – that is, about 500,000. Approximately 50–100 people arrive in Lviv every day on evacuation trains. Some of them go abroad, while others seek refuge within the region (Evacuation.City, 2023). There are more than 400,000 IDPs in the Zakarpatska Oblast, and more than 200,000 people are officially registered as IDPs (UKRINFORM, 2023).

Therefore, today in the Zakarpatska Oblast, every 4th inhabitant of the region is an IDP; in the Lvivska Oblast – every 6th inhabitant; and in the Volynska Oblast – every 14th inhabitant. This has a strong impact on the socio-economic development of the border regions at war due to the weak social security of IDPs, their financial vulnerability, the search for a place of temporary stay, and the significant burden on the social infrastructure and economy of hromadas, etc. At the same time, IDPs are also an important asset, an additional potential resource for the economic development of local hromadas, whose effective use minimises socio-economic challenges and at the same time guarantees positive results in terms of ensuring the employment and self-sufficiency of IDPs, engaging their potential in the development of the economy and infrastructure, running local business stimulation programmes, and organising the following: training courses, professional development, seminars for IDPs, systematic involvement of IDPs in public projects, events within the volunteer movement, and the implementation of cross-border programmes for financing business and social projects of IDPs (Public Space, 2022).

The Lvivska Oblast is ahead of the Volynska and Zakarpatska Oblasts in terms of GRP and GRP per capita. At the same time, GRP per person in the Lvivska Oblast is 90.4% of its average value in Ukraine.

In the conditions of crises and external shocks, an important role in the development of regions is played by their administrative structure. In 2014, decentralisation reform began in Ukraine, with the adoption of the Concept of Reform of Local Self-Government and Territorial Organisation of Power in Ukraine, dated April 1, 2014, No. 333 (Verkhovna Rada of

Ukraine, 2014.). It aims to establish a three-tier system of administrative and territorial organisation: hromada (community); raion (district); oblast (region). On June 12, 2020, the Cabinet of Ministers of Ukraine adopted 24 orders on the definition of administrative centres and approval of the territories of hromadas in Oblasts. As a result, 1,469 territorial hromadas were created in the country. On October 25, 2020, the first elections of local heads and deputies of local councils were held in 1,420 out of 1,469 hromadas (Decentralization, 2020).

As a result of the reform, instead of more than 11,000 local councils, 1,469 capable territorial hromadas were formed, and instead of 490 raions, 140 new raions were formed. Administrative and territorial reform was accompanied by budgetary and financial decentralisation. The public administration system of Ukraine is still being reformed in accordance with the new system of administrative-territorial division and updated roles. The implementation of the reform (changes in the administrative and territorial structure, budget decentralisation, sectoral reforms, etc.) is intended to become a catalyst for positive changes at all levels of society.

The number of administrative-territorial units in the border regions of Ukraine as of January 1, 2022, is shown in Table 4.2.

The economic growth of regions is largely determined by the efficiency of labour markets. In 2020–2021, the COVID-19 pandemic led to significant changes in labour markets around the world, including Ukraine. During 2019–2021, the number of the economically active decreased by 744,400, and the number of employed population decreased by 968,300. At the same time, the level of economic activity decreased from 63.4% to 61.8% and the level of employment from 58.2% to 55.7%. The unemployment rate increased from 8.2% to 9.9%.

As of 2021, in all border regions of Ukraine, the share of the workforce to the population aged 15–70 was lower than its level in the country as a whole. Furthermore, the regions lag behind significantly in terms of the average monthly salary. At the same time, the unemployment rate in Lvivska Oblast in 2021 was 2.2% lower than the national average (see Table 4.3 and Figure 4.1).

The structure of employment of the population of Ukrainian border regions in 2021 is shown in Figure 4.2.

Table 4.2 Number of administrative and territorial units as of January 1, 2022

	Raions	*Territorial hromadas*	*Cities*	*Raions in cities*	*Urban type settlements*	*Rural type settlements*
Ukraine	**140**	**1469**	**461**	**108**	**881**	**28369**
Volynska Oblast	4	54	11	–	22	1054
Lvivska Oblast	7	73	44	6	34	1850
Zakarpatska Oblast	6	64	11	–	19	578

Source: State Statistics Service of Ukraine (accessed: 25.02.2023).

Table 4.3 The characteristics of the labour market in the border regions, 2021

	Labour force aged 15–70 years old		*Unemployed population aged 15–70 years old (by ILO methodology)*		*Average monthly nominal wages of regular employees, UAH*
	thousand persons	*% to the population aged 15–70 years*	*thousand persons*	*% to the workforce aged 15–70*	
Ukraine	**17,321.6**	**61.8**	**1,711.6**	**9.9**	**14,014**
Volynska Oblast	**412.6**	**55.5**	**52.4**	**12.7**	**11,445**
Lvivska Oblast	**1,114.4**	**60.4**	**85.7**	**7.7**	**12,530**
Zakarpatska Oblast	**544.1**	**59.5**	**60.6**	**11.1**	**12,235**

Source: State Statistics Service of Ukraine (accessed: 23.02.2023).

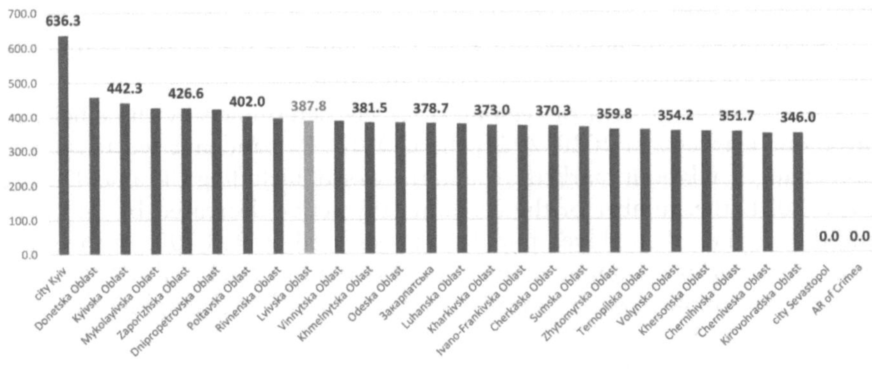

Figure 4.1 Average monthly nominal salary of regular employees by region of Ukraine in 2021 (in Euros).

Source: State Service of Statistics of Ukraine; National Bank of Ukraine (accessed: 21.02.2023).

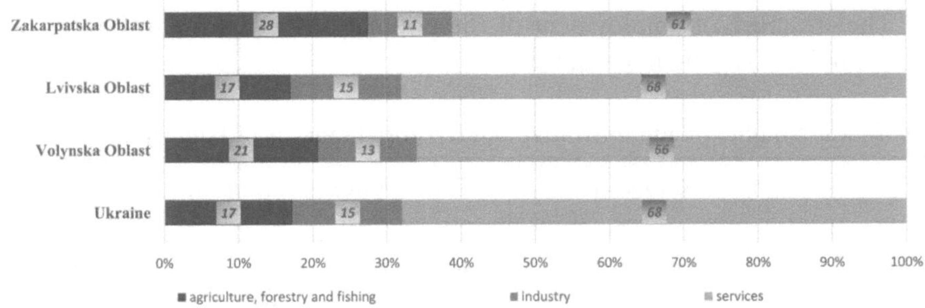

Figure 4.2 Employed population, by type of economic activity (in percentage terms).

Source: State Statistics Service of Ukraine (accessed: 03.03.2023).

The lower level of urbanisation in the Volynska and Zakarpatska Oblasts relative to Ukraine in general means more people are involved in agriculture, forestry, and fisheries. At the same time, in the Lvivska Oblast, the number of employed people in the primary sector is lower than in Ukraine as a whole, and the number of people employed in industry and services is higher, respectively. The Lvivska Oblast is one of the regions of Ukraine in which the IT sector is actively developing; a powerful IT cluster has been formed. As of 2022, about 18% of specialists in computer industries were concentrated in this region.

In 2022, the consequence of the full-scale Russian invasion of Ukraine was a significant narrowing of the labour market in Ukraine: many enterprises in the country closed, and many people lost their jobs. Only some companies were able to move the entire team or part of the staff to safe regions or other countries and continue working. These were mainly employees of the IT sector. The loss and damage of production assets and infrastructure and the interruption of supply chains of trade networks weakened the potential of the labour market, leading to "disruptions" and the loss of employment opportunities for the majority of Ukrainians (Razumkov Centre, 2022). Relocation and forced migration led to a change in the regional structure of the labour market, as well as the structure of offers and the saturation of specialists in the region. In the regions most affected by the military aggression of the Russian Federation, the number of jobs decreased, and competition increased. The imbalance between labour supply and demand has become significant. The demand for labour has decreased dramatically due to the inability to work in war zones, reduced demand for goods and services, logistical problems, and uncertainty about the future. If during January–September 2021, the State Employment Service of Ukraine registered 582,486 vacancies, then for the same period in 2022, only 325,145, that is, the demand for labour force fell by 1.8 times. During this period, the applicants per vacancy increased from 1.7 to 2.4 people, primarily due to a sharp drop in the number of registered vacancies and, to a lesser extent, due to an increase in the number of people who had the status of unemployed.

As of September 1, 2022, the largest discrepancy between the demand for labour and its supply in terms of professional and qualification was observed among technical employees (25 people applied for one vacancy), qualified agricultural workers (19 people), employees and managers (18 people), and trade and service workers (14 people). In terms of types of economic activity, as of October 1, 2022, the greatest load per vacancy was observed in the spheres of financial and insurance activities (84.3 people), information and telecommunications (17.3 people), and public administration and defence (16.2 people).

In addition, there is a significant level of irregular employment in the labour market in the country – many vacancies are offered without registration, such as part-time work, etc. Due to the war, there has been a decrease in wages, because there are far more unemployed people than there are vacant jobs. The share of the population with incomes lower than the actual living wage, which for working-age persons in 2022 was UAH 2,481 (67.6 Euros according to the Euro exchange rate as of October 2022), can be as high as 70%.

According to the data of the Main Department of Statistics in Volynska Oblast, the number of people employed in the 15–70 age group in 2021, compared with 2020, decreased by 3,900 and amounted to 360,200 people. The employment rate in the 15–70 age group decreased from 48.9% to 48.5%. The number of unemployed people (according to the ILO methodology) aged 15–70 in 2021, compared with 2020, increased by 500 people and amounted to 52,400 people. The unemployment rate (according to the ILO methodology) in the 15–70 age group increased from 12.5% to 12.7% of the workforce. In January–March 2023, 9,500 jobseekers used the services of the State Employment Service in the Volynska Oblast, of which 6,800 people were registered as unemployed. 4,700 people received unemployment benefits. According to the types of jobs, most citizens are employed in trade (27.8%) and the processing industry (17.8%). According to professional groups, 21.6% are trade and service workers, 17.1% are unskilled workers, and 13.1% are specialists. In terms of job vacancies, most are in the wholesale and retail trade (31.6%) and in the processing industry (18.4%).

As of April 1, 2023, on average in the Volynska Oblast, two unemployed people applied for one job vacancy (as of April 1, 2022 – 11 people). The largest discrepancy between the demand for labour and its supply in terms of professional qualifications was observed among qualified workers in the financial and insurance sectors (22 persons) (Volyn Regional Employment Centre, 2023).

The number of people employed in the Lvivska Oblast aged 15–70 in 2021, compared with 2020, decreased by 10,200 people and amounted to 1,028,700 people. The employment rate in the 15–70 age group decreased from 56.0% to 55.8% (in Ukraine – from 56.2% to 55.7%). The number of unemployed (according to the ILO methodology) aged 15–70 in 2021, compared with 2020, increased by 800 people and amounted to 85,700 people. The unemployment rate (according to the ILO methodology) among the 15–70 age group increased from 7.6% to 7.7% of the workforce (in Ukraine, from 9.5% to 9.9%).

As of April 1, 2023, the number of vacancies reported by employers to the Lviv Regional Employment Service amounted to 4,600 units, which is 1.6 more than on April 1, 2022 (2,800). As of April 1, 2023, on average, one unemployed person applied for one vacant job in the region (as of April 1, 2022, four people); in Ukraine, on average, there were four people. The imbalance in the registered labour market is observed only by professionally qualified groups of agricultural and forestry workers, as well as managers; two unemployed people applied for every one vacancy (Lviv Regional Employment Center, 2023).

According to the State Statistics Service of Ukraine, the average number of employed people aged 15–70 in Zakarpatska Oblast in 2021 was 483,500. The employment rate of the population aged 15–70 was 52.8%. The number of unemployed (according to the ILO methodology) aged 15–70 in 2021 was 60,600. The unemployment rate among the 15–70 age group was 11.1% of the workforce. As of April 1, 2023, the number of vacancies reported by employers to the headquarters and branches of the Zakarpattia Regional Employment Service was 506. By type of economic activity, most vacancies were in the processing industry (32.1%), in wholesale and retail trade (16.6%), in transport, warehousing, postal and courier activities (12.1%).

The imbalance between labour supply and demand in the Zakarpatska Oblast remains significant. As of April 1, 2023, on average, in the region, five unemployed people applied for one job vacancy (as of April 1, 2022 – seven unemployed). The greatest discrepancy between the demand for labour and its supply in terms of professional qualifications was observed among qualified rural workers (12 people applied for one vacancy) and workers in trade and services (8 people). The greatest difficulties with employment were experienced by sellers of food products, assemblers, workers in forestry works, auxiliary workers, sales consultants, and sellers of non-food products (Zakarpattia Regional Employment Center, 2023).

According to the data of mobile operators, during April–September 2022, the number of people who were outside Ukraine amounted to approximately 3.2 million people. At the same time, 23% of those fleeing the war managed to keep their jobs in Ukraine and work remotely. Most intend to return to Ukraine. As of February 21, 2023, according to the UN, more than eight million Ukrainian citizens were abroad due to the war.

In July 2022, the Ministry of Defence of Ukraine announced that, in total, more than 1,000,000 people support the security and defence sector.

Measures to increase the flexibility of the labour market, optimise labour relations, stimulate employment, relocate enterprises, etc. contribute to slowing down the growth of unemployment indicators.

The revitalisation of economic activity both in the production sector and in the service sector, adaptation of employers to new conditions of economic activity contributed to a recovery of activity on the labour market in recent months. Thus, the number of current vacancies on the Work.ua portal increased by 14% in July (compared with the previous month of the current year), by 20% in August, and by 16% in September. Kyiv, Lviv, Dnipropetrovsk, Odesa, and Ivano-Frankivsk regions hold the lead in the offer of vacant jobs.

Further imbalance of supply and demand in the labour market, particularly in the long term, will increase the burden on the state budget and social security. This can lead to an acute shortage of workers in certain industries and deepen existing disparities in the labour market.

Such a deepening should also be expected during the recovery period, when there will be a projected increase in demand for specialists in the construction industry (planners, architects, designers, masons, etc.) and related sectors of the economy (logistics, drivers of motor vehicles, engineering and technical personnel, specialists in production of building materials). If the trend towards the development of the IT sector continues, the demand for specialists in this field will increase. In post-war times, the demand for medical workers will be significant. However, given the extent of destruction of industrial enterprises and the duration of restoration of destroyed facilities, the demand for workers in industrial activities will be relatively weak for some time.

In the conditions of martial law, the state authorities took a number of measures to stabilise the situation on the labour market of Ukraine, provided for in the regulatory and legal acts, in particular (Scientific and Analytical Report, 2022): (1) introduction of annual basic paid leave for all employees lasting 24 calendar days, (2) expansion of the autonomy of employers in decision-making regarding the conclusion of labour contracts, accounting of working hours, etc., (3) ensuring the possibility of submitting an application for granting the status of unemployed, for the appointment of unemployment benefits and for terminating the registration of the unemployed through the mobile application of the Diya Portal, and (4) guaranteeing employers compensation for labour costs of UAH 6,500 per month for each employed person, for whom a single contribution to mandatory state social insurance is paid, during wartime and within 30 calendar days after its cancellation or termination.

The functioning of the labour market is also determined by the specifics of the development of foreign economic activity of the regions. The border regions are characterised by a more open economy relative to Ukraine in general. According to the indicators of the share of exports and imports in GRP, the economy of the Zakarpatska Oblast is the most open (see Figure 4.3).

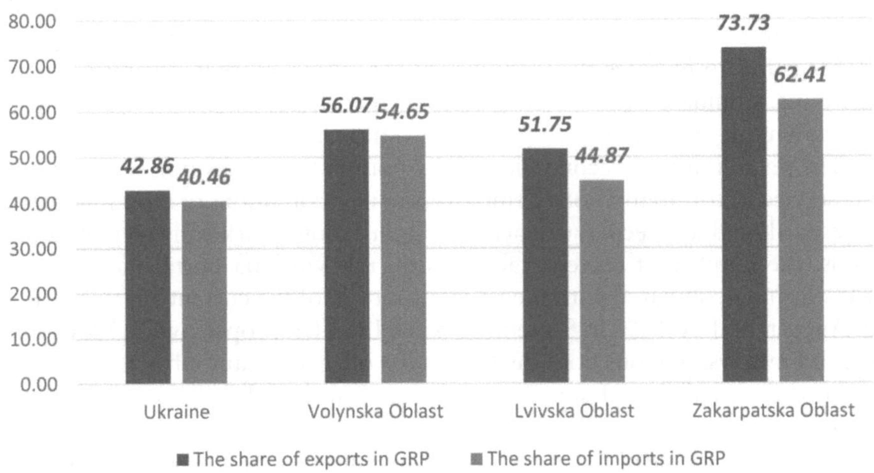

Figure 4.3 The share of exports and imports of Ukraine and its border regions in their GDP in 2021 (in percentage terms).

Source: State Statistics Service of Ukraine (accessed: 06.03.2023).

The analysis of the export commodity structure of the border regions showed that in all regions the largest share of export goods belongs to commodity group XVI. Machines, equipment and mechanisms, electric and technical equipment, as of 2021, account for 30% of all exports in Volynska Oblast, 20.2% in Lvivska Oblast, and 61.9% in Zakarpatska Oblast.

In the Volynska Oblast, goods in groups IX – wood and articles made from wood (25.7%) – and group XX – various industrial goods (11.3%) – also have a large share of exports. In the Lvivska Oblast, a significant share of exports falls on goods in group II: plant products (16%) and XX: various industrial goods (14.6%). In the Zakarpatska Oblast, the export of goods in group IX, wood and articles made from wood (9.2%), is also significant.

In the structure of imports for the Volynska and Lvivska Oblasts, goods in group V – mineral products (34.7% and 19.3%, respectively) – take precedence. A significant share of imports to the Volynska Oblast are goods in group XVII – means of land transport, aircraft, boats (26.3%) – and group XVI – machines, equipment and mechanisms, electrical equipment (12.1%). The Lvivska Oblast imports about 15.1% of goods in group XVI – machines, equipment and mechanisms, electrical equipment – and 12.4% of goods in group XI – textile materials and textile products. In the import structure of the Zakarpatska Oblast, the greatest volume of goods is from groups XVI – machines, equipment and mechanisms, electrotechnical equipment (49.7%) – as well as group VII – polymeric materials, plastics, and products from them (10.8%) – and XVII – means of land transport, aircraft, and boats (7.8%).

The main trade partners of Ukrainian border regions are neighbouring countries. In particular, 55.1% of all export-import operations of the Volynska Oblast in 2021 were accounted for by Belarus (18.1%), Poland (16.1%), Germany (12.1%), and Lithuania (8.8%). The main partners of the Lvivska Oblast were Poland (21%), Germany (11%), China (8%), Belarus (7.7%), and Turkey (5.1%). Hungary (34.7%), China (12%), and Germany (9.1%) account for about 56% of all foreign trade with the Zakarpatska Oblast.

A number of international transport corridors (ITCs) pass through the Ukrainian border regions, which help strengthen interregional integration within the country and encourage foreign business by facilitating access to international markets. In particular, the Baltic Sea-Black Sea ITC passes through the Volynska Oblast, which has an approximate length of 271.4 km. Three ITCs pass through the Lvivska Oblast: Pan-European transport corridor III and V, and "Europe-Asia". The total length of corridors in the region is 344.7 km. The Pan-European transport corridor V and Europe-Asia pass through the Zakarpatska Oblast. In addition, in order to improve the logistics of Ukraine's export deliveries, in July 2022, Ukrainian logistics routes were included in the Trans-European Transport Network (TEN-T). The routes of the four TEN-T will now pass through Ukraine and will be able to apply for their inclusion in the EU financial plans for the development of these corridors (Directorate-General for Mobility and Transport, 2022):

- The North-Baltic Corridor was extended through Lviv and Kyiv to Mariupol.
- The Baltic-Black Sea-Aegean Corridor was extended through Lviv, Chernivtsi (Romania and Moldova) to Odessa.
- The Baltic Sea-Adriatic Sea and Rhine-Danube Corridors will pass through Lviv.

The development of transport networks in the region can become an effective tool for ensuring spatially balanced and more sustainable regional economic development and improving people's well-being. At the macro level, the transport network is linked to national output, employment, and income. At the micro level, transport networks connect producers and consumers and affect human well-being, including poverty reduction through increased output and wages, job creation, and lower costs and higher prices for products. Transport networks also facilitate access to education, work, healthcare, and other social and cultural institutions (Quium, 2019).

A cross-country analysis of 60 countries over the period 1980–2010, which compared them by indicators of improved mobility (through investment in motorways and expressways), accessibility (investment in local roads that provide more direct connections to destinations), and economic growth, has demonstrated that, in particular, the improvement of mobility contributes to economic growth due to the increase of exports in countries with a medium and high level of development (Ng et al., 2017).

A study conducted in Southeast Asian countries based on a gravity model showed that the development of cross-border road infrastructure had a positive effect on intra-regional trade in basic goods with an elasticity in the range of 0.6–1.4. A similar influence on the growth of trade was substantiated in a study conducted among the countries of Eastern Europe. Using a gravity model, it was found that road upgrades can increase regional trade by 50% from the baseline, exceeding the expected effects of tariff reductions or trade facilitation programmes (Fujimura & Edmonds, 2006).

The development of cross-border transport infrastructure along ITCs reduces transaction costs. A study conducted in Asian countries showed that a 10% reduction in border transaction costs increases exports by about 2%. This will be facilitated by the effective functioning of the network of checkpoints, improvement of transit procedures, etc. (De, 2011).

In 2023, Regulation (EU) 2023/1077 was adopted regarding the temporary opening of the European market for goods originating from Ukraine; the Agreement between the European Union and Ukraine on Road Freight Transport (Special Agreement on the Liberalisation of Road Transport) was signed. On October 1, 2022, Ukraine began to apply the Convention on

Common Transit and the Convention on Simplification of Formalities in Trade in Goods (international application of NCTS).

Transport development is also linked to many Sustainable Development Goals (SDGs) and can be used as a tool to achieve some of them. For example, the development of corridors and transport networks can affect the achievement of Goal 9. Industry, innovation, and infrastructure (objectives 9.1–9.4) and Goal 10. Reducing inequality (objectives 10.3–10.4).

The general characteristics of the development of the transport network of border regions are shown in Table 4.4.

The loss of part of the transit potential and the closed borders in the east and north of the country are changing the priorities of planning and restoring the transport infrastructure and forming new transport corridors. Logistics routes have also undergone significant changes. To replace the existing ITCs in circumstances of geopolitical change, new initiatives to form new ITCs are already being actively developed. One of the few alternatives to transit traffic along the main route of the New Silk Road, which travels through the Russian Federation, is currently the Middle Corridor (through Kazakhstan, Azerbaijan, and Georgia). Last year, the volume of railway cargo that passed through this corridor increased by 52% (Logist.Today, 2022). This increase is expected to be even higher this year due to growing interest in the corridor as an alternative multimodal route between Europe and China.

Therefore, Ukraine should not only actively participate in new initiatives regarding the development of ITC but also initiate the creation of new partnerships along the important Europe-Caucasus-Asia trade route. The development of ITC and the efficiency of its functioning have a direct impact on the surrounding territories.

The high density of highways and railway tracks due to proximity to the state border and a favourable geographical location at the intersection of the

Table 4.4 Characteristics of the transport network of the border regions of Ukraine, 2020

Indicators	*Ukraine*	*Volynska Oblast*	*Lvivska Oblast*	*Zakarpatska Oblast*
Length of paved roads, 1,000 km	158.7	5.8	8.2	3.4
Density of paved public roads, km per 1,000 km^2 of territory	283	288	376	266
The average categorisation of motor roads*	3.71	3.69	3.64	4.07
Density of public railway tracks, km per 1,000 km^2 of territory	35	29	58	47
Operational length of railway tracks for general use, km	19,791	593	1,263	601

Source: Scientific and Analytical Report (2023).

* categories of roads I–V, where I is the category of roads with the highest intensity of traffic and the maximum calculated speed of traffic on flat terrain – 130 km/h

main European and world transport arteries mean that the border regions have immense potential for the transport of goods. If logistics and transport infrastructure are developed effectively, regional development will accelerate, and the competitiveness of regions on national and global markets will grow.

The reorientation of the main international and transit cargo transportation towards the western border of Ukraine increased the load on the border infrastructure of the border regions. This affected the periodic formation of huge queues of trucks and railway wagons at checkpoints. At the border with the EU, 21 international checkpoints for cargo transportation currently operate, of which 11 are for road traffic and ten are for rail.

In the Volynska Oblast, there are three checkpoints for cargo transportation: one – for road, and two – for rail. There are six checkpoints for cargo transportation in the Lvivska Oblast: four by road and two by rail. In the Zakarpatska Oblast, there are nine operating checkpoints for freight transportation, of which five are railway checkpoints.

All automobile checkpoints on the border with Poland tend to suffer a significant overload of the actual throughput compared to their design capacity. The checkpoints on the border with Slovakia, Hungary, and Romania are operating at the limit of their design capacity. Some process fewer vehicles relative to their design capacity.

Regionally, the Zakarpatska Oblast has the largest checkpoint design capacity (33.5% – for road traffic, 72.4% – for rail traffic). At the same time, as of 2021, 38% of trucks and 38.6% of all cargo passed through automobile checkpoints in the Lvivska Oblast. The development of the network of checkpoints for cargo transportation in the Lvivska Oblast should consider the peculiarities of how the entire network of checkpoints functions along the Ukraine-EU border.

Among the border regions of the Western region of Ukraine, the Lvivska Oblast features the most developed transport networks. The rest of the regions are above the Ukrainian average. In the post-war period, the reconstruction and development of transport communications and transport infrastructure (interchanges, bridges, etc.) must consider the needs of domestic and foreign markets regarding the volume and logistics of freight transportation and provide for the active implementation of smart and energy-efficient transport technologies.

In general, the following economic development trends can be identified:

- From February 24, 2022, a state of war was declared in Ukraine, along with general mobilisation. The economy of the regions is gradually being reoriented to the needs of the country at war; fewer people are in employment due to mobilisation, and enterprises have been relocated from regions of active hostilities.
- In the period up to 2022, the leading branch of the Volynska Oblast's economy was the agrarian and industrial sector, which provided almost half of its total output. Agriculture specialised in animal husbandry for

the meat and dairy sector, as well as in the production of grain, sugar beet, vegetables, and potatoes. The leading branches of industry were food, machine building, fuel, chemicals, and building materials. In the Lvivska Oblast, more than half of the industrial production was provided by the food industry, processing of agricultural products, machine building, production, and distribution (transportation) of energy carriers. Mechanical engineering was one of the main industries of the region. Significant capacity for the production of buses, forklifts, cranes, overhead conveyors, oil and gas industry, machine tool engineering, and agricultural machinery was concentrated here. Zakarpattia is one of the regions of Ukraine with a predominantly rural population. Therefore, agriculture occupies a leading place in the economy of the region; it creates 15% of the gross added value. In the Zakarpatska Oblast, agricultural production has its own specifics and features, as the region is land-poor.

- Since the beginning of the full-scale aggression, according to the relocation programme, about 800 enterprises have moved to safer regions. Of these, 623 companies have already resumed work. Another 239 enterprises are currently searching for a new location. Therefore, about 24% of enterprises relocated to the Lvivska Oblast, while 14.5% moved to the Zakarpatska Oblast.
- In total, since the beginning of the full-scale invasion, 225 enterprises have relocated to the Lvivska Oblast, of which 164 are up and running. Most of the others have already returned to their previous locations or have opened branches in the region. The largest number of relocated enterprises are in light industry, mechanical engineering, metalworking, and food industry. As of the end of September 2022, 422 enterprises have moved to Zakarpattia, of which 378 are operational and 44 are still in the process of moving, installing, and connecting equipment. Of the total number of enterprises relocated to the region, 18.7% are processing industry enterprises.
- In the circumstances of war, the transport and logistics system plays a decisive role in ensuring the humanitarian, social, food, energy, and, above all, military security of Ukraine. In this context, the border regions have a significant potential to increase international and transit cargo transportation. An important prerequisite is the formation of an effective institutional environment, integrated into the European economic space by ensuring that the requirements stipulated by the Association Agreement between the EU and Ukraine are met in terms of transport, adaptation of the European and Ukrainian freight transport markets to the requirements of the European Green Plan, as well as the development of cooperation within the Eastern Partnership (EaP) transport panel, which is also focused on making the EaP regional transport network compatible with the TEN-T network. The improvement of the state border crossing infrastructure, in particular in terms of increasing the throughput capacity of the Ukraine-EU customs border, should optimise and encourage rail

freight transportation, restore and increase the production capacities for cargo handling at railway terminals, develop a network of intermodal and transshipment terminals, create border "dry ports" and cross-border logistics hubs with the introduction of joint control by the authorities of neighbouring countries, and simplify border crossing procedures during multimodal and contra-rail transportation. The development of the logistics and transport infrastructure of the border regions of Ukraine will act as a catalyst for economic, social, and environmental development both regionally and nationally.

4.3 Comparative Analysis of Regional Competitiveness in the Polish-Ukrainian Borderland

Globalisation of world economic processes and increased competition in product sales markets in conditions of limited resources strengthen the role of competitiveness as a determining factor in the development of the economy of the country, region, and enterprises. In recent years, regions have become powerful players in world markets and global production networks. Therefore, a key component of the development and implementation of regional development strategies are their competitive advantages.

According to the OECD definition, "A competitive region is one that can attract and maintain successful firms and maintain or increase standards of living for the region's inhabitants. Skilled labour and investment gravitate away from 'uncompetitive' regions towards more competitive ones".

Regional economic competitiveness aims to provide sustainable economic growth, namely developing leading sectors in accordance with the potential and needs of the area to improve people's welfare (Widiastuti, 2020).

The Lvivska Oblast is one of the most developed regions of the country in terms of its economy, tourism, culture, and science. It is an administrative-territorial unit (oblast) located in the far west of Ukraine. The Lvivska Oblast borders the Volynska, Rivnenska, Ternopilska, Ivano-Frankivska, and Zakarpatska Oblasts and has access to the state border with the Republic of Poland. It borders the Lublin (common border length ≈ 72 km) and Subcarpathian Voivodeships of Poland (common border length ≈ 206 km).

The Lvivska Oblast covers 21,800 km^2 (3.6% of the country's area) (see Table 4.5) and is divided into seven districts and 73 territorial communities. As of 2020, the population of the Lvivska Oblast was 2,497,800 (2,478,100 in 2021), including 1,526,800 (61.1%) urban and 970,980 (38.9%) rural residents. The average life expectancy is 72.42 years: 67.4 for men and 77.57 for women.

The Lvivska Oblast is smaller in area compared with the Lublin Voivodeship, but it is larger than the Subcarpathian Voivodeship. In terms of population, the region dominates both the Lublin and Subcarpathian Voivodeships. The population density of the Lvivska Oblast is almost the same as the population density of the Subcarpathian Voivodeship. At the same time, if the

Table 4.5 Comparative characteristics of the socio-economic development of the Lvivska Oblast and the Lublin and Subcarpathian Voivodeships, 2020

	*Ukraine**	*Lvivska Oblast**		*Poland***	*Lublin Voivodeship***		*Subcarpathian Voivodeship***	
	total	*total*	*Ukraine=100*	*total*	*total*	*Poland=100*	*total*	*Poland=100*
AREA								
Area in km²	603549	21831	**3.6**	312705	25123	**8**	17846	**5.7**
POPULATION								
Population in thousands	41588.3	2497.8	**6.02**	38265	2095.3	**5.5**	2121.2	**5.5**
urban areas	28959.5	1526.8	**5.3**	22905.1	971.7	**4.2**	877.4	**3.8**
rural areas	12628.8	970.98	**7.7**	15359.9	1123.5	**7.3**	1243.8	**8.1**
per 1 km²	69	114.4	**165.8**	122.37	83.4	**68.2**	118.86	**97**
Natural increase (decrease) per one thousand population	−8.1	**−6.1**		−3.2	**−4.4**		**−2.1**	
Migration increase (decrease) per one thousand population	0.51	**0.34**		0.1	**−2.1**		**−0.9**	
LABOUR MARKET								
Employed persons in thousands	15915.3	1038.9	**6.5**	15682.2	855.9	**5.5**	868.1	**5.5**
Average monthly gross wages in EUR	376.5	334.5	**88.8**	1175.76	1050.36	**89.33**	1015.04	**86.3**
EDUCATION								
Higher education institutions (HEI)	515	33	**6.4**	349	16	**4.59**	14	**4.01**
Students of HEI	1 141 889	95 364	**8.4**	1218046	68634	**5.64**	45804	**3.76**
TRANSPORT INFRASTRUCTURE								
Railway lines operated, in km	19791	1263	**6.4**	19422	1092	**5.6**	978	**5**
Hard surface public roads, in km	158.7	8.2	**5.2**	313.6	23.9	**7.6**	17.6	**5.6**

(*Continued*)

Table 4.5 (Continued)

	Ukraine[*]	*Lvivska Oblast*[*]		*Poland*[**]	*Lublin Voivodeship*[**]		*Subcarpathian Voivodeship*[**]	
	total	*total*	*Ukraine=100*	*total*	*total*	*Poland=100*	*total*	*Poland=100*
REGIONAL ACCOUNTS								
Gross domestic product (current prices), in mln EUR	137132.8	7673.61	**5.6**	515928.50	19583.11	**3.8**	20091.79	**3.9**
Per capita in EUR	3285	3063.45	**93.26**	13440.65	9310.43	**69.3**	9450.819	**70.7**
UNITS OF THE NATIONAL ECONOMY								
Units of the national economy, in thousands	1980.8	128.6	**6.5**	4663.4	192.7	**4.1**	188.4	**4.0**
incl. natural entities-entrepreneurs	1606.5	107.6	**6.7**	3326.8	145.7	**4.4**	140.7	**4.2**

Source: Regions of Ukraine (2020; 2021); Statistical Yearbook of the Republic of Poland (2021); Narodowy Bank Polski (2020); Urząd Statystycny w Lublinie (2021); Statistical Yearbook of the Lublin Voivodeship (2020); Urząd Statystyczny w Lublinie (2020); Statistical Yearbook of the Subcarpathian Voivodeship (2021).

[*] Data as of January 1, 2021
[**] Data as of December 31, 2020

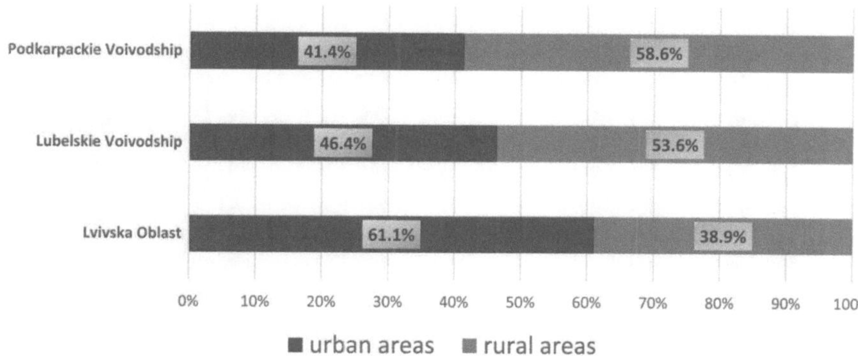

Figure 4.4 The structure of the population by place of residence in 2020 (in percentage terms).

Source: State Statistics Service of Ukraine; Statistical Yearbook of the Lublin Voivodeship (2020); Statistical Yearbook of the Subcarpathian Voivodeship (2020) (accessed: 06.03.2023).

population density in the Lvivska Oblast is higher than average for the country, then in both border voivodeships, it is lower than average in Poland. The comparative characteristics of the Lvivska Oblast, compared with the Lublin and Subcarpathian Voivodeships, regarding the structure of the population by place of residence, are shown in Figure 4.4.

In recent years, the population of Ukraine has been decreasing; during 2015–2021, the overall rate of natural decline increased from –4.2 to –11.2 (per 1,000). A similar trend is observed in the Lvivska Oblast; during 2015–2021, the overall coefficient of natural decline increased from –2 to –8.2.

A population decrease has also been observed in Poland, but at a slower pace; between 2015 and 2020, the overall coefficient of natural reduction increased from –0.7 to –3.2 (per 1,000). In the Lublin Voivodeship, indicators of population decrease are higher compared with average values in the country as a whole: in 2015, the total coefficient of natural decrease was –1.5; in 2019, it was –1.8; in 2020, it was –4.4. The Subcarpathian Voivodeship is characterised by lower rates of decline: in 2020, the total coefficient of natural decrease was –2.1. At the same time, in previous years, there was an increase in the population of the region: 1.7 in 2010; 0.1 in 2015; and 0.3 in 2019.

An increase in migration has been observed in both countries: in Ukraine, the total coefficient of migration increases in 2020 was 0.51; in Poland, it was 0.1. Such an increase in migration is characteristic of the Lvivska Oblast as well. At the same time, in the two border voivodeships of Poland, there was a reduction in migration: –2.1 in the Lublin Voivodeship and –0.9 in Subcarpathian.

The average life expectancy in the studied border regions for men and women is shown in Figure 4.5.

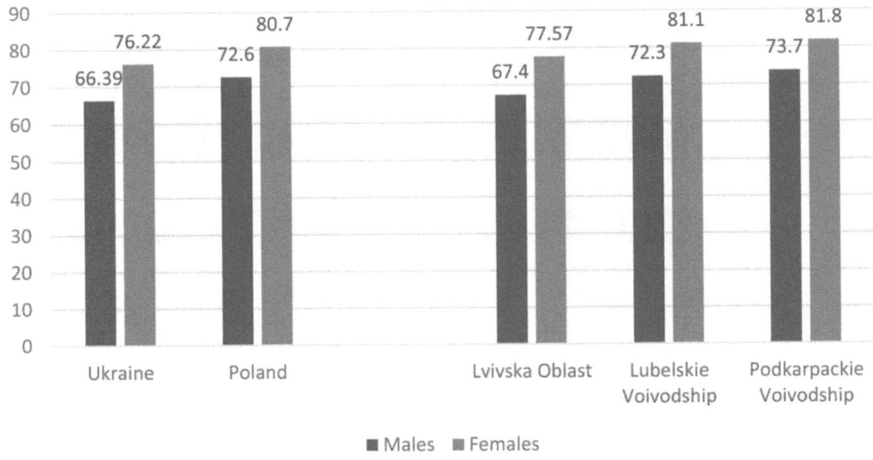

Figure 4.5 Average life expectancy in Ukraine, Poland, and their border regions in 2020.

Source: Statistical Yearbook "Regions of Ukraine" (2021); Statistical Yearbook of the Republic of Poland (2021); Statistical Yearbook of the Lublin Voivodeship (2020); Statistical Yearbook of the Subcarpathian Voivodeship (2020) (accessed: 06.03.2023).

Until 2019, with variable trends, the average life expectancy in Ukraine and the Lvivska Oblast, in particular, increased to 72.01 and 73.45 years, respectively (both sexes). Over the following two years, this decreased, and in 2021, it was 69.77 and 71.51 years, respectively. Similar trends are to be found in Poland and border voivodeships.

On average, as of 2020, compared with Ukraine, women in Poland will live six years longer, and men four years longer. At the regional level, this difference is five–six years and four years, respectively. At the same time, in the border regions of both Ukraine and Poland, the average life expectancy is equal to or higher than the national average.

The dynamics of the number of employed persons is also characterised by changing trends both in Ukraine and in Poland (see Figure 4.6). The labour markets of Ukraine and Poland are comparable in terms of the number of those in employment, while Ukraine has a higher employment rate, which was 56.2% in 2020. In the Lvivska Oblast, the number of those in employment is approximately 200,000 more than in the Lublin and Subcarpathian Voivodeships.

In 2021, the largest contributors of personal income tax and, accordingly, the largest employers in Lviv Oblast were:

- The regional branch of "Lviv Railway" JSC "Ukrzaliznytsia" – provision of services for transportation of goods and passengers (Regional branch "Lviv Railway" JSC Ukrzaliznytsia, 2021).
- Leoni Ltd. – production of electrical equipment for engines and vehicles. Cable networks manufactured at the LEONI plant in Ukraine are

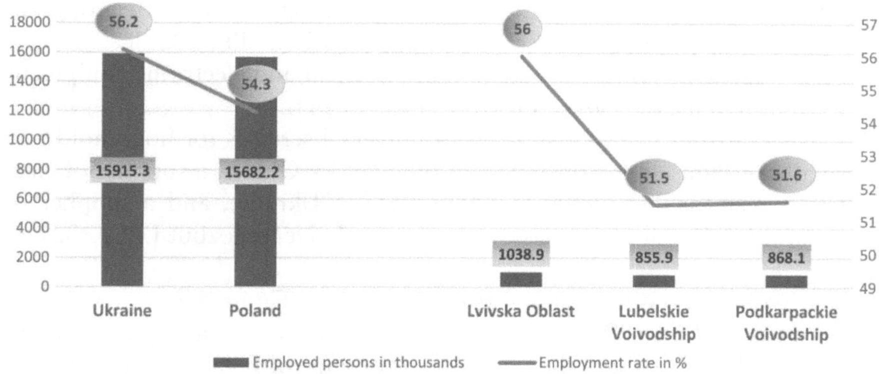

Figure 4.6 Employed persons and employment rate in Ukraine, Poland, and their border regions in 2020.

Source: Statistical Yearbook "Regions of Ukraine" (2021); Statistical Yearbook of the Republic of Poland (2021); Statistical Yearbook of the Lublin Voivodeship (2020); Statistical Yearbook of the Subcarpathian Voivodeship (2020) (accessed: 06.03.2023).

supplied to factories in Poland, Slovakia, Hungary, the Czech Republic, Germany, Spain, Portugal, Italy, Belgium, Great Britain, the USA, and Austria, where they complete the assembly of cars of the global brands "Opel", "Porsche", "Volkswagen", "Audi", and "Lamborghini" (LEONI in Ukraine, 2021).

- "Bader Ukraine" Ltd. – production of car seats from genuine leather for the premium segment for international car manufacturers (Audi, BMW).
- Lvivgaz PJSC – transportation of natural gas through distribution pipelines; maintenance and repair of gas networks and their facilities; design and construction of gas supply systems using steel and polyethylene gas pipelines; installation, verification, and repair of gas metres, etc. (The company's activities, 2021).
- Silpo-Food Ltd. – a chain of food supermarkets in Ukraine, which is a flagship business of FOZZY GROUP (Silpo, 2021).
- "ATB-Market Ltd" – the largest Ukrainian supermarket chain both in terms of turnover and number of stores (ATB, 2021).
- "Electrokontakt Ukraine" LLC – manufacturer of electric cable networks for BMW, General Motors, VW, Daimler cars; a subsidiary of the German company "Elektrokontakt GmbH", which belongs to the French concern Nexans (Electrokontakt Ukraine, 2021).
- Lviv Municipal Utility Company "Lvivvodokanal" – a municipal enterprise of the city of Lviv, whose main task is the uninterrupted provision of water supply and drainage to the residents of the city (Lvivvodokanal, 2021).
- Nova Poshta Ltd. – the leader in the express delivery market in Ukraine, providing services for fast, convenient, and reliable delivery of documents, parcels, and goods to any point of the country (Nova Poshta, 2021).

- "Zachidnyi Bug" PE – one of the largest producers and exporters of grain and oil crops in Western Ukraine ("Zachidnyi Bug" PE, 2021).
- "ODV-Elektrik" Ltd. – production of electrical and electronic equipment for motor vehicles ("ODV-Elektrik" Ltd., 2021).
- Lvivenergozbut LLC – a supplier of universal services for household and small non-household consumers in the Lvivska Oblast, a supplier of electric power for consumers at a free price in Ukraine, and a supplier of natural gas for all categories of consumers (Lvivenergozbut LLC, 2021).

The average monthly nominal wage is shown in Figure 4.7.

Between 2010 and 2020, the gap between the average monthly gross wages in the Lvivska Oblast and the border voivodeships of Poland increased from 500–550 Euros in 2010 to almost 700 Euros. The increase in the gap was influenced by the sharp devaluation of the Hryvnia, starting in 2014. During the studied period, the Euro exchange rate increased from 10.5 hryvnias for one Euro to 32.31 hryvnias in 2021. The level of average monthly gross wages in the Lvivska Oblast fluctuated at around 85–90% of the average in the country: 90% in the Lublin Voivodeship; 85.4–86.5% in the Subcarpathian Voivodeship.

The development of educational and scientific potential is an important prerequisite for increasing the competitiveness of regions. Ukrainian border regions tend to have relatively few children attending preschool education institutions. At the same time, according to the number of students in general secondary education per 10,000 population, they significantly exceed the average for Ukraine. The Lvivska Oblast is the leader among the rest of the regions in terms of the number of institutions of general secondary education and professional pre-higher education; it ranks second after Dnipropetrovska Oblast in terms of the number of professional (vocational and technical) education institutions. The Lvivska Oblast plays the role of an important

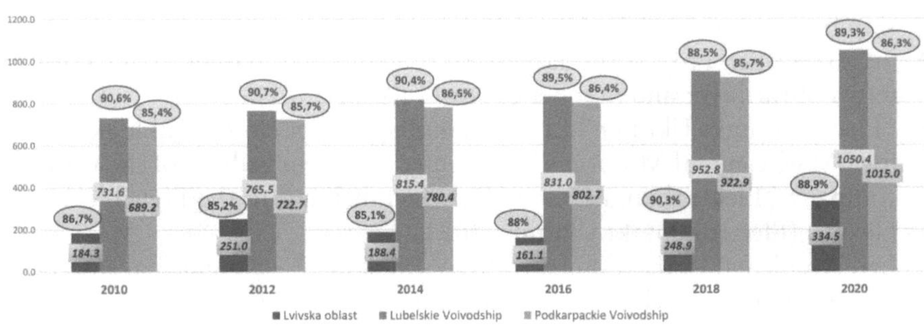

Figure 4.7 Dynamics of average monthly nominal wages in Ukraine, Poland, and their border regions in 2010–2020.

Source: Regions of Ukraine (2020–2021); Statistical Yearbook of the Subcarpathian Voivodeship (2012–2021); Statistical Yearbook of the Lublin Voivodeship (2013–2020).

Table 4.6 General characteristics of the development of education

Numbers in education	*Ukraine*	*Volynska Oblast*	*Lvivska Oblast*	*Zakarpatska Oblast*
Children in preschool educational institutions, as a percentage of the number of children of the corresponding age, 2021	65	58	58	53
Secondary educational institutions, at the beginning of the academic year, 2021/2022: units	13,991	561	1,130	586
Pupils at secondary educational institutions per 10,000 population, at the beginning of the academic year, 2021/2022: persons	1,028	1,419	1,167	1,375
Vocational (professional and technical) training institutions, by the end of 2021: units	694	14	53	16
Students at vocational (professional and technical) training institutions per 10,000 population, by the end of 2021: persons	60	79	85	47
Institutions of professional pre-tertiary education, at the beginning of the academic year, 2021/2022: units	248	6	20	7
their students: persons	282,319	7,912	18,312	7,506
Institutions of tertiary education, at the beginning of the academic year, 2021/2022: units	386	8	21	7
their students: persons	1,046,669	19,269	90,385	17,394

Source: Statistical Yearbook "Regions of Ukraine" (2020–2021) (accessed: 14.03.2023).

scientific and educational centre in Ukraine. The main indicators of the development of education in the border regions are shown in Table 4.6.

The Lvivska Oblast traditionally occupies one of the leading places in Ukraine in terms of its level of development of educational and scientific potential. During the 2020/2021 academic year, 33 higher education institutions, including 18 universities, nine institutes, and six academies, trained specialists with higher education in the Lvivska Oblast. Comparative characteristics of the number of higher educational institutions and the number of students per 1,000 population are shown in Figure 4.8.

The Lvivska Oblast is characterised by the highest number of students per 1,000 population. In terms of the number and level of training of highly qualified scientists, the Lvivska Oblast ranks first in Ukraine. As of 2019, more than half of all organisations that conducted research work in the country were concentrated in the Kyiv (339 units), Kharkiv (139 units), Lviv (69 units), Dnipropetrovsk (57 units), and Odesa (51 units) regions. A number of positive trends have appeared in the scientific and scientific-technical

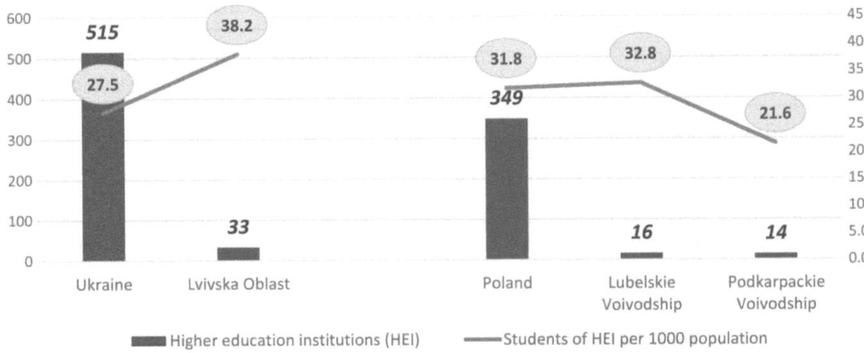

Figure 4.8 Comparative characteristics of the educational potential of Ukraine, Poland, and their border regions at the beginning of the 2020/2021 academic year.

Source: Statistical Yearbook "Regions of Ukraine" (2021); Statistical Yearbook of the Republic of Poland (2021); Statistical Yearbook of the Lublin Voivodeship (2020); Statistical Yearbook of the Subcarpathian Voivodeship (2021) (accessed: 15.03.2023).

activity of the region in recent years; there is an extensive network of scientific organisations with strong scientific potential and an increase in the volume of scientific and scientific-technical work, as well as in completed developments.

The high density of highways and railway tracks due to the proximity to the state border and a favourable geographical location at the intersection of the main European and world transport arteries combine to create a powerful transit potential for the border regions of Ukraine. Its effective implementation, based on the development of logistics and transport infrastructure, will accelerate regional development and increase the competitiveness of regions in national and global markets.

The length of railway tracks in Ukraine and Poland is practically the same and amounts to around 20 thousand km. However, the length of paved roads in Poland is almost twice that of Ukraine. Some indicators of transport infrastructure development are shown in Figure 4.9.

The Lvivska Oblast has an extensive network of transport communication. International European highways pass through the region, which contributes to its transit potential and determines its strategic importance for the development of the country's economy and its integration into the European community. International transport communications connecting Ukraine with Poland, Romania, Slovakia, and Hungary pass through the Lvivska Oblast: the international Cretan transport corridor No. 9 (Helsinki – Kyiv – Lyubashivka/Rozdilna – Chisinau – Bucharest – Dimitrovgrad Alexandroupolis); international transport corridor No. 5 (Venice-Trieste-Ljubljana-Budapest-Uzhhorod-Lviv); international transport corridor No. 3 (Berlin/Dresden-Wroclaw-Lviv-Kyiv); highways of international importance (M-06 Kyiv – Chop, M-09 Lviv – Rava-Ruska, M-10 Lviv – Krakovets, M-11 Lviv – Shehyny, M-12 Stryi – Ternopil – Kropyvnytskyi – Znamyanka).

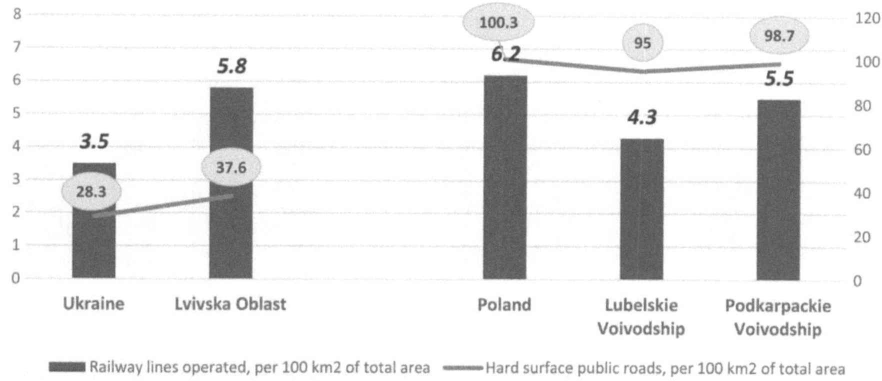

Figure 4.9 Some indicators of the development of transport infrastructure in Ukraine, Poland, and their border regions in 2020.

Source: Statistical Yearbook "Regions of Ukraine" (2021); Statistical Yearbook of the Republic of Poland (2021); Statistical Yearbook of the Lublin Voivodeship (2020); Statistical Yearbook of the Subcarpathian Voivodeship (2021) (accessed: 15.03.2023).

Lviv International Airport, named after Danylo Halytskyi, is of strategic importance for the region; it is the largest airport in Western Ukraine in terms of passenger traffic and has a route network consisting of 60 destinations.

The successful location and presence of ITCs, as well as the main railways, has played a leading role in increasing freight transport and developing the transport hub (logistics hub) of the region.

Comparative economic characteristics of adjacent border regions of Ukraine and Poland demonstrate the deepening of the gaps in their development. Between 2011 and 2020, the GRP of the border voivodeships of Poland was 2.5–4 times higher than the GRP of the Lvivska Oblast (see Figure 4.10).

The economic crisis in Ukraine in 2014–2015, provoked by Russian aggression, affected the sharp devaluation of the Hryvnia and the decline of the country's economy. Therefore, the gap in the level of GRP per person in Ukraine and Poland during the studied period mostly grew (see Figure 4.11).

There is also a significant difference in the value of the level of GRP per person in the border regions of both countries. During the studied period, the difference between these values in the Lvivska Oblast and the Lublin and Subcarpathian Voivodeships fluctuated between three and five times (see Table 4.7).

At the national level, the border regions of Poland show larger deviations from their average value in terms of the level of GRP per capita; as of 2020, the level of GRP per capita of the border voivodeships was 68–69% of their average level in the country as a whole. At the same time, in the Lvivska Oblast, this indicator was 93.3% of its average value in Ukraine.

The structure of the gross added value of Ukraine, Poland, and their border regions is shown in Table 4.8.

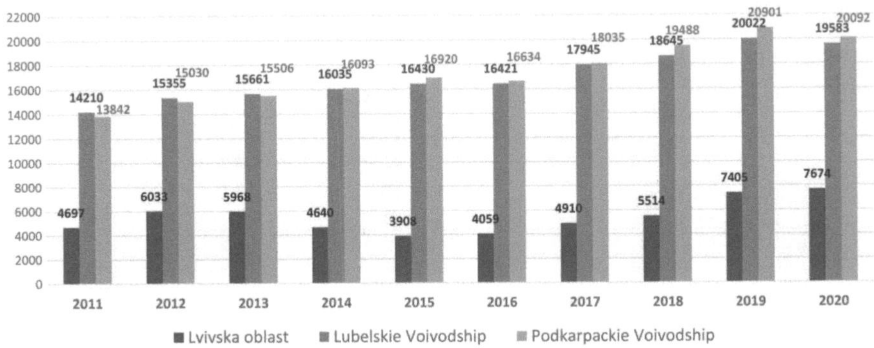

Figure 4.10 GRP of the Lvivska Oblast and the Lublin and Subcarpathian Voivodeships (in million Euros).

Source: Statistical Yearbook "Regions of Ukraine" (2020–2021); Statistical Yearbook of the Subcarpathian Voivodeship (2012–2021); Statistical Yearbook of the Lublin Voivodeship (2013–2020) (accessed: 15.03.2023).

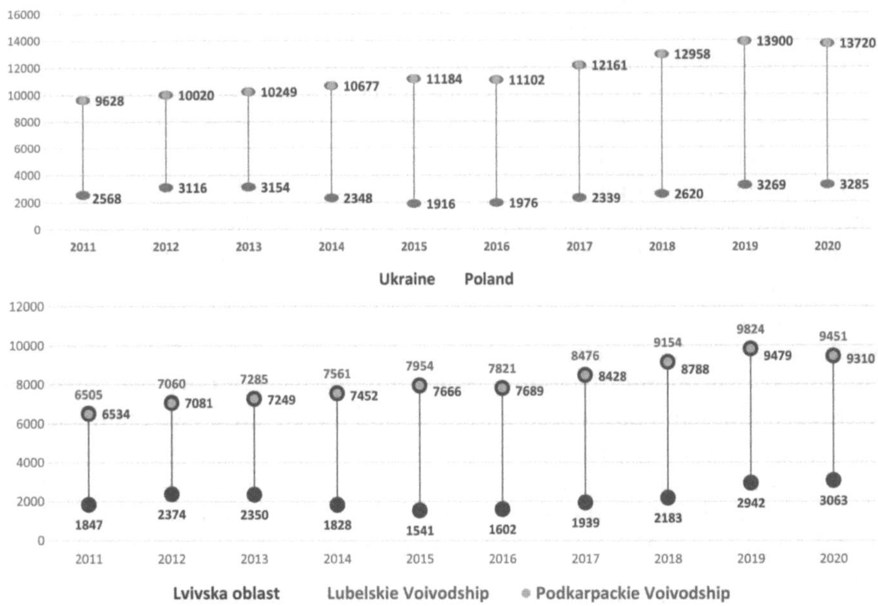

Figure 4.11 *(a)* GRP per person in Ukraine and Poland – national level (in Euro); *(b)* GRP per person in regions: Lvivska oblast, Lubelskie Voivodship and Podkarpackie Voivodship (in Euro).

Source: State Statistics Service of Ukraine; Statistical Yearbook of the Republic of Poland (2012–2021) (accessed: 14.03.2023).

Table 4.7 Comparative characteristics of the economic development of the Lvivska Oblast and the Lublin and Subcarpathian Voivodeships

	2011	*2013*	*2015*	*2017*	*2019*	*2020*
Gross Domestic Product, per capita in EUR						
Lvivska Oblast	1847	2350	1541	1939	2942	3063
Lublin Voivodeship	6534	7249	7666	8428	9479	9310
Subcarpathian Voivodeship	6505	7285	7954	8476	9824	9451
GDP per capita in border regions relative to the average level in the country, %						
Lvivska Oblast	71.9	74.5	80.4	82.9	90.0	93.3
Lublin Voivodeship	67.9	70.7	68.5	69.3	68.2	67.9
Subcarpathian Voivodeship	67.6	71.1	71.1	69.7	70.7	68.9
The difference between the level of GRP per capita in the Lvivska Oblast and border voivodeships, EUR						
compared to Lublin Voivodeship	4687	4899	6125	6489	6537	6247
compared to Subcarpathian Voivodeship	4658	4935	6413	6537	6882	6387

Source: Statistical Yearbook "Regions of Ukraine" (2020–2021); Statistical Yearbook of the Subcarpathian Voivodeship (2012–2021); Statistical Yearbook of the Lublin Voivodeship (2013–2020) (accessed: 15.03.2023).

Table 4.8 Gross value added by kind of activity in 2020 (current prices) (in % of total)

	Ukraine	*Lvivska Oblast*	*Poland*	*Lublin Voivodeship*	*Subcarpathian Voivodeship*
Total	100	100	100	100	100
Agriculture, forestry, and fishing	***10.8***	***8.4***	2.8	5.9	1.7
Industry	***17.1***	***16.1***	25.3	20.9	30
Construction	***3.3***	***4.6***	7.4	7.1	7.4
Trade; repair of motor vehicles; transportation and storage; accommodation and catering; information and communication	30.1	31.7	29.3	27.8	26.9
Financial and insurance activities; real estate activities	11	10.4	9.4	9.1	7.6
Other services	27.7	28.8	25.8	29.2	26.4

Source: Statistical Yearbook "Regions of Ukraine" (2021); Statistical Yearbook of the Republic of Poland (2021); Statistical Yearbook of the Lublin Voivodeship (2020); Statistical Yearbook of the Subcarpathian Voivodeship (2021) (accessed: 17.03.2023).

The share of agriculture, forestry, and fishing in Ukraine and the Lvivska Oblast significantly exceeds its value in Poland and the border regions. At the same time, the shares of industry and construction are significantly lower compared with the neighbouring country and its border regions. Shares of the service sector are almost the same.

The development of the economy depends on the number of economic units. As of 2020, 2.5 times more business units were operating in Poland than in Ukraine. Including in the Lvivska Oblast, the number of business units is 1.5 times smaller compared with the Lublin and Subcarpathian Voivodeships.

4.4 Labour Migration from Ukraine to the EU in 2014–2021

In 2014, the Association Agreement between the European Union and Ukraine was signed. Democratisation of public life, respect for human rights, and focus on integration into the European Union, including a visa-free regime with the EU, have opened up opportunities for Ukrainian citizens to freely move and travel abroad for employment, study, and to enjoy tourism and leisure activities. Temporary labour migration has been evolving into permanent migration; the willingness of Ukrainians to emigrate has increased, while Ukraine's attractiveness for immigrants has remained low (IOM, 2021).

Since 2014, the number of Ukrainian migrants moving to the European Union (EU) has increased significantly, especially after the outbreak of the armed conflict in eastern Ukraine. In 2021 alone, Ukrainian nationals received 875,794 residence permits for remunerated activities across the member states – the largest external labour force in the EU. The reliance of member state economies on workers from Ukraine has thus reached significant levels, as exemplified by the labour shortage seen during the COVID-19 crisis that forced the EU to shut down its borders (Dubenko & Kravchuk, 2021). During the period 2014–2021, almost five million Ukrainian nationals received first-time residence permits for the EU-28. Of these permits, 84% (4,130,777) were issued for remunerated activities.

Almost three million first residence permits were issued in the EU to non-EU citizens in 2021. Ukrainians topped the ranking of first residence permits issued in 2021 (875,800 beneficiaries), accounting for 30% of all permits issued in the EU (Eurostat, 2022). More than half (57%) of all first residence permits issued in the EU in 2021 were issued to citizens of the top ten countries (see Figure 4.12).

In 2021, compared with 2020, among the ten most popular citizenships, the highest relative increases were observed for Belarus (up 135%), Ukraine (up 46%), and Russia (up 42%). Only in the cases of Syria and Brazil, the number of first residence permits issued shrank, down by 14% and 2%, respectively (Eurostat, 2022).

There are several factors that influence the destination chosen by citizens of non-EU countries granted residence permits; these include: geographical

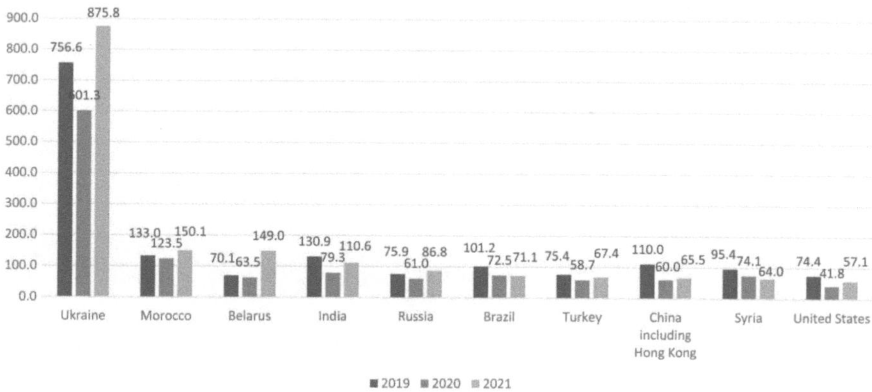

Figure 4.12 Developments in the top ten countries, whose citizens received a first residence permit, by country of citizenship, EU, 2019–2021 (in thousands).

Source: Eurostat (2019–2021).

proximity (for example, a high number of Ukrainians sought residence in Poland, Estonia, Latvia, or Lithuania) (Eurostat, 2022).

Poland was the principal destination for Ukrainian citizens, as 83% of all resident permits issued to Ukrainians in the EU in 2021 were issued in this country (see Figure 4.13).

Figure 4.14 shows in more detail the reasons for granting permits to Ukrainian citizens. Almost nine out of ten Ukrainians who were granted a

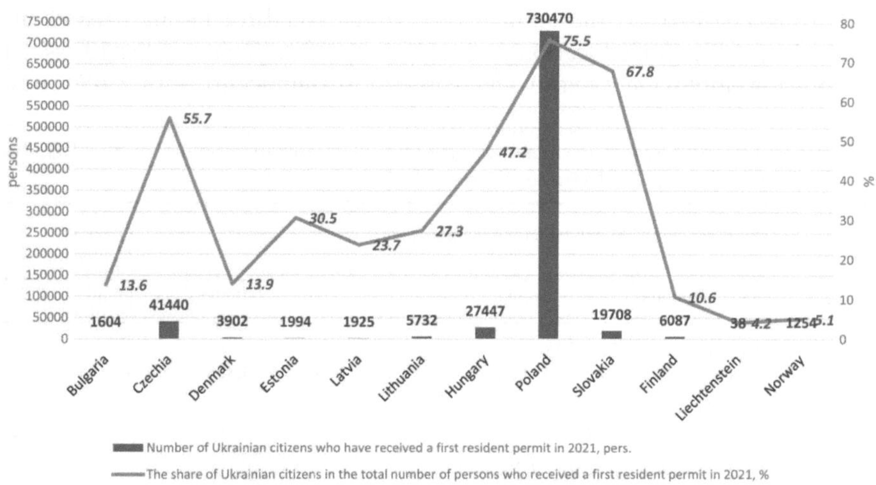

Figure 4.13 Ukrainian citizens who received a first resident permit in 2021, by EU Member State and EFTA country.

Source: Eurostat (2021).

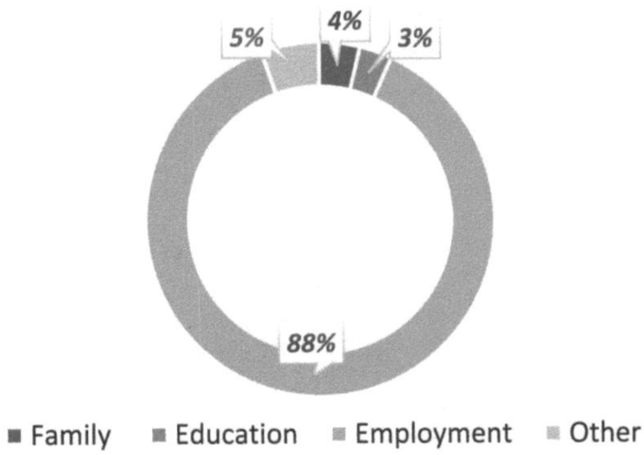

Figure 4.14 The first residence permits that have been received by Ukrainian citizens in the EU, by reason, 2021.

Source: Eurostat (2021).

residence permit in the EU in 2021 received their permit for employment-related reasons.

In 2021, Poland was the leading country in the EU in terms of the number of permits issued to Ukrainians for education, employment, and other reasons, and the second country in terms of the number of permits issued for family reasons (see Table 4.9).

During 2014–2021, an upward trend was observed regarding the number of permits issued to Ukrainians in Poland. In 2021, permits were issued to 730,470 Ukrainians. In the structure of issued permits, permits issued for employment reasons prevail and account for ≈90% (see Figure 4.15).

During 2014–2021, the number of permits issued for family reasons increased by 64%; for educational reasons – by 23%. The number of issued permits for employment reasons increased most significantly – by 3.69 times.

Table 4.9 The first residence permits issued to Ukrainian citizens in the EU, by reason and EU Member States, 2021

EU permits issued (number)	Three leading EU Member States issuing permits									*Other EU Member States*	
	First	(number)	(%)	Second	(number)	(%)	Third	(number)	(%)	(number)	(%)
PERMITS ISSUED FOR FAMILY REASONS											
33451	Czechia	7,631	22.8	Poland	6,407	19.2	Italy	3,818	11.4	15,595	46.6
PERMITS ISSUED FOR EDUCATIONAL REASONS											
26 208	Poland	18,986	72.4	Slovakia	1,850	7.1	Czechia	1,395	5.3	3,977	15.2
PERMITS ISSUED FOR EMPLOYMENT REASONS											
769 429	Poland	666,295	86.6	Czechia	31,535	4.1	Hungary	26,832	3.5	44,767	5.8
PERMITS ISSUED FOR OTHER REASONS											
46 694	Poland	38,782	83.1	Spain	2,039	4.4	Italy	1,527	3.3	4,346	9.3

Source: Eurostat (2021).

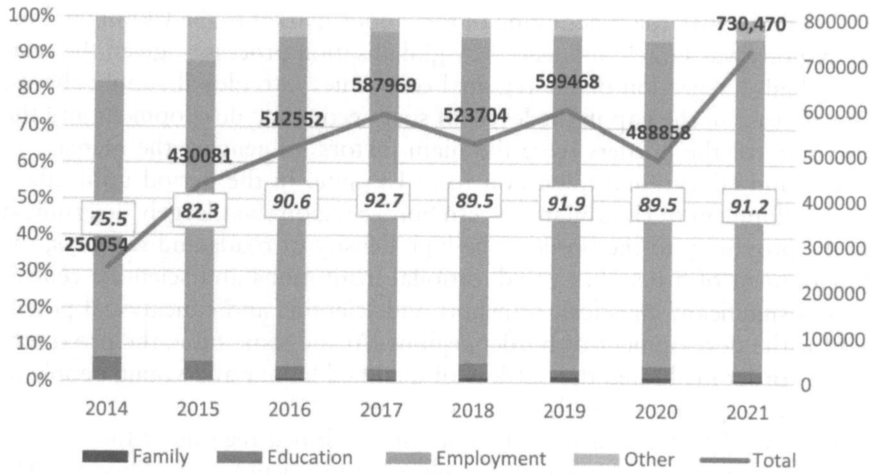

Figure 4.15 Number of first residence permits issued by reason to Ukrainian citizens in Poland in 2014–2021.

Source: Eurostat (migr_resfirst, 2021).

The number of permits issued for other reasons slightly decreased during the research period – by 10%.

More than 70% of all permits issued to Ukrainians in the EU for educational, employment, and other reasons are issued in Poland.

4.5 Conclusions

Among the border regions of Ukraine, Lvivska Oblast is characterised by a favourable economic and geographical location near the border with the EU, the presence of border checkpoints, a developed transport network, and the international airport "Lviv", named after Danylo Halytskyi. The economy of the region has a high level of diversification. These strengths are supported by such opportunities as the strengthening of European integration processes, including foreign economic relations between the Lvivska Oblast and EU member states, increasing cross-border cooperation, using the transit and transport potential of the Lvivska Oblast, and attracting foreign investments in high-tech industries (Strategy for the development of the Lvivska Oblast for the period 2021–2027).

According to estimates of State Statistics Service of Ukraine, the GDP of Ukraine in 2022 fell by 29.1%. The war has narrowed the Ukrainian labour market: around eight million Ukrainians have left for abroad, around seven million are IDPs, and hundreds of thousands of Ukrainians are engaged in combat. The border regions of Ukraine have become a refuge for hundreds of thousands of IDPs and a place of business relocation, primarily from the eastern and southern regions of the country. The economy of all regions is developing, considering the provision of primary military needs.

Before the war, the functioning of the labour market in the Ukrainian border regions was largely influenced by globalisation processes, given the relatively high integration of the regional economies into global supply chains. The increase in the gap in the levels of socio-economic development and the proximity of the borders were the main factors influencing the increase in labour and educational migration from Ukraine. In the period until 2022, the development of Ukrainian western border regions was largely determined by the proximity to the border. The high density of roads and railways, the development of a network of educational institutions and scientific centres offered significant logistical, transport and scientific and educational potential for the development of border regions. At the same time, the proximity to the border facilitated the outflow of qualified labour and young people to the border regions of neighbouring countries.

The Lvivska Oblast is one of the most developed regions of the country in terms of its economy, tourism, culture, and science. Yet between 2010 and 2020, the gap between the average monthly gross wages in the Lvivska Oblast and the border voivodeships of Poland increased from 500–550 Euros in 2010 to almost 700 Euros. The growing disparities in the level of average monthly gross wages were caused, in particular, by the systematic increase in the minimum wage in Poland, especially noticeable in the regions of Eastern Poland, where regional economies are characterised by lower wages compared to the national average. The increase in the gap was influenced by the sharp devaluation of the Hryvnia, starting in 2014. During the studied period, the Euro exchange rate increased from 10.5 hryvnias for one Euro to 32.31 hryvnias in 2021. The level of average monthly gross wages in the Lvivska Oblast fluctuated at around 85–90% of the average in the country.

During 2012–2021, the development of the labour market in Ukraine was characterised by a reduction in the labour supply, an increase in its demand, low wages, a lack of highly productive workplaces, a mismatch of the professional and general competencies of employees with the needs of employers, irregular employment of the population, etc. In 2022, the consequence of the full-scale Russian invasion of Ukraine was a significant narrowing of the labour market in Ukraine: many enterprises in the country closed and many people lost their jobs. Relocation and forced migration led to a change in the regional structure of the labour market, as well as the structure of offers and the saturation of specialists in the region. In the regions most affected by the military aggression of the Russian Federation, the number of jobs decreased and competition increased. The imbalance between labour supply and demand has become significant.

In 2022, the situation on the labour market of the Ukrainian border regions has fundamentally changed. General mobilisation continues in the country, there is a shortage of male personnel, new categories of job seekers have appeared, and gradually, previously "male" professions are becoming "female".

Although the Lviv Oblast in particular is more competitive compared to the border regions of Poland by certain socio-economic indicators (in terms of employment level, number of higher education institutions, number of students per 1,000 inhabitants, etc.), the gap between wage levels and GRP per capita is only increasing. These factors contribute to the further development of migration processes from Ukraine to Poland. In the post-war period, migration processes will also be caused by increased competition with foreign employers for mobile, highly qualified labour.

As of April 1, 2023, on average in the Volynska Oblast, two unemployed people applied for one job vacancy (as of April 1, 2022 – 11 people). The largest discrepancy between the demand for labour and its supply in terms of professional qualifications was observed among qualified workers in the financial and insurance sectors (22 persons). The number of vacancies reported by employers to the Lviv Regional Employment Service was 4,600, which is 1.6 times greater than on April 1, 2022 (2,800). As of April 1, 2023, on average, one unemployed person applied for one vacant job in the region (as of April 1, 2022, four people); in Ukraine, on average, there were four people. The imbalance in the registered labour market has only been experienced by professionally qualified groups of agricultural and forestry workers, as well as managers; two unemployed people applied for one vacancy. The imbalance between labour supply and demand in the Zakarpatska Oblast remains significant: five unemployed people applied for one job vacancy (as of April 1, 2022 – seven unemployed). The greatest discrepancy between the demand for labour and its supply in terms of professional qualifications was observed in the qualified agricultural workers' market (twelve people applied for one vacancy) and workers in trade and services (eight people). The greatest difficulties with employment are experienced by sellers of food products, assemblers, workers in forestry works, auxiliary workers, sales consultants, and sellers of non-food products.

In the current conditions, the determining factor affecting the development of the labour market in the Ukrainian border regions is the security factor. The level of the security situation in the regions affects the structure of labour supply and demand, the level of employment, the level of wages and, of course, the dynamics of both internal and external migration processes. Now the western border regions of Ukraine are safer and, accordingly, more favourable and comfortable for people to live, organise, and do business.

Since 2014, after the signing of the Association Agreement between the European Union and Ukraine, the visa-free regime with the EU, etc., the temporary labour migration of Ukrainian citizens has been evolving into permanent one. The number of Ukrainian migrants to EU countries increased significantly after Russia's occupation of Crimea and the beginning of the armed conflict in eastern Ukraine. Ukrainians topped the ranking of first residence permits issued in 2021 (875,800 beneficiaries), accounting for 30% of all permits issued in the EU. Poland was the principal destination for Ukrainian citizens, as 83% of all resident permits issued to Ukrainians in the EU in 2021 were issued in this country. Common historical and cultural heritage, closeness of languages, geographic location, etc. make Poland particularly attractive for Ukrainian migrants.

Since 2014, the number of Ukrainian labour migrants moving to the EU has increased significantly, especially after the outbreak of the armed conflict in eastern Ukraine. In 2021 alone, Ukrainian nationals received 875,794 residence permits for remunerated activities across the member states – the largest external labour force in the EU. The reliance of member state economies on workers from Ukraine has thus reached significant levels, as exemplified by the labour shortage seen during the COVID-19 crisis that forced the EU to close its borders. During the period 2014–2021, almost five million Ukrainian nationals received first-time residence permits for the EU-28. Of these permits, 84% were issued for remunerated activities.

Poland was the principal destination for Ukrainian citizens, as 83% of all resident permits issued to Ukrainians in the EU in 2021 were issued in this country. Today in the Zakarpatska Oblast, every fourth inhabitant of the region is an IDP, in the Lvivska Oblast – every sixth inhabitant, and in the Volynska Oblast – every 14th inhabitant.

References

ATB. (2021). *About the Company*. https://www.atbmarket.com/contact. Accessed in 2023.

De, P. (2011). Why is trade at borders a costly affair in South Asia? An empirical investigation. *Contemporary South Asia*, *19*, 441–464.

Decentralization. (2020). *Territorial Hromadas*. https://decentralization.gov.ua/newgromada. Accessed in 2023.

Decree of the Cabinet of Ministers of Ukraine of December 24, 2019, No. 1396-r. *On the approval of the main directions of the implementation of state policy in the field of employment of the population and stimulation of the creation of new jobs for the period until 2022*. https://zakon.rada.gov.ua/laws/show/1396-2019-%D1%80#Text. Accessed in 2023.

Scientific and Analytical Report. (2023). *Development of the Logistics and Transport Infrastructure of the Border Regions of the Western Region of Ukraine. Comparative Systematic Assessment*. http://ird.gov.ua/irdp/p20230031.pdf. Accessed in 2023.

Directorate-General for Mobility and Transport. (2022). *Commission amends TEN-T proposal to reflect impacts on infrastructure of Russia's war of aggression against Ukraine*. European Commission. https://transport.ec.europa.eu/news/commission-amends-ten-t-proposal-reflect-impacts-infrastructure-russias-war-aggression-against-2022-07-27_en. Accessed in 2023.

Dubenko, L., & Kravchuk, P. (2021). *Ukrainian Labour Migration to the EU: Analytical Report*. https://www.pragueprocess.eu/en/resources/repository/33-reports/287-ukrainian-labour-migration-to-the-eu. Accessed in 2023.

Electrokontakt Ukraine. (2021). *Company History*. http://eku.com.ua. Accessed in 2023.

EU. (2023). *Regulation (EU) 2023/1077 of the European Parliament and of the Council of 31 May 2023 on Temporary Trade-liberalisation Measures Supplementing Trade Concessions Applicable to Ukrainian Products under the Association Agreement between the European Union and the European Atomic Energy Community and Their Member States, of the One Part, and Ukraine, of the Other Part.* https://eur-lex.europa.eu/legal-content/EN/TXT/?uri=CELEX%3A32023R1077. Accessed in 2023.

Eurostat (MIGR_RESFIRST). (2021). *First Permits by Reason, Length of Validity and Citizenship.* https://ec.europa.eu/eurostat/databrowser/view/MIGR_RESFIRST__custom_5107111/default/table?lang=en. Accessed in 2023.

Eurostat. (2019–2021). *First Permits by Reason, Length of Validity and Citizenship.* https://ec.europa.eu/eurostat/databrowser/view/MIGR_RESFIRST__custom_3167082/bookmark/table?lang=en&bookmarkId=bcfa1528-242b-4756-8607-1d783c5acc4f. Accessed in 2023.

Eurostat. (2021). *First Permits by Reason, Length of Validity and Citizenship.* https://ec.europa.eu/eurostat/databrowser/view/MIGR_RESFIRST__custom_3167087/bookmark/table?lang=en&bookmarkId=f55685f4-5c11-4779-9df0-e36704e6d90e&page=time:2021. Accessed in 2023.

Eurostat. (2022). *Residence Permits – Statistics on First Permits Issued during the Year.* https://ec.europa.eu/eurostat/statistics-explained/index.php?title=Residence_permits_-_statistics_on_first_permits_issued_during_the_year&oldid=584076. Accessed in 2023.

Evacuation.City. (2023). *Twice as Many People as Registered: How Many Displaced People Did Lvivska Oblast Take In?* https://evacuation.city/articles/262969/jmovirna-kilkist-mozhe-syagati-500-tisyach-skilki-pereselenciv-prijnyala-lvivschina. Accessed in 2023.

Fujimura, M., & Edmonds, C. (2006). *Impact of cross-border road infrastructure on trade and investment in the Greater Mekong Subregion.* ADBI Discussion Paper No. 48. Asian Development Bank Institute.

Hansen, N. M. (1976). *The Economic Development of Border Regions.* IIASA Research Memorandum. https://core.ac.uk/download/pdf/33892119.pdf. Accessed in 2023.

IOM. (2021). *Migration in Ukraine: Facts and Figures.* https://ukraine.iom.int/sites/g/files/tmzbdl1861/files/documents/migration_in_ukraine_facts_and_figures_2021-eng_web-1.pdf. Accessed in 2023.

IOM. (2023). *Ukraine Crisis 2022-2023: 1 Year of Response. Annual report.* https://www.iom.int/sites/g/files/tmzbdl486/files/documents/2023-02/IOM_Ukraine_Regional_Response-1_Year_Special_Report.pdf. Accessed in 2023.

Kyiv City State Administration. (2022). *Monitoring of the Social and Economic Development of the Regions for 2021.* https://dei.kyivcity.gov.ua/files/2022/6/17/rejtyngova-oczinka-za-2021-rik-prezentaczijni-materialyza.pdf. Accessed in 2023.

LEONI in Ukraine. (2021). https://www.leoni-ukraine.com/en/leoni-in-ukraine/general-information/. Accessed in 2023.

Logist.Today. (2022). *Transportation through the Middle Corridor Bypassing the Russian Federation is on the Rise.* https://logist.today/uk/dnevnik_logista/2022-04-01/perevozki-po-srednemu-koridoru-v-obhod-rf-nahodyatsya-na-podeme/. Accessed in 2023.

Lviv Regional Employment Center. (2023). *The Situation on the Labor Market and the Activities of the Lviv Regional Employment Service in January–March 2023.* https://lviv.dcz.gov.ua/analitics/69. Accessed in 2023.

Lvivenergozbut LLC. (2021). https://www.lez.com.ua/aboutus. Accessed in 2023.

Lvivvodokanal. (2021). https://lvivvodokanal.com.ua. Accessed in 2023.

Ministry of Social Policy of Ukraine. (2023). *Internally Displaced Persons.* https://www.msp.gov.ua/timeline/Vnutrishno-peremishcheni-osobi.html. Accessed in 2023.

Narodowy Bank Polski (2020). https://www.nbp.pl/homen.aspx?f=/kursy/kursyen.htm

National Bank of Poland. (2022). https://nbp.pl/en. Accessed in 2023.

National Bank of Ukraine. (2022). https://bank.gov.ua/en. Accessed in 2023.

Ng, C. P., Law, T. H., Wong, S. V., & Kulanthayan, S. (2017). Relative improvements in road mobility as compared to improvements in road accessibility and economic growth: A cross-country analysis. *Transport Policy*, *60*, 24–33.
Nova Poshta. (2021). *About Company*. https://novaposhta.ua/o_kompanii. Accessed in 2023.
ODV-Elektrik Ltd. (2021). https://odw-elektrik.business-guide.com.ua. Accessed in 2023.
Public Space. (2022). *Integration of IDPs and Relocated Businesses into Hromada Life: How to Use All the Advantages*? https://www.prostir.ua/?news=intehratsiya-vpo-ta-relokovanoho-biznesu-v-zhyttya-hromady-yak-vykorystaty-usi-perevahy. Accessed in 2023.
Quium, A. (2019). Transport corridors for wider socio–economic development. *Sustainability*, *11*(19), 5248. https://www.mdpi.com/2071-1050/11/19/5248
Razumkov Centre. (2022). *The Labor Market in Wartime Conditions: Main Trends and Directions of Stabilization*. https://razumkov.org.ua/images/2022/07/18/2022-ANALIT-ZAPIS-PISHULINA-2.pdf. Accessed in 2023.
Regional branch “Lviv Railway” JSC Ukrzaliznytsia. (2022). https://www.uz.gov.ua/about/general_information/entertainments/lviv_railway
Silpo. (2021). https://silpo.ua. Accessed in 2023.
State Statistics Service of Ukraine. (2022). https://www.ukrstat.gov.ua. Accessed in 2023.
Statistical Yearbook “Regions of Ukraine”. (2020). *State Statistics Service of Ukraine, Part I-II*. https://www.ukrstat.gov.ua. Accessed in 2023.
Statistical Yearbook “Regions of Ukraine”. (2021). *State Statistics Service of Ukraine, Part I-II*. https://www.ukrstat.gov.ua. Accessed in 2023.
Statistical Yearbook of the Lublin Voivodeship. (2013–2020). https://lublin.stat.gov.pl/en/publications/statistical-yearbook/statistical-yearbook-lubelskie-voivodship-2022,1,21.html
Statistical Yearbook of the Republic of Poland. (2012). https://stat.gov.pl/cps/rde/xbcr/gus/SY_statistical_yearbook_of_Poland_2012.pdf. Accessed in 2023.
Statistical Yearbook of the Republic of Poland. (2013). https://stat.gov.pl/en/topics/statistical-yearbooks/statistical-yearbooks/statistical-yearbook-of-the-republic-of-poland-2013,2,8.html. Accessed in 2023.
Statistical Yearbook of the Republic of Poland. (2014). https://stat.gov.pl/en/topics/statistical-yearbooks/statistical-yearbooks/statistical-yearbook-of-the-republic-of-poland-2014,2,9.html. Accessed in 2023.
Statistical Yearbook of the Republic of Poland. (2015). https://stat.gov.pl/en/topics/statistical-yearbooks/statistical-yearbooks/statistical-yearbook-of-the-republic-of-poland-2015,2,10.html. Accessed in 2023.
Statistical Yearbook of the Republic of Poland. (2016). https://stat.gov.pl/en/topics/statistical-yearbooks/statistical-yearbooks/statistical-yearbook-of-the-republic-of-poland-2016,2,16.html. Accessed in 2023.
Statistical Yearbook of the Republic of Poland. (2017). https://stat.gov.pl/en/topics/statistical-yearbooks/statistical-yearbooks/statistical-yearbook-of-the-republic-of-poland-2017,2,17.html. Accessed in 2023.
Statistical Yearbook of the Republic of Poland. (2018). https://stat.gov.pl/en/topics/statistical-yearbooks/statistical-yearbooks/statistical-yearbook-of-the-republic-of-poland-2018,2,19.html. Accessed in 2023.
Statistical Yearbook of the Republic of Poland. (2019). https://stat.gov.pl/en/topics/statistical-yearbooks/statistical-yearbooks/statistical-yearbook-of-the-republic-of-poland-2019,2,21.html. Accessed in 2023.
Statistical Yearbook of the Republic of Poland. (2020). https://stat.gov.pl/en/topics/statistical-yearbooks/statistical-yearbooks/statistical-yearbook-of-the-republic-of-poland-2020,2,22.html. Accessed in 2023.

Statistical Yearbook of the Republic of Poland. (2021). https://stat.gov.pl/en/topics/statistical-yearbooks/statistical-yearbooks/statistical-yearbook-of-the-republic-of-poland-2021,2,23.html#. Accessed in 2023.

Statistical Yearbook of the Subcarpathian Voivodeship (2012–2021). https://rzeszow.stat.gov.pl/en/publications/statistical-yearbook/statistical-yearbook-of-podkarpackie-voivodship-2023,1,17.html

Statistical Yearbook of the Subcarpathian Voivodeship (2020). https://rzeszow.stat.gov.pl/en/publications/statistical-yearbook/statistical-yearbook-of-podkarpackie-voivodship-2020,1,14.html

Statistical Yearbook of the Subcarpathian Voivodeship (2021). https://rzeszow.stat.gov.pl/en/publications/statistical-yearbook/statistical-yearbook-of-podkarpackie-voivodship-2021,1,15.html

Strategy for the development of the Lvivska Oblast for the period 2021–2027. (2022). https://www.minregion.gov.ua/wp-content/uploads/2020/05/strategiya-rozvytku-lvivskoyi-oblasti-na-period-2021-2027-rokiv.pdf. Accessed in 2023.

The company's activities. (2021). https://lv.dsoua.com/ua/informacija-pro-kompaniju/dijalnist-kompaniji/id/dijalnist-kompaniji-6631. Accessed in 2023.

Scientific and Analytical Report. (2022). *The Economy of the Regions of Ukraine in the Conditions of War: Risks and Directions of Ensuring Stability.* http://ird.gov.ua/irdp/p20220033.pdf. Accessed in 2023.

UKRINFORM. (2023). *In Zakarpatska Oblast, the Most Displaced People Are from Kharkivska, Donetska and Zaporizshska Oblasts.* https://www.ukrinform.ua/rubric-regions/3707255-na-zakarpatti-najbilse-pereselenciv-iz-harkivsini-doneccini-ta-zaporizkoi-oblasti.html. Accessed in 2023.

Urząd Statystyczny w Lublinie (2021). Data on Voivodeship. https://lublin.stat.gov.pl/en/information-about-voivodship/voivodship

Urząd Statystyczny w Lublinie. (2022). *Major Data on the Voivodeship.* https://lublin.stat.gov.pl/files/gfx/lublin/en/defaultstronaopisowa/512/1/1/wazniejsze_dane_o_wojewodztwie_blubelskie.pdf. Accessed in 2023.

Verkhovna Rada of Ukraine. (2014). *Concept of Reform of Local Self-government and Territorial Organization of Power in Ukraine dated April 1, 2014 No. 333.* http://zakon5.rada.gov.ua/laws/show/333-2014-%D1%80. Accessed in 2023.

Verkhovna Rada of Ukraine. (2021). *STATE PROGRAM for the Development of Cross-Border Cooperation for 2021–2027.* https://zakon.rada.gov.ua/laws/show/408-2021-%D0%BF#Text. Accessed in 2023.

Volyn Regional Employment Center. (2023). *The Situation on the Labor Market and the Activities of the Volyn Regional Employment Service in January-March 2023.* https://vol.dcz.gov.ua/analitics/66. Accessed in 2023.

Volyn Regional State Administration. (2023). *Internally Displaced Persons in the Territory of Volyn.* https://voladm.gov.ua/article/vnutrishno-peremischeni-osobi-na-teritoriyi-volini8. Accessed in 2023.

Widiastuti, W. (2020). *Comparative Study of the Regional Competitiveness of Semarang City and Surakarta City in Central Java Provinc.* https://proceedings.undip.ac.id/index.php/icrd/article/viewFile/189/49. Accessed in 2023.

Word and deed. (2023). *The Ministry of Reintegration Told How Many Displaced Persons Are Registered in Ukraine.* https://www.slovoidilo.ua/2023/02/07/novyna/suspilstvo/minreintehracziyi-rozpovily-skilky-ukrayini-zareyestrovano-vnutrishno-peremishhenyx-osib. Accessed in 2023.

Zachidnyi Bug PE. (2021). https://zahbug.com/. Accessed in 2023.

Zakarpattia Regional Employment Center (2023). *Demand and Supply on the Registered Labor Market of Zakarpatska Oblast in January-March.* https://zak.dcz.gov.ua/analitics/70. Accessed in 2023.

5 The Socio-Economic Situation of the Polish-Ukrainian Borderland with Particular Emphasis on the Cross-Border Labour Market

5.1 Introduction

Poland has gone through a period of very intense growth and development of labour markets – after separating from the Eastern Block in the 90s of the 20th century, the average income per capita has doubled (from 38% to 76% of the EU average) while simultaneously achieving a relatively low unemployment rate (approx. 3%) and a higher employment rate (74%) in comparison with the average in the EU (ILO Web Page). Since accession to the European Union in 2004, Poland has been the recipient of a strong inflow of migrant labour. In recent years, due to the amendment of provisions in 2016, resulting in allowing temporary employment without the necessity of obtaining a work permit due to the ratification of Directive 2016/801/EU on the conditions of entry and residence of third-country nationals for the purposes of research, studies, training, voluntary service, pupil exchange schemes or educational projects, and au pairing (EU, 2016), it became a country of temporary and circular immigration for third-country nationals from Ukraine, Belarus, Russia, Moldova, Georgia, and Armenia. After the outbreak of armed conflict in 2014, these opportunities have been taken advantage of primarily by Ukraine citizens (Kall et al., 2020), and the OECD data suggests that, as early as in 2017, Poland was at the world's top in terms of the number of accepted temporary migrants (Kall et al., 2020, as in OECD, 2019). In 2019, 93,000 new long-term migrants arrived in Poland (for a period of over 12 months, i.e., 8.3% more than in 2018), 61.5% of whom were labour migrants, 15.5% their family members, 2.1% students, and 20.9% others. The number of temporary and seasonal labour migrants amounted to a total of 568,000, and 19,000 applications were from students. In 2020, approximately 800,000 migrants (which correspond to 2.2% of the country's population) arrived in Poland. By country of origin, 34% were born in Ukraine, 12% in Germany, and 12% in Belarus – thus, in total, 46% of the migrants came from two neighbouring countries bordering Poland on the east. Concurrently, in 2020, the number of emigrants year-on-year dropped by 8% to 150,000 people. The main destinations of emigrant Poles were Germany (42%), the Netherlands (18%), and Great Britain (9%) (OECD, 2021, p. 294).

DOI: 10.4324/9781003471646-5

Labour markets in eastern Poland have been so far considered less attractive and, as is the case with other eastern regions of the European Union that joined the Community in 2004, are classified as Lagging Low-Income countries (an average of 6.7% per year between 2003 and 2017), with low GDP and high long-term GDP growth rate per capita. In total, they cover 14.5% of regions NUTS-3 in the EU, and 96.9% of them are NUTS-3 regions in countries included in the grouping after 2004 (Ganau & Kilroy, 2023). In comparison with other Central European countries (the Czech Republic and Slovakia), Poland is characterised by smaller internal convergence, and the regions of eastern Poland are characterised by their inadequate infrastructure, primarily in the scope of transport and communication. In consequence, these differences translated into a greater effectiveness of European Union financing on the supply side of Poland's economy in comparison with neighbouring countries (Mogila et al., 2022).

The chapter provides a detailed characterisation of the situation and processes defining the labour market in the eastern borderland regions of Poland, specifically the Lublin and Subcarpathian Voivodeships, which constitute the eastern external border of the European Union. The analysis includes a comparative assessment of poverty on the Polish-Ukrainian borderland of Polish regions (Lublin Voivodeship and Subcarpathian Voivodeship) as well as Zakarpattia Oblast, Volyn Oblast, and Lviv Oblast in Ukraine. Additionally, the study examines cross-border movements of people between Ukraine and Poland after 2011.

The core of the chapter revolves around addressing main research questions:

- What are the specifics of the Polish-Ukrainian borderland with particular emphasis on the economy and cross-border flows, including the labour market?
- Were the Polish border regions prepared to perform new roles regarding war migration after the Russian aggression on Ukraine?

To deepen the answers to these questions, an additional, detailed question was applied: What was the participation and areas of activity of Ukrainian citizens in the Polish-Ukrainian cross-border labour market before the escalation of the conflict in Ukraine in February 2022? The answers to these research questions are derived from analyses and comparisons of indicators characterising the macroeconomic development of the regions, as well as descriptions of demand and supply issues in the labour market. To ensure comparability, the analysis of the labour market situation in Poland was conducted using the same framework as in the case of Ukraine.

5.2 Economy and Labour Market in the Borderland Region in Poland

Within its current borders, due to historic conditions, the regions of Eastern Poland (including the Polish-Ukrainian borderland voivodeships) belong to the weakest regions of the country in terms of economy. The lagging economies of these lands were already described in political and economic treaties in the period between the two world wars, in which the necessity of establishing an industrial zone on those lands administered by Lviv was emphasised (then within the border of the Second Polish Republic, currently Western Ukraine) (Kwiatkowski, 2011). Also currently, despite large financial resources to stimulate development of the five administrative regions of Eastern Poland (including the Lublin and Subcarpathian Voivodeships addressed by this analysis) from funds allocated to the cohesion of the EU, the disproportionate development of these lands is still noticeable, as is true in other countries of the eastern part of the EU. However, these regions have had a period of significant progress – between 2004 and 2020 in the Lublin and Subcarpathian Voivodeships, supported by the Operational Programme Eastern Poland 2014–2020 (Eastern Poland Programme Web Page). Subsequently, development disproportions were diminished by 12.6% (Annual Regional Programme 2021…).

Subsidising the development of the EU borderland regions with the intention of increasing its economic cohesion contributed to an increase in economic disparity. It resulted in undertaking pilot cross-border measures between the Subcarpathian Voivodeship and the Lviv Oblast implemented in the scope of eliminating legal and administrative barriers at the external border within b-solutions INTERREG-A NUTS III (Medeiros et al., 2022). It is important to note that, in the case of the studied regions whose character is mainly rural, the economic growth of these regions is driven mainly by the growth of the share of industry in GVA, including within the FDI (which, in the case of regions other than rural areas, constitutes only one of many economic growth factors). Economic growth in the eastern regions of the European Union that are predominantly rural results from the replacement of agriculture with industry and the influx of FDI, whose importance is growing (Ganau & Kilroy, 2023).

It should be underlined that the Polish-Ukrainian borderland area is marked by a difficult history of separatist and nationalist movements (nationalisms: German, Great Russian, Ukrainian, and Polish) resulting in mass ethnic cleansing in the former multicultural area of Europe (Kęsik, 2002; Torzecki, 1993) as well as consequences thereof in the form of mutual distrust and the development level of cross-border cooperation. In terms of development of the cooperation organisation system, the region of Lublin Voivodeship is characterised by a governance culture based on exchange and leadership and not cooperation, dialogue, or solidarity. The progressing centralisation of the country, financial transfers, and investments in the region favour, however, reinforcing regional identity by building foundations for the process of regionalisation in Central-Eastern Europe (Gajewski, 2022).

Research on resilience and susceptibility to shocks of the European Union regional labour markets implies that post-socialist regions without a capital city constitute the most sensitive EU market (Borsekova & Korony, 2022; Borsekova et al., 2021). Such regions include the Lublin Voivodeship, whereas the Subcarpathian Voivodeship turns out to be at a lower risk in the face of crises, and thus should focus on mitigating susceptibility to threats (e.g., through sectoral diversification) and reinforcement of resilience (e.g., due to increasing the efficiency of work or employment rate) (Borsekova & Korony, 2022). However, in the face of the necessity of post-crisis recovery of GDP per capita after the financial crisis in 2008, a model of individual countries prevailed, which was especially noticeable in France, Portugal, Austria, Poland, and Germany, whereas, regional features were of minor importance – regions situated within one country usually have similar opportunities for recovery (Pontarollo & Serpieri, 2017; 2020).

The eastern regions of the European Union bordering Ukraine belong to the poorest regions of the grouping; however, the wealth therein is diverse. A comparison of GDP per capita has at constant prices in 2020 in all regions located along the border with Ukraine been presented in Figure 5.1. In none of the border regions with Ukraine has GDP per capita exceeded 50% of that of the average of the 27 EU Member States

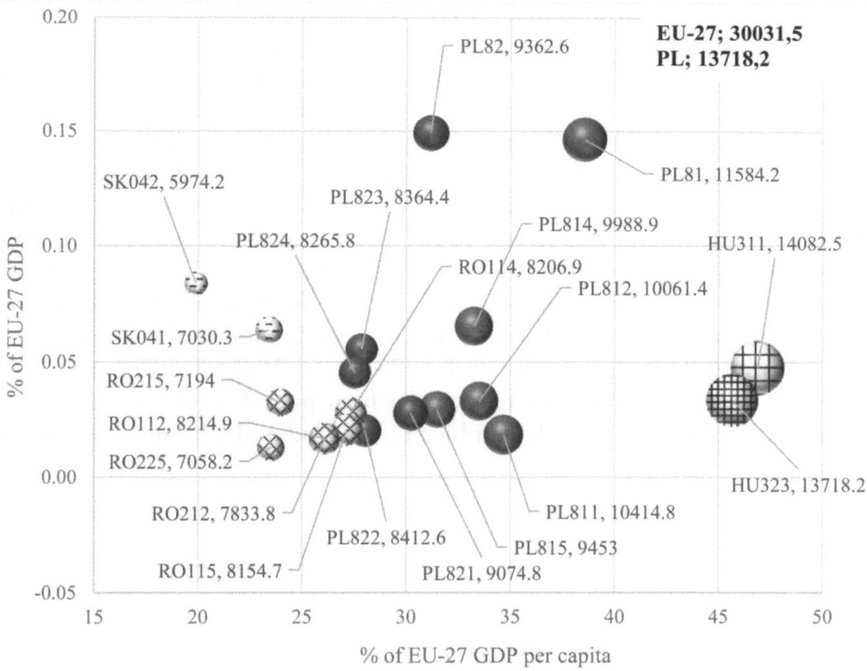

Figure 5.1 Per capita income in 2021 by NUTS 3 regions* (in Euro per capita).

Source: Own elaboration based on Eurostat (2021). Gross domestic product (GDP) at current market prices by NUTS 3 regions, https://doi.org/10.2908/NAMA_10R_3GDP (accessed: 23.03.2023).

* EU27 – European Union 27 Member States (from 2020); HU311 – Borsod-Abaúj-Zemplén, HU323 – Szabolcs-Szatmár-Bereg; PL81 – Lublin; PL811 – Biała; PL812 – Chełm and Zamość; PL814 – Lublin; PL815 – Puławy; PL82 – Subcarpathian; PL821 – Krosno; PL822 – Przemyśl; PL823 – Rzeszów; PL824 – Tarnobrzeg; RO112 – Bistrița-Năsăud; RO114 – Maramureș; RO115 – Satu Mare; RO212 – Botoșani; RO215 – Suceava; RO225 – Tulcea; SK041 – the Prešov Region; SK042 – the Košice Region.

(OX axis; in 2020 EU-27 = EUR 30,031.5 per capita) – the difference between extreme regions was as much as EUR 8,108.3 per capita (the wealthiest: the Košice Region SK – EUR 14,082.5 per capita; the least wealthy: Botoşani County RO – EUR 5,974.2 per capita, i.e., 42.42% of the average in the wealthiest borderland region and only 19.89% of the average of that of the EU-27).

Significant heterogeneity also characterised the community of Polish border regions. The wealthiest subregions of voivodeship cities, Lublin (PL814) and Rzeszów (PL823), had a per capita income of, respectively, EUR 12,364.1 and EUR 11,584.2. The least wealthy was Przemyśl (PL822). Chełm and Zamość (PL812) attained a per capita income of: EUR 7,058.2 and EUR 7,194.0 (i.e., slightly over 50% of per capita income in Poland as a whole – EUR 13,718.2).

Over the decade (2011–2020), the unemployment rate in eastern Poland regions decreased by 6.7% (from 11.0% to 4.3%), and average income per person in a household in 2020 did not exceed PLN 1,700 (approx. EUR 363/person), which ranked these voivodeships in five last places among 16 Polish Voivodeships (Annual Regional Programme, 2021…).

Changes in the availability of workers on the national labour market in 2010–2021 were not as intense as those observed in Ukraine. The labour market in Poland was characterised by significant stability. In the period between 2010 and 2015, two trends beneficial for the development of this market were observed: the first was related to the increase in the total number of people actively employed (from 17,153,000 in 2010 to 17,489,000 in 2015), and the second was related to the increase in the percentage of people actively employed in (economically active population – women aged 15–59, men aged 15–64). In the years 2010–2015, the share of people actively employed increased by 4.1% (from 65.4% to 69.5%), and in the entire period of analysis by 8.2% (up to the level of 73.6% in 2021) (see Figure 5.2). It is worth underlining the fact that in the final period of analysis in 2021, the number of people actively employed in Poland and Ukraine (affected by

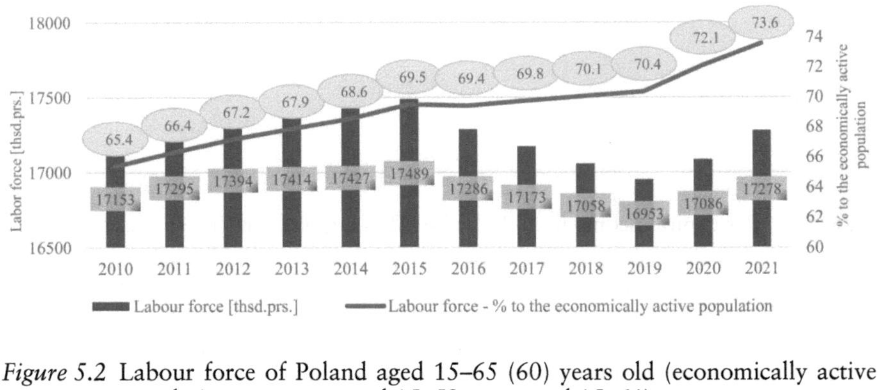

Figure 5.2 Labour force of Poland aged 15–65 (60) years old (economically active population – women aged 15–59, men aged 15–64).

Source: Statistics Poland, Local Data Bank of Statistics Poland, https://bdl.stat.gov.pl/bdl/start (accessed: 12.02.2023).

the annexation of Crimea in 2015) was similar – 17,278,000 in Poland and 17,321,000 in Ukraine.

In the years 2016–2019, the country experienced a drop of 0.5 million in the number of people actively employed (from approximately 17,500,000 people to almost 17 million), which has been caused by the departure the elderly from the labour market and an insufficient supply of younger replacements, as well as the social policy conducted by the national government. Dependent on the level of income, benefits for families with children have resulted in the outflow of women from the labour market to the group of economically inactive people; the low birth rate resulting from the demographic structure of Poland after World War II, as a consequence of the post-war baby boom and the cyclical echo of this boom, appeared. After this period, changes in the 500+ programme (departure from making support dependent on family incomes) resulted in professional re-activation and an increase in the number of workers to 17,278,000 in 2021 (see Figure 5.3).

In 2010–2021, the number of working people in Poland was growing. After growing slowly from 15.56 million to 15.71 million workers in 2010–2013 (after the crisis of 2008), in 2014–2015 the growth rate of the number of workers rose significantly to 16.28 million, followed in 2020 by a gradual increase to 16,560,000. In 2021, the number of workers increased by approximately 225,000 to 16,780,000.

The beneficial situation on the labour market is confirmed by data on unemployment. The number of unemployed in the analysed time frame decreased by 2/3rds from 1,600,000 in 2010 (6.1% of all economically active people) to almost 500,000 in 2021 (2.1% of people of working age). In principle, apart from regional/local deviations, the national labour market is healthy. After the crisis in 2008–2012, during which the number of unemployed reached a maximum of – 17,570,000, the level of unemployment dropped gradually until 2020, when, as a result of the uncertainty caused by the COVID-19 pandemic, a small increase was observed (by approx.

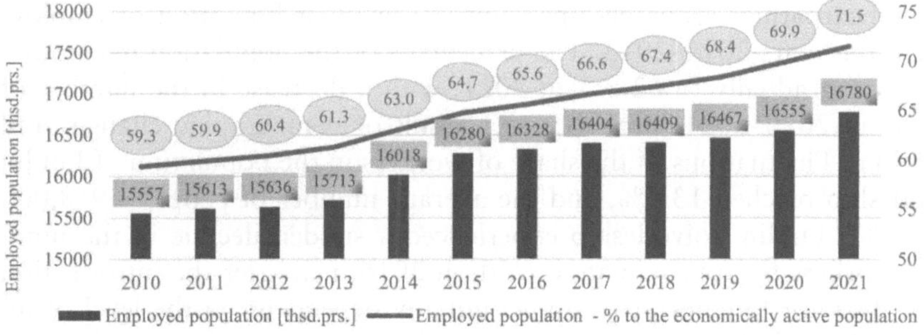

Figure 5.3 Employed population of Poland aged 15–65 (60) years old (economically active population – women aged 15–59, men aged 15–64).

Source: Statistics Poland, Local Data Bank of Statistics Poland, https://bdl.stat.gov.pl/bdl/start (accessed: 12.02.2023).

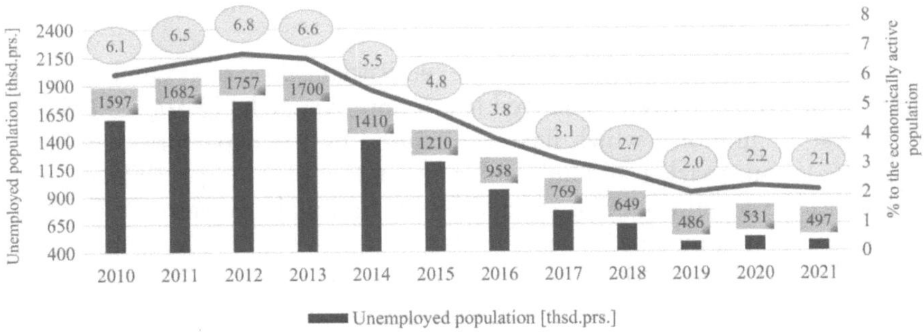

Figure 5.4 Unemployed population of Poland aged 15–65 (60) years old (economically active population – women aged 15–59, men aged 15–64).

Source: Statistics Poland, Local Data Bank of Statistics Poland, https://bdl.stat.gov.pl/bdl/start (accessed: 12.02.2023).

50 thousand year-on-year, on the national scale), which confirms that the national economy is stable (see Figure 5.4).

The labour market in districts in south-west Poland differed markedly. The figures regarding actively employed people in the Subcarpathian Voivodeship did not reflect the changes on the national market. In the period between 2010 and 2021, the Subcarpathian Voivodeship was characterised by significant stability of the share of actively employed people in the population at working age, at a level of approximately 65% (± 2.5%). The number of actively employed people has been dropping. During the study period, it dropped from 938,000 in 2010 to 854,000 in 2021. The greatest decrease was in 2014 (approx. 63,000 people) (see Figure 5.5).

The trends in the number of people employed in the regions are clearly noticeable (see Figure 5.6). The Subcarpathian Voivodeship saw smaller fluctuations in the percentage of working people (8.4% between 2014 and 2021) and the level of employment (an average of 819,000 persons ± 5.3%). Data from Subcarpathian Voivodeships shows an explicit limitation of employment in the years 2014–2015. The percentage of the population in employment grew gradually to 62.8% in 2021, with a decrease in the number of workers in 2020–2021 (probably as a result of demographic changes and migration). Fluctuations of the share of workers in the population of Lublin Voivodeship reached 13.4%, and the average number of people – 958,000 (± 10.9%). Lublin Voivodeship experienced a sudden decline in the number of workers by approximately 1/5th in 2016, i.e., after the introduction of the 500+ for families programme, initially dependent on the level of incomes in households and stabilisation of the level of employment for over 900,000 people. It is estimated that approximately 65,000–70,000 people remain professionally passive voluntarily or engage in unregistered work. After the ending of the income criterion in the programme 500+, since 2017,

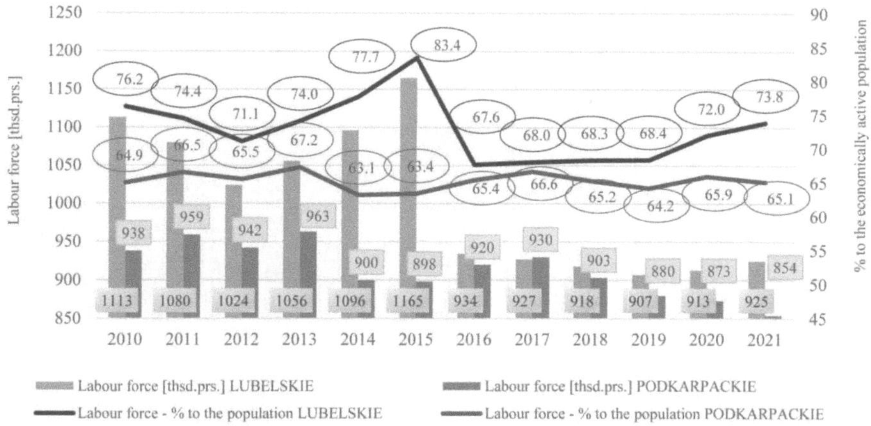

Figure 5.5 Labour force of Lublin and Subcarpathian Voivodeships aged 15–65 (60) years old (economically active population – women aged 15–59, men aged 15–64).

Source: Statistics Poland, Local Data Bank of Statistics Poland, https://bdl.stat.gov.pl/bdl/start (accessed: 12.02.2023).

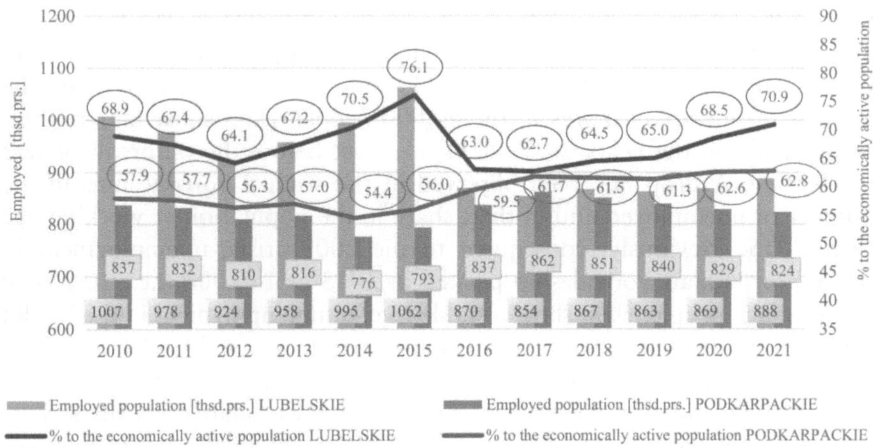

Figure 5.6 Employed population of Lublin and Subcarpathian voivodeships aged 15–65 (60) years old (economically active population – women aged 15–59, men aged 15–64).

Source: Statistics Poland, Local Data Bank of Statistics Poland, https://bdl.stat.gov.pl/bdl/start (accessed: 12.02.2023).

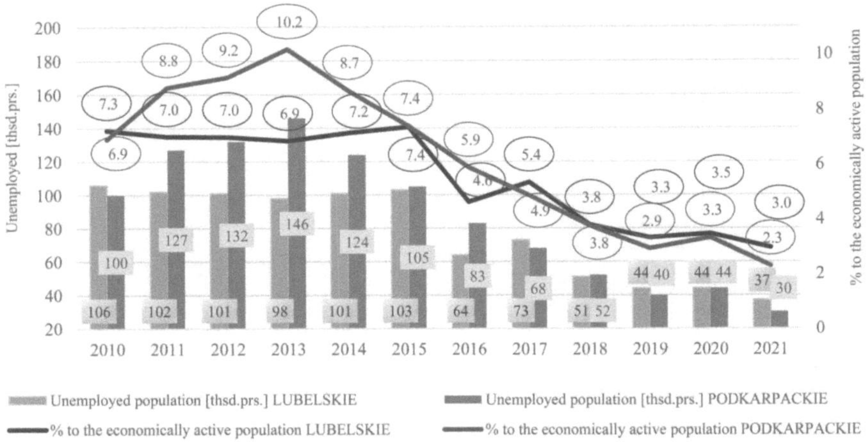

Figure 5.7 Unemployed population of Lublin and Subcarpathian voivodeships aged 15–65 (60) years old (economically active population – women aged 15–59, men aged 15–64).

Source: Statistics Poland, Local Data Bank of Statistics Poland, https://bdl.stat.gov.pl/bdl/start (accessed: 12.02.2023).

a gradual increase in the number of workers and the share of workers in population has been observed; however, they are still significantly lower than before the intervention within this programme.

Unemployment readings (see Figure 5.7) show a very favourable situation on the labour market in both voivodeships. In 2021, in the Lublin and Subcarpathian Voivodeships, the percentage of people of working age who were unemployed did not exceed 3% (3% and 2.3%, respectively), and the number of unemployed was below 40,000 people. Data show minimal unemployment in the years 2018–2021, i.e., just before the outbreak of war in Ukraine. A drop has been observed in the studied voivodeships in the number of unemployed and in their share in the population at working age since 2015. Previously, consequent to the 2008 crisis, unemployment in the Subcarpathian Voivodeship peaked in 2013 at 146,000, i.e., 10.2% of working-age people. Data show a stable level of unemployment in the Lublin Voivodeship (between 98,000 and 106,000 people, i.e., 6.9%–7.4%).

The employment structure in the economy of the studied regions of the eastern part of Poland is primarily characterised by a lower share of workers in the service sector – in sectors G–K (activities related to wholesale and retail; repair of motor vehicles; transport and warehouse management; activity related to accommodation and catering; information and communication; and finance and insurance) and in sectors related to specialist activity: M and N (i.e., related to professional, scientific and technical activity, managing services, and support). At the same time (by 2–4%), the share of employment in the studied regions in Sectors O, P, and Q related to public administration and government service (i.e., in public administration, national defence, law enforcement, education, healthcare, and social welfare) was observed to be significantly higher than the national average. Furthermore, it was noted that the Lublin Voivodeship had a higher share of people employed in the agriculture sector compared with the share of agricultural employment throughout Poland and in the Subcarpathian Voivodeship. Also noted was a slightly higher share of employment in Sector F (activity related to construction), as well as a share of employment in Sector C (manufacturing) significantly lower than the national average and in the Subcarpathian Voivodeship (in 2021, by 4.1% and 9.5%, respectively). However, the share of people in the Subcarpathian Voivodeship who were employed in Sectors B+C+D+E (activity related to mining and excavation; manufacturing; production and supply of utilities; water supply; waste and sewage management, and restoration) was 4.46% higher than the national average and 6.12% greater than the employment figures for the same sectors in the Lublin Voivodeship (see Table 5.1).

In the period between 2010 and 2021, average monthly remuneration in Poland increased by 76.2% (from EUR 676 to EUR 1,191). In the analogous period, remuneration in the Lublin Voivodeship increased by 73.4% (from EUR 613 to EUR 1,063), and in the Subcarpathian Voivodeship by 80.2% (from EUR 777 to EUR 1,040). Therefore, disproportion in remuneration in the Lublin Voivodeship grew by 1.4% (from 89.2% to 90.6%) as against the national figures, and the wages gap between the Subcarpathian Voivodeship and Poland diminished by 1.9% (from 85.4% to 87.3%). In 2021, the average monthly remuneration in regions covered by the analysis was smaller than the national average: by 10.8% in the Lublin Voivodeship and by 12.7% in the Subcarpathian Voivodeship (see Figure 5.8).

In Poland, in the years 2017–2021, remuneration in the entrepreneurial sector increased by 30%. During this timeframe, a similar increase was observed in the studied regions – by 29% in Lublin Voivodeship and by 30% in Subcarpathian Voivodeship. The remuneration in the aforementioned regions was lower than the national average (85% and 83%, respectively). However, the average monthly gross wages and salaries of regular employees in the entrepreneurial sector in the two voivodeships in 2021 were the highest in the sector. The average remuneration in the Lublin Voivodeship was EUR 1,051; in manufacturing, it was EUR 1,150; in construction, it was EUR 978; in trade and vehicle repair, it was EUR 920. In the Subcarpathian Voivodeship, the diversification of remuneration was narrower: the average monthly remuneration was EUR 1,023, whereas in industry it was EUR 1,072, in construction it was EUR 959, and in trade and vehicle repair it was EUR 935 (see Figure 5.9).

In Poland, the years 2010 and 2021 witnessed a constant increase in the number of jobs (a total increase of 3,135,000 jobs) and a remarkably high volatility of increase. In general, a clear growth trend was noted in Poland between 2012 and 2017. The years 2018–2019 saw this dynamism inhibited. Furthermore, jobs were lost nationwide as well as in the studied regions during the year of the COVID-19 pandemic (2020) (see Figure 5.10). In 2021,

Table 5.1 Structure of unemployment by type of economic activity (in percentage terms)

	POLAND				*LUBLIN*				*SUBCARPATHIAN*			
	2012	*2015*	*2018*	*2021*	*2012*	*2015*	*2018*	*2021*	*2012*	*2015*	*2018*	*2021*
In total [thousands of jobs]	9,719.6	9,823.0	10,606.2	10,874.7	391.4	390.4	412.2	424.2	412.5	409.1	442.3	451.6
Average employment by sector – percentage structure*, ** [%]												
Sector A	1.47	1.48	1.39	1.50	2.19	2.19	2.15	2.69	1.26	1.24	1.19	1.14
Sector: B+C+D+E	27.51	27.54	27.39	27.03	24.88	25.06	25.96	25.37	30.81	31.22	31.91	31.49
Sector C	22.82	23.36	23.65	23.38	18.34	18.55	19.73	19.37	27.89	28.57	29.31	28.87
Sector F	6.90	6.03	6.04	6.16	7.17	5.85	6.24	6.72	6.86	6.20	6.29	6.84
Sector G	16.04	16.25	16.28	16.02	15.89	15.64	15.12	15.00	15.63	15.09	15.02	14.84
Sector H	6.08	6.21	6.69	7.11	4.19	4.74	5.19	5.80	3.08	3.36	3.72	4.32
Sector I	1.80	1.75	1.84	1.83	1.24	1.26	1.29	1.36	1.31	1.34	1.48	1.48
Sector J	2.10	2.33	2.52	2.87	0.70	0.79	0.89	1.02	1.75	1.68	1.27	1.40
Sector K	2.94	2.73	2.53	2.33	2.39	2.00	1.65	1.37	1.28	1.21	1.20	0.81
Sector L	1.46	1.44	1.39	1.31	1.43	1.48	1.37	1.34	1.11	1.20	1.09	1.03
Sector M	3.56	3.81	4.03	4.37	2.21	2.22	2.23	2.36	2.12	2.00	2.10	2.21
Sector N	3.66	4.09	4.53	4.23	0.94	1.29	1.40	1.47	2.53	2.76	3.33	2.97
Sector O	6.48	6.31	5.86	5.76	8.43	8.64	8.13	7.89	7.42	7.41	6.88	6.65
Sector P	10.75	10.65	10.28	10.29	16.01	15.97	15.33	14.83	13.21	13.08	12.64	12.84
Sector Q	6.86	6.82	6.61	6.55	10.00	10.28	10.40	10.10	9.39	9.59	9.20	9.24
Sector R	1.33	1.23	1.19	1.18	1.35	1.35	1.37	1.33	1.48	1.36	1.27	1.24
Sector S	1.05	1.32	1.42	1.46	0.98	1.26	1.27	1.34	0.77	1.25	1.41	1.50

Source: Statistics Poland, Local Data Bank of Statistics Poland, https://bdl.stat.gov.pl/bdl/start (accessed: 12.02.2023).

* A. Agriculture, forestry, hunting, and fishery; B. Mining and excavation; C. Manufacturing; D. Electricity, gas, water steam, hot water, and air for air-conditioning production and supply; E. Water supply; waste and sewage management, and restoration-related activity; F. Construction; G. Wholesale and retail; repair of motor vehicles, including motorcycles; H. Transport and warehouse management; I. Activity related to accommodation and catering services; J. Information and communication; K. Finance and insurance; L. Activity related to servicing the real estate market; M. Professional, scientific and technical activity; N. Activity in the scope of management and support services; O. Public administration and national defence; mandatory social security; P. Education; Q. Healthcare and social welfare; R. Activity related to culture, entertainment, and recreation; S. Other services.

** Other, unspecified – in total below 0.00%: T. Households hiring workers; households manufacturing goods and providing services for their own purposes and U. Exterritorial organisations and teams.

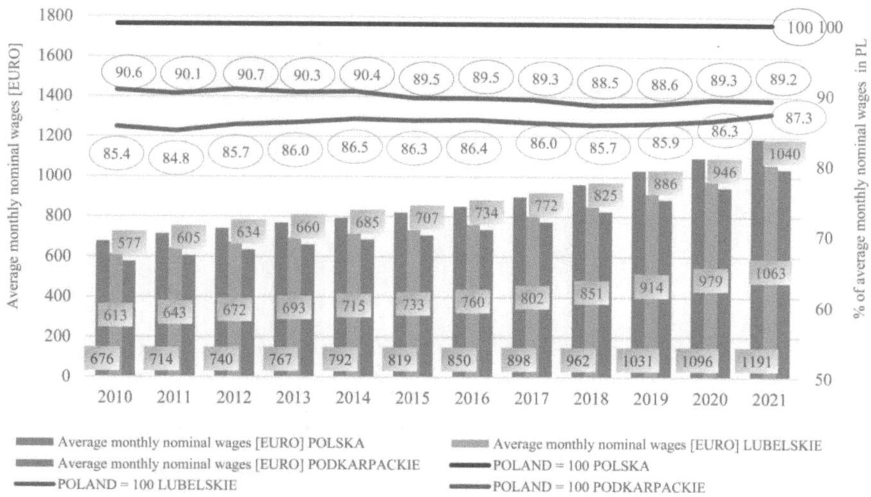

Figure 5.8 Average monthly gross wages of regular employees of Lublin and Subcarpathian voivodeships and Poland in general, in Euro.

Source: Statistics Poland, Local Data Bank of Statistics Poland, https://bdl.stat.gov.pl/bdl/start (accessed: 19.02.2023).

a recovery occurred; the dynamics of the number of jobs doubled (dynamics index on a fixed basis, in comparison with 2010). General trends in the country and studied regions were similar, with the exception of 2017 and 2018, when, in contrast to the national trend, the economy of the Lublin Voivodeship showed further increase in dynamics, until reaching a maximum level in 2019 (dynamics in comparison with 2010 equals 415).

In the studied period between 2010 and 2021 in Lublin and Subcarpathian Voivodeships, 111,000 and 114,000 jobs were created, respectively. The highest increases were noted in 2015–2019, before the pandemic. An average of 14,000 jobs were added yearly in the Lublin Voivodeship, and in the Subcarpathian Voivodeship, an average of 13,900 were added yearly. In 2021, 14,900 jobs were added in Lublin Voivodeship and 13,500 were added in Subcarpathian Voivodeship. It is also worth underlining that, in 2020, in both regions (as in the entire country), despite the crisis and dramatic slowdown, there was a positive balance between new job creation and job loss. Based on this data, it can be said that labour markets in Polish regions of the Polish-Ukrainian borderland continue to witness growth despite fluctuations related to the national and international economic situation. This suggests that the market is absorbing new workers.

In 2021, poviats covered by the research reported a total demand for 46,656 jobs and activation of the unemployed, which translated into 3.5 unemployed people for every job opening (in the Lublin Voivodeship – 3.1 of unemployed people per one job offer, whereas in the Subcarpathian Voivodeship – 3.9). Women were a small majority of the unemployed (51.6%), while a significant

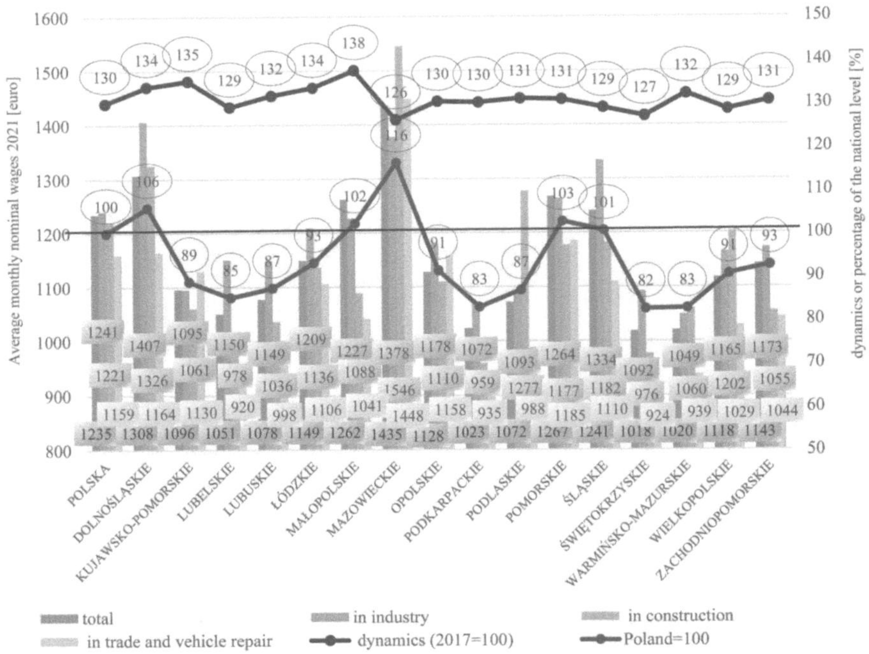

Figure 5.9 Average monthly gross wages and salaries of regular employees in the entrepreneurial sector according to selected PKD 2007 codes by voivodeships of Poland in 2021, in Euro*.

Source: Statistics Poland, Local Data Bank of Statistics Poland, https://bdl.stat.gov.pl/bdl/start (accessed: 19.02.2023).

* The line graph presents the dynamics (2017=100) and the percentage share in relation to the average in Poland in 2021.

discrepancy was noted in particular poviats. In the Subcarpathian Voivodeship, depending on the poviat, the number of unemployed per one job opening fluctuated from 1.5 (Rzeszów), through 7.3 (Przemyśl) and 9.6 (Brzozów Poviat) to 15 (Przemyśl Poviat), while high rates reflect the small number of reported vacancies. In the Subcarpathia Voivodeship, the highest share of women among the unemployed was in Przeworsk poviat (57.1%). A slightly higher share than the average in the studied region in 2021 was also noted in the poviats of Jarosław (53.7%) and Bieszczady (52.7%), whereas the share of women in the group of the unemployed was relatively low in Lesko poviat (46.5%) and Lubaczów poviat (47.1%). The Lublin Voivodeship was also distinguished by internal diversification in particular poviats, but it was not as extreme as in the case of poviats in the Subcarpathian Voivodeship, where the number of unemployed per one vacancy ranged from 1.6 (Zamość) and 1.7 (Biała Podlaska) to 6.3 (Zamość poviat) and 6.4 (Krasnystaw poviat). A high percentage of women among the unemployed was noted in the following poviats: Parczew (56.6%), Łęczna (55.8%), Chełm (54.5%), and in the city of Chełm (54.4%) (see Table 5.2).

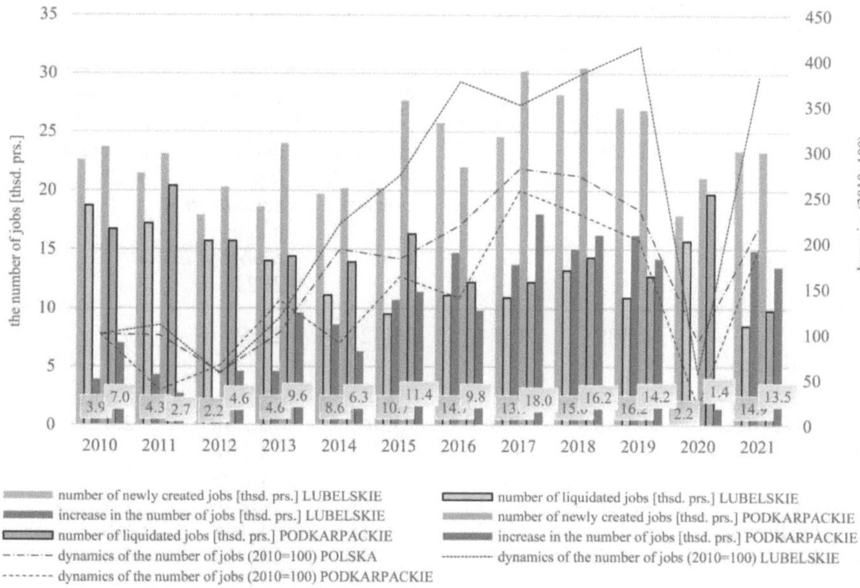

Figure 5.10 Number of created jobs* (in thousands) in Lublin and Subcarpathian Voivodeships** and graphic representation of the number of jobs (2010= 100) compared to Poland in general.

Source: Statistics Poland, Local Data Bank of Statistics Poland, https://bdl.stat.gov.pl/bdl/start (accessed: 19.02.2023).

* Newly created jobs are jobs created because of organisational changes, expansion or change of a business profile, and all jobs in newly established units.

** The data does not include those working in budgetary units operating in the field of national defence and public security.

The unemployed registered in 2021 in Labour Offices in the studied regions indicated a lack of trained or exercised profession among the most frequently declared professional competences: in the Lublin Voivodeship – 14.5%, and in the Subcarpathian Voivodeship – 10.1% of declarations. Trades the most frequently given by the unemployed included salesperson, cook, and car mechanic. In both regions covered by the analysis, the lack of structural fit between competences of unemployed people and jobs needing to be filled is noticeable. Employers from the region were searching for low-skilled employees (salesperson, warehouseman, assistant construction worker, catering assistant, hand packer, office cleaning lady, assistant worker in manufacturing) or people with specific qualifications or technical skills (delivery truck driver, welder, locksmith, nursery school teacher assistant, operators of machines, devices, or CNC tools). A higher demand for work performed by operators of machines and warehousemen is evident in the Subcarpathian Voivodeship, which may demonstrate the need to extend employment opportunities in this type of enterprise in the region (see Table 5.3).

Table 5.2 Demand and supply on the labour market in Lublin and Subcarpathian Voivodeships (Poland), in 2021

	Registered unemployed (in 2021)	*Registered unemployed as of 31.12.*	*Registered unemployed people as of 31.12. – women*	*The number of vacancies and professional activation places reported in 2021*	*The number of unemployed per one job offer*
Lublin Voivodeship*	54,339	70,546	36,324	22,660	3.1
by poviats:					
Bielsko Poviat	4,988	7,980	3,960	3,288	2.4
Biała Podlaska	2,816	4,226	2,054	2,548	1.7
Biłgoraj Poviat	4,352	4,384	2,332	1,578	2.8
Chełm	4,528	4,348	2,364	2,256	1.9
Chełm Poviat	6,034	6,630	3,616	1,146	5.8
Hrubieszów Poviat	4,812	6,586	3,320	1,922	3.4
Krasnystaw Poviat	3,154	6,110	2,940	952	6.4
Łęczna Poviat	2,662	2,706	1,510	1,028	2.6
Parczew Poviat	2,040	1,906	1,078	558	3.4
Świdnik Poviat	3,336	4,346	2,144	842	5.2
Tomaszów Poviat	3,995	5,014	2,664	1,436	3.5
Włodawa Poviat	2,578	4,096	2,178	1,036	4.0
Zamość Poviat	5,644	7,474	3,814	1,180	6.3
Zamość	3,400	4,740	2,350	2,890	1.6
Subcarpathian Voivodeship*	62,560	93,060	48,174	23,996	3.9
by poviats:					
Bieszczady Poviat	2,108	2,368	1,248	396	6.0
Brzozów Poviat	4,538	8,564	4,418	890	9.6
Jarosław Poviat	8,458	10,762	5,774	2,356	4.6
Lesko Poviat	2,682	3,490	1,624	716	4.9
Leżajsk Poviat	4,896	7,312	3,802	1,354	5.4
Lubaczów Poviat	3,650	4,112	1,936	1,082	3.8
Łańcut Poviat	5,406	6,594	3,270	1,112	5.9
Przemyśl Poviat	4,424	7,422	3,848	496	15.0
Przemyśl	3,090	5,814	2,980	792	7.3
Przeworsk Poviat	5,650	7,702	4,400	1,776	4.3
Rzeszów Poviat	6,532	11,356	5,880	2,868	4.0
Rzeszów	7,052	12,588	6,478	8,490	1.5
Sanok Poviat	4,074	4,976	2,516	1,668	3.0
Studied poviats – in total	116,899	163,606	84,498	46,656	3.5

Source: Own elaboration based on the Portal of *Public Employment Services*, Ministry of Family and Social Policy, https://psz.praca.gov.pl/rynek-pracy/statystyki-i-analizy/zatrudnianie-cudzoziemcow-w-polsce (accessed: 14.12.2022).

* Data for poviats covered by the research.

Table 5.3 Structural adjustment of labour demand and supply of jobs according to type of work, demand for work reported in 2021

	Lublin Voivodeship	*Subcarpathian Voivodeship*
Total unemployed registered during the reporting period, total including:*	54,339	62,560
without trade	7,854	6,303
salesperson	2,392	2,870
cook	1,097	1,210
car mechanic	761	825
assistant construction worker	780	763
locksmith	588	884
economic technician	594	868
hairdresser	564	699
public administration specialist	534	591
warehouseman	477	634
maintenance worker	514	571
mechanical technician	472	600
IT technician	508	467
The total number of vacancies and professional activation places (reported in the reporting period), including:*	22,660	23,996
salesperson	822	1,371
warehouseman	644	950
other office employees	790	481
assistant construction worker	501	731
maintenance worker	528	646
office worker	447	505
catering assistant	458	471
hand packer	512	363
assistant worker in manufacturing	784	37
delivery truck driver	613	201
office cleaning lady	390	385
other workers performing simple work not classified	314	404
welder	178	416
truck driver	235	289
cook	215	289
warehouse worker	227	196
locksmith	124	295
nursery schoolteacher assistant	224	181
sales representative	153	246
driver mechanic	393	4
operator of machines for the production of wire goods, ropes, nets, and cables	8	375
other operators of machines and devices for metal production and processing	34	334
operator of numerically controlled machine tools	49	297

Source: Own elaboration based on WORTAL Publicznych Służb Zatrudnienia (Public Employment Services), Ministry of Family and Social Policy, https://psz.praca.gov.pl/rynek-pracy/statystyki-i-analizy/zatrudnianie-cudzoziemcow-w-polsce (accessed: 14.12.2022).

* professions represented in large numbers.

5.3 Comparative Poverty Assessment in the Polish-Ukrainian Borderland

Polish and Ukrainian institutions set different poverty levels: "legal" poverty, absolute and relative poverty levels; therefore, one should approach interpretation of these values with caution. The legal poverty rate in Ukraine means the share of households with average per capita equivalent monthly incomes below the legally established subsistence minimum (EUR 71.99 in 2019). State social assistance is assigned and paid in cash to low-income families who permanently live in Ukraine and have an average monthly total income lower than the subsistence minimum for the family. In Poland, the legal poverty rate is the amount that, pursuant to the binding act, authorises citizens to apply for social assistance (in 2019 for a single-person household, it amounted to EUR 164.61 monthly and EUR 123.99 per person in multi-person households). The definition of the absolute poverty level is different too in Ukraine than in Poland. In Ukraine, it is the share of households with average per capita equivalent total monthly incomes below the actual subsistence minimum (EUR 138.56 in 2019), and in Poland, the subsistence minimum is established by the level of needs' satisfaction, below which there is a biological threat to life and psychological and physical development of a human (in 2019, for a family with one younger child, it amounted to EUR 357.14, i.e., EUR 119.05 per person, in a single-person household; for a person at working age, the minimum was estimated at EUR 144.78 and for a single retired person – EUR 137.38).

The statutory poverty threshold in Poland, in 2019, constituted over double the amount in Ukraine. In 2019, 9% of households in Poland qualified as poor as defined by statute, whereas in the analysed regions, 12.6% of households (Lublin Voivodeship) and 12.9% of households (Subcarpathian Voivodeship) were defined as poor. In Ukraine, only 1% of households received benefits (0.4% in Zakarpattia Oblast, 0.5% in Lviv Oblast, and 3.8% in Volyn Oblast). Data on the absolute poverty level and relative poverty level in Poland and Ukraine seem to be more reliable and to reflect the economic reality of the poorest population more accurately (see Table 5.4). In 2019, in Ukraine, 23.3% of the population – three times as many as in 2013 – were classified as living at the absolute poverty level, indicating extreme conditions below the level of minimal subsistence. In Volyn Oblast, the situation was even worse, with as many as 30.9% of all households – four times more than in 2013 – classified as at the level of absolute poverty. In the same period of time (2013–2019), in Poland, only 4.2% of households faced similar hardship. The percentage of such households in the eastern voivodeships of Poland was higher than elsewhere in Poland (Lublin – 6.8%, Subcarpathian – 5.3%).

Additional information for the purposes of international comparison is provided by the relative poverty level estimated for Ukraine and adjusted to criteria used in Poland, which emphasises the scale of incomes. In 2019,

Table 5.4 Poverty rate in Ukraine and Poland and its border regions (in percentage terms)

	Legal poverty rate			*Absolute poverty level*			*Relative poverty level****		
	2013	*2019*	*2013=100*	*2013*	*2019*	*2013=100*	*2013*	*2019*	*2013=100*
Ukraine	6.9	1.0	14.7	6.9*	23.3	*338.9*	4.69	7.6	*162.1*
Zakarpattia Oblast	9.8	0.4	3.8	9.8	17.4	177.6	4.97**	4.6	92.2
Volyn Oblast	7.5	3.8	50.5	7.5	30.9	411.5	2.86	8.6	*301.4*
Lviv Oblast	8.6	0.5	6.3	8.6	16.7	194.2	4.17	6.7	*159.5*
Poland	12.8	9.0	70.3	7.4	4.2	56.8	16.2	13	80
Lublin Voivodeship	17.6	12.6	71.6	9.4	6.8	72.3	21.5	17.5	81
Subcarpathian Voivodeship	16.9	12.9	76.3	9.4	5.3	56.4	20.9	18.6	89

Source: Statistics Poland, Central Statistical Office of Poland, https://bdl.stat.gov.pl/bdl/start (accessed: 19.02.2023).; Expenditure and resources of households of Ukraine in 2019 according to the data of a sample survey of the living conditions of households in Ukraine. Statistical collection. State Statistics Service of Ukraine, https://www.ukrstat.gov.ua/druk/publicat/kat_u/2020/zb/06/zb_vrd_19_ue.pdf; Households of Lviv Oblast in 2019. Statistical collection, https://www.lv.ukrstat.gov.ua/ukr/publ/2020/ZB1720200101.pdf; Households of Lviv Oblast in 2013. Statistical collection, https://www.lv.ukrstat.gov.ua/ukr/publ/2015/ZB1520150101.pdf; Expenditures and resources of households of Ukraine by each region), https://ukrstat.gov.ua/operativ/menu/menu_e/virdg.htm; Expenditure and resources of households in Volyn Oblast in 2013, http://www.lutsk.ukrstat.gov.ua/domogosp_pb.html (accessed: 24.02.2023).

* In 2013, the amount of legally established subsistence and the actual subsistence minimum were almost the same (EUR 42.15 and EUR 41.14).

** Data as of 2017. Data for 2013 is not available publicly. An official request can be made.

*** The data is presented in accordance with the definition given in Polish Statistics – the share of households with average per capita equivalent total income per month below 50% of the average level of total income. Ukraine: EUR 106.28 in 2019; Poland: (in a single-person household, EUR 201.48, in four-person households – EUR 136.02 per person in 2019); amounts in EUR were calculated on the basis of average exchange rates of UAH and PLN as on 31.12.2019 according to the National Bank of Ukraine and the National Bank of Poland.

in Ukraine, where the income structure is less diverse, 7.6% of households were rated as living in relative poverty (4.6% of households in Zakarpatia Oblast, 8.6% in Volyn Oblast, and 6.7% in Lviv Oblast). Likewise, in 2019, in Poland, with its greater economic disparity, 13% of households were rated as living in relative poverty. The percentage of such households was significantly higher in the southeastern areas of Poland that share a border with Ukraine (17.5% of all households in Lublin Voivodeship, 18.6% of all households in–Subcarpathian Voivodeship).

5.4 Cross-Border Movements of Persons between Ukraine and Poland

In the literature, there are numerous references to cross-border flows between Poland and Ukraine before the outbreak of war in 2022, which mainly concerned persons, capital, and goods and services as well as such issues as smuggling and other forms of organised crime, or even bilateral visits of participants in Polish-Ukrainian cross-border projects. The data analysis implies that citizens of Ukraine were travelling to Poland much more frequently (in 2001, it was once a month, in 2011 it was several times a week) than Poles to Ukraine (in 2001, it was less frequently than once a month, and in 2011 there were several visits a month). While comparing the years 2001 and 2011, H. Powęska (2013) underlines explicit asymmetries concerning, for example, cross-border movement of persons dealing with, for example, borderland trade.

Furthermore, more recent data from the Polish Border Service (Border Guard Poland, Statistical Service) confirm that Ukrainians constitute the largest group of people crossing the Polish border. In 2013, border traffic from this country accounted for 40.4% of total traffic on the Polish part of the EU's external border into the EU (8.46 million in total). In the following years (after the annexation of Crimea in 2014), this increased by additional few percentage points to 47.7% – to maximum of 11.44–11.50 million people in 2016–2017. The dynamics of passenger border traffic from Ukraine towards Poland was characterised by the following trends: stable growth in 2014–2017, which slackened off in 2018–2019, and a clear decline during the period of restrictions related to the COVID-19 pandemic in 2020–2021 (to 3.89 million in 2020). Russia's attack on Crimea in 2014, apart from the increase in passenger traffic from Ukraine to Poland, resulted in a significant increase in local border traffic by 44 percentage points between 2013 and 2015. The COVID-19 pandemic caused the scale of local border traffic to decrease by more than 1/3 in 2018–2019 compared to 2017 (see Table 5.5). However, this was accompanied by an increase in the number of people coming from Ukraine to Polish regions located beyond the border zone (an increase from 3.56 million in 2013 to 7.2–7.7 million in 2018–2019). This proves the intensification of economic migration of Ukrainian citizens to Poland (Border Guard Poland, Statistical Service).

Table 5.5 Total border traffic – number of crossings of sections of the EU external border

		2013	2014	2015	2016	2017	2018	2019	2020	2021	2022
total movement of people from Ukraine (to Poland)	amount	8456102	8961100	10685108	11 444 158	11 502 576	10 857 578	10 894 450	3 891 480	4 386 910	9 677 248
	fluctuation (2013=100)	100	106.0	126.4	135.3	136.0	128.4	128.8	46.0	51.9	114.4
total movement of people (to Poland) – EU external border	amount	20927209	21760389	23161022	23 985 163	25 495 088	26 195 802	27 151 162	8 924 419	9 735 646	19 619 119
	fluctuation (2013=100)	100	104.0	110.7	114.6	121.8	125.2	129.7	42.6	46.5	93.7
participation of Ukrainian citizens in the total border traffic to Poland	*percentage*	*40.4*	*41.2*	*46.1*	*47.7*	*45.1*	*41.4*	*40.1*	*43.6*	*45.1*	*49.3*
movement of people from Ukraine – to Poland (foreigners)	*amount*	7288695	7952084	9602956	10 287 753	10 431 421	9 860 223	9 983 562	465 286	4 145 434	9 436 203
	fluctuation (2013=100)	100	109.1	131.8	141.1	143.1	135.3	137.0	6.4	56.9	129.5
movement of people from Ukraine – from Poland (foreigners)	*amount*	7147780	7745048	9373572	10 039 620	10 279 590	9 735 839	9 929 753	465 609	4 100 072	7 376 721
	fluctuation (2013=100)	100	108.4	131.1	140.5	143.8	136.2	138.9	6.5	57.4	103.2
local border traffic from Ukraine – to Poland (foreigners)	*amount*	3731438	4207974	5367484	4 910 015	4 238 211	2 639 955	2 238 579	465286	67 216	317 689
local border traffic from Ukraine – from Poland (foreigners)	*amount*	3731325	4207338	5367475	4 910 315	4 238 698	2 640 020	2 238 486	465609	67 159	317 096
excluding local border traffic from Ukraine – to Poland (foreigners)	*amount*	3557257	3744110	4235472	5377738	6193210	7220268	7744983	0	4078218	9118514
	percentage	*48.8*	*47.1*	*44.1*	*52.3*	*59.4*	*73.2*	*77.6*	*0.0*	*98.4*	*96.6*
excluding local border traffic from Ukraine – from Poland (foreigners)	*amount*	3416455	3537710	4006097	5129305	6040892	7095819	7691267	0	4032913	7059625
	percentage	*47.8*	*45.7*	*42.7*	*51.1*	*58.8*	*72.9*	*77.5*	*0.0*	*98.4*	*95.7*

Source: Border Guard (Poland), Zarząd Graniczny KGSG, https://www.strazgraniczna.pl/pl/granica/statystyki-sg/2206,Statystyki-SG.html (accessed: 19.07.2023).

5.4.1 Perspectives before the COVID-19 Pandemic – Years 2011–2019

Whereas, in 2011, main goods purchased by the participants in the borderland trade of Ukrainian nationality in Poland were construction materials, Poles were mainly brining fuel from Ukraine (Powęska, 2013). A majority of persons (both citizens of Poland and Ukraine) whose main purpose for crossing the Polish-Ukrainian border was to visit shops resided in the area located within 50 km from the border (Peciakowski & Gizicki, 2021; Powęska, 2011). O. Charucka refers to the research conducted in 2015, according to which the number of such persons amounted to over 71% (Charucka, 2016) of foreigners and almost the same number of Poles. The cross-border movement of persons is also related to economic transfer, i.e., transferring money to a neighbouring country. In the case of the Polish-Ukrainian borderland, one can notice a difference in transferring by Ukrainian citizen's financial means as of arriving in Poland – persons arriving in Poland before 2014 transferred much more money to Ukraine than persons who arrived after 2014 (Szast, 2019). The year 2014 can be considered the beginning of the military aggression of the Russian Federation on Ukraine and the related increase in interest in migration to Poland. M. Wosek and R. Kata underline that over the past years migration flows covered not only borderland areas but also the entire area of Ukraine and the concentration of labour migration streams to Poland concerned more than just the regions localised at the border. These regions did play the role of temporary places of residence from which migrants moved to more developed regions of Western and Central Poland (Wosiek & Kata, 2019). For some of them, Poland was only a transit country (Kuzior & Lobanova, 2017).

Before 2022, the cross-border movement of persons in the Polish-Ukrainian borderland also concerned tourists. While comparing the general number of departures through borders and tourist traffic in both ways – from Poland to neighbouring countries and vice versa, M. Więckowski states that arrivals of neighbours from the East prevail in the balance. The largest disproportion concerns the tourist traffic between Poland and Ukraine (8.5 times more Ukrainians arrived in Poland than Poles in Ukraine). Such disproportions in movement were caused by the fact that for Poles the western part of Ukraine had features of a reception area for sentimental tourism popular in the 90s of the previous century (Więckowski, 2011). The main motive for Ukrainians to arrive in Poland was not only the eagerness to visit a European Union Member State but also, for example, to visit relatives and friends staying in Poland or researching possibilities of economic migration to Poland.

Cross-border movements were also related to the mobility of students, which resulted from the development of the educational offer of Polish universities for students from the East. While analysing the movements of students in the Polish-Ukrainian borderland, U. Bronisz stated that the one-way influx of Ukrainians to Poland could be observed (Bronisz, 2017). As written by P. Długosz, the fact that it was worth coming to Poland to study, since the educational level was higher, was more often supported by Ukrainian students in Rzeszów (52%) and Przemyśl (43%) than in Krakow (22%). Results of the comparisons show that students choosing universities in Przemyśl and Rzeszów were under the influence of attracting factors, and people studying in Krakow were subject to push factors (Długosz, 2018). In many cases, Ukrainian students were also active on the Polish labour market. There are several Polish scholarship programmes for Ukrainian citizens to pursue education in Poland after 2022: Solidarity with Ukraine, Anders NAWA, Banach NAWA, CEEPUS, POLONISTA, NAWA Summer Courses. These programmes offered over 4,500 thousand scholarships in 2022. The most popular programmes were: Solidarity with Ukraine and NAWA Summer Courses (Ministry of Education and Science; National Agency for Academic Exchange).

As far as the employment of Ukrainian migrants in Poland is concerned, detailed trends in recent years are illustrated by the data of the Ministry of Family and Social Policy (Ministry of Family and Social Policy, 2021). The information implies that in 2016, as many as 82.8% foreigners who received a work permit in Poland, came from Ukraine. In consecutive years, stabilisation was noted and then a drop in this scope, a stable trend, a downward trend and a percentage of work permits issued to Ukrainians in Poland was the following: 2017 – 84.5%, 2018 – 74.4%, 2019 – 74.7%, 2020 – 73.2%, 2021 – 68.5%. It means that in the years 2016–2021, citizens of Ukraine constituted the gross majority of foreigners applying for a work permit in Poland.

Data on work permits issued in Poland to Ukrainian citizens confirm that they are the largest group to apply for, and obtain, work permits in Poland (see Figure 5.11). The number of permits issued after the annexation

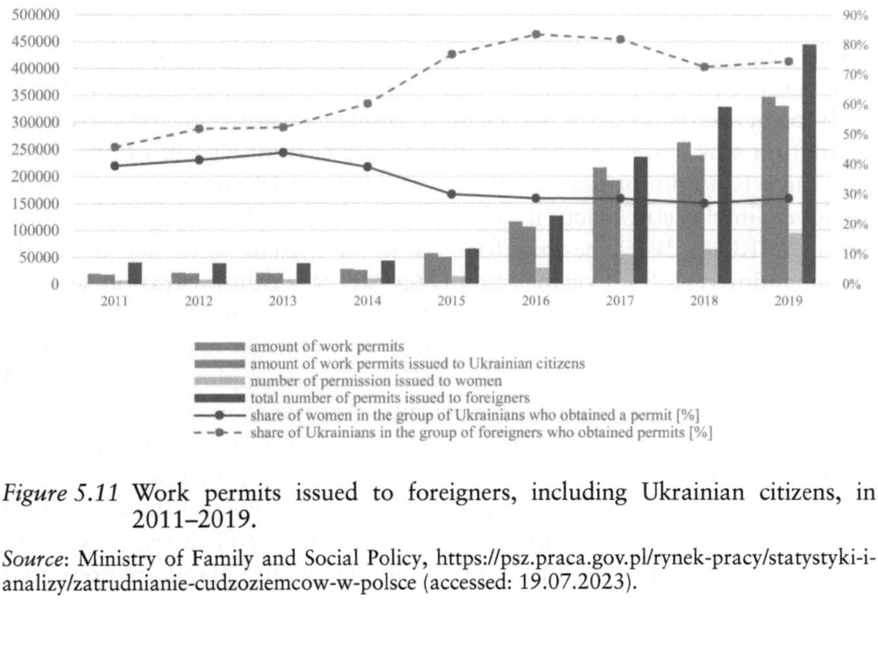

Figure 5.11 Work permits issued to foreigners, including Ukrainian citizens, in 2011–2019.

Source: Ministry of Family and Social Policy, https://psz.praca.gov.pl/rynek-pracy/statystyki-i-analizy/zatrudnianie-cudzoziemcow-w-polsce (accessed: 19.07.2023).

of Crimea by Russia in 2014 soared – in the 2014–2019 period there was a more than a 12-fold increase (to over 102,000 permits in 2019) with 1.1% applications refused. Throughout the 2011–2019 period, the vast majority were type A permits issued for a period not longer than three years (for foreigners working in Poland, under a contract with an employer from Poland) (information and service website for entrepreneurs: biznes.gov.pl) – see Table 5.6.

In the period before the outbreak of the COVID-19 pandemic, women represented no more than 20%. Before February 2022, the Ukrainian economic migration in Poland was mainly represented by young men, less educated, but in general speaking Polish fluently, mainly engaged in physical labour (work in agriculture, work as a qualified worker), staying in Poland without their families, mainly for earning purposes, less frequently educational, treating their stay in Poland as a temporary situation. Their total length of stay in Poland usually comprised several stays during which they were extending their social networks (relations with other migrants from Ukraine, as well as Poles), which provided them with support in the process of searching for employment (Górna & Jaźwińska, 2019).

Before the annexation of Crimea and the intensification of migration flow, workers from Ukraine in 2013 mainly worked in Poland as skilled (27.9%) or unskilled workers (23.5%). In 2019, this structure was still dominated by professions related to the manufacturing sector: industrial workers and craftsmen (38.2%), unskilled workers (28.8%), machine and equipment operators and fitters (21.1%), and there was a visible shift towards better-educated employees (medium or higher up to 8%), including specialists, technicians, and others, including office workers – see Table 5.7.

Between 2013 and 2019, there was a change in the rules for qualifying professions by the Polish Employment Services, so it is not possible to directly compare data on the structure of industries in which the Ukrainian population was employed before 2014 to the current classification. However, there is no doubt that significant numbers of Ukrainian citizens were employed in the construction (17.3%) and household help (22.3%) sectors in 2013. In 2019, permits for Ukrainian citizens were issued mainly in four industries: F – Construction (26.4%), N – Administration services and support activities (22.6%), C – Industrial processing (22.5%), and H – Transport and warehousing (16.3%). In terms of border regions, these were also the industries in which foreigners were mainly employed in 2019, and in the Lublin Voivodeship the most permits were issued in section H (5,156, i.e., 39.7%), followed by F (4,050, i.e., 31.2%), while in the Subcarpathian Voivodeship there are three industries: F (2,831, i.e., 33.1%), N (2,608, i.e., 30.5%), and H (1,530, i.e., 17.9%). Statistics Poland does not have data on permits issued to Ukrainian citizens in the NUTS2 region system. Detailed data on work permits issued to foreigners in Poland are presented in Table 5.8.

Table 5.6 Work permits issued to Ukrainian citizens in 2011–2019 – indicators

	2011	*2012*	*2013*	*2014*	*2015*	*2016*	*2017*	*2018*	*2019*
number of work permits issued to Ukrainian citizens	7921	9091	9430	11100	17158	33412	62404	71718	102033
fluctuation in the number of work permits issued to Ukrainian citizens (2011=100)	100	114.8	119.1	140.1	216.6	421.8	787.8	905.4	1288.1
type of work permit in percentages									
A	98.8%	98.5%	98.0%	97.6%	97.6%	98.0%	99.0%	98.0%	97.3%
B	0.8%	0.7%	0.7%	0.6%	0.4%	0.1%	0.1%	0.2%	0.2%
C	0.3%	0.3%	0.9%	1.7%	1.9%	1.7%	0.7%	1.4%	2.3%
D	0.1%	0.4%	0.4%	0.0%	0.1%	0.1%	0.1%	0.2%	0.1%
E	0.0%	0.0%	0.0%	0.0%	0.0%	0.0%	0.1%	0.2%	0.1%
ratio of refusals to issued permits – total	0.9%	2.4%	1.7%	0.9%	1.3%	0.8%	0.8%	0.7%	1.0%
ratio of refusals to issued permits – Ukrainian citizens	0.8%	3.1%	2.3%	0.9%	1.1%	0.8%	0.9%	0.7%	0.8%
ratio of revocations of work permits to extensions – total foreigners	1.35	1.00	0.98	1.49	3.22	3.83	4.68	3.15	2.22
ratio of revocations of work permits to extensions – Ukrainian citizens	1.04	1.28	1.07	1.58	3.29	4.36	5.12	3.04	1.89

Source: Own study based on data from the Ministry of Family and Social Policy, https://psz.praca.gov.pl/rynek-pracy/statystyki-i-analizy/zatrudnianie-cudzoziemcow-w-polsce (accessed: 19.07.2023).

Table 5.7 Trends in work permits issued to Ukrainian citizens in 2013, 2019 – according to profession

		Poland – foreigners in total	*Lublin – foreigners in total*	*Subcarpathian – foreigners in total*	*Poland – Ukrainian citizens*	*Lublin – Ukrainian citizens*	*Subcarpathian – Ukrainian citizens*	*Percentage of Ukrainians among refugees (%)*	*Types of visa and professions performed by Ukrainian citizens in Poland (%)*
Total work permits issued in 2019 (situation preceding COVID-19		444738	12981	8551	330495	6946	6751	74.3	100.0
according to main classifications of professions and specialisations -2019	representatives of public authorities, senior officials and managers	2513	36	19	860	12	8	34.2	0.3
	specialists	11724	139	84	4471	96	68	38.1	1.4
	technicians and other skilled staff	11961	380	113	7925	250	82	66.3	2.4
	office workers	17107	127	253	13911	112	53	81.3	4.2
	service and sales staff	15349	157	133	10095	95	98	65.8	3.1
	farmers, gardeners, forest rangers and fishermen	2682	403	38	2227	204	38	83.0	0.7
	industrial workers and craftsmen	172172	5150	4306	126137	3153	3255	73.3	**38.2**
	machine and equipment operators and fitters	88879	5531	2173	69619	2154	2056	78.3	**21.1**
	unskilled workers	122351	1058	1432	95250	870	1093	77.8	**28.8**

(*Continued*)

Table 5.7 (Continued)

		Poland – foreigners in total	*Lublin – foreigners in total*	*Subcarpathian – foreigners in total*	*Poland – Ukrainian citizens*	*Lublin – Ukrainian citizens*	*Subcarpathian – Ukrainian citizens*	*Percentage of Ukrainians among refugees (%)*	*Types of visa and professions performed by Ukrainian citizens in Poland (%)*
according to work permit type – 2019	Type A	429497	12720	8431	322654	6840	6682	75.1	**97.6**
	Type B	745	10	9	412	2	5	55.3	0.1
	Type C	9426	251	71	5529	104	28	58.7	1.7
	Type D	2869	0	20	1087	0	20	37.9	0.3
	Type E	2201	0	20	813	0	16	36.9	0.2
Total work permits issued in 2013 (before Russia's annexation of Crimea)		39078	1320	553	20416	761	408	52.2	100.0
according to work classification	management staff, advisors, experts	3026	70	55	575	23	27	19.0	2.8
	including: functions on the management boards of legal entities	567	40	23	150	17	12	26.5	0.7
	skilled workers	10700	557	290	5696	334	226	53.2	**27.9**
	unskilled workers	5761	9	29	4801	6	29	83.3	**23.5**
according to work permit type	Type A	35843	1261	527	19495	742	396	54.4	**95.5**
	Type B	860	49	22	225	19	12	26.2	1.1
	Type C	1952	5	4	537	0	0	27.5	2.6
	Type D	271	5	0	143	0	0	52.8	0.7
	Type E	152	0	0	16	0	0	10.5	0.1

Source: Own study based on data from the Ministry of Family and Social Policy, https://psz.praca.gov.pl/rynek-pracy/statystyki-i-analizy/zatrudnianie-cudzoziemcow-w-polsce (accessed: 07.07.2023).

Table 5.8 Trends in work permits issued to Ukrainian citizens in 2013, 2019 – data by industry

		Poland – foreigners in total	*Lublin – foreigners in total*	*Subcarpathian – foreigners in total*	*Poland – Ukrainian citizens*	*Lublin – Ukrainian citizens*	*Subcarpathian – Ukrainian citizens*	*Percentage of Ukrainians among refugees (%)*	*Types of visa and professions performed by Ukrainian citizens in Poland (%)*
Total work permits issued – 2019		444738	12981	8551	330495	6946	6751	74.3	100.0
Total by PKD business code classification*	A	5552	293	46	3659	200	46	65.9	1.1
	B	296	9	8	252	9	8	85.1	0.1
	C	101588	1012	1100	74260	679	881	73.1	**22.5**
	D	39	1	0	35	1	0	89.7	0.0
	E	2418	8	5	1907	8	5	78.9	0.6
	F	113040	**4050**	**2831**	87214	2646	2341	77.2	**26.4**
	G	14698	421	123	10538	321	84	71.7	3.2
	H	70155	**5156**	**1530**	54025	1844	1493	77.0	**16.3**
	I	15505	137	155	9897	63	110	63.8	3.0
	J	4692	19	26	1486	11	26	31.7	0.4
	K	487	0	0	221	0	0	45.4	0.1
	L	615	11	3	452	11	3	73.5	0.1
	M	5397	81	19	3215	30	16	59.6	1.0
	N	99488	1643	**2608**	74806	1032	1670	75.2	**22.6**
	O	73	3	0	66	3	0	90.4	0.0
	P	604	31	4	291	7	2	48.2	0.1
	Q	1856	27	2	1642	23	2	88.5	0.5
	R	1027	31	34	469	14	22	45.7	0.1
	S	3376	24	50	2437	20	35	72.2	0.7
	T	3831	24	7	3622	24	7	94.5	1.1
	U	1	0	0	1	0	0	100.0	0.0

(*Continued*)

Table 5.8 (Continued)

		Poland – foreigners in total	*Lublin – foreigners in total*	*Subcarpathian – foreigners in total*	*Poland – Ukrainian citizens*	*Lublin – Ukrainian citizens*	*Subcarpathian – Ukrainian citizens*	*Percentage of Ukrainians among refugees (%)*	*Types of visa and professions performed by Ukrainian citizens in Poland (%)*
Total work permits issued – 2013		39078	1320	553	20416	761	408	52.2	100.0
Total by selected PKD business code classification	agriculture, forestry, hunting and fishing	1842	29	6	1381	23	6	75.0	6.8
	industrial processing	1897	9	10	1049	5	8	55.3	5.1
	building	5054	87	158	3533	61	156	69.9	17.3
	wholesale and retail	7164	266	57	1815	163	48	25.3	8.9
	transport and storage	3380	580	73	1926	312	73	57.0	9.4
	accommodation and catering services	3029	44	68	675	11	9	22.3	3.3
	information and communication	758	13	4	208	7	2	27.4	1.0
	finance and insurance	251	0	0	58	0	0	23.1	0.3
	professional, scientific and technical activity	1849	34	10	779	19	4	42.1	3.8
	education	356	12	5	61	2	0	17.1	0.3
	healthcare and social work	343	12	7	211	10	6	61.5	1.0
	households with employees	5014	68	9	4558	59	9	90.9	22.3

Source: Own study based on data from the Ministry of Family and Social Policy, https://psz.praca.gov.pl/rynek-pracy/statystyki-i-analizy/zatrudnianie-cudzoziemcow-w-polsce (accessed: 19.07.2023).

* sections of the Polish Classification of Business Activities (PKD 2007): A. Agriculture, forestry, hunting, and fishery; B. Mining and excavation; C. Manufacturing; D. Electricity, gas, water steam, hot water, and air for air-conditioning production and supply; E. Water supply; waste and sewage management and restoration-related activity; F. Construction; G. Wholesale and retail; repair of motor vehicles, including motorcycles; H. Transport and warehouse management; I. Activity related to accommodation and catering services; J. Information and communication; K. Finance and insurance; L. Activity related to servicing the real estate market; M. Professional, scientific and technical activity; N. Activity in the scope of management and support services; O. Public administration and national defence; mandatory social security; P. Education; Q. Healthcare and social welfare; R. Activity related to culture, entertainment, and recreation; S. Other services; T – Households with employees; households producing products and providing services for their own needs; Section U – Extraterritorial organisations and teams.

5.4.2 Perspective after the COVID-19 Pandemic – 2020–2022

In the period immediately preceding Russia's attack on Ukraine in February 2022, 64.5% of all work permits issued in Poland in 2021 were given to Ukrainians, and two-thirds of this group were men. Similar to other foreigners, this work migration especially concerned younger people in the mobile age brackets (44 years and younger) or middle-aged people (a significant number of 45–54-year-olds), which shows that the distribution of economic migrants from Ukraine was flatter than for foreigners taken as a whole (see Table 5.9), dominated by the 25–44 age group. The probable cause of the flattening and shifting of the distribution towards middle age in the case of Ukrainian citizens was the need to emigrate due to the difficult economic situation facing families even before the outbreak of full-scale conflict. Regionally, the age structure of foreigners obtaining work permits is consistent with the structure throughout the country (see Table 5.9).

In 2021, there was no visible seasonality in issuing work permits for employees from Ukraine across the country. The change in the rules for employing Ukrainian citizens in 2022, including the Act on Assistance to Citizens of Ukraine, waived the necessity to apply for a work permit in Poland (see Figure 5.12). More reliable information on the attractiveness of labour markets in terms of region is provided by data on permits issued in 2021 that show the dominance of four voivodeships: Masovian (54,152 permits), Greater Poland (47,565 permits), Silesia (39,465 permits), and Lower Silesia (33,334 permits), which, considering the economic structure of these regions, leads to the conclusion that what attracts people to work is the availability of jobs in non-agricultural sectors. In the case of men (predominant in the group of Ukrainian workers), the key factor was the availability of job opportunities in the industrial sector (see Figure 5.13).

The structure of industries in which Ukrainian citizens took up employment after the end of pandemic restrictions differed from 2019, but was consistent with the sectors chosen by other groups of foreigners. In 2021, Ukraine employees largely determined the structure of employment of foreigners in Poland due to their numbers, mainly in the following sectors: C, F, N, and H. In the case of Ukrainian citizens, the statistics for the numbers of work permits issued for these sections of the economy read as follows: F – 76,283, C – 74,433, H – 71,018, and N – 69,303. The number of permits issued by industry in the border regions varied due to the structure of their economies – sections H and F were dominant. In the Lublin Voivodeship, where 27,278 permits were issued to foreigners in 2021, 11,402 people (41.6%) were granted for section H. Sections F (8,043 permits, 29.4%), N (2,813 permits, 10.3%), and C (2,738 permits, 10.0%) were less important. In the Subcarpathian Voivodeship, 7,414 people obtained work permits: 2,404 (32.4% of permits issued to foreigners in 2021) in section H,

Table 5.9 Number of work permits for foreigners issued in 2021–2022 in the Polish-Ukrainian border regions by type of contract (data by age groups)

Place of work		*Lublin – 2021*	*Subcarpathian – 2021*	*Poland – 2021*	*Lublin – 2022*	*Subcarpathian – 2022*	*Poland – 2022*	*Ukrainian citizens – 2021*	*Ukrainian citizens – 2022*
women	below 25	609	179	22127	326	83	9976	**17661**	4418
	25–34	1002	242	**34604**	719	219	22202	**23018**	5739
	35–44	1032	250	**34762**	585	210	18758	**26183**	6586
	45–54	711	179	25671	339	94	9563	**22029**	5660
	55–59	179	42	5274	65	13	1609	4763	1211
	60–64	66	12	1674	16	2	516	1505	410
	over 64	15	4	412	2	3	141	355	107
	Total	3614	908	124524	2052	624	62765	95514	24131
men	below 25	2343	870	**54719**	1909	745	47953	**32346**	7838
	25–34	**7767**	**2072**	**135258**	6289	1782	121597	**74053**	18925
	35–44	**7972**	**2021**	**113884**	6019	1312	90765	**68126**	18633
	45–54	**4510**	**1211**	**61670**	2736	558	35640	**44537**	12273
	55–59	884	228	10740	452	90	5043	8131	2380
	60–64	235	93	2909	140	33	1441	2184	755
	over 64	53	11	468	22	3	286	322	139
	Total	23764	6506	379648	17567	4523	302725	229699	60943
Total		27378	7414	**504172**	19619	5147	365490	**325213**	85074

Source: Own study based on data from the Ministry of Family and Social Policy, https://psz.praca.gov.pl/rynek-pracy/statystyki-i-analizy/zatrudnianie-cudzoziemcow-w-polsce (accessed: 19.07.2023).

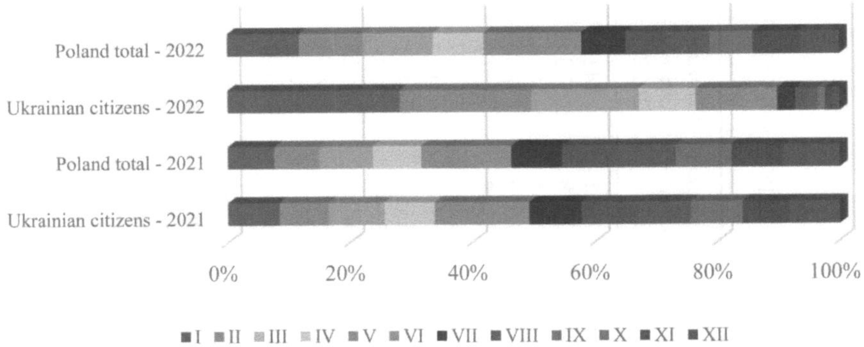

Figure 5.12 Work permits for foreigners (including Ukrainian citizens) issued in 2021–2022 by month of issue.

Source: Own study based on data from the Ministry of Family and Social Policy, https://psz.praca.gov.pl/rynek-pracy/statystyki-i-analizy/zatrudnianie-cudzoziemcow-w-polsce (accessed: 19.07.2023).

2,074 (28.0%) in section F, 1,379 (18.6%) in section N, and 841 (11.3%) in section C. This structure should be assumed to meet the regional labour market demand for external workers – see Figure 5.14.

Complex both in economic and social terms, the geopolitical situation after Russia's aggression on Ukraine opened another field for research concerning

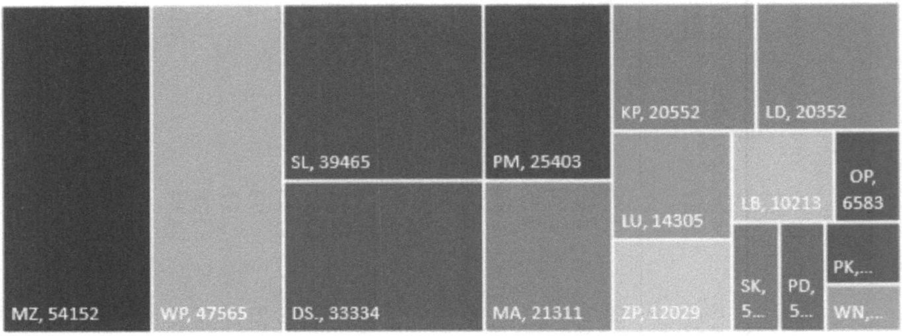

Figure 5.13 The structure of work permits for Ukrainians issued in 2021 by Polish Voivodeships. Voivodeships are indicated in accordance with the ISO 3166-2:PL standard: DS – Lower Silesia, KP – Kuyavian-Pomeranian, LB – Lubusz, LD – Łódź, LU – Lublin, MA – Lesser Poland, MZ – Masovian, OP – Opole, PD – Podlaskie, PK – Subcarpathian, PM – Pomeranian, SK – Świętokrzyskie, SL – Silesia, WN – Warmian-Masurian, WP – Greater Poland, ZP – West Pomeranian.

Source: Own study based on data from the Ministry of Family and Social Policy, https://psz.praca.gov.pl/rynek-pracy/statystyki-i-analizy/zatrudnianie-cudzoziemcow-w-polsce (accessed: 19.07.2023).

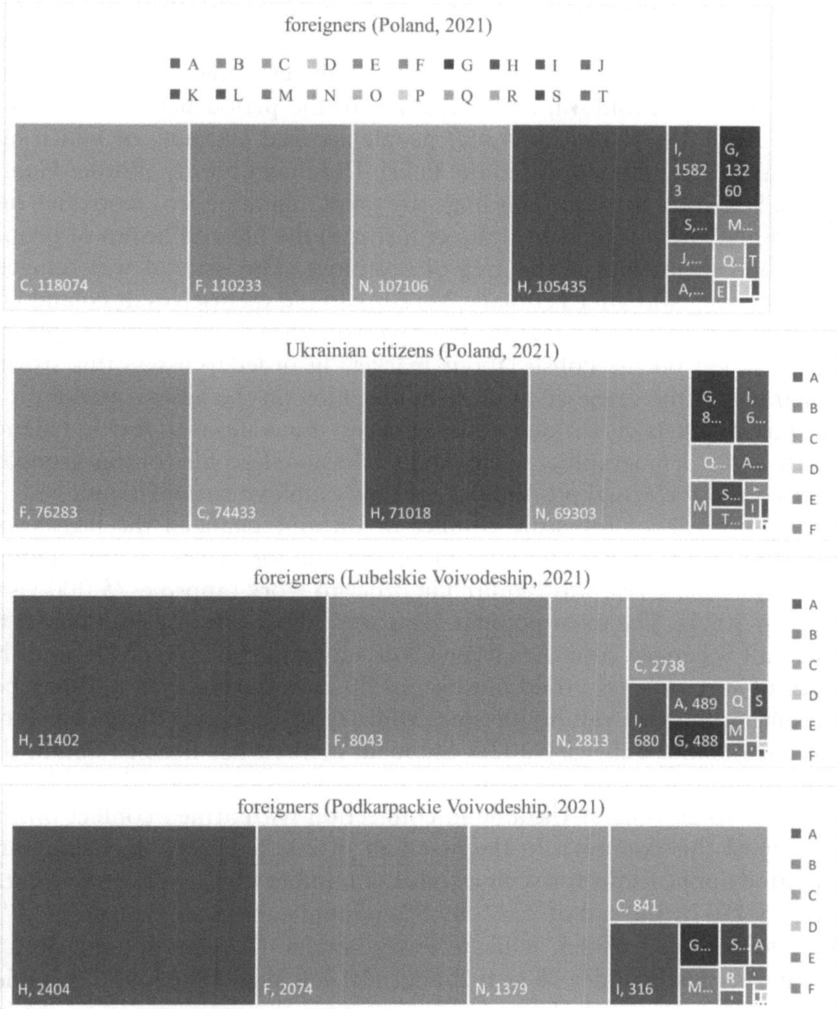

Figure 5.14 Structure of work permits for foreigners issued in 2021 in the Polish-Ukrainian border regions by sector of the economy*.

Source: Own study based on data from the Ministry of Family and Social Policy, https://psz.praca.gov.pl/rynek-pracy/statystyki-i-analizy/zatrudnianie-cudzoziemcow-w-polsce (accessed: 19.07.2023).

* sections of the Polish Classification of Economic Activities (PKD 2007): A. Agriculture, forestry, hunting, and fishery; B. Mining and excavation; C. Manufacturing; D. Electricity, gas, water steam, hot water, and air for air-conditioning production and supply; E. Water supply; waste and sewage management and restoration-related activity; F. Construction; G. Wholesale and retail; repair of motor vehicles, including motorcycles; H. Transport and warehouse management; I. Activity related to accommodation and catering services; J. Information and communication; K. Finance and insurance; L. Activity related to servicing the real estate market; M. Professional, scientific and technical activity; N. Activity in the scope of management and support services; O. Public administration and national defence; mandatory social security; P. Education; Q. Healthcare and social welfare; R. Activity related to culture, entertainment, and recreation; S. Other services; T – Households with employees; households producing products and providing services for their own needs; Section U – Extraterritorial organisations and groups.

the issue of war migration in Central-Eastern Europe in the 21st century. As soon as the day after the Russian invasion started, the swiftly growing stream of migrants from Ukraine crowded border crossings with Poland, Slovakia, Hungary, Moldova, and Romania. In the period between February 24 and April 19, 2022, 5,034,439 people escaped Ukraine, of which approximately 2.8 million crossed the Polish-Ukrainian border (Border Guard Poland, Statistical Service). This huge stream of migration was motivated not by economic premises but by a direct threat to the life and health of people who found themselves in the area of hostilities. The issue of war refugees from Ukraine, who after February 24, 2022 found themselves in Poland not by choice but coerced by fear for their lives and health, sheds more light on their situation on the Polish labour market. In order to assess this stream of migrants in the category of cross-border flow on the labour market, it is necessary to take a closer look at the refugees' motivations to stay in Poland, as well as the demographic, social, and professional profiles of this group of migrants and the actual possibilities for their employment in Poland.

The outbreak of full-scale conflict in Ukraine changed the legislation enabling non-EU citizens to work in Poland and the Schengen area. Before February 2022, a visa was required in order to work (approx. 75,000 visas issued in 2021). The most popular visas were those offering entitlement to stay in all Schengen countries (type C) or stay and travel (type D), and the length of stay or stays could not exceed 90 days during each 180-day period during the visa validity period (Ministry of Foreign Affairs of Poland Web Page). Since February 2022, the main method has been to obtain the status of a foreigner on the basis of the provisions of a special act (Act on assistance to citizens of Ukraine in connection with armed conflict on the territory of this country). In the first half of 2022, 1,201,706 Ukrainians submitted applications for such a status, a number that had risen to a total of 1,505,350 by the end of 2022. 69.8% of applicants were women (47.7% were women aged 18–65, while 7% were under 18 years of age). 30.2% were male, mostly under 18 years of age (10.4% aged 18–65, 18.7% under 18 years of age), which dramatically disrupted the proportions on the labour market (Ministry of Digital Affairs).

By April 19, 2022, in the Lublin and Subcarpathian Voivodeships, 65,552 Ukrainians had taken advantage of the opportunity to apply for foreigner status under the special act (Act on Assistance to Citizens of Ukraine), which translates into only 6.8% of all those who acquired this status in the analysed period throughout Poland. In the border regions, the spatial distribution of migrant registrations at the county level is not uniform, due to the lack of internal relocation mechanism in the country (see Table 5.10). The largest number of applications for this status was in the following poviats: Lublin (9,000), Rzeszów (6,900), Przemyśl (3,500), Jarosław (3,200), Lublin (3,100), and Puławy (2,500). Moreover, the proportion of women among the applicants was uneven (from 55.3% in Strzyżów Poviat to 70.4% in Parczew Poviat) (see Table 5.10).

Table 5.10 Detailed statistics on people in the register of Ukrainian citizens and their family members who were granted foreigner status on the basis of the Special Act*

Voivodeship	*Poviat*	*TOTAL*			*Percentage of women*
		women	*men*	*total*	
Lublin	Bialski	827	445	1272	65.0
	Biłgorajski	1062	541	1603	66.3
	Chełmski	841	520	1361	61.8
	Hrubieszowski	402	264	666	60.4
	Janowski	209	124	333	62.8
	Krasnostawski	554	328	882	62.8
	Kraśnicki	549	299	848	64.7
	Lubartowski	781	445	1226	63.7
	Lubelski	2040	1086	**3126**	65.3
	Łęczyński	618	327	945	65.4
	Łukowski	749	368	1117	67.1
	Opolski	1070	539	1609	66.5
	Parczewski	476	200	676	70.4
	Puławski	1607	923	**2530**	63.5
	Radzyński	324	163	487	66.5
	Rycki	493	309	802	61.5
	Świdnicki	969	557	1526	63.5
	Tomaszowski	660	363	1023	64.5
	Włodawski	578	386	964	60.0
	Zamojski	1011	639	1650	61.3
	Biała podlaska	526	345	871	60.4
	Chełm	363	233	596	60.9
	Lublin	5542	3470	**9012**	61.5
	Zamość	420	265	685	61.3
Subcarpathian	Bieszczadzki	490	236	726	67.5
	Brzozowski	173	106	279	62.0
	Dębicki	823	405	1228	67.0
	Jarosławski	1928	1278	**3206**	60.1
	Jasielski	301	181	482	62.4
	Kolbuszowski	157	91	248	63.3
	Krośnieński	473	249	722	65.5
	Leżajski	293	168	461	63.6
	Lubaczowski	319	219	538	59.3
	Łańcucki	389	231	620	62.7
	Mielecki	960	450	1410	68.1
	Niżański	258	186	444	58.1
	Przemyski	991	665	1656	59.8
	Przeworski	489	318	807	60.6
	Ropczycko-sędziszowski	352	162	514	68.5
	Rzeszowski	948	565	1513	62.7
	Sanocki	657	416	1073	61.2
	Stalowowolski	591	340	931	63.5
	Strzyżowski	131	106	237	55.3
	Tarnobrzeski	182	129	311	58.5
	Leski	470	287	757	62.1
	Krosno	351	225	576	60.9
	Przemyśl	2035	1442	**3477**	58.5
	Rzeszów	4380	2560	**6940**	63.1
	Tarnobrzeg	361	225	586	61.6
LU + PO Voivodeships total		41173	24379	65552	62.8
LU + PO Voivodeships total (percentage PL=100%)		6.7%	7.1%	6.8%	-
Poland total		616872	341248	958120	64.4

Source: Data from the Ministry of Digital Affairs, https://dane.gov.pl/pl/institution/333,ministers two-cyfryzacji?page=1&per_page=20&q=status%20UKR&sort=relevance (accessed: 15.07.2023).

* Act of 12 March 2022 on assistance to citizens of Ukraine in connection with armed conflict on the territory of this country (Journal of Laws of 2022, item 583, as amended).

5.5 Conclusions

The eastern regions of the EU are some of the poorest in the Union. Although the significant heterogeneity of the Polish NUTS3 subregions is noticeable, the annual income per capita in 2020 was a maximum of 41.2% of the median income of the EU as a whole, and in the very poorest region, it was 23.5% of the median income in the EU-27. The regions of eastern Poland are poorer than other areas within Poland itself, with between 55.5% and 97.2% of median income in 2020 of EUR 13,718.2. Due to the development policy directed towards eastern Poland, among other areas of the country, the region is addressing development inequalities. Nevertheless, despite a significant reduction of the unemployment rate and a significant increase in household disposable income, the low earnings within the region put eastern Poland in last place in the country in terms of personal income.

The studied regional markets are dissimilar to others in eastern Poland and within Poland as a whole. The number of people actively employed in the Subcarpathian Voivodeship dropped from 938,000 in 2010 to 854,000 in 2021, and the average number of people employed between 2014 and 2021 was 819,000 ± 43. The number of workers in the region has seen a steady increase. There were an average of 958,000 workers in the Lublin Voivodeship in the analysed period (± 104 thousand). In 2021, the unemployment rate in the studied regions did not exceed 3% (it should be assumed that it was not higher than the natural rate of unemployment). Before 2015, unemployment had constituted a significant hindrance in these voivodeships.

There was lower employment in market services and specialist activities in the economies in the southeastern regions of Poland and higher employment in administration, healthcare, and public services. Employment in agriculture was slightly greater in Lublin Voivodeship than elsewhere, whereas in the Subcarpathian Voivodeship, there was more employment in mining and excavation, manufacturing, and wastewater treatment. The lower average remuneration in the two southeastern regions of Poland is related to the low level of vocational and professional specialisation. Furthermore, in the case of the Lublin Voivodeship, in the years 2010–2021, the trend of a deepening disproportion of wages by 1.4% in comparison with the country was noticeable due to the decrease in the gap between average remuneration in the Subcarpathian Voivodeship and in Poland by 1.9% (from 85.4% to 87.3%). In 2021, average remuneration in the analysed regions was still 10.8%–12.7% lower than the national average, whereas in 2017–2021, remuneration in the entrepreneurial sector increased at a rate of approximately 30%, on par with the rest of Poland. This served to exacerbate the disadvantage of the disparity in remuneration within the studied regions. The highest remuneration was for employees in the industrial sector.

Between 2010 and 2021, 111,000 jobs were created in the Lublin Voivodeship, and 114,000 jobs were created in the Subcarpathian Voivodeship. Despite periodic small discrepancies, regional labour markets experienced constant quantitative increases. Labour markets enjoyed significant absorptivity and demand for employees, especially those low-skilled or with specific qualifications or technical skills. It has been noticed that there is a structural misalignment between the demand for qualified workers and their supply in southeastern Poland.

The cross-border flow of people between Ukraine and Poland varied in the analysed years 2011–2022, stricken by shock events for the labour markets, which largely affected employment for Ukrainian citizens in Poland. Five specific periods should be mentioned: before the annexation of Crimea by Russia (2014), between the annexation of Crimea and the occurrence of the COVID-19 pandemic (2015–2019), the period of the strongest restrictions related to the pandemic (2020), the post-pandemic period (2021), and after Russia's attack on Ukraine in 2022.

The economic migration of Ukrainian citizens to Poland before the outbreak of the war mainly involved men seeking employment in manufacturing and construction. In the period after the annexation of Crimea (2014–2019), the number of work permits issued to Ukrainian citizens increased 12-fold (to over 102,000 permits in 2019), while the structure of migrants also changed. Individuals working based on permits issued in 2019 accounted for 1.04% of the total working population in Poland in 2019. Considering that the average duration for which these permits are issued is three years, the estimated share of Ukrainian workers likely exceeded 2% of the working population in Poland during that period. Work permits for Ukrainian citizens in 2019 were issued mainly within four industries: F – Construction, N – Administration services and support, C – Industrial processing, and H – Transport and warehousing. In 2021, the industries remained the same, but their order changed (F, C, H, N).

The beginning of the second decade of the 20th century in terms of work for Ukrainian citizens in Poland is associated with manual labour performed mainly by young men in manufacturing and construction. The attack on Crimea and the eastern (relatively well-developed) regions of Ukraine in 2014 significantly influenced the number and structure of people arriving in Poland, gradually shifting the age limit of these people towards older generations and attracting more highly qualified workers. The share of women in the migrant group still did not exceed 20%. During the period of restrictions on movement during the COVID-19 pandemic, as a result of political decisions, the relationality of the labour market between countries grew smaller. In the last period before Russia's aggression against Ukraine in February 2022, probably as a result of poverty caused by the need to defend the country's eastern regions against Russia's military actions, there was a visible increase in disproportions in the level of wages and opportunities provided by the labour markets. The migration of Ukrainian citizens to Poland began to gather momentum. In 2021, there was an increase in the migration of young women, probably for economic reasons, but disproportionate to the number of women with children fleeing the war in 2022.

Economic migrants from Ukraine were mainly employed in highly industrialised and better-developed regions of the country with plenty of job vacancies and better employment conditions. About 50% of Ukrainian citizens gained employment in businesses located in the Masovian, Greater Poland, Silesian, and Lower Silesian Voivodeships – regions of Western Poland and the capital. Previous contact with these regions and the existence of a strong Ukrainian diaspora in their major cities were additional factors that attracted refugees to these regions after the outbreak of a full-scale war in February 2022. The structure of work permits for foreigners in the eastern regions of Poland did not correspond to the national structure. The same economic sectors dominated, but most permits were issued in sections H, followed by F, N, and C. In 2021, over 3.5 times more foreigners were employed in the Lublin Voivodeship (27,378 permits) than in the Subcarpathian Voivodeship (7,414 permits).

References

Act of 12 March 2022 on assistance to citizens of Ukraine in connection with armed conflict on the territory of that country; Journal of Laws of 2022, item 583, as amended.

Annual Regional Programme 2021. (2022, May). *Sprawozdanie z realizacji Programu Operacyjnego Polska Wschodnia 2014-2020 za rok 2021*. https://www.polskawschodnia.gov.pl/strony/o-programie/raporty/sprawozdania-z-realizacji-programu/#/domyslne=1/10533=1757. Accessed in 2023.

Border Guard (Poland). Zarząd Graniczny KGSG. https://www.strazgraniczna.pl/pl/granica/statystyki-sg/2206,Statystyki-SG.html. Accessed in 2023.

Borsekova, K., & Korony, S. (2022). Resilience and vulnerability of regional labour markets: Principal component analysis of labour market efficiency in the EU. *Regional Studies*, *57*(12), 2373–2390. https://doi.org/10.1080/00343404.2022.2042507.

Borsekova, K., Korony, S., & Nijkamp, P. (2021). Traces of the iron curtain: A multivariate analysis of regional cohesion in Europe. *Socio-Economic Planning Sciences*, *78*, 10104. https://doi.org/10.1016/j.seps.2021.101040.

Bronisz, U. (2017). Higher education as a factor of Polish-Ukrainian cross-border cooperation. In *Challenges in the development of the Polish-Ukrainian borderland*. Norbertinum.

Charucka, O. (2016). Inter-regional and cross-border cooperation between Poland and Ukraine. *Zeszyty Naukowe Uczelni Vistula*, *47*(2), 34–59.

Długosz, P. (2018). Integration of Ukrainian students studying in Poland. *Studia Migracyjne-Przegląd Polonijny*, *168*(2), 67–92.

Eastern Poland Programme. http://www.polskawschodnia.gov.pl. Accessed in 2023.

EU. (2016). Directive (EU) 2016/801 – Consolidated Text of Directive (EU) 2016/801 of the European Parliament and of the Council of 11 May 2016 on the Conditions of Entry and Residence of Third-country Nationals for the Purposes of Research, Studies, Training, Voluntary Service, Pupil Exchange Schemes or Educational Projects and au pairing (recast). ELI: http://data.europa.eu/eli/dir/2016/801/2021-11-17. Accessed in 2024.

Eurostat (2021). *Gross Domestic Product (GDP) at Current Market Prices by NUTS 3 Regions*. https://doi.org/10.2908/NAMA_10R_3GDP.

Gajewski, R. (2022). The strategic-relational formation of regional and metropolitan scales: Studying two Polish regions undergoing transformation. *Regional Studies, Regional Science*, *9*(1), 280–301. https://doi.org/10.1080/21681376.2022.2071165.

Ganau, R., & Kilroy, A. (2023). Detecting economic growth pathways in the EU's lagging regions. *Regional Studies*, *57*(1), 41–56. https://doi.org/10.1080/00343404.2022.2050200.

Górna, A., & Jaźwińska, E. (2019). Ukrainian Migrants in Warsaw Agglomeration: Social and Demographic Features and Social Relations. Report on the Research. *Cmr Working Papers*, 115/173.

ILO. *About the ILO in Poland*. https://www.ilo.org/budapest/countries-covered/poland/WCMS_476068/lang–en/index.htm. Accessed in 2023.

Information and Service Website for Entrepreneurs: Biznes.gov.pl. https://www.biznes.gov.pl/pl. Accessed in 2023.

Kall, K., Brzozowska, A., Lillie, N., Matuszczyk, K., & Salamońska, J. (2020). *Regional Case Study from Ukraine to Finland and Estonia via Poland: Migration and Posting of Third Country Nationals. Regional Case Study*. Work package 4, Con-3Post – Posting of Third Country Nationals. Mapping the Trend in the Construction Sector, Project Number: VP/2018/011/0019, 20–21.

Kęsik, J. (2002). Ogólny bilans strat ludności w wyniku ukraińsko-polskiego konfliktu narodowościowego w latach II wojny światowej. In Polska-Ukraina. Trudne pytania. Vol. 9. Światowy Związek Żołnierzy Armii Krajowej.

Kuzior, A., & Lobanova, A. (2017). The issue of migration – Ukrainian and Polish experiences. *Zeszyty Naukowe. Organizacja i Zarządzanie/Politechnika Śląska*, *112*, 219–228.

Kwiatkowski, E. (2011). *Dysproporcje. Rzecz o Polsce przeszłej i obecnej*. Wydawnictwo ANTYK.

Medeiros, E., Ramírez, M. G., Dellagiacoma, C., & Brustia, G. (2022). Will reducing border barriers via the EU's b-solutions lead towards greater European territorial integration? *Regional Studies*, *56*(3), 504–517. https://doi.org/10.1080/00343404.2021.1912724.

Ministry of Digital Affairs. Republic of Poland. https://dane.gov.pl/pl and https://dane.gov.pl/pl/institution/333,ministerstwo-cyfryzacji?page=1&per_page=20&q=status%20UKR&sort=relevance. Accessed in 2023.

Ministry of Education and Science. Republic of Poland. https://dane.gov.pl/pl. Accessed in 2023.

Ministry of Family and Social Policy. *Public Employment Services*. https://psz.praca.gov.pl/rynek-pracy/statystyki-i-analizy/zatrudnianie-cudzoziemcow-w-polsce. Accessed in 2023.

Ministry of Family and Social Policy. (2021). *Information on Employment of Foreigners in Poland*. https://stat.gov.pl/en/topics/labour-market/studies/work-permits-for-foreigners-in-poland-in-2021,12,5.html. Accessed in 2023.

Ministry of Foreign Affairs. Republic of Poland. https://dane.gov.pl/ and https://www.gov.pl/web/dyplomacja/wizy. Accessed in 2023.

Mogila, Z., Miklošovič, T., Lichner, I., Radvanský, M., & Zaleski, J. (2022). Does cohesion policy help to combat intra-country regional disparities? A perspective on Central European countries. *Regional Studies*, *56*(10), 1783–1795. https://doi.org/10.1080/00343404.2022.2037541.

National Agency for Academic Exchange – NAWA. *Badania i analizy*. https://nawa.gov.pl/badania-i-analizy. Accessed in 2023.

National Bank of Poland. https://nbp.pl/en. Accessed in 2022 and 2023.

National Bank of Ukraine. https://bank.gov.ua/en. Accessed in 2022 and 2023.

National Bank of Poland. *Archiwum kursów*. https://nbp.pl/archiwum-kursow. Accessed in 2022 and 2023.

OECD. (2019). *International Migration Outlook*. https://doi.org/10.1787/1999124x. Accessed in 2022 and 2023.

OECD. (2021). *International Migration Outlook*, 294. https://doi.org/10.1787/1999124x. Accessed in 2022 and 2023.

Peciakowski, T., & Gizicki, W. (2021). Identity dimension of cross-border cooperation between Poland and Ukraine. Studies on the collective awareness of borderland areas' citizens. *Athenaeum. Polskie Studia Politologiczne*, *70*, 175–195.

Pontarollo, N., & Serpieri, C. (2017). *The Renewal Capacity of EU Regions*. JRC Research Reports JRC109647, Joint Research Centre (Seville site).

Pontarollo, N., & Serpieri, C. (2020). Towards regional renewal: A multilevel perspective for the EU. *Regional Studies*, *54*(6), 754–764. https://doi.org/10.1080/00343404.2019.1640357.

Powęska, H. (2011). Commodity structure of cross-border trade at the Polish-Ukrainian borderland. *Roczniki Naukowe Stowarzyszenia Ekonomistów Rolnictwa i Agrobiznesu*, *13*(2), 371–376.

Powęska, H. (2013). Frequency of crossing the border by border trade participants vs commodity structure of cross-border purchases at the Polish-Ukrainian borderland. *Roczniki Naukowe Stowarzyszenia Ekonomistów Rolnictwa i Agrobiznesu*, *15*(4), 337–343.

State Statistics Service of Ukraine. *Expenditures and Resources of Households of Ukraine by Regions*. https://ukrstat.gov.ua/operativ/menu/menu_e/virdg.htm. Accessed in 2023.

State Statistics Service of Ukraine. Main Statistical Office in Lviv Region. *Households of Lviv Oblast in 2013*. https://www.lv.ukrstat.gov.ua/ukr/publ/2015/ZB1520150101.pdf. Accessed in 2023.

State Statistics Service of Ukraine. Main Statistical Office in Lviv Region. *Households of Lviv Oblast in 2019*. https://www.lv.ukrstat.gov.ua/ukr/publ/2020/ZB1720200101.pdf. Accessed in 2023.

State Statistics Service of Ukraine. Main Statistical Office in Volyn Region. *Expenditure and Resources of Households in Volyn Oblast in 2013*. http://www.lutsk.ukrstat.gov.ua/domogosp_pb.html. Accessed in 2023.

Statistics Poland, Central Statistical Office of Poland. https://stat.gov.pl/. Accessed in 2023.

Statistics Poland, Local Data Bank of Statistics Poland. https://bdl.stat.gov.pl/bdl/start. Accessed in 2023.

Szast, M. (2019). Human capital transfer between Ukraine and Poland – a challenge or a threat to social security of both countries? *Athenaeum. Polskie Studia Politologiczne*, *62*, 97–110.

Szast, M. (2019). Transfer kapitału ludzkiego pomiędzy Ukrainą a Polską – Wyzwanie czy zagrożenie dla bezpieczeństwa społecznego obu krajów? *Athenaeum. Polskie Studia Politologiczne*, *62*(1), 9–17. https://doi.org/10.15804/athena.2019.62.06

Torzecki, R. (1993). *Polacy i Ukraińcy. Sprawa ukraińska w czasie II wojny światowej na terenie II Rzeczypospolitej*. Wydawnictwo Naukowe PWN.

Więckowski, M. (2011). Wybrane aspekty rozwoju turystyki transgranicznej w sąsiedztwie zewnętrznej granicy strefy Schengen. *Zeszyty Naukowe Wyższej Szkoły Społeczno-Przyrodniczej w Lublinie*, *12*, 122–140.

WORTAL of Public Employment Services, Ministry of Family and Social Policy. https://psz.praca.gov.pl/web. Accessed in 2023.

Wosiek, M., & Kata, R. (2019). Trade at the Polish – Ukrainian Borderland – Selected economic aspects. *Wiadomości Statystyczne*, *64*(2), 44–63. https://ws.stat.gov.pl/Article/2019/2/044-063

6 Activities of Polish Self-Governments Mitigating the Refugee Crisis

6.1 Self-Government in Poland – Selected Social Tasks Addressed at Migrants

In the Polish legal system, public administration is divided into government administration (centralised) and self-government administration (decentralised) (Dolnicki, 2021). Government administration representatives operate in the territory of the entire country (e.g., the president, prime minister, ministers) or in the area of voivodeships (voivode). Self-government administration operates at the voivodeship level (regional council, marshal), poviat level (poviat council, starost), urban municipality level (town or city council, mayor or president), or rural municipality level (parish council, bailiff). Each of these administration levels has assigned public tasks which fall within their exclusive competences, but implementation of many tasks, including social policy tasks, requires cooperation of government and self-government administration bodies. In the Polish system of state organisation, within the mechanism of authority decentralisation, some tasks and authorities are delegated from the national level (a sphere of the government activity) to the regional level (voivodeship self-government) or local level (poviat, municipality, or rural municipality). No authority can implement tasks reserved for higher-level authorities or violate independence of lower-level authorities.

Local self-governments, including regional poviat and municipality self-governments, play a special role in extraordinary situations, which certainly include the crisis situation caused by a sudden inflow of war refugees from Ukraine to Poland after February 24, 2023. On the one hand, it is determined by direct proximity and connection to citizens represented by self-governments in the system of a democratic state, and at the same time, direct relations maintained by these self-governments with many regional, poviat, and local stakeholders, including social environment institutions. Both of these elements confirm the crucial role of self-government in reacting to identified needs of the local community concerning, among others, social support (among others: nursing home cares, healthcare facilities, and crisis intervention centres), law and order enforcement (among others: city guards, cooperation with the state fire brigade and the police), and preventing the risk

DOI: 10.4324/9781003471646-6

of various crisis situations and minimising effects thereof (e.g., introducing crisis management procedures, direct protection of citizens and property in hazardous situations, e.g., flood, fire, terrorist attacks, etc.).

Position of self-governments and their strong social mandate especially favour inspiring various types of activities and bottom-up processes that allow identification and proper use of the potential of citizens and other local stakeholders to engage in various forms of assistance in extraordinary situations. In Polish conditions, they have been until now associated with natural disasters such as fires or floods. Such crisis situations triggered local communities to provide the affected with immense support in the scope of a shelter, care, as well as taking care of their basic needs, and self-governments usually coordinated this aid by cooperating with donors and volunteers.

Regardless of the possibilities and scale of support from local stakeholders, self-governments are obliged to implement tasks and authorities vested in them regarding elements of strategic management and operational management, including social assistance, law and order enforcement, and crisis management. Table 6.1 presents selected examples of measures undertaken in the scope of social assistance and implemented in Poland by various levels of administration, which can concern support for, among others, foreigners staying in the territory of Poland, including migrants and refugees. Although these tasks have been assigned both to self-government and government administration, in many cases they require the aforementioned cooperation and coordination at various levels.

Table 6.1 shows that many social and related tasks of local significance, which can also concern support for war refugees, are assigned for implementation by, among others, municipalities and poviats. Therefore, the local self-governments should have at their disposal officials, including social assistance and labour market specialists, who are prepared to provide migrants and refugees with proper support. It should be emphasised that before the outbreak of war in Ukraine, economic migrants, among others from Ukraine, prevailed in Poland, who very rarely had the opportunity to meet with local self-government representatives. The purpose of their stay in Poland was predominantly gainful and temporary, and even seasonal. Migrants usually left their families in their countries of origin and arrived in Poland alone. They primarily maintained relations with Poles in their professional lives (the employer and co-workers). During their stay in our country, they devoted almost all of their time to professional work. They primarily integrated with other migrants staying in the same environment and, to a much smaller extent, with the local community. In general, migrants did not form a social group on which the attention of local self-governments focused, unless their behaviours violated the law and order, which resulted in specific sanctions.

The above deliberations show that before the outbreak of war in Ukraine, Polish self-government officials had hardly any contact with economic migrants or refugees. Refugees who arrived in Poland during the period of the refugee procedure were placed in centres for foreigners and taken care of

Table 6.1 Selected tasks of public administration in the scope of social assistance and other related tasks addressed at, among others, migrants

Public administration unit	*Selected tasks in the scope of social assistance and other related tasks addressed at, among others, migrants*
Urban municipality Rural municipality	• Implementation of a municipal strategy for solving social issues. • Granting and payment of benefits. • Providing shelter, meals, and necessary clothing to persons devoid thereof (e.g., refugees). • Providing social assistance services. • Additional nourishment. • Running social assistance centres and nursing home cares. • Drawing up and implementing social projects. • Cooperation with poviat employment office in the scope of distributing job offers and information on vacancies, distributing information on professional counselling services and trainings. • Protection of the level of life of persons, families, and social groups and providing them with specialist assistance. • Granting and payment of designated benefits, as well as providing foreigners staying in Poland shelter, meals, and necessary clothing on the basis of separate provisions. • Granting and payment of designated benefits, as well as providing shelter, meals, and necessary clothing to foreigners, who have been given a stay permit due to humanitarian reasons or a tolerated stay permit in the territory of the Republic of Poland. • Cooperation with crisis management of the public administration authorities. • Cooperation and activity for the benefit of non-governmental organisations, as well as cooperation with local and regional communities of other states.
Poviat	• Running specialist counselling. • Helping foreigners who have received a refugee status in the Republic of Poland, subsidiary protection, or temporary residence permit granted on the basis of separate provisions, in the scope of individual integration programme, and paying for such persons' healthcare insurance contributions stipulated in the provisions on healthcare benefits funded with public resources. • Running crisis intervention centres. • Giving information on rights and entitlements. • Running the poviat family support centre. • Providing foreigners staying in Poland with assistance in the scope of crisis intervention. • Preventing unemployment and activation of the local labour market. • Preventing extraordinary threats to people's lives and health.

(*Continued*)

Table 6.1 (Continued)

Public administration unit	*Selected tasks in the scope of social assistance and other related tasks addressed at, among others, migrants*
Voivodeship	• Implementation of programmes for social exclusion prevention, equal opportunities for people with disabilities, social assistance, preventing and resolving alcohol problems, and cooperation with non-governmental organisations. • Professional training for social assistance staff. • Diagnosing and monitoring selected social problems in the region. • Inspiring and promoting new solutions in the scope of social assistance.
Voivode	• Coordinating measures undertaken in the scope of the integration of foreigners who have received a refugee status, subsidiary protection, or temporary residence permit in the Republic of Poland granted on the basis of separate provisions, in particular, in the scope of indicating a place of residence, as well as keeping a register of approved individual integration programmes for foreigners. • Coordinating, within the social assistance system, measures undertaken in the scope of preventing human trafficking and support provided to victims thereof. • Public security, including crisis management. • Preventing unemployment and activation of the local labour market.
Minister	• Developing the conception and stipulating the directions of development in the social assistance area. • Financially supporting selected programmes in the social assistance area implemented by local self-government units or authorised entities. • Co-operating with non-government organisations.

Source: Act of 5 June on Voivodeship Self-Government... (1998), Act of 5 June 1998 on Poviat Self-Government... (1998), Act on Commune Self-Government... (1990).

by the Office for Foreigners. In compliance with the provisions, the refugee procedure should take 3–3.5 months, but in practice, it was often prolonged for 24 months. During this time, refugees should have been preparing for independent life outside the centre. After receiving a positive result from the procedure implemented by the Office for Foreigners, refugees could apply for an individual integration programme. It was implemented by poviat family assistance units and supervised by the Ministry of Family, Labour and Social Policy. Having left such centres, refugees usually arrived in large cities, where it was easier for them to search for a job and become independent of social assistance benefits (The Polish Institute of International Affairs, 2016). The presented path of refugees' independence in Poland shows that self-governments were engaged in these measures to a very small extent (only poviat family assistance centres); therefore, at the outbreak of war in Ukraine, there was a lack of practical experience in proceeding with war refugees. The refugee crisis triggered by the unprecedented inflow of a huge wave of refugees in Poland, in a very short period of time, disclosed a lack of the country's readiness to react to such a situation. Self-governments had neither the organisational nor financial potential to receive such a large wave of war refugees, whom it was impossible to provide with a sufficient number of places in centres. Moreover, there were no specific guidelines for managing such situations at a local level. In 2015, the Supreme Audit Office already indicated that there was a shortage of integrated solutions for refugees' integration in Poland (NIK o systemie pomocy..., 2015). Among others, the insufficient coordination of measures between state authorities obliged to perform tasks in this scope, e.g., the Office for Foreigners and ministries responsible for labour market and social affairs, was emphasised. The period of refugees' stay in centres was not used to learn the language, and after leaving such centres, refugees were not ready to start working and living in local communities. It resulted in not many people managing to find employment, while others were forced to benefit from social assistance. The Supreme Audit Office recommended undertaking swift measures regarding, among others, developing a coherent, continuous, and motivating system for learning Polish; implementing solutions allowing allocating flats to refugees, especially where they had the possibility of gaining employment; and more effective professional activation, in particular using the acquired and developed qualifications of refugees. However, nothing of importance changed until 2020.

In 2020, a diagnostic document titled "Poland's migration policy – diagnosis of the baseline" was drawn up, which was aimed at providing grounds for agreements and recommendations for the new migration policy of Poland (Polityka migracyjna Polski..., 2021). In this document, a lot of space was devoted to the refugees' integration, which should allow them to independently function in Poland, prepare to start employment and become independent of social benefits and assistance. Furthermore, the relation between the refugees' integration process and proper preparation of the education system, public services, integration programmes, citizenship, information measures addressed at the receiving community, and crime was emphasised. This document of a diagnostic nature became the basis for developing a framework programme proposition titled Poland's migration policy – directions and measures for 2021–2022; however, the bill of the Council of Ministers on adoption of this document was withdrawn in the fourth quarter of 2022.

Polish lawyers and employers believe that currently, Poland does not have a migration policy (Prawo migracyjne trafi do kosza..., 2021). A single and comprehensive document is missing, which would discuss the subject matter of migration policy, including the integration policy. It indicates a lack of perspective on long-term measures in this scope, despite many new experiences in the field of refugees' integration resulting from the crisis situation after the outbreak of war in Ukraine. It seems that, in the case of

Poland, the hitherto lack of a large population of migrants in comparison to Western European countries, resulted in reactiveness of measures rather than a well-thought-out implementation of the European Union law. This state of affairs was paradoxically linked, among others, with the fact that before the outbreak of war, the largest group of working and living foreigners were the citizens of Ukraine, who, due to the geographical and cultural proximity or linguistic similarity, did not need thus far-reaching support in the scope of integration (Tutak, 2023). The new reality in which Poland found itself after the outbreak of war in Ukraine showed that these assumptions were wrong.

6.2 Polish Self-Governments in the Face of the Outbreak of War in Ukraine

The inflow of war refugees to Polish regions bordering Ukraine, triggered by the Russian attack on Ukraine, and later the spreading of this wave onto the entire country, was an unprecedented phenomenon in the post-war history of Poland. The presented above process of shaping Polish migration policy indicates that Polish public administration was not properly prepared for the crisis situation caused by war in Ukraine. No specific preparations for the possibility of a larger inflow of refugees from Ukraine in Poland were made in advance. When the first Ukrainian war refugees appeared at the Polish border, measures at the self-government level generally fell within tasks and entitlements specified by legal provisions, but in many aspects, they were implemented rather intuitively or even experimentally.

It is worth referring here to crucial conditions, which as of the beginning of the crisis, determined the approach to refugees. First of all, Polish-Ukrainian relations have for many years been encumbered with historical circumstances which, in some members of Polish society, triggered an ambivalent or even negative approach to economic migrants from Ukraine. After the outbreak of war, this approach has changed, whereas the Poles' attitude to refugees was shaped under a huge influence of the geopolitical situation in the entire region after the outbreak of war and was strongly characterised with the fear of conflict spreading onto the neighbouring countries, among others, Poland (Public Opinion Research Center, 2023). Therefore, Ukrainian strategic plans to strongly oppose Russian aggression and not even consider a possible capitulation were initially met with varied reception in the Polish society, which remained under a huge shock caused by the first, after World War II, military conflict at the Polish border. Secondly, the amount and scope of support for refugees depended on the level of sensitivity of self-government authorities and other local decision-makers to the problems experienced by migrants and accessibility of budget funds and other resources, e.g., council houses and social housing. Thirdly, effective support for people in a crisis situation each time requires providing them with care by specialists who have the knowledge, skills, and experience related to a given subject matter.

Meanwhile, Polish self-government employees responsible for developing support instruments for refugees at the local level had not previously had any experience with this type of a crisis situation and acted to a large extent intuitively in the face of the inflow of refugees to municipalities. Fourthly, the scale of the refugee crisis faced by Polish self-governments after the outbreak of war in Ukraine was so large that solving many problems was possible only due to the cooperation with other stakeholders at the level of the municipality or poviat. These were, e.g., non-governmental organisations or volunteers who offered their resources to additionally support refugees. It was crucial, since the formal scope of support allowing meeting the refugee's needs that could be offered by self-governments was not sufficient to implement all measures urgently necessary from the first weeks of war in Ukraine. A lot of such initiatives implemented bottom-up and spontaneously or loosely related to statutory tasks of self-governments became examples of good practices in the scope of supporting refugees at the local level. They have been the subject of in-depth analysis in the further part of the study.

Findings concerning the situation in local self-governments at the moment of Russia's invasion of Ukraine indicate that formal and theoretical frameworks for measures and the scope of tasks, in charge of which were particular state and self-government administration units, were present in the Polish legal system; however, support in the scope of indicating sources of financing aid measures implemented for those units and detailing regulations directly concerning the situation of Ukrainian refugees after crossing the Polish border was missing. As it is known, previously binding procedures concerning placement of refugees in designated centres could not have been implemented in this specific situation. Although refugees who were headed to other countries, e.g., Western European countries, and were passing through Poland, were usually placed in designated centres, another assumption was made in Poland from the very beginning. Thanks to the hospitality of citizens and engagement of local self-governments, the majority of arriving Ukrainians were successfully placed in Polish families, or permanent and temporary reception camps. Polish citizens or entrepreneurs and self-governments hosting refugees received funds from the state for accommodation and maintenance of refugees (Regulation of the Minister of the Interior…, 2022). Before, however, refugees arrived in places of temporary stay, it was necessary to receive them in Poland after crossing the border and legalising their stay. In this aspect, the most difficult situation was faced by self-governments performing the function of first centres receiving refugees on the Polish side, such as Chełm, Przemyśl, Lublin, or Rzeszów. They became natural relocation hubs for refugees, and as the first ones, they faced challenges regarding providing this specific group of migrants with support. Self-governments cooperated with voivodes, but since no refugees' relocation system coordinated by the state functioned at that time, the entire process was chaotic, and the responsibility for managing refugees' movement was vested in self-governments (Dziennik Gazeta Prawna, 2023).

The accelerated legislation process allowed adopting the Act on assistance to citizens of Ukraine in connection with armed conflict on the territory of that country (Act of 12 March 2022 on assistance to citizens of Ukraine…, 2022) three weeks after the outbreak of the conflict. This Act specifies general rules of cooperation and scopes of duties of public units and services. The detailed role in the implementation of this Act was vested in voivodes, who were obliged to coordinate "measures of public authorities, as well as non-governmental organisations and entrepreneurs in the scope of providing citizens of Ukraine with assistance" (Act of 12 March 2022 on assistance to citizens of Ukraine…, 2022, Article 12, par. 2). Furthermore, the scope of possible support of voivodes has been specified in the Act: organisation of accommodation, provision of daily collective maintenance, transport to places of accommodation, financing travel by means of public transport and specialist transport, providing cleaning and hygiene supplies, organisation of places of providing emergency medical care, ensuring healthcare staff, and other necessary forms of assistance (Act of 12 March 2022 on assistance to citizens of Ukraine …, 2022, Article 12, par. 1). Support for these tasks can be provided by other public administration authorities, subordinate units or units supervised by the latter, public finance units, and other bodies of public authorities. It should be mentioned that in order to improve the process of helping funding tasks, which in compliance with legal provisions should be performed under the public procurement procedure, standard procedures in the scope specified in the Act on the public procurement law (Act of 11 September 2019 – Public Procurement Law…, 2019) were resigned from. Moreover, the voivode, local self-government units, and organisational units subject to public authorities received the right to commission some public tasks to non-governmental and public benefit organisations with omission of standard procedures of the open competition.

Passing the Act on assistance to citizens of Ukraine in connection with armed conflict on the territory of that country (Act of 12 March 2022 on assistance to citizens of Ukraine…, 2022) in total required amendment of 23 of other binding legal acts, among others, concerning the rules of undertaking measures by self-governments due to this crisis. With regard to the entry into force of this Act, changes were introduced in the self-governments' activity concerning such matters as: consular issues, undertaking anti-terrorist measures, crisis management concerning foreigners, census rules, public finance, taxes, issues of access to healthcare, education, and higher education, or the refugees' right to work in regulated professions (Act of 12 March 2022 on assistance to citizens of Ukraine…, 2022). Development of the legal frameworks for handling movement of migrants in Poland and providing them with social support required adoption of 18 executive acts (mainly in the form of regulations of relevant ministers or the Council of Ministers) in first weeks following the invasion of Ukraine, as well as 18 consecutive acts amending the initially adopted regulations. Therefore, this was an accelerated process of shaping a new, formal-legal framework of operations of local self-governments in the conditions of an already ongoing crisis and simultaneously in conditions of high uncertainty regarding principles for support of lower-level units by government administration. It should also be mentioned that an important aspect of all measures undertaken by self-governments towards refugees must be the compliance thereof with a series of other legal acts concerning the issue of Poland's defence, i.e.:

- Defence of the Homeland and executive acts regulating the issue of defence preparations in the non-military sphere (Act of 11 March 2022 on defence of the Homeland…, 2022).
- Crisis management (Act of 26 April 2007 on crisis management…, 2007).
- State of emergency or martial law (Act of 21 June 2002 on state of emergency…, 2002; Act on martial law…, 2002).
- Stay of foreign troops on the territory of Poland (Act of 23 September 1999 on the rules of stay of foreign troops on…, 1999).

The aforementioned legal acts constitute a complex structure of legal regulations regarding security, which has never been tested before under the conditions of an actual threat. Apart from specific provisions, also standard provisions regulating matters of public finance (Act of 27 August 2009 on public finance…, 2009), public procurement (Act of 11 September 2019 – Public Procurement Law…, 2019), rules of administrative procedures (Act of 14 June 1960 – Code of Administrative Procedure…, 1960), etc. apply in the self-governments' activity in times of a crisis.

Local self-governments are obliged to implement tasks in compliance with the competence specified in the state organisation structure at the poviat level (Act of 5 June 1998 on poviat self-government…, 1998) or municipal level (Act of 8 March 1990 on Commune Self-Government …, 1990). Act on assistance to citizens of Ukraine allows initiatives of self-governments, as well as inter-municipal unions and metropolitan unions to the benefit of providing refugees with assistance within held funds. Additionally, auxiliary tasks can be imposed on self-governments by order of a voivode, and such tasks can also be delegated by national administration. They are funded by subsidies (Act of 12 March 2022 on assistance to citizens of Ukraine…, 2022, Article 12, par. 10, 16).

6.3 Engagement of Self-Governments in the Process of Refugees' Adaptation in Their Place of Stay in Poland

Engagement of self-government in helping Ukrainians arriving in Poland following the outbreak of war was the subject of previous scientific research concerning, among others, activities undertaken by self-governments with regard to the inflow of refugees (Staniszewski et al., 2022), legal and financial aspects of measures undertaken to the benefit of refugees (Kowalska, 2022), as well as the impact of refugee crisis on public sector (Firlit-Fesnak et al., 2022). Furthermore, numerous documents of analytical nature were written, concerning, among others: the resilience of democracy of Central European countries to crises in the years 2019–2022 (K-Monitor, 2023), mutual perception and relations between Poles and refugees from Ukraine, as well as challenges of integration, the socio-economic condition of the Polish-Ukrainian cooperation (e.g., Report on the socio-economic situation of Subcarpathian Voivodeship, 2022), as well as the model of local policy for inclusion of migrants in city life (Centre of Migration Research, University of Warsaw, 2023). The research on the impact of war migration on society and self-governments in Poland was also participated by non-governmental organisations, among others, Migration Consortium (Jarosz & Klaus, 2023), the Paweł Adamowicz Centre for Analysis and Research of the Union of Polish Metropolises (Paweł Adamowicz Centre for Analysis and Research of the Union of Polish Metropolises..., 2022), Batory Foundation (Biała Księga, 2022), and others. The analysis of Polish self-governments' attitudes regarding the crisis in Ukraine was also the subject of a public debate that served, among others, as an opportunity for exchanging good practices in the scope of manners of supporting refugees, optimisation of logistical connections, and organisation of frameworks for communication in a crisis. Such discussions were held, among others, during the largest all-Poland economic events, e.g., the 8th European Congress of Local Governments within the Economic Forum (8th European Congress of Local Governments). A separate set of information in this scope is provided by reports on measures undertaken by self-governments and funds incurred by them, drawn up by self-government entities and institutions obliged to inform on the scope and scale of spending public funds.

The analysis of media reports from 2022 confirms the multifaceted and authentic engagement of Polish self-governments in providing support for refugees arriving in Poland (Dziennik Gazeta Prawna, 2023; Krzos, 2023; Radio Wrocław, 2022). These were often measures undertaken in response to the expedience, preceding legal regulations formally introduced under the Act of 12 March 2022 (Act of 12 March 2022 on assistance to citizens of Ukraine..., 2022). The direct support from Polish self-governments concerned, first of all, is the provision of necessary humanitarian and administrative assistance (e.g., obtaining PESEL (Personal Identification Number), applying for due benefits, etc.), as well as medical and psychological aid, and creating social and living conditions in Poland. Secondly, it consisted of assistance in the integration with the local community and assistance in activation on the labour market. Indirect support from self-governments was primarily provided by coordination of cooperation between various institutions and entities at the local level, which simultaneously undertook measures to the benefit of refugees, e.g., labour market institutions, schools and nursery schools, and non-governmental organisations. Due to the engagement of self-governments in these measures, higher effectiveness and synergy resulting from, among others, parcelling support could be achieved.

Polish self-governments reacted to the Ukrainian crisis swiftly and intuitively, as well as comprehensively. Regardless of the aforementioned statutory tasks from the period before the outbreak of war in Ukraine, which to a certain extent also concern satisfying the needs of migrants staying in Poland, in the face of the new crisis, Polish self-governments assigned additional funds from their budgets to help Ukrainians. Furthermore, all held provisions of resources and social capital, among others, to provide refugees with social and living conditions were activated. It was executed with a significant engagement of many local stakeholders, i.e., entrepreneurs, non-governmental organisations, and informal groups of citizens, including Ukrainians living in Poland. These stakeholders joined various forms of support, among others, provided refugees with the most necessary products, emergency assistance, as well as shelter in private reception camps and their own homes. It proves the high social support for self-government initiatives aimed at supporting refugees. Moreover, attention should be paid to the organisational effort of self-governments, many of which took on themselves the role of an intermediary and coordinator of assistance measures with regard to bottom-up initiatives undertaken by local entrepreneurs, non-governmental organisations, or citizens. Self-governments joined, among others, activities of labour market institutions and informed refugees of the terms and conditions of searching for employment in Poland and vacancies available in local companies. Support warehouses, apartments' exchanges, and care for nursery school and school kids were organised for refugees, and information-counselling points were activated, providing a wide scope of support for migrants. Also, Ukrainians who stayed in the warfare zone were not forgotten. A lot of Polish self-governments organised individually or in cooperation with non-governmental organisations convoys of offerings sent to Ukraine. They usually transported to territories attacked by Russians with material support such as generators, batteries, torches, power banks, first aid kits, basic medical resources (vitamins, painkillers, cough, and cold medicine), long shelf life foods, water, blankets, sleeping bags, cleaning supplies, clothing, paper towels, soaps, toothpastes, tooth brushes, and other everyday use hygiene supplies. Also, material aid for hospitals was sent to Ukraine (medical rescue sets, dressings, aseptic materials, emergency blankets, sleeping bags, and even ambulances and portable X-ray machines). This support was allocated to, among others, cure Ukrainian war veterans. Help was also given to firefighters, who were sent helmets, gloves, water nozzles, jumpsuits, motor pumps, and even fighting fire trucks (Faliński, 2023).

It can be stated that the crisis triggered a new potential for international cooperation of local self-governments. An example can be the Greater Poland's municipality – Gizałki, which did not previously have any partnership contacts with Ukrainian municipalities, but in cooperation with foreign partners from France (Anor municipality), Belgium (Momignies municipality), and Germany (Apen municipality) collected a lot of offerings which were transported to Ukraine via the Polish Governmental Agency for Strategic

Reserves. Whereas, the Masurian municipality – Olecko, which before Russia's aggression on Ukraine had an agreement on partnership cooperation with Russian Gusev, terminated this agreement in a gesture of protest against Russian aggression on March 7, 2022. This is one of many examples of attitudes of Polish self-governments that clearly communicated their approach to Russia's behaviour towards Ukraine. Another example can be the approach of the Węgrowo City Council, which on February 24, 2022, took a standpoint condemning Russia's aggression on Ukraine and forwarded it to befriended and partner Ukrainian local communities (Faliński, 2023).

In the first weeks following the Russian attack on Ukraine, the largest wave of war refugees arrived in Polish borderland voivodeships, i.e., Lublin and Subcarpathian, which were the first to face the new situation that required an immediate reaction. These regions had to a significantly higher extent than other Polish regions provided the so-called first aid for refugees crossing the Polish border from the Ukrainian side. A particular challenge was to relocate refugees crossing the border in Lublin and Subcarpathian Voivodeships, since it was necessary to provide them with a temporary place to rest and sleep and then activate their further transport deep into Poland. It resulted from the fear of refugees accumulating near border crossings and blocking the humanitarian aid points, which had to be ready for arrival of Ukrainians who were just waiting for the opportunity to cross the Polish border. Therefore, in two Polish Voivodeships, Lublin and Subcarpathian, the highest demand for specific first aid for refugees, in particular humanitarian aid, occurred.

An example of a self-government which was one of the first to face challenges related to the reception of refugees in Poland was the city of Lublin. In the first weeks of war, over 1.2 million of Ukraine's citizens stopped there on their journey, whereas approximately 138 thousand spent at least one night there. For the needs of refugees in Lublin, 16 collective accommodation points were organised in boarding schools, dormitories, and sports facilities. These measures were implemented by the City Council in cooperation with the Municipal Family Assistance Centre and with the support of volunteers from Lublin Social Committee to Aid Ukraine. Until February 15, 2023, approximately 13.5 thousand Ukrainian citizens benefited from municipal overnight stops. In total, over 307 thousand of overnight stays were provided in Lublin, and additionally, many refugees found shelter in private homes. Whereas Rzeszów, a city with approximately 200 thousand of citizens, at the peak of the refugee crisis hosted 100 thousand of refugees from Ukraine, simultaneously sending hundreds of thousands of tonnes of humanitarian aid to Ukraine (Krzos, 2023). Some self-governments supporting refugees, e.g., Przemyśl and Rzeszów, received humanitarian aid from the President of Ukraine with the title of City-Rescuer. Humanitarian aid was sent to the war zone both within cooperation of partnership cities, e.g., Przemyśl – Lviv, Lublin – Kamianets-Podilskyi, etc., but also as a result of these cities' coordination of sending humanitarian aid to Ukraine from other foreign partners cooperating with Polish cities, e.g., German cities, etc. Lublin's self-government transferred aid to Ukraine from, among others, Nancy, Münster, Lancaster, and Windsor.

Reports on aid granted to Ukraine by Lublin Voivodeship show that the weight of goods transferred to refugees amounts to 3,000 tons, that is, 251 thousand units of various types of products. The total value of provided financial support amounted to PLN 570.9 million (including PLN 31.7 million from funds of the Lublin Voivodeship self-government). Aid was given to 3.7 million of refugees from Ukraine (including 67% of women), who crossed the border through border crossings in the region, of whom: 300 thousand of refugees were provided services at reception points; 171 thousand benefited from overnight stays or accommodation; 23.7 thousand started working in the region; and 1.74 thousand of refugees were hospitalised (Departament Strategii i Rozwoju, Urząd Marszałkowski Województwa Lubelskiego, 2022). There is a lack of an analogous study summarising measures undertaken in the Subcarpathian Voivodeship, but the statements of self-government authorities show that, among others, the voivodeship self-government provided support from its budget for 2022 with designated subsidies in the total amount of PLN 850,000 within the programme of financial aid for local self-government units for the task related to the refugee crisis caused by the war in Ukraine. This subsidy was entrusted to: the city of Przemyśl and poviats: Przemyśl, Jarosław, Lubaczów, Bieszczady, and Leżajsk municipality (Report on the condition of the Subcarpathian Voivodeship in 2022, 2023).

As of the moment when first refugees arrived in Poland, self-governments receiving them from borderland areas undertook a series of measures in order to provide incomers with basic social and living, as well as psychological support. Development of warfare in Ukraine and, in consequence, further inflow of refugees to Poland resulted in high pressure on their swift relocation from the borderland to other Polish regions or abroad. Self-governments also engaged in logistical operations, among others, by providing a rolling stock, as well as food and healthcare during travel. Such measures prevented blocking overnight stays near the border considering the further, intensive inflow of migrants, among them many people in need of medical care, and provided them with places in hospitals. Several factors were of vital importance for swift and efficient reaction of self-governments to the new crisis situation: previous experiences concerning measures to the benefit of local integration of migrants; experiences of cooperation with Ukrainian partners, e.g., within cooperation of partner cities or with regard to the implementation of cross-border projects; existing channels of cooperation between self-government administration, social organisations, media, and local leaders (e.g., town councillors, village administrators, etc.), from whom many personally engaged in helping refugees (Jarosz & Klaus, 2023).

Local self-governments that were the closest to the crisis situation triggered by the war in Ukraine, played a particularly important role in counteracting unfavourable consequences of the inflow of refugees to Poland, both in terms of the situation of refugees and their impact on the environment in which they found themselves. A crucial challenge for the self-government was, on the one hand, supporting refugees in their independence and, on the other hand, ensuring their integration with the local community. Certain regulations in this scope were introduced by the Act on assistance to citizens of Ukraine in connection with armed conflict in the territory of that country (Act of 12 March 2022 on assistance to citizens of Ukraine..., 2022), which transferred certain tasks from the national and regional levels to local self-governments. It primarily concerned formal entitlements for self-governments to undertake measures providing migrants with necessary humanitarian aid on the premises, e.g., an overnight stay, and support in the organisation of further travel to places where they would like to stay temporarily. Such measures were, in the first place, undertaken by self-governments in borderland areas with Ukraine.

The research conducted in the largest Polish city centres (The Paweł Adamowicz Centre for Analysis and Research of the Union of Polish Metropolises) shows that citizens of Rzeszów and Lublin assess assistance provided to refugees from Ukraine by self-government authorities better than assistance provided by the government (respectively, 94% and 79% of positive assessments of Rzeszów citizens; and respectively, 87% and 78% of positive assessments in the case of Lublin). Especially the engagement of self-governments in collecting offerings is appreciated (Paweł Adamowicz Centre for Analysis and Research of the Union of Polish Metropolises, 2022). Whereas, the research conducted by the University of Warsaw, concerning social perception of refugees, shows that Polish society accepts certain legislative solutions within the package for refugees from Ukraine (covering refugees with public healthcare, Ukrainian children's access to the education system, a single aid benefit in the amount of PLN 300, about EUR 64, covering the costs of accommodation and maintenance), whereas the level of acceptance regarding refugees' use of family support funds (including the monthly benefit for each child in a family in the amount of PLN 500, about EUR 107), or social assistance, including benefits, is lower. The research shows a lack of objections against refugees living in Poland (approx. 80% of respondents support these solutions), welcoming them to the family (64% of respondents support these solutions), or inviting them to their own flat/house (50% of respondents support these solutions). Furthermore, after the outbreak of war, the social perception of Ukrainians in Poland improved in comparison to the previous period (78% of positive answers in April/May 2022 in comparison with 41% of positive answers in January 2022), and the percentage of people declaring negative approach decreased (8% in April/May 2022 in comparison to 25% in January 2022) (Staniszewski et al., 2022). Results of this research provide valuable observations useful in formulating conclusions concerning directions for shaping future policies regarding migrants and refugees developed both at the government level and at regional and local self-government levels. Moreover, the research shows social approval for Ukrainian refugees' activation on the Polish labour market.

In the context of conclusions drawn up from the literature analysis as well as assessment of legal frameworks determining possibilities of self-governments operating in the conditions of a crisis caused by the war in Ukraine, an especially interesting subject matter seems to be tracking such activities of self-governments in Polish borderland regions. Given the diverse dynamics of the refugee crisis related to warfare in Ukraine, activities of self-governments in Polish borderland regions were assessed from the perspective of two periods: the first weeks of the conflict in Ukraine (February and March 2022), characterised by high dynamics and high level of uncertainty, as well as another period covering the time of relative stabilisation of the situation and gradual adaptation of refugees to living conditions in Poland (August–December 2022).

6.4 Self-Governments' Support for War Refugees on the Polish Labour Market – Research Results

Research conducted by the co-authors of publications showed that before the outbreak of war in Ukraine over half of studied municipalities stayed in contact with Ukrainian self-governments. Partnerships were usually concluded between self-governments localised in near proximity to the border and were of a different nature, e.g., cooperation within cross-border projects, cooperation of partner cities and municipalities, exchange of letters of intent, etc. Such contacts were maintained by, among others: Bełżec, Brzozów, Hrubieszów, Jarosław, Krasnystaw, Leżajsk, Łańcut, Przemyśl, Przeworsk, Radymno, Sanok, Tomaszów Lubelski, Zamość. Ukrainian partners of Polish self-governments included: Belz, Bohuslav, Boryslav, Chortkiv, Drohobych, Ivano-Frankivsk, Kamienets-Podilskyi, Koziatyn, Lviv, Novoiavorivsk, Rudky, Sambor, Sokal, Świdyn, Truskavets, Turiisk, Uman, Uzhhorod, Vasylkiv, Volodymyr-Volynskyi, Yavoriv, Zhovkva. Some of the studied municipalities had no relations with Ukrainian partners before the outbreak of war. This issue was discussed in the research, based on the assumption that Polish self-governments, which had good relations with Ukraine before war, could be more engaged in supporting refugees and even offer additional support to citizens of partnership cities. Nevertheless, the research has not settled this issue unambiguously, which can be indicated by the fact that Ukrainian population's escapes in the direction of Polish border following the outbreak of war were spontaneous acts, not directly coordinated by self-governments of cities which refugees came from.

Apart from the aforementioned partner contacts with Ukraine, also the scope of statutory tasks imposed on municipalities, legal requirements, and a sense of duty, empathy, and compassion for people running away from the armed conflict could have an impact on swift self-organisation of self-governments in Polish borderland areas in order to provide refugees with required support.

Leading types of assistance offered to Ukrainians after the outbreak of the refugee crisis in 2022 have been presented in Figure 6.1.

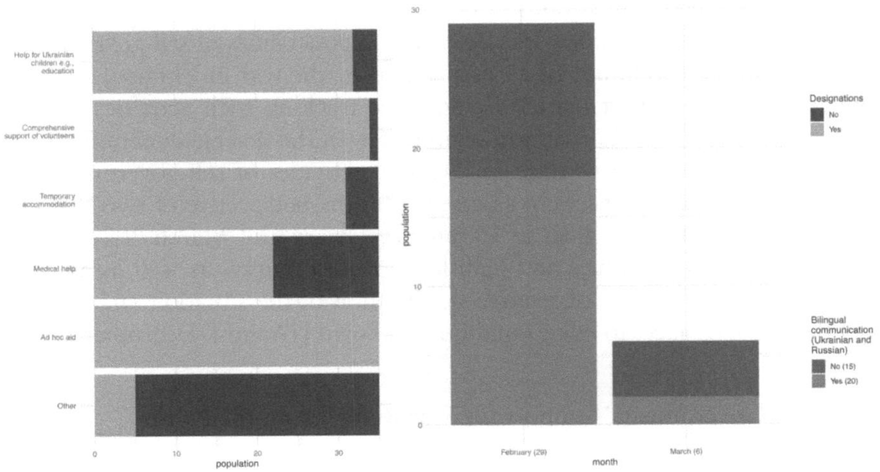

Figure 6.1 Types of self-governments' support for war refugees from Ukraine, the moment of activating support and information on languages in which support is provided.

Source: Own elaboration based on the results of the study.

As many as 82.9% of studied self-governments activated assistance for refugees in the first week of war (February 2022), and another 17.1% of self-governments undertook such measures with a certain delay, i.e., in March 2022. As far as the pace of activating assistance is concerned, the research showed that previous experiences in cooperation with the Ukrainian side had only a minimal impact on the swiftness of measures. Furthermore, close relations with Ukrainian partners from before the outbreak of war did not translate into the pace of activating bilingual assistance. In this aspect, municipalities, which did not have previous relations with the Ukrainian side coped better. In February, 58.8% of such municipalities organised bilingual aid, i.e., assistance in Russian and Ukrainian. Other studied municipalities, which did not have relations with Ukrainian partners, did not activate such assistance at all. While 44.4% of self-governments that had partner relations with Ukraine before the outbreak of war activated bilingual assistance in February, whereas in the period between February and March 2022, such assistance was activated by 55.6% of Polish municipalities, which had cooperated with Ukraine before the war. It is worth mentioning here that the condition for activating bilingual assistance by municipalities was the availability of people fluent in Polish and Ukrainian or Russian in the area of such a municipality who could be employed, e.g., in information points for refugees established in municipality offices. In many cases, such people recruited themselves from among refugees or local Ukrainian economic migrants who came to Poland before the war and managed to learn Polish. Refugees' employment in order to provide Ukrainians with bilingual assistance was practised in the case of eight studied self-governments (22.9%).

The criterion of maintaining partner relations with Ukraine before the outbreak of war did not significantly diversify municipalities in terms of intensity and variety of assistance offered to refugees. All self-governments cooperating with Ukraine participated in organising ad hoc aid; a vast majority also offered a wide support provided by volunteers (97.1%) and temporary accommodation (88.6%). Voluntary service in the scope of information support and other forms of assistance for refugees was also offered by all municipalities without any regular contact with Ukraine. Moreover, studied municipalities provided Ukrainian children with, e.g., educational assistance (94.4%), medical help (66.7%), and other forms of assistance (22.2%), such as providing medicine, warehouse points, transport, workshops, and cultural events.

Support for refugees was also provided by self-governments due to the cooperation of self-governments with non-governmental organisations that dealt with aid for Ukrainians. Such cooperation took place in the area of 77.1% of studied municipalities (see Table 6.2).

In all municipalities in which non-governmental organisations provided various forms of support for refugees, they could count on understanding and assistance from self-governments. Relations between studied self-governments and cooperating non-governmental organisations were mainly of an informal nature and based on mutual trust and direct communication at the operational level. Agreements concerning cooperation in the implementation of specific tasks were made during personal meetings, on the phone, or

Table 6.2 Activity of self-governments in cooperation with non-governmental organisations (2022)

	In total	*Are there non-governmental organisations in the municipality that provide assistance to Ukrainians?*	
		No	*Yes*
In total	35	8	27
Percentage (%)	100%	22.86%	77.14%
		including percentage of answers in municipalities, in which non-governmental organisations supporting Ukrainians:	
		do not exist	exist
Does the municipality organise any cultural initiatives for refugees from Ukraine?			
No	42.86%	87.50%	29.63%
Yes	57.14%	12.50%	70.37%
Does the municipality cooperate with non-governmental organisations?			
No	22.86%	100.00%	0.00%
Yes	77.14%	0.00%	100.00%

Source: Own elaboration based on the results of the study.

via email. This cooperation concerned not only humanitarian aid but also the organisation of cultural events aimed at the refugees' integration with the local community and distracting them from their feelings of war trauma that many of them experienced. The research shows that culture became an important element in establishing relations between the local community and war refugees. Such measures consisted not only in familiarising newcomers with local traditions and customs, as well as including them in various types of local celebrations and events, but also in allowing them to present their own culture, tradition, customs, cuisine, etc. These measures were aimed at getting to know better the local community and refugees, who often temporarily resided not only in local collective accommodation facilities but also in citizens' homes. Other occasions for meetings happened during school festivities in educational establishments attended by refugees' children or local companies where migrants from Ukraine were employed.

As far as crisis management by self-governments from Polish borderland areas is concerned, in 2022, with a consideration of the fluctuating intensity of inflow of refugees to Poland (Duszczyk & Kaczmarczyk, 2022), the role of those self-governments in providing refugees with assistance mainly consisted in coordination of all support processes at the local level. Exceptions were the largest cities in these regions, among others: Lublin and Rzeszów, where self-governments coordinated activity of refugees' reception points in Poland and additionally managed the refugees' traffic in order to avoid blocking this infrastructure, which had to be at all times ready to receive other Ukrainians. Self-governments of smaller rural and urban municipalities were responsible for operational planning (including setting aims to support people who declared the will to stay in those municipalities) and further organisation of the support process, as well as monitoring of ongoing measures. The key areas of support include providing material support, organising of accommodation, establishing a base of services provided for people in need of specific support, and preparing a logistics system related to the further reallocation of refugees. The exclusive decision-making of self-governments regarding coordination of assistance for refugees translated into various models of reacting and organising support for them, both in terms of formal leadership in this process and distributing tasks among units engaged in providing assistance to refugees. The responsibility for coordination of measures on behalf of self-governments was usually taken by existing superior authorities in the municipality or municipal aid institutions. Usually these were a bailiff, mayor (23% of studied self-governments), or municipality's secretary (20% of studied self-governments). Among units subject to a municipality, in 20% of cases, the task was entrusted to heads or directors of social assistance centres; in 11%, the function of a coordinator was performed by a team or a person appointed to implement tasks in the scope of crisis management; and in other cases (11%), this function was entrusted to heads/directors/managers of departments within municipality offices or city councils (for social affairs, civil affairs, and education). In one of the studied municipalities, this function was performed by the Director of the Centre of Common Services, whereas in another – the Commandant of City Guards. Only in the case of three self-governments, working teams for refugees' assistance were appointed (Sanok, Przemyśl, and Jarosław), whereas in the municipality of Radymno, no coordinator was appointed (measures were managed ad hoc by appointed employees of the city council).

Almost in all studied municipalities, educational establishments, and social assistance centres were engaged in organisation of assistance for refugees. To a smaller extent, the following units were also engaged: community centres, sports and recreation centres, firefighters, nursery schools, libraries, farmers' wives' associations, local traffic undertakings, public utility enterprises, and family assistance centres.

The scope and intensity of support provided depended on the current inflow of refugees and their needs. Furthermore, the financial potential of studied self-governments, that is, the capability to cover costs of support from the local budget and funds provided by other entities, e.g., local entrepreneurs, was of great importance. In general, funding outreach activities pursuant to the adopted Act on assistance to citizens of Ukraine in connection with armed conflict on the territory of that country could proceed with the use of resources coming from subsidies granted by higher-level organisations (regional, national). This act also allowed the use of own resources by municipal self-governments (Act of 12 March 2022 on assistance to citizens of Ukraine, 2022). Studied self-governments activity used resources mainly from public subsidies granted by regional authorities (including the established aid fund) or national authorities. Every fifth studied self-government indicated significant material assistance from non-governmental organisations from Poland (the Polish Red Cross) and/or abroad (England, France, Germany). Funds were also allocated by partner cities and individual donors from Poland and abroad. Furthermore, studied self-governments cooperated with volunteers from Poland and abroad who supplied municipalities with collected funds or material aid. Moreover, several self-governments benefited from institutional or logistical support, including poviats (a superior level in state organisation).

As far as challenges and fields of activity in the scope of self-governments' support for refugees are concerned, the research shows that since the beginning of the crisis in 2022, the issue of providing them with temporary accommodation in the area of the municipality was of key importance. Decisions were made under conditions of high uncertainty regarding the period of time for which this support should be planned. Polish self-governments wield specific housing resources (council houses, social houses, premises established by social housing associations, etc.) for meeting the living needs of municipalities' citizens. At the same time, self-governments manage subservient organisational units (e.g., schools and other educational facilities, boarding schools, and cultural institutions), which can be in special conditions temporarily adapted for collective overnight points. Availability of such facilities is, however, very diverse in the area of municipalities. Therefore, after the inflow of refugees to municipalities and especially to the largest cities, housing resources quickly started running out. In single cases, there were issues with financing refugees' stay for over 120 days (due to the legal provisions concerning housing benefits only for the period of three months). A sudden increase in the number of citizens of cities and municipalities due to the temporary stay of refugees (situation on the route of migration) also led to the destabilisation of the waste management system. In the borderland regions, there were also cases of collecting benefits on the Polish side despite actual, permanent stay in the territory of Ukraine. Furthermore, attempts at coercing undue assistance by people using Ukrainian passports were noted. Despite the aforementioned cases of negative behaviour of migrants, every third self-government does not report any problems related to the inflow of refugees to a municipality.

Another challenge for representatives of local self-governments was providing the possibility of communicating with refugees in Ukrainian or Russian, since the majority of migrants did not speak Polish or English well. It required engagement of competent personnel not only with relevant linguistic background but also relevant communication and interpersonal skills, showing appropriate level of empathy to newcomers, who often had very difficult experiences and could not always explicitly articulate their needs.

Furthermore, the research proved the occurrence of certain difficulties in providing Ukrainian children with education. According to government guidelines, children were supposed to be allocated to the so-called mixed grades. Classes in such grades were conducted in Polish, but Ukrainian pupils had the right to use the support of Ukrainian assistants if they had been employed. Ukrainian children joining Polish grades caused challenges not only due to the language barrier but also curriculum differences and a lack of properly trained teachers. The integration process of Ukrainian pupils in Polish schools was also hindered by war trauma experienced by many of them, and the lack of psychological and pedagogical support in Ukrainian (Public Information Bulletin of the Commissioner for Human Rights, 2023). Eventually, in many cases, carers decided that they should continue education remotely in Ukrainian and in compliance with the Ukrainian curriculum.

The majority of self-government officials stated that in the perspective of the studied period (February–September 2022), refugees' needs did not change (63.9%, i.e., 22 respondents). Other studied representatives of municipalities specified primarily two tendencies:

- Decreasing the scale of the demand for support,
- A change in the type of declared needs (lower demand for social, material, and accommodation needs, and higher demand for support in searching for a job).

Moreover, several respondents emphasised the inhomogeneity of groups of refugees that arrived in municipalities in 2022. In the period following the outbreak of war, affluent people arrived in municipalities (especially people who had previously established business or social relations in Poland), and then poor people who required immediate social assistance came. The described differences indicate that organisational structures for reacting to the needs of people in a refugee crisis require a significant flexibility in approach.

An important challenge for studied self-governments remains establishing or maintaining contact with Ukrainian municipalities. Only 51.4% of studied self-governments maintained such relations at the end of 2022. In the majority, these contacts concerned transferring humanitarian aid directly between self-governments or non-governmental or religious organisations. Communication mainly proceeded on the phone or via email, whereas due to the risk caused by the war in Ukraine, only in the case of five municipalities (urban municipalities: Łańcut, Przemyśl, Tomaszów Lubelski, and Zamość, rural municipality: Bełżec) mutual personal visits were also practised. In compliance with the results of the research conducted in December 2022, in the case of the majority of studied self-governments (71.4%), the inflow of war refugees did not cause significant development problems in municipalities. In cases where such difficulties were identified, main transitional problems were noted, concerning warranting accommodation or funds for refugees' maintenance. Furthermore, issues of a decrease in the level of safety (including road safety), a negative impact of privatisation of municipal ownership on the possibility of self-governments' reaction in the scope of organising temporary accommodation for refugees, an increase in the costs of waste disposal burdening municipalities and remaining outside the municipalities' financial support system in the period of migration crisis, or difficulties in delegating employees to assist refugees, were indicated. Furthermore, self-governments indicated the possibility of growing tensions between population and refugees due to equalising social rights for migrants with rights for Polish citizens. In a wider context, the following were also indicated: destruction of roads or a potential issue related to the evacuation of a large number of people in the case of a direct threat (e.g., threat resulting from the spreading armed conflict in Ukraine or, e.g., fire hazard, etc.). Opinions of studied self-government officials concerning a decrease in the level of security are confirmed by statistical data of Statistics Poland (Local Data Bank of Statistics Poland, 2022) concerning the number of crimes recorded in the country and in studied regions, which shows an increase in the number of recorded criminal events in the second and fourth quarters of 2022. In compliance with data included in Table 5.3, a higher increase in crime was noted in borderland regions than in the country in general. It concerned both serious events (criminal, against life and health, against family) and against activity of state institutions or local self-government.

Furthermore, the significance of the inflow of refugees from Ukraine compared to the changes in the level of unemployment in borderland regions was analysed in a public debate. However, the statistical data concerning unemployment in particular quarters of 2022 rather indicates seasonality of this phenomenon than an important impact of migrants on the increase in the number of the unemployed. Whereas, data concerning the level of the use of resources shows a positive stimulation of the sector of tourism in the period after the outbreak of a fully-fledged war (both in comparison to December 2021 and to the period before COVID-19, i.e., December 2019), which to a large extent can result from accommodating migrants in overnight facilities in borderland regions (see Table 6.3).

As far as the approach of the local community towards refugees is concerned, all studied self-governments assessed that, as of the first days of war, it was unequivocally positive. It was manifested in the huge engagement of the local community in helping Ukrainians. Despite the prolonged

Table 6.3 The impact of war migration on safety, unemployment, and use of overnight facilities in Polish borderland regions and in the country in 2022

		Poland	*Lublin*	*Subcarpathian*
Recorded crime (1st quarter of 2022 = 1.00)				
In total	2nd quarter	1.15	1.21	1.25
	3rd quarter	0.72	0.90	0.86
	4th quarter	0.88	1.07	1.20
of criminal nature	2nd quarter	1.10	1.17	1.45
	3rd quarter	0.85	0.91	1.01
	4th quarter	1.07	1.12	1.49
against life and health	2nd quarter	1.11	1.05	1.46
	3rd quarter	0.85	0.78	0.98
	4th quarter	1.17	1.01	2.02
against family and care	2nd quarter	1.34	1.22	1.57
	3rd quarter	0.90	0.76	0.83
	4th quarter	1.05	0.80	1.30
against activity of state institutions and local self-governments	2nd quarter	1.04	1.20	2.35
	3rd quarter	0.85	1.33	3.11
	4th quarter	0.96	1.59	1.37
The number of the unemployed registered in Labour Offices (1st quarter of 2022 = 1.00)				
	2nd quarter	0.91	0.91	0.90
	3rd quarter	0.89	0.88	0.88
	4th quarter	0.90	0.91	0.90
The extent of using tourist overnight facilities – a change in time				
In total	December 2021 = 1.00	1.25	1.31	1.22
	December 2019 = 1.00	1.00	1.06	1.01
hotel facilities in total	December 2021 = 1.00	1.35	1.40	1.46
	December 2019 = 1.00	0.99	1.09	1.08
other facilities in total	December 2021 = 1.00	1.13	1.15	1.05
	December 2019 = 1.00	1.00	1.00	0.95

Source: Own elaboration on the basis of the Local Data Bank of Statistics Poland (accessed: 26.11.2023).

armed conflict, over half of the studied self-governments (18) in the period between February and September 2022 did not notice a change in the citizens' approach towards Ukrainians, whereas in 13 cases it was explicitly indicated that the approach continued to be positive, but the community's engagement in helping refugees was visibly smaller. In four municipalities, negative opinions were expressed concerning continuing to provide assistance to Ukrainians, but such opinions were not prevailing. According to the respondents, the reasons for giving negative opinions regarding refugees were single cases of abusing assistance by them or a feeling of unequal treatment of citizens due to the wide range of possibilities provided for the Ukrainian population, e.g., on the labour market or in the scope of social assistance. In compliance with the research results from the end of 2022, some self-governments felt more explicitly discouraged and tired with the prolonged conflict and the state of uncertainty, which resulted in a smaller acceptance and a decrease in support for prolonged assistance (as stated by seven studied municipalities).

6.5 Conclusions

In the Polish legal system, local self-governments play a special role in extraordinary situations, which include the refugee crisis after the outbreak of war in Ukraine on February 24, 2023. They remain in close proximity and maintain communication with the local environment, and have competences to coordinate cooperation with stakeholders representing various sectors, e.g., in a crisis situation. Social and other tasks that can concern assistance for refugees are primarily assigned to municipalities and poviats, but in many situations, they also require cooperation and coordination at various levels, among others regarding the engagement of voivodes. A lack of specific legal regulations concerning proceeding with refugees hindered planning, organisation, and coordination of necessary measures directly after the outbreak of war. The hitherto regulations in compliance with which refugees were placed in assigned centres for the time of the legalisation procedure of their stay in Poland were not legitimate in this situation. New solutions were necessary, but they were usually searched for on an ongoing basis while using the great social mobilisation. As a result of the above, among others, a solution was introduced, according to which the state refunded Polish citizens for the expenses related to hosting Ukrainians at their homes.

At the moment of Russia's attack on Ukraine, Polish self-governments were not properly prepared to provide assistance to a huge wave of war refugees continuously incoming to Poland through border crossings in Lublin and Subcarpathian Voivodeships. The undertaken measures generally fell within the tasks and authorisations of self-governments, but comprehensive top-down regulations concerning the migration and integration policy were missing. Only three weeks after the outbreak of war (March 12, 2022), the Polish Parliament adopted the Act on assistance to citizens of Ukraine in connection with armed conflict on the territory of that country (Act of 12 March 2022 on assistance to citizens of Ukraine…, 2022). This legal act specifies general rules for cooperation and scopes of duties of public units and services with regard to accepting Ukrainian refugees in Poland. It imposes on self-governments specific tasks but also opens the path for using a simplified mode of commissioning certain tasks to, e.g., non-governmental organisations. Self-governments cooperated the closest with voivodes in the scope of set tasks.

The manner of receiving refugees in a given municipality and the scope of support in 2022 were conditioned by, among others: social approach to Ukrainians; financial capacities of the local self-government; availability of specialists prepared to work with refugees: the interest of local stakeholders in cooperation with the self-government. The fluctuating dynamics of the Russian-Ukrainian conflict hindered self-governments' planning of a relevant scale of measures supporting refugees and providing relevant funds for financing them.

Special tasks were allocated to self-governments located the closest to the Polish-Ukrainian border, e.g., cities such as Chełm, Przemyśl, Lublin, or Rzeszów. They became reception points, i.e., the first aid points for refugees crossing the Polish border, and relocation hubs. A special task of borderland self-governments also comprises, among others, managing refugees' traffic, i.e., supporting swift movement of refugees from border crossings deep into Poland and not allowing them to block the infrastructure near border crossings and hubs (e.g., Polish State Railways' stations and bus stops), where other refugees were constantly incoming.

The analysis of measures implemented by borderland self-governments in 2022 allows distinguishing two key stages of providing assistance to refugees:

- Support after crossing the border, including, among others: legalisation of stay in Poland, providing medical help and proper sanitary conditions, maintenance, clothing, place for rest, psychological support, logistical support, and assistance in relocation to the place of temporary stay.
- Support at the place of temporary stay, including, among others: providing shelter and a sense of security, as well as basic social and living conditions, providing medical care and conditions for education, socialisation, and integration with the local community, and activation on the labour market.

An additional task of many self-governments comprised coordination of outreach activities with regard to bottom-up initiatives undertaken by local entrepreneurs, non-governmental organisations, or citizens, as well as cooperation with labour market institutions. It was carried out with a large social support. A lot of citizens engaged in voluntary activities concerning, e.g., collecting offerings, providing refugees with overnight stays and maintenance, working in information points for refugees, etc. The level of social approval of refugees' activation on the Polish labour market was also high.

One should also remember the increase in the significance of international cooperation of self-governments in a gesture of solidarity with Ukraine, which came down to, among others, organising by Polish self-governments collections of offerings and funds from partner cities from around the world and further transport thereof to Ukraine in independently organised convoys or with the support of the Governmental Agency for Strategic Reserves. Some municipal councils also passed symbolic resolutions in solidarity with Ukraine and terminated agreements on cooperation with Russian self-governments.

No single prevailing model of coordination of assistance to refugees at a local level has been identified. The decision-making exclusivity of self-governments in this scope translated into various models of reacting and organising support regarding formal leadership (e.g., a bailiff, mayor, president, or another appointed person) and division of tasks among public units (e.g., a city council, social assistance centre, educational establishments) and partners from other sectors engaged in helping refugees (e.g., labour market institutions or non-governmental organisations).

Maintenance of various types of partner relations between self-governments and Ukrainian municipalities before the outbreak of war did not have a significant impact on their engagement in helping refugees in 2022. The pace of activating assistance as of the outbreak of war was diverse, depending on current needs and financial capacities of the self-government, but also, e.g., availability of specialists with relevant competences. Furthermore, the majority of self-governments provided refugees with temporary accommodation, as well as educational and care support for Ukrainian children. To a lower extent, medical help and bilingual communication (Ukrainian or Russian) were provided. Incompatibility of Polish and Ukrainian educational systems also became a reason for difficulties in Ukrainian children's adaptation to Polish schools, which the self-governments tried to solve by employing, among others, Ukrainian assistants (Pogorzała, 2023, pp. 113–121). Furthermore, some self-governments employed Ukrainians, including refugees, who were familiar with Polish legal provisions and spoke Polish well. They performed functions of translators and advisors, mainly employed in information points for refugees. A lot of municipalities also received significant aid from non-governmental organisations in many support areas exceeding capacities of self-governments. Moreover, some municipalities undertook social initiatives, among others: organised cultural events, which were aimed at better integration of the local community and refugees. These self-governments intended to provide refugees with possible best adaptation to the living conditions in Poland, since, contrary to the belief of a large number of Ukrainians, they reckoned with the possibility that, in the face of prolonged warfare, their stay in Poland could last much longer than it initially seemed.

Although the majority of refugees stayed in Lublin or Subcarpathian Voivodeship only temporarily, some of them chose borderland as their destination, where they settled for the period of their stay in Poland. Self-governments provided those people primarily with ad hoc aid (overnight stay, maintenance, clothing, benefits, etc.), as well as comprehensive support of volunteers. Given the limited resources of council flats and premises for temporary adaptation for overnight purposes, a huge challenge was to provide refugees with temporary accommodation. These issues were intensified by the asymmetry in the number of refugees staying in cities and rural municipalities. The largest number of refugees wanted to settle in larger agglomerations where it was easier to find a job, but it was more difficult to obtain a council flat or find a flat for rent. Whereas, premises were available in rural municipalities, but there was a shortage of interested refugees. The uneven allocation of refugees led to the increase in the prices of flats for rent in cities and destabilisation of the waste management system. Moreover, some Ukrainians staying in borderland areas tried to collect benefits or benefit from other forms of support from Poland despite their actual, permanent stay in the territory of Ukraine. Another problem was the decrease in the level of safety (including road safety) and an increase in crime, as well as growing tensions between citizens and refugees benefiting from social rights at an equal level with Polish citizens. However, no relation between the inflow of refugees from Ukraine and the increase in unemployment in borderland regions was noted. As a result of accommodating migrants in overnight facilities, a positive stimulation of the tourism sector was observed. Despite the diverse impact of the refugee crisis on the functioning of local communities, every third studied self-government did not record any issues related to the inflow of refugees to the municipality.

In the perspective of the analysed period (February–September 2022) refugees' needs did not significantly change, but the following two tendencies have been more explicitly observed:

- A decrease in the scale of the demand for support.
- A change in the type of declared needs (a lower demand for social, material, and accommodation needs, and higher demand for support in searching for a job).

Solidarity with Ukraine in the situation of the refugee crisis did not translate into establishing new relations with municipalities on the other side of the border; however, this issue did not have any impact on the mass and spontaneous nature of assistance provided to Ukrainian refugees who arrived in Poland. At the same time, humanitarian aid was also sent to the areas affected by warfare in Ukraine. Despite a lack of a coordinated migration policy, Polish self-government showed self-agency and high effectiveness of independent activities, as well as the ability to coordinate support offered to migrants in many various aspects. The analysis of research results inclines to draw first conclusions regarding the necessity to use experiences from the refugee crisis in order to regulate in more detail the subject matter of self-governments' tasks and procedures of implementation thereof in the case of similar crises in the future.

References

Act of 14 June 1960 – Code of Administrative Procedure; Journal of Laws of 1960, No. 30, item 168, as amended.

Act of 8 March 1990 on Commune Self-Government (Article 7); Journal of Laws of 1990, No. 16, item 95, as amended.

Act of 5 June 1998 on Poviat Self-Government (Article 4); Journal of Laws of 1998, No. 91, item 578, as amended.

Act of 5 June 1998 on Voivodeship Self-Government (Article 14); Journal of Laws of 1998, No. 91, item 576, as amended.

Act of 23 September 1999 on the Rules of Stay of Foreign Troops on the Territory of the Republic of Poland and the Rules of Their Movement within the Territory of the Country; Journal of Laws of 1999, No. 93, item 1063, as amended.

Act of 21 June 2002 on State of Emergency; Journal of Laws of 2002, No. 113, item 985, as amended.

Act of 26 April 2007 on Crisis Management; Journal of Laws of 2007, No. 89, item 590, as amended.

Act of 27 August 2009 on Public Finance; Journal of Laws of 2009, No. 157, item 1240, as amended.

Act of 11 September 2019 – Public Procurement Law; Journal of Laws of 2022, items 1710, 1812, 1933, and 2185.

Act of 11 March 2022 on defence of the Homeland; Journal of Laws of 2022, item 655, as amended.

Act of 12 March 2022 on Assistance to Citizens of Ukraine in Connection with Armed Conflict on the Territory of That Country; Journal of Laws of 2022, item 583, as amended.

Biała Księga. (2022). *Wyzwania systemowego wsparcia uchodźców na poziomie lokalnym i krajowym.* https://www.batory.org.pl/wp-content/uploads/2022/06/Okragly_stol_Biala-ksiega_www_S.pdf

Centre of Migration Research, University of Warsaw. (2023). *'Model lokalnej polityki włączania migrantów i migrantek w życie miast. Założenia i rekomendacje' ('A model of Local Policy for Inclusion of Migrants in City Life. Assumptions and Recommendations').* https://www.migracje.uw.edu.pl/publikacje/model-lokalnej-polityki-wlaczania-migrantow-i-migrantek-w-zycie-miast-zalozenia-i-rekomendacje

Departament Strategii i Rozwoju, Urząd Marszałkowski Województwa Lubelskiego. (2022). *Raport o pomocy udzielonej Ukrainie przez Województwo Lubelskie (Report on aid provided to Ukraine by Lublin Voivodeship).* https://strategia.lubelskie.pl/rot/opracowania/raport.wsparcie.ua.pdf

Dolnicki, B. (2021). *Samorząd terytorialny (local self-government).* Wolters Kluwer.

Duszczyk, M., & Kaczmarczyk, P. (2022). The war in Ukraine and migration to Poland: Outlook and challenges. *Intereconomics*, *57*(3), 164–170.

Dziennik Gazeta Prawna. (2023). *Jak samorządy poradziły sobie z kryzysem uchodźczym i co jeszcze je czeka?* gazetaprawna.pl. https://www.gazetaprawna.pl/perlysamorzadu/artykuly/8665348,jak-samorzady-poradzily-sobie-z-kryzysem-uchodzczym-i-co-jeszcze-je-czeka.html

Faliński, S. (2023). Samorząd terytorialny jako nowa jakość w stosunkach międzynarodowych. Agresja na Ukrainę jako czynnik weryfikujący (Local self-government as the new quality in international relations. Aggression on Ukraine as a verifier). *Political Science Studies/Studia Politologiczne*, *67*, 56–73.

Firlit-Fesnak, G., Jaroszewska, E., Łotocki, Ł., Łukaszewska-Bezulska, J., Ołdak, M., Zawadzki, P., Żołędowski, C., & Żukowski, T. (Eds.). (2022). *Inwazja Rosji na Ukrainę. Społeczeństwo i polityka wobec kryzysu uchodźczego w pierwszym miesiącu wojny. Raport roboczy – Working paper*. Uniwersytet Warszawski. https://wnpism.uw.edu.pl/wp-content/uploads/2022/04/Kryzys-uchodzczy-2022-raport-KPS.pdf

Jarosz, S., & Klaus, W. (2023). *Przyjęcie osób uchodźczych z Ukrainy w Polsce w 2022 roku*. Polska Szkoła Pomagania. Konsorcjum Migracyjne. https://konsorcjum.org.pl/wp-content/uploads/2023/04/Polska-Szkola-Pomagania-raport-1.pdf

K-Monitor. (2023). Local governance in the crosshairs: An overlooked front of the struggle for European democracy. *K-Monitor Working Papers*, *1*. http://localgov.k-monitor.hu

Kowalska, I. (2022). Finansowanie przez jednostki samorządu terytorialnego zadań w zakresie pomocy uchodźcom z Ukrainy na przykładzie wybranych miast. *Finanse Komunalne*, 6, 7–19. https://assets.contenthub.wolterskluwer.com/api/public/content/d498e805713a434e87daf215a593d5f1?v=52022269

Krzos, M. (2023). *Wysiłek i solidarność polskich samorządów z potrzebującymi*. rp.pl. https://www.rp.pl/gospodarka/art38016341-wysilek-i-solidarnosc-polskich-samorzadow-z-potrzebujacymi

Local Data Bank of Statistics Poland. (2022). https://bdl.stat.gov.pl/bdl/start

NIK o systemie pomocy społecznej dla uchodźców (The Supreme Audit Committee on the system of social assistance for refugees). (2015). https://www.nik.gov.pl/aktualnosci/nik-o-systemie-pomocy-spolecznej-dla-uchodzcow.html

Paweł Adamowicz Centre for Analysis and Research of the Union of Polish Metropolises. (2022). *Sąsiedzka pomoc Mieszkańcy 12 największych polskich miast o pomocy uchodźcom z Ukrainy. Raport z badania*. https://metropolie.pl/fileadmin/news/2022/09/SasiedzkaPomoc_2.pdf

Pogorzała, E. (2023). System oświaty w Polsce wobec napływu dzieci-uchodźców wojennych z Ukrainy po 24 lutego 2022 roku (Education system in Poland vs inflow of children – War refugees from Ukraine after 24 February 2022). *Acta Politica Polonica*, *55*, 113–121. www.wnus.edu.pl/ap

Polityka migracyjna Polski – diagnoza stanu wyjściowego (Poland's migration policy – diagnosis of the baseline). (2021). https://www.gov.pl/web/mswia/polityka-migracyjna-polski–diagnoza-stanu-wyjsciowego

Prawo migracyjne trafi do kosza, podobnie jak wcześniej polityka migracyjna? (Will the migration law be thrown away as was the case with the previous migration policy?). (2021). https://www.prawo.pl/kadry/polityka-migracyjna-polski,522248.html

Public Information Bulletin of the Commissioner for Human Rights. (2023). https://bip.brpo.gov.pl/pl/content/rpo-mein-problemy-edukacja-uczniowie-ukraina-odpowiedz

Public Opinion Research Center. (2023). *Poles vs War in Ukraine and the Grain Crisis*. Communication on Research no. 69/2023.

Radio Wrocław. (2022). *Samorządowcy przekazali prezydentowi Białą Księgę dot. wsparcia samorządów wobec kryzysu uchodźczego*. radiowroclaw.pl. https://www.radiowroclaw.pl/articles/view/120630/Samorzadowcy-przekazali-prezydentowi-Biala-Ksiege-dot-wsparcia-samorzadow-wobec-kryzysu-uchodzczego

Regulation of the Minister of the Interior and Administration of 16 March 2022 on a Template of an Application for the Cash Benefit for Providing Citizens of Ukraine Staying in the Territory of the Republic of Poland Due to Warfare with Accommodation and Maintenance; Journal of Laws, items 608 and 617.

Staniszewski, R. et al. (2022). *Social perception of refugees from Ukraine, migrants and measures undertaken by the government of Mateusz Morawiecki – Report on public opinion survey*. Wydział Nauk Politycznych i Studiów Międzynarodowych, Uniwersytet Warszawski. https://doi.org/10.13140/RG.2.2.17930.34243

The Polish Institute of International Affairs. (2016). *Samorządy w Polsce wobec kryzysu uchodźczego (Self-Governments in Poland vs Refugee Crisis)*. https://pism.pl/publikacje/Samorz_dy_w_Polsce_wobec_kryzysu_uchod_czego

Tutak, G. (2023). Polityka integracyjna cudzoziemców w Polsce – znaczenie, aspekty prawne, instrumenty (Integration Policy of Foreigners in Poland – Significance.

7 Labour Market Institutions in a Situation of Inflow of War Refugees from Ukraine to Polish Border Regions

7.1 Tasks of Selected Labour Market Institutions in Poland

Labour market institutions are key players responsible for the implementation of active labour market policies. According to the OECD definition (OECD, 2023), these policies serve to expand access to jobs and improve professional development prospects by enhancing motivation and incentives to seek employment, improving job readiness, and helping in finding suitable employment. From the perspective of the employee, active labour market policies should be tailored to the needs and capabilities of different target groups, which require appropriate activation measures. From the perspective of the employer, active labour market policies support the processes of human resources management by facilitating the recruitment of competent employees and providing them with professional development prospects, which can benefit both the employer and the employee. From a macroeconomic perspective, active labour market policies have a key impact on shaping the employment area, which determines the overall socio-economic development of the country. They also regulate the inflow of labour into a given country (Blanchard, 2006) and make it easier for citizens to seek employment abroad, which is inter alia affected by the attractiveness of the domestic labour market and labour markets in other, e.g., neighbouring, countries, as well as the level of flexibility of the labour market institutional environment (Lehmann & Muravyev, 2012). Specific target groups to which active labour market policies are addressed include, inter alia, prisoners and people with disabilities, but also migrants and refugees. Thanks to special labour market support, gaining employment can be for them a way out of isolation and a means of social adaptation. Staying legalisation and getting a job becomes crucial, especially for refugees, from the perspective of becoming independent in their new place of residence (Sałtykowa-Wołkowicz, 2023, p. 59).

In Polish conditions, pursuant to the Act on employment promotion and labour market institutions of 2004 (Act of 20 April 2004 on employment promotion and labour market institutions, 2004), the tasks of the state regarding employment promotion, alleviation of the effects of unemployment, and professional activation targeted at Polish citizens and foreigners with

DOI: 10.4324/9781003471646-7

the refugee status in Poland are exercised by labour market institutions (Bogacz-Wojtanowska, 2007, p. 11). The aim of activities of these institutions is to strive for full and productive employment and high-quality work, to strengthen social integration and solidarity, as well as to develop human resources and increase labour market mobility (Cyranowicz, 2023, p. 27). These institutions are obliged to react not only to the changing economic situation but also to important social and economic factors affecting the labour market, such as, e.g., rural depopulation, educational and labour migration abroad, changes in old-age pension legislation, or labour migration of foreigners. According to I. Ostój, the primary role of the labour market institutions should be to develop, under given conditions and at given times, relatively stable rules governing interpersonal interactions on the domestic labour market (Ostoj, 2010, p. 534). For this purpose, the labour market institutions have a system of laws, standards, and customary rules creating restrictions or incentives that affect individual decisions on the exchange of labour services and wage levels (Kuźmar, 2015, p. 354). These institutions are responsible for monitoring the labour market situation and taking measures to promote a balance between labour demand and supply. They should react in a timely manner to factors distorting the labour market balance. In recent years, these were such events as the COVID-19 pandemic (2020–2023) or the outbreak of war in Ukraine in February 2022. Both of these crises have significantly affected labour markets and forced countries to take non-standard stabilisation measures (Cortes & Forsythe, 2023, pp. 30–55).

Such situations certainly included the refugee crisis after the outbreak of war in Ukraine, which resulted in an inflow of specific groups of refugees (mainly mothers with children) and an inflow of labour, inter alia, to industries that needed seasonal workers. At the same time, there was noted a small outflow of Ukrainians who had stayed in Poland before the outbreak of the war as economic migrants and, after the Russian attack, returned to their country to enlist in the army. This situation has temporarily destabilised the Polish labour market, e.g., in the transport or construction industries (Machniewski, 2022). Significant impediments to the efficient planning of measures mitigating the impact of the refugee crisis on the labour market in Poland included the unpredictability of the development of the conflict in Ukraine but also the numerous barriers to the professional activation of refugees, which labour market institutions had to face for the first time on such a scale (Uchodźcy na rynku pracy w Polsce, 2022). Thus, the key task of these institutions in Poland after the outbreak of war in Ukraine was to stabilise the labour market in the face of the turbulence.

Institutions responsible for implementation of the labour market policy in Poland are of diverse nature and are represented by all sectors – public, private, and social (Frączek et al., 2015, pp. 25–40). This group includes public employment services, Voluntary Labour Corps, employment agencies, training institutions, social dialogue institutions, and local partnership institutions. They exercise tasks resulting from their statutory obligations or the specificities of their activities. The key role in labour market development in Poland is played by public employment services. These institutions are distinct in formal and organisational terms and report to the government or self-government administration, respectively.

The general labour market policy is drafted and coordinated at the national (government) level by the ministry competent for labour and social policy, while at the regional level, it is conducted by voivodes and voivodeship offices managed by them (16). In turn, within the self-government structure, there are voivodeship labour offices (16) at the regional level and poviat labour offices (340) at the local level (Przeklasa, 2021, p. 349). Voivodeship and poviat labour offices determine and coordinate regional and local labour market policies according to the needs of a given area. In practice, they play a key role in supporting unemployed persons and jobseekers.

Voivodeship labour offices determine regional employment and human resources development policies, coordinate professional activation programmes, and carry out labour market research and analysis, including monitoring of deficit and surplus occupations. They develop vocational counselling and cooperate with poviat labour offices in the organisation of trainings, as well as professional preparation for adults and vocational education for youth, in accordance with the labour market needs. An important area of their activity is the exercise of tasks related to the free international movement of workers, which is currently of particular importance for solving the problems of Ukrainian refugees on the Polish labour market (Górniak, 2015).

The task of poviat labour offices is to balance the labour demand and supply on a microscale, i.e., in local markets. For this purpose, they carry out, inter alia, such activities as job placement and assisting employers in recruiting employees, vocational counselling for the unemployed, implementation of employment promotion and local labour market activation programmes, provision of the labour market information, financing of lifelong education of employees and organisation of trainings and professional preparation of adults, and monitoring of deficit and surplus occupations on a local scale. An important area of their activity is to register the unemployed persons and jobseekers and to administer the unemployment benefits (Górniak, 2015).

The vast majority of activities of poviat labour offices are addressed to the unemployed, including foreigners wishing to take up employment in Poland, as well as to employed persons and employers (Rollnik-Sadowska, 2019, pp. 98–99). The scope of tasks performed by poviat labour offices largely includes direct support for jobseekers (Poles and foreigners) but is also based on close cooperation with employers, self-governments, and other labour market institutions, e.g., Voluntary Labour Corps, employment agencies, training institutions, social dialogue institutions, and local partnership institutions. Poviat labour offices also perform tasks resulting from the right to free movement of workers between countries, including, inter alia, activities of the EURES network (Kalmár, 2015, pp. 47–57), participation in EURES cross-border partnerships, participation in proceedings on issuing work permits for foreigners, and performance of tasks related to taking up employment by foreigners in the territory of the Republic of Poland. An important area of their involvement is also the implementation of projects in the fields of employment promotion, counteracting unemployment, and professional activation of the unemployed, resulting from operational programmes co-financed by the European Social Fund and the Labour Fund.

The presented tasks of the voivodeship and poviat labour offices are carried out depending on the specificity and needs of the labour market in a given area. Regional and local labour market development policies are generally developed from a long-term perspective; however, events such as the outbreak of war in Ukraine required a rapid and coordinated response. This exceeded the previously outlined framework for the implementation of these policies, the planned objectives and measures, as well as instruments assigned to them.

The inflow of a large wave of refugees to Poland meant the need to take urgent ad hoc measures to facilitate the professional activation of migrants on the Polish labour market, but also to prepare a legal and organisational framework for systemic support of this group. The phenomenon of war migration that occurred in Poland after February 24, 2022, significantly differed from the much better-recognised phenomenon of economic migration. This wave of war refugees is mainly characterised by Bieniek-Majka and Stupałkowska (2022, pp. 169–182) and Długosz et al. (2022):

- A specific purpose of migration (fleeing an armed conflict rather than an economic purpose, as in the case of economic migrants).
- A different structure of the target group (mostly female refugees with under-age children, and not, as in the case of economic migration, mainly persons arriving on their own, without family obligations on the spot in Poland).
- Large scale of difficulties in professional activation (in the case of refugees it was, inter alia, the problem of providing childcare, difficulties in finding accommodation, and lack of motivation for jobseeking, while economic migrants were mostly better prepared for their stay in Poland and motivated to look for a job).
- Poor competences for jobseeking in Poland (incompatibility of competences and qualifications with the needs of the Polish labour market, poor knowledge of the Polish language by refugees, while economic migrants were much more attractive on the Polish labour market and mostly knew Polish at least on a communicative level).
- Temporary nature of stay (refugees declared, as a rule, a stay in Poland not longer than six months, while economic refugees usually stayed in Poland for a longer period).

7.2 Statutory Regulations on Opening the Polish Labour Market to Refugees from Ukraine

The problem of foreigners' employment is extremely complex because political, social, ethical but also economic reasons for or against opening the labour market to migrants intermingle here (Castles & Miller, 2009). The research (Heckman & Pagés, 2000; Nickell & Layard, 1999, p. 3068) confirmed the negative impact of employment protection on labour demand and, as a result, on employment decline and economic growth. Other research on the relationship between the measures undertaken by the labour market institutions and employment levels has shown that restrictive labour market protection regulations have a negative impact on employment and contribute to an increase unemployment among young workers (Lehmann & Muravyev, 2012, p. 254). Social arguments in favour of foreigners' access to the domestic labour market or limiting such access often result from radically different viewpoints (Majka et al., 2022). On the one hand, it is argued that foreigners' employment allows them to replenish the labour force, especially in lower-paid occupations, and can be a recipe for the demographic crisis that haunts many countries. On the other hand, opponents of migrants' employment often draw attention to cultural differences that hamper adaptation to work and life in the host country, as well as increased competition on the labour supply side, which can result in lower wage rates. In the case of the Ukrainian wave of war refugees that flowed into Poland after the outbreak of war in Ukraine in February 2022, the public discourse was dominated from the beginning by arguments for the need to provide comprehensive support to those fleeing Russian aggression, all the more so because they were mainly women with children and seniors. Refugees arriving in Poland were almost immediately provided with social, but also psychological and healthcare. Not only the Polish government, self-governments, public institutions, and NGOs but also, to a very large extent, informal groups and many individuals were involved in such actions. Labour market institutions have also started activities facilitating the professional activation of war refugees, allowing them to be employed during their stay in Poland.

Pursuant to Polish regulations from before the outbreak of the war in Ukraine, employment of a foreigner in Poland could take place on the basis of a work permit, a seasonal work permit, and a declaration of entrusting work to a foreigner (registered by a starost for up to 24 months for citizens of Armenia, Belarus, Georgia, Moldova, and Ukraine).

Due to the military aggression of Russia against Ukraine, urgent legislative work was undertaken in Poland to facilitate employment of refugees from across the eastern border. Under a special law, i.e., the Act of 12 March 2022, on assistance to citizens of Ukraine in connection with armed conflict on the territory of that country, the employment of a Ukrainian citizen in Poland may take place on the basis of the so-called notification of entrusting work to a Ukrainian citizen (Panasiuk et al., 2023, p. 97). The mentioned

Act regulates legal residence in Poland for war refugees from Ukraine and opens their access to the Polish labour market, education, health, and social care, as well as social benefits (Kałuża-Kopias, 2023). The Act grants Ukrainians legally residing on the territory of Poland the right to take advantage of services of public institutions dealing with the employment of workers. They may register at poviat labour offices as unemployed or jobseekers (also Ukrainian citizens of retirement age, i.e., 65 years for men and 60 years for women), and take advantage of job placement, vocational counselling, training, cash and non-cash benefits (periodic allowance, purpose-specific allowance for food, care services, sheltered housing, specialised counselling, and crisis intervention), free psychological assistance, child-care benefit, and one-off cash benefit for the most urgent expenses (Flaszyńska et al., 2022, p. 86).

The Act has granted the right to legal employment to all Ukrainian citizens whose stay on the territory of Poland was legal, either due to entry to Poland after February 24, 2022, or on other grounds (e.g., if they hold a temporary residence permit, visa, etc.). As a rule, an employer recruiting a Ukrainian citizen is obliged to notify the poviat labour office of this fact within 14 days from the day the foreigner takes up employment. This obligation does not apply to the employment of a Ukrainian citizen who legally performs work in Poland, e.g., on the basis of a work permit or an appropriate temporary residence permit, and if he or she has the right to work in Poland due to his or her residence status (e.g., he or she has been granted refugee status) (Stowarzyszenie Interwencji Prawnej, 2023).

The Act also regulates the specific conditions under which refugees from Ukraine may:

- Continue their studies.
- Take up employment as a doctor or dentist, teacher, academic teacher, and psychologist.
- Learn Polish language free of charge if they are subject to compulsory education.

Refugees from Ukraine may also undertake and carry out their own business activity in Poland on the same conditions as Polish citizens, including the right to apply for a refund/support in the form of additional funds for undertaking business activity in accordance with the provisions of the Act on employment promotion and labour market institutions of 2004 (Act of 20 April 2004 on employment..., 2004). The efficiency of forms of support for Ukrainian refugees on the Polish labour market provided for in the Act of 12 March 2022 on assistance to citizens of Ukraine in connection with the armed conflict on the territory of that country depends, on the one hand, on migrants' willingness to take up employment and, on the other hand, on the activity and commitment of the Polish employment services, which were enabled by the Act to undertake specific measures in this respect.

Even before the Act of 12 March 2022 was passed in Poland, the so-called temporary protection for persons fleeing the conflict in Ukraine had already been launched throughout the European Union on March 4, 2022. The decision of the Council of the European Union defined the circle of persons covered by this protection more broadly than the Act passed in Poland on March 12, 2023. Pursuant to this decision, temporary protection on the territory of Poland was granted to Ukrainian nationals residing in Ukraine who left for Poland on or after February 24, 2022, in connection with the Russian invasion, including those who crossed the border illegally, as well as nationals of third countries who benefited from international protection on the territory of Ukraine (refugees) who left Ukraine on or after February 24, 2022, family members of the above-mentioned two groups of persons, and third-country nationals who, before February 24, 2022, legally resided in Ukraine on the basis of a valid permanent residence permit, and who are unable to return in safe and durable conditions to their country or region of origin (Stowarzyszenie Interwencji Prawnej, 2023). In light of this decision of the Council of the European Union, the circle of refugees who could potentially seek activation on the Polish labour market has further expanded, as, according to the international legal order, the Polish law may not limit the right to protection of persons to whom it has been granted under the decision of the Council of the European Union. All persons who have fulfilled the conditions for temporary protection could receive a relevant certificate from the Head of the Office for Foreigners.

In order to better prepare labour market institutions in European Union Member States for the professional activation of migrants, on June 14, 2022, the European Commission issued a communication providing guidance for access to the labour market, vocational education and training, and adult learning for persons fleeing Russia's war of aggression against Ukraine. The European Commission stressed that fast and effective labour market integration was important both for the host communities and for those fleeing Russia's war of aggression against Ukraine, for whom such integration meant an opportunity to rebuild their lives and further develop their skills. This will be for the benefit of the persons concerned, the European Union and eventually for the reconstruction of Ukraine (European Commission Communication…, 2022). The Commission stressed that all beneficiaries of temporary protection had the right to access the EU labour market, vocational education and training, and adult education. The Commission's guidance includes, inter alia, the following recommendations for refugees' activation in the labour market:

- Ensuring refugees fast and effective access to and integration into the labour market (e.g., prompt registration in labour offices; employing refugees in professions in which they can support other war migrants, e.g., doctor; raising awareness about diversity in the workplace and providing civic/social-cultural orientation courses).

- Preventing exploitation and undeclared work.
- Taking into account the perspective of persons with disabilities on the labour market.
- Obliging public employment services to facilitate the integration of refugees into the labour market, providing information, inter alia, using the EURES network, as well as acting as matchmakers between jobseekers and employers, in active cooperation with other stakeholders such as national administrations, municipalities, social partners, and civil society organisations, including migrant and Ukrainian diaspora organisations.
- Creation of entrepreneurship support programmes for refugees, including, e.g., training, mentoring, coaching, and networking support, as well as microfinance or a combination of financial and non-financial support measures.
- Mapping skills and speedy recognition of qualifications.
- Ensuring swift access to initial vocational education and training, including apprenticeships and, in cooperation with social and economic partners, expanding the provision of quality work-based learning and apprenticeship opportunities, in line with the vocational preparation programmes.
- Supporting providers of vocational education and training.
- Recognising previous learning experiences and qualifications by using existing validation processes.
- Gaining access to general education, including through second chance schooling.

The presented recommendations were applied to measures taken by the Polish public employment services, which, together with self-governments took measures to support refugees in entering the Polish labour market. The process and forms of supporting the unemployed refugees by poviat labour offices are presented in Table 7.1.

Irrespective of the above-described framework support for refugees entering the Polish labour market, resulting from the legal regulations, public employment services, in cooperation with other partners, have provided additional forms of support, with the use, inter alia, of European Union funds and other means and local resources. Examples of such activities are presented in the next part of this work.

7.3 Selected Activities of Public Employment Services for War Refugees from Ukraine in Polish Border Regions

Since the outbreak of war, refugees from Ukraine have been supported by various institutions and organisations in Poland; however, their activation on the Polish labour market is the responsibility of public employment services, i.e., mainly voivodeship labour offices and poviat labour offices. The

Table 7.1 The process and forms of support for unemployed refugees by poviat labour offices

Step 1	Registration at the poviat labour office	A refugee legally residing in Poland registers online or in person at the poviat labour office as an unemployed, jobseeker, and before registration, he or she can also obtain general information about the Polish labour market.
Step 2	Interview with the Customer Adviser	A Customer Adviser (vocational counsellor or job placement officer) interviews the unemployed refugee and identifies his or her professional potential (professional experience, level and field of education, professional skills, and certificates, job expectations (profession, shifts, remuneration), etc.).
Step 3	Development of an Individual Action Plan	The Customer Adviser prepares, together with the unemployed refugee, an Individual Action Plan, which contains information about activities of the poviat labour office aimed to help the refugee find a job and about activities the refugee needs to carry out to get a job. The Individual Action Plan is accompanied by a timetable.
Step 4	Implementation of the Individual Action Plan and its monitoring by the poviat labour office	As part of the Plan, the unemployed refugee may take advantage of: • Job placement (Central Job Offer Database and ePraca application). • Vocational counselling (choice of profession, professional reorientation, balance of competences, and aptitudes, career development plan, assistance in applying for a job, preparation to start a business. • Vocational training and retraining. • Polish language training for foreigners. • Financing the costs of nostrification proceedings or proceedings to confirm the completion of studies. • Funding for starting business activity. • Reimbursement of travel and accommodation costs to and from the place of work. • Reimbursement of costs of care for a child under seven or a dependent person. • Referral to subsidised jobs (vouchers, internships, intervention works, and public works).
Step 5	Completion of the Individual Action Plan	The Individual Action Plan should end with the refugee taking up employment.

Source: Own study based on https://wuplublin.praca.gov.pl/pomocdlaukrainy/wsparcie (accessed: 27.11.2023).

involvement of each of these offices in activities supporting Ukrainians depends on at least several factors, such as:

- The number of refugees residing in a given district (poviat) and the scale of their interest in using the jobseeking support.
- The level of employers' interest in employing refugees.
- Available funds for professional activation of refugees.
- Competences of the public employment services to work with refugees, e.g., communication skills, empathy, the ability to overcome the language barrier, and build trust in relations with refugees.

In general, it can be assumed that since the start of the war in Ukraine, the voivodeship labour offices have made strategic decisions related to the scope of support for refugees in the regional labour markets and coordinated activities undertaken in this field in each region, inter alia, in cooperation with self-governments and poviat labour offices. The tasks of the voivodeship labour offices also included monitoring the current situation on the regional labour market, providing training support to employees of poviat labour offices serving refugees, undertaking key projects relevant to the support for war migrants across the region, as well as promoting nationwide activities such as:

- A special nationwide helpline of labour offices, the so-called Green Line (tel. 19524).
- The internet portal: https://pomagamukrainie.gov.pl/ where one can find comprehensive information about the possibility to take advantage of various forms of support.
- Legal guide for Ukrainian citizens in Poland (Guide on the situation of Ukrainian citizens on the territory of Poland under the current legal state, June 5, 2023). The guide covers issues of legality of stay, work, and access to benefits.
- Central Job Offer Database available via computer, phone, or other mobile devices with access to the Internet.
- The free ePraca application, which allows to browse job offers in an intuitive way.

The Lublin and Subcarpathian Voivodeships, located directly on the border with Ukraine, have established information and welfare points that serve all war migrants crossing the Polish border. These migrants included persons who then decided to relocate to other regions of Poland or to other countries, as well as those who, for various reasons, decided to stay in the Polish-Ukrainian border area. Already at these points, refugees could obtain basic information about the social, psychological, and vocational support available to them in Poland. The voivodeship labour offices have also developed their own regional websites dedicated to refugees, available in Ukrainian, which collected local job offers. Refugees who have remained in the Lublin and Subcarpathian Voivodeships, after being provided with social and subsistence security, were further encouraged to contact voivodeship labour offices and poviat labour offices for professional activation. During occupational interviews with refugees, employees of public employment services identified their competences and professional experience, as well as their motivations for seeking jobs in the border regions. The most frequently indicated motivations were: familiarity with the area due to previous arrivals for tourist or economic purposes, having family or friends in the area, the desire to stay in an area that is culturally and linguistically close, and the desire to stay as close as possible to the borders of one's home country.

According to a report drawn up by the Lublin Voivodeship on employment support for Ukrainians in this voivodeship, 21,000 refugees took up employment there from the beginning of the war until the end of 2022 (Departament Strategii i Rozwoju, Urząd Marszałkowski Województwa Lubelskiego, 2022). In connection with the war in Ukraine, the Voivodeship Labour Office, in cooperation with poviat labour offices, has taken a number of measures aimed at professional and social activation of Ukrainian citizens who have arrived in the region. Examples of such measures include the creation of a network of information points offering all kinds of assistance in finding suitable employment and taking advantage of aid provided by various institutions. In order to reach as many people in need of support as possible, information campaigns have been organised, e.g., the Open Day for Ukrainian citizens, and EU and national funds have been used to organise further activities dedicated to this group. According to data provided by the Voivodeship Labour Office in Lublin, by October 31, 2022, a total of almost PLN 4.3 million was allocated from the Labour Fund and the EU PO WER programme to support employment of refugees from Ukraine.

Similar activities were conducted in the Subcarpathian Voivodeship. According to data from the Voivodeship Labour Office in Rzeszów, at the end of March 2023, as many as 963 entrepreneurs in the voivodeship declared their willingness to employ, inter alia, Ukrainian citizens in 3,345 job positions. A total of 2,763 Ukrainian citizens have been registered in poviat labour offices, including 2,679 persons as unemployed and 84 persons as jobseekers. 526 active unemployed persons (citizens of Ukraine) have been registered as of March 31, 2023, in Subcarpathian Voivodeship, and 1,191 citizens of Ukraine took advantage of the labour market offers, including 441 persons who have been referred to work, 549 people who have been referred to internships, 124 persons – to intervention work, 65 persons – to public works, and 12 persons who have received one-off funds for starting a business. Since the beginning of 2022, 24,441 Ukrainian citizens have taken up legal employment in Subcarpathian Voivodeship. 30,152 persons have been granted the status of UKR foreigner (with PESEL) due to the conflict in Ukraine, on the territory of the Subcarpathian Voivodeship (currently holding the status of UKR foreigner) (Terczyńska, 2023).

War refugees interested in taking up employment in Poland could also register at poviat labour offices as unemployed persons, who could take advantage of labour market services and instruments on the same basis as Polish citizens. Poviat labour offices first of all offered refugees individual support by so-called Customer Advisers, who helped them in setting individual professional goals (e.g., verification of qualifications and professional experience, as well as knowledge of Polish language, assessment of professional predispositions, etc.) (Bieniek-Majka & Stupałkowska, 2022, pp. 169–182). These offices obtained knowledge from the local authorities about the scale of refugees' interest in temporary residence in the area and were thus better able to address them, in particular, with information about the possibility of obtaining specific assistance from other public institutions/non-governmental organisations operating in the area. After getting acquainted with the foreigner's legal situation (residence title held, work permits, if any), the vocational counsellors tried to indicate to refugees the best possible area of job search and supported them in taking the next steps according to the procedure outlined in Table 7.1.

The analysis of measures taken by public employment services in 2022 allowed to identify good practices that concerned various forms of support for refugees by poviat labour offices. These are described in Table 7.2.

Irrespective of the above-described framework support for refugees entering the Polish labour market, resulting from the legal regulations, public employment services in cooperation with other partners have provided additional forms of support, with the use, inter alia, of European Union funds and other means, e.g., public and private. Examples of such measures are presented in Tables 7.3 and 7.4.

The presented examples of additional initiatives, mainly projects, confirm the commitment to professional activation and employment promotion of refugees from Ukraine, which exceeded the obligations imposed by law on public employment services and also fostered the involvement of other partners. The diversity and comprehensiveness of support for refugees depended, inter alia, on the commitment of employees of public employment services, the availability of funds for this purpose, as well as the interest of refugees themselves in professional activation and in taking advantage of opportunities offered to them.

7.4 The Involvement of Public Employment Services in the Activation of Refugees on the Polish Labour Market – Results of Interviews

As mentioned earlier, the effects of the increased inflow of Ukrainian refugees into Poland first affected Polish border regions and their public employment services. The situation resulted in the strengthening of cooperation between these institutions and self-governments as well as social organisations, which have jointly supported war migrants. This was due to the mixed nature of the support expected by refugees. They were interested

Table 7.2 Good practices with regard to the form of support for unemployed refugees by poviat labour offices in border regions

No	*Name*	*Description*
1	Launch of a network of information points	"First contact" points to recognise the refugee's situation and offer comprehensive assistance both in the registration as an unemployed person and in obtaining other types of support from various institutions. Points operated by employees fluent in Ukrainian, Russian, and English.
2	Assistance in drawing up an Individual Action Plan	Trained Customer Advisers worked with refugees to prepare professional activation plans (the so-called Individual Action Plans), presenting them earlier with the whole spectrum of available labour market instruments together with an indication of future employment opportunities in Poland. This helped to ensure that the plans were realistic and tailored to the individual potential of the unemployed migrants, and also took into account the planned duration of their stay in Poland.
3	Short-term information and promotion campaigns	Most often 1-day campaigns, undertaken in cooperation with business partners (companies, chambers of commerce), social partners (self-governments, NGOs) as well as local media and social media (also in Ukrainian). They aimed to arouse refugees' interest in selected labour market instruments, e.g., internships, public works, trainings, language courses, etc.
4	Creating a diversified employment offer	A diversified employment offer has been prepared for refugees, taking into account their personal plans related to the duration of their stay in Poland: • Short-term offer (e.g., seasonal work, public works, intervention work). • A long-term offer (e.g., internships together with vocational training and language courses).
5	Individual support in applying for employment	In cooperation with businesses, municipalities, and NGOs, databases of local job offers have been created and published on websites in Ukrainian (e.g., www.gospodarczy.lublin.eu/ukraina). Persons interested in applying for jobs received expert support in preparing their application documents and the poviat labour office also covered the cost of their travel to the interviews.
6	Mapping potential refugee employment sites and informing employers about the benefits of hiring Ukrainians	After identifying the competences of refugees interested in taking up employment in the area, employees of poviat labour offices individually contacted companies operating in the relevant sector and inquired about their interest in employing unemployed Ukrainians, also informing entrepreneurs about possible support for those newly employed, e.g., funding of commuting to work or childcare, funding of courses and training, or covering the costs of creating a workplace for a Ukrainian employee.

Source: Own study based on https://wuplublin.praca.gov.pl/pomocdlaukrainy/wsparcie; https://rzeszow.uw.gov.pl/pomagamukrainie (accessed: 27.11.2023).

Table 7.3 Example of measures for professional activation of Ukrainian war refugees in the Lublin Voivodeship (2022–2023)

No	*Title of the project*	*Objective of the project*	*Description of measures*
1	"Zapytaj o pracę" (Ask for a job) – Labour market activation programme responding to the inflow of refugees from Ukraine	Creation of a transparent and simple system for employers to provide information on vacancies and willingness to hire refugees from Ukraine. Sending a clear message to refugees with little knowledge of the realities of the Polish labour market, who chose to seek employment on their own.	1 A promotional campaign in the media and through a dedicated website, carried out in cooperation with business support institutions, indicating how employers interested in employing refugees can communicate with Ukrainians looking for a job. 2 Development and dissemination of a uniform graphic symbol, which has become a form of expression of the willingness of companies in the region to employ Ukrainian citizens immediately; distribution – business support institutions. 3 Placing the symbol on the doors, signs, advertisements, and fences of businesses that have participated in the migrant employment action. 4 Informing refugees that there are job offers waiting for them in the places marked with this symbol. 5 Adequate preparation of recruiters responsible for hiring Ukrainians in the companies concerned to communicate with migrants.
2	Professional aptitude verification system as an instrument of assistance for inactive people	Professional activation of the long-term unemployed people and persons under 30 years of age who are unemployed, as well as migrants from Ukraine – pilot initiative of the Ministry of Family and Social Policy "Stable work – strong family"	1 Introducing a so-called "vocational test", giving the unemployed a package of benefits, i.e., a free vocational counselling service and an opportunity to observe the profession they would like to pursue in the future under natural working conditions ("testing" both the candidate under natural working conditions and his or her perception of the profession). 2 Unemployed refugees participating in the project also received references from a potential employer, specifying their aptitude for a particular profession. 3 The project participant was "paired" with a selected employer and, after confirming his or her aptitude for a particular job, was given the chance to stay with the company, where he or she took a vocational test. 4 Employers received a package of benefits in the form of a cash bonus of PLN 1,000 (reimbursement of costs related to the presence of a project participant during "testing"), but could also easily acquire in this way an employee with the right competences. This allowed to reduce recruitment costs and quickly introduce an employee to work (training).

(*Continued*)

Table 7.3 (Continued)

No	*Title of the project*	*Objective of the project*	*Description of measures*
3	Polish-Ukrainian Meeting for Jobs	Direct exchange of information between refugee jobseekers and employers representing different sectors.	Organisation of a job fair with participation of ca 80 employers, interpreters, advisers, and specialists providing, inter alia, legal advice to refugees (ca. 3,500 people). The programme included: 1 Presentation of current information about potential employers, their potential, job offers, recruitment plans, and requirements for future employees. 2 Workshop on self-presentation during a job interview. 3 Instruction in the preparation of documents for setting up a business.

Source: Voivodeship Labour Office in Lublin.

Table 7.4 Example of measures for professional activation of Ukrainian war refugees in the Subcarpathian Voivodeship (2022–2023)

No	*Title of the project*	*Objective of the project*	*Description of measures*
1	Subcarpathian Centre for Integration of Foreigners	Active integration of Ukrainian refugees through the establishment of the Subcarpathian Centre for Integration of Foreigners	Activities of the Subcarpathian Centre for Integration of Foreigners include the following offer for refugees: 1 Learning the Polish language (at various levels). 2 Interpreter services. 3 Psychological support. 4 Legal advice. 5 All kinds of specialised courses needed to improve qualifications/competences. 6 Assistance in the nostrification of diplomas and certification of competences. 7 Care for dependants (children and elderly) during training or other support under the project. 8 Organisation of support for refugee children: workshops in schools, summer camps, and half-day camps for children with Polish language lessons.

(*Continued*)

Table 7.4 (Continued)

No	*Title of the project*	*Objective of the project*	*Description of measures*
2	"Razem Możemy Więcej" (Together We Can Do More) – Activation Programme for Foreigners in Subcarpathian Voivodeship	Increase in attractiveness of unemployed Ukrainian refugees on the labour market	1 Meetings with a vocational counsellor and working out a support path for the unemployed person and his or her family during their stay in Poland. 2 Meetings with a psychologist. 3 Polish language courses. 4 Workshops on active job search. 5 Workshop on conducting business in Poland. 6 Advice on finding and applying for available training, courses, or other forms of education. 7 Support and financing of formalities related to the recognition of education and qualifications (nostrification of foreign university diplomas).
3	Subcarpathian Support Centre for Ukrainian Citizens	Social, administrative, and professional adaptation of Ukrainian citizens migrating to Poland.	1 Legal support: accepting legal cases and their follow-up in cooperation with solicitors and legal counsels, assistance in the preparation of documents, letters, and contracts, and legal information. 2 Administrative support: assistance in filling in official documents and forms as well as setting up a trusted profile and using other official platforms, assistance with other official matters. 3 Employment support: assistance in filling in employment forms and their follow-up in administration offices, assistance in acquiring job offers, assistance in starting a business.

Source: Voivodeship Labour Office in Rzeszów.

both in legalising their stay in Poland and obtaining a PESEL number, as well as in the conditions to be fulfilled to apply for benefits, the possibilities of the labour market activation, and obtaining other forms of assistance, e.g., psychological support, medical assistance, and free clothing or food. With such a large wave of refugees, it could not reasonably be expected to refer each person to separate institutions for individual information, as this would significantly delay the whole process of providing support. Therefore, many labour offices acted as a comprehensive information centre for migrants who contacted them to get help not only with work issues but also with family or housing issues. These institutions cooperated closely with poviat family assistance centres, social affairs departments in cities, and municipal offices, and also with non-governmental organisations, e.g., Caritas, PCK, and Polish Humanitarian Action, as well as social economy entities and professional integration centres, in order to provide migrants with the most comprehensive support possible.

Thanks to the fact that it was possible to introduce, in a relatively short period, legal regulations facilitating the support of refugees on the Polish labour market, information chaos was avoided, and Ukrainians were provided with basic social and living conditions and prospects of taking up employment in Poland on the same basis as citizens of the European Union Member States. At the same time, cross-regional consultations were held between various labour market institutions in order to develop a common approach to the professional activation of war migrants.

Limiting factors in this respect included the lack of knowledge about the specific nature of war refugees, and mainly female war refugees, as a target group in the labour market. This group was clearly different from economic migrants from Ukraine, who have been present on the Polish labour market for many years. It should be mentioned here that all surveyed poviat labour offices have at least several years of experience in mediating between Ukrainian employers and Polish employees, as well as in other activities related to the international flow of employees, inter alia within the EURES network, e.g., the EU Talent Pool sub-site dedicated to employees from Ukraine (Eures, 2023). Previous analyses of the cross-border labour market carried out by these institutions focused on assessing the inflow of labour from Ukraine to Poland, but they only took into account economic migration. Thus, there was no detailed knowledge on how to activate war migrants in the labour market. In addition, shortly after the outbreak of the war (March–April 2022), border regions recorded an outflow of economic migrants from Ukraine who returned to their country to take part in the fighting. They were mostly men employed in occupations such as, for example, drivers in passenger and freight transport, construction workers, and IT professionals. However, this temporary destabilisation of the labour market disappeared after a few months (Dębkowska et al., 2023) when the vacancies were filled by Polish employees.

The analysis of the involvement of Polish labour market institutions in assistance for Ukrainians should take into account the fact that the outbreak of the war in Ukraine overlapped with intensive involvement of the staff of these institutions in accounting for the support of entrepreneurs by the state within the framework of the so-called "anti-crisis shield", which was set up in connection with the negative impact of COVID-19 pandemic on the economy (Dębkowska et al., 2021). Meanwhile, after February 24, 2022, public employment services in Poland also had to quickly get acquainted with the new terms of employment of Ukrainians in Poland, which were introduced by the Act of March 12, 2022, and then launch an information campaign on these legislative solutions at the level of voivodeships and poviats, addressed primarily to refugees but also to employers, business support institutions, the media, NGOs, or self-government units. These measures were carried out within the existing budgets, as labour market institutions did not receive any additional funds from the state, e.g., for increased services for the unemployed or vocational counselling for Ukrainian migrants. Such funds were later obtained, inter alia, from the reserve of the Labour Fund and were used to support unemployed foreigners. They were used, inter alia, for work placements for migrants, refunds for workplace equipment, or costs of migrants' start-ups.

According to interviews with representatives of labour market institutions from the Polish border regions, the issue of getting a job was not a priority for Ukrainians arriving at reception and information points. More important were issues of livelihood, housing, social security, etc. Therefore, labour market institutions gained time to properly prepare themselves for the growing wave of interest in finding a job by Ukrainian migrants. The process of their professional activation was often difficult and multi-stage. The largest number of migrants contacted poviat labour offices in former voivodeship cities: Zamość, Chełm, and Biała Podlaska, but also Lublin and Rzeszów.

The first cumulation of Ukrainian refugees' interest in taking up employment in the Polish border regions was noted in April 2022, when a relatively large group of migrants had already arrived in Poland. Some of them expected vocational counselling and guidance on how to seek employment as close to the Ukrainian border as possible in order to return to their country. During the period of field and seasonal work (May–September 2022), the refugee labour supply could be satisfied by engaging at least some of them in agricultural, horticultural, or processing work. According to the Voivodeship Labour Office in Lublin, almost every third employer of Ukrainians was involved in growing trees, fruit bushes, and vegetables, agri-food processing, warehousing, and storage of goods. At the same time, employers from the Lublin and Subcarpathian Voivodeships were gradually increasing their demand for the employment of migrants in simple jobs in catering, warehousing, housekeeping, caring, as well as cosmetic and hairdressing services, i.e., where the language barrier was relatively easy to overcome.

In connection with the inflow of Ukrainian refugees to Poland, both voivodeship and poviat labour offices faced challenges regarding the provision of specific vocational counselling services to migrants whose professional experience, often solid, was not much useful in the Polish labour market (e.g., accountants, accounting specialists, etc.) due to different business conditions. Such persons had to be offered, in the first instance, supplementary education or new qualifications, taking into account the barometer of expected shortage and surplus professions in Poland. For migrants interested in improving their professional qualifications, it is possible to use the National Training Fund with the participation of interested employers. This required, however, an assurance from the migrant that he or she intended to take up employment for a longer time. A significant factor reducing refugees' attractiveness on the labour market was the temporary stay in Poland announced by them, which discouraged some employers from investing in their skills development and offering them permanent employment. The experience of the labour offices shows that in 2022, in the vast majority of cases, migrants were unfortunately working below their professional qualifications.

As regards the impact of the war in Ukraine on the activities of public employment services in border voivodeships, interviews conducted in 2022 with representatives of these institutions show that:

- Labour market institutions in the Lublin and Subcarpathian Voivodeships had been noting increased interest in economic migration of Ukrainians to Poland for several years. They knew the typical professional profiles of persons arriving in border regions from Ukraine and were aware of the demand of entrepreneurs in the region for migrants' employment. They also knew the motivations and expectations of this group towards employment in Poland, but they did not have any recognition of war refugees from Ukraine as a separate target group in the labour market.
- Economic migrants arriving from Ukraine to seek work most often filled gaps in labour supply in low-paid, though not always shortage occupations, but also in occupations where labour shortage was noted in the local environment; in this way, migrants contributed to a certain equilibrium in the labour market in the border regions, while the arrival in these regions of a large wave of war refugees, mainly women caring for children, changed the state of play in this market.
- Ukrainian economic migrants were well informed on the situation on the Polish labour market and usually looked for a job on their own, most often coming to a specific employer who offered them employment, while refugees initially had a very poor knowledge of the Polish labour market and required very large individual support.
- The arrival of war migrants in the Polish border regions has, in a way, obliged the employees of the poviat and voivodeship labour offices to take up new challenges connected with a different type of migration and other expectations of unemployed persons who expected the labour market support.
- Not all procedures and instruments of support for war migrants were introduced from the first days of the war in Ukraine, many measures were only taken as a response to the situation, when there were indications for such support to be expected or useful.
- The professional provision of support to refugees also required specific competences on the part of the staff (communicative and substantive), which had yet to be developed, e.g., through consultation or training.
- Public employment services sought to use the EU funds at their disposal until the end of 2022 and involved both Polish and Ukrainian unemployed persons in activation measures.

- In the face of the refugee crisis, public employment services were motivated to intensify their cooperation with various types of partners: social and business ones, which complemented their capacity to provide war migrants with the expected support.
- In view of the high dynamics of events, the professional activation of war migrants was carried out under conditions of uncertainty because some migrants decided overnight to return to their country and did not continue employment, training, internships, etc. This caused a number of formal problems in assessing the efficiency of the support provided.
- In the absence of a specific and coherent national strategy for dealing with refugees in the labour market, individual institutions developed in parallel their own ad hoc solutions, and for this reason, the extent and availability of support in different parts of the border regions could differ.

As regards the expectations of war refugees from Ukraine towards employment in Poland as recorded by the public employment services in the Polish border regions, the survey focused primarily on two issues:

- Refugees' expectations of the support provided by public employment services in Poland.
- Barriers to the professional activation of refugees in Poland.

The results of the survey should be read in the context of the specific nature of the target group of war refugees who were to be supported by Polish labour market institutions. The survey revealed that in 2022, in the Polish border regions, the group of Ukrainian refugees was by far outnumbered by women. The largest group of female-refugees interested in taking up a job were in the 25–44 age bracket and had specialised qualifications and professional experience in positions such as manager, doctor, teacher, engineer, lawyer, etc. There were far fewer women performing simple manual jobs or with no professional qualifications. Most of the surveyed poviat labour offices declared that the majority of migrants had professional experience in commercial companies, and it was only in a few labour offices that a predominance of people with experience in employment in the budgetary sphere was observed. The majority of migrants coming to Poland knew foreign languages (English and Russian), but only at a basic level, and the did not have communicative knowledge of Polish.

The clearly defined professional profile of most female war refugees and their experience of working in narrowly specialised positions did not facilitate finding employment in Poland, inter alia, due to the different conditions for many professions (e.g., teacher and lawyer), the necessity to nostrify diplomas (e.g., doctor), or the lack of knowledge of Polish, impeding, inter alia, work with the customer. This was one of the key reasons for the demotivation of many migrant women to seek jobs in Poland.

In all poviat labour offices surveyed in 2022, female-refugees interested in employment declared their willingness to work full-time, but in the vast majority of cases, they did not declare a period of employment, or declared a period of one to three months. This was one of the barriers limiting the possibilities of their professional activation in Poland. The expected net remuneration was PLN 2,000–3,000, while there were also expectations regarding other benefits (see Table 7.5).

Most of the benefits in respect of employment listed in Table 7.5 were included in job offers available in the surveyed poviat labour offices; however, in each case, their availability depended on the terms agreed upon between the unemployed person and the prospective employer. For example, although all surveyed offices offered refugees the possibility to take advantage of vocational courses and trainings, in many cases, the lack of an unequivocal migrants' decision as to the duration of their planned stay in Poland became a real obstacle to finding an employer interested in their additional professional training and contributing to the cost of such training. There were also identified other barriers to refugees becoming economically active (see Table 7.6).

The majority of refugees visiting labour offices, after learning about the working conditions and the requirements to be fulfilled by candidates for different positions, including formal requirements regarding, e.g., education,

Table 7.5 Additional benefits in respect of employment of interest to Ukrainian refugees seeking jobs in Poland

No	*Type of benefit (X – present)*	*The surveyed poviat labour offices according to subsection 3.3 – random order*															
		1	*2*	*3*	*4*	*5*	*6*	*7*	*8*	*9*	*10*	*11*	*12*	*13*	*14*	*15*	*16*
1	Discretionary bonus				X					X		X	X	X	X		
2	Overtime bonus				X					X			X				
3	Subsidies for vocational training and language learning					X									X	X	X
4	Child care	X	X	X		X	X	X	X	X					X		X
5	Vocational guidance and courses								X			X	X				
6	Flexible working hours	X	X					X		X		X		X		X	
7	Reimbursement of commuting expenses		X				X			X	X				X		
8	Additional medical care		X														

Source: Research findings.

Table 7.6 Barriers hindering Ukrainian refugees from seeking jobs in Poland

No	*Type of barrier (X – present)*	*The surveyed poviat labour offices according to subsection 3.3. – random order*															
		1	2	3	4	5	6	7	8	9	10	11	12	13	14	15	16
1	Poor knowledge of the Polish language	X	X		X	X	X	X	X	X				X			X
2	Lack of documented education	X	X		X					X	X	X	X			X	
3	Lack of childcare facilities		X			X								X			
4	Poor housing conditions						X	X	X		X						
5	Poor knowledge of the labour market in Poland			X		X	X					X	X	X			X
6	Lack of suitable job opportunities								X	X	X	X	X	X	X	X	X

Source: Research findings.

and taking into account the barriers presented in Table 7.6, have decided to be employed only in positions related to the performance of simple tasks. These included the following positions: cook and kitchen helper, maintenance worker for cleaning work, warehouseman, child, and elderly carer, production worker, waiter, bartender, salesperson, beautician, hairdresser, as well as nurse and salesperson. These positions were filled by people who either had suitable qualifications (e.g., nurse, hairdresser, and cook) or the positions involved such simple tasks that a short apprenticeship was sufficient.

According to the voivodeship and poviat labour offices, migrants from Ukraine who were interested in employment in Poland received sufficient support from these institutions in terms of:

- Vocational counselling.
- Assistance in finding job offers and preparing for job applications.
- Training to improve existing professional competences and enable vocational reorientation.
- Language training.
- Psychological and motivational support.
- Internships and apprenticeships to get better acquainted with the conditions of employment for specific positions in Poland.

This support corresponded to the scale of interest in refugees activation in the labour market and even exceeded the declared interest. There were no situations in which persons waiting for support did not receive it from the public employment services, but there were cases where, due to a mismatch between qualifications and job offers, a language barrier, an inability to meet the conditions for employment (e.g., through childcare or psychological trauma caused by the war), as well as a change of residence or a return to the country – support and employment have not been materialised. In the case of refugees, there was a high degree of variability in decisions about the place of residence. During the first contact related to the start of support, it was difficult to determine which refugees would decide to stay in the border regions and want to further receive the support of the labour market institutions and which would decide to relocate to another region of Poland and at that point the support provided by the labour market institution would be discontinued.

Certainly not all migrants have received the job offers they expected. According to the interviews, some refugees did not want to take up employment at the rates offered to them, often at the level of the minimum national wage. The underemployment of Ukrainian refugees who wanted to work was also due to a number of other reasons, including some of the barriers outlined in Table 5.9. At the same time, the new tasks imposed by the legislator on the voivodeship and poviat labour offices (Act of 12 March 2022) required the employees of these institutions to be even more involved in the tasks carried out than during the passing pandemic period. In this respect, such measures were taken as were possible.

Using the funds available to labour market institutions for the organisation of intervention works and public works, employment was also offered to refugees with a background in, e.g., office work or as teaching assistants (e.g., in schools and kindergartens) in city and poviat offices and subordinate units. In addition, e.g., at the Poviat Labour Office in Zamość, persons of Ukrainian nationality who were fluent in Ukrainian have been employed as job placement officers for contacts between refugees and Polish employers. These employees have also maintained social media accounts in Ukrain.

According to the representatives of labour market institutions surveyed in 2022, it should be expected that in the long term, some Ukrainian migrants would adapt to the Polish labour market and develop their professional careers here, as well as become involved in social and local life, perhaps bring their families and settle permanently. The increase in multiculturalism and the inflow of migrants into the Polish labour market also require a number of adaptation measures on the part of employers, ranging from changes in organisational culture to changes in interpersonal relations (e.g., getting rid of stereotypes and national antagonisms) and to changes in the way employees are motivated and in internal communication within companies. Developing positive relations between foreigners seeking employment in Poland and their future employers is one of the new strategic challenges for labour market institutions in Poland.

7.5 Conclusions

In the period 2022–2022, Polish labour market institutions had to meet the challenges connected with the labour market stabilisation in the face of turbulence caused by at least two crises: the COVID-19 pandemic and the very rapid inflow of refugees to Poland after February 24, 2022. In particular, the latter crisis has changed the supply side of the labour market. The wave of wartime migration from Ukraine differed fundamentally from migration of persons who had arrived in Poland from across the eastern border before February 24, 2022, primarily in terms of a conviction of the temporary nature of their stay in Poland, weaker motivation to take up gainful employment, and insufficient preparation for entering the labour market in Poland.

The appearance of war migrants on the Polish labour market, as a new and previously poorly recognised target group in Poland, required a new approach to active labour market policies. This has resulted in swift learning on the part of public employment services, an increase in the organisational agility of these institutions, a reduction in resistance to change, and a greater openness to innovative, even experimental, tools for the professional activation of refugees. An important organisational benefit for all labour market institutions was also the development of networking with a wide range of public, social, and business partners, which took place on such a large scale. The voivodeship labour offices and poviat labour offices were closest to the problems of refugees on the Polish labour market and took measures at the local level to activate war migrants in cooperation with the voivodes.

The border voivodeships – Lublin and Subcarpathian – have provided increased support to refugees, because they dealt with all war migrants crossing the Polish border. Most Ukrainians then decided to relocate to other regions of Poland or to other countries, but many remained in the Polish-Ukrainian border area. The most frequently indicated motivations to stay in the border area were: familiarity with the area due to previous arrivals for tourist or economic purposes, having family or friends in the border area, the desire to stay in an area that is culturally and linguistically close, and the desire to stay as close as possible to the borders of one's home country.

Poland's role as a frontline state has compounded the challenges connected with the need to efficiently plan the measures aimed to mitigate the impact of the refugee crisis on the labour market. This was influenced by:

- The unpredictability of the development of the conflict in Ukraine and the threat of its spilling over into neighbouring countries.
- The specific role of Poland in taking care of the refugees as soon as they cross the borders of the European Union, e.g., legalising the stay of Ukrainians on the territory of the European Union, providing them with first medical assistance, providing them with a place to rest, etc.
- Logistical tasks related to further directing the movement of refugees from the Polish border regions inland, as well as to other EU countries.

All these circumstances also determined the activities of public employment services in Poland.

The efficient performance of tasks related to the activation of refugees was greatly influenced by the special Act on assistance to citizens of Ukraine in connection with the armed conflict on the territory of that country, passed by the Polish Parliament on March 12, 2022. Under the previous conditions of foreigners' employment pursuant to the Act of 20 April 2004 on employment promotion and labour market institutions, it would be difficult for war refugees from Ukraine to find jobs in Poland, inter alia due to the high competition from migrants better prepared to take up employment in Poland. The Act of 12 March 2022 on assistance to citizens of Ukraine in connection with the armed conflict on the territory of that country has equalised the rights of Ukrainian refugees with those of citizens of the European Union. It has simplified a number of formal issues related to the employment of Ukrainians in Poland but also gave labour market institutions real tools to enable the professional activation of refugees. Migrants have acquired several rights to various forms of support for their professional development in Poland, on an equal footing with EU citizens. Poviat and voivodeship labour offices could address to them similar forms of labour market support. In many situations, additional, even innovative, measures have been also taken to support refugees in their search for job offers (e.g., by the Voivodeship Labour Office in Lublin or the Poviat Labour Office in Zamość). Good practices in this area were learnt from, inter alia, the European Commission's guidelines as well as by exchanging experiences of activities carried out by individual voivodeship and poviat labour offices and their cooperating partners.

The decentralised model of operation and the clear division of tasks carried out at poviat and voivodeship levels, as well as the time reserve between the moment refugees arrived in Poland and the period in which they started looking for a job, allowed to ensure efficient support for war refugees by labour market institutions. Finding employment was not a priority for Ukrainian war refugees, who primarily sought refuge in Poland from Russian aggression and only secondarily took steps to secure a livelihood during their stay in Poland.

A very good tool to support refugee jobseekers proved to be Individual Action Plans, which the war migrants drew up for themselves in cooperation with their customer advisers, i.e., vocational counsellors and job placement officers in poviat labour offices. They have structured the activation process of many refugees on the Polish labour market and have comprehensively identified career opportunities for them in Poland.

Polish public employment services have also shown a great deal of initiative and creativity when preparing special support tools for migrants, tailored to identified needs, such as creating a diversified employment offer (short-term and long-term), mapping potential refugee employment sites, engaging refugees to test professions for a trial period, etc.

Numerous barriers to the professional activation of refugees have been identified, including some that labour market institutions had to face for the first time on such a scale. These are mainly concerned with:

- The need to get acquainted with new statutory regulations on the employment of migrants from Ukraine and to implement them in labour market institutions.
- Poor knowledge of the phenomenon of war migration and difficulties in matching support to the actual needs of refugees (at least in the first months of the war).
- A shortage of professionals who had a background in vocational counselling for refugees.
- Internal migration of Ukrainians between different regions in Poland made it difficult to provide support.
- The mismatch between the competences and qualifications of migrants and the needs of the labour market in Poland and insufficient knowledge of the Polish language.
- Lack of childcare.

In addition, in many cases, wage expectations and expectations of other wage benefits (bonuses, reimbursement of commuting expenses, etc.), as well as non-acceptance of the offered job (often below the migrant's qualifications), stood in the way of the migrant's successful employment. A variety of job offers awaited Ukrainian migrants in Poland; however, despite many labour market activation measures, the inability to document education or professional qualifications in many cases proved to be a barrier to taking up employment. The results of the interviews also indicate another very important factor determining the motivation for labour market activation – the declared duration of stay in Poland. A very large number of war migrants stipulated in advance that they planned to stay in Poland for only a few months, did not associate their future with Poland, and planned to return to their country once the military threat ceased. Such declarations made it difficult or even impossible to take advantage of certain labour market instruments, e.g., internships, trainings, and courses, as people taking advantage of such forms of support were expected to stay longer in their jobs. Employers were also interested in hiring refugees who have declared a desire for professional development in the long term and showed a high level of motivation to get a job. Migrants who were determined to stay in Poland for as short a time as possible had much weaker motivation to find a job.

References

Act of 20 April 2004 on Employment Promotion and Labour Market Institutions; Journal of Laws of 2023, item 735.

Act of 12 March 2022 on Assistance to Citizens of Ukraine in Connection with Armed Conflict on the Territory of That Country; Journal of Laws of 2022, item 583, as amended.

Bieniek-Majka, M., & Stupałkowska, U. (2022). Uchodźcy z Ukrainy na powiatowym rynku pracy. Studium przypadku. *Nierówności Społeczne a Wzrost Gospodarczy*, *71*, 169–182.

Blanchard, O. (2006). European unemployment: The evolution of facts and ideas. *Economic Policy*, 21(45), 6–59.

Bogacz-Wojtanowska, E. (2007). *Modele współpracy lokalnych instytucji a rozwiązywanie problemów rynku pracy*. Wydawnictwo Uniwersytetu Jagiellońskiego.

Castles, S., & Miller, M. J. (2009). *The age of migration. International population movements in the modern world*. Palgrave Macmillan.

Cortes, G. M., & Forsythe, E. (2023). Heterogeneous labor market impacts of the COVID-19 pandemic. *ILR Review*, *76*(1), 30–55.

Cyranowicz, Ż. (2023). Pośrednictwo pracy teraz i po wejściu w życie przepisów ustawy o aktywności zawodowej. *Rynek Pracy*, *184*(1), 27–38.

Dębkowska, K., Kłosiewicz-Górecka, U., Szymańska, A., Ważniewski, P., & Zybertowicz, K. (2021). *Tarcza Antykryzysowa... Koło ratunkowe dla firm i gospodarki?* Polski Instytut Ekonomiczny. https://pie.net.pl/tarcza-antykryzysowa-kolo-ratunkowe-dla-firm-i-gospodarki/

Dębkowska, K., Kłosiewicz-Górecka, U., Szymańska, A., Wejt-Knyżewska, A., & Zybertowicz, K. (2023). *Wpływ wojny w Ukrainie na działalność polskich firm*. Polski Instytut Ekonomiczny. https://pie.net.pl/wp-content/uploads/2023/02/Wplyw-wojny-na-PL-firmy.pdf

Długosz, P., Kryvachuk, L., & Izdebska-Długosz, D. (2022). *Uchodźcy wojenni z Ukrainy – życie w Polsce i plany na przyszłość*. Wydawnictwo Academicon.

EURES. (2023). *EU Talent Pool Pilot*. https://eures.ec.europa.eu/eu-talent-pool-pilot_en

European Commission Communication of 14.06.2022 C(2022) 4050 final entitled Guidance for access to the labour market, vocational education and training and adult learning of people fleeing Russia's war of aggression against Ukraine. https://eur-lex.europa.eu/legal-content/EN/TXT/?uri=CELEX%3A52022XC0616%2801%29

Flaszyńska, E. et al. (2022). Pracownicy z Ukrainy–perspektywa polska i europejska. *Edukacja Ustawiczna Dorosłych*, *116*(1), 79–101.

Frączek, M. et al. (2015). Praktyka realizacji polityki rynku pracy w Polsce a współzarządzanie publiczne. *Zarządzanie Publiczne*, 32, 25–40.

Górniak, J. (2015). *Polski rynek pracy – wyzwania i kierunki działań*. Polska Agencja Rozwoju Przedsiębiorczości.

Heckman, J., & Pagés, C. (2000). The cost of job security regulation: Evidence from latin American labor markets. *Economia*, *1*(1), 1–44.

Kalmár, A. (2015). Viewpoints to labour mobility development. *Journal of Contemporary Economic and Business Issues*, 2(1), 47–57.

Kałuża-Kopias, D. (2023). Atrakcyjność powiatów grodzkich dla migrantów zarobkowych z Ukrainy z perspektywy rozwoju społeczno-gospodarczego. *Migracje i rozwój regionu*, *179*, 167–184.

Kuźmar, S. (2015). Rola instytucji rynku pracy w Polsce w latach 2000–2011. *Nierówności społeczne a wzrost gospodarczy*, 42, 353–366.

Lehmann, H., & Muravyev, A. (2012). Labor market institutions and labor market performance: What can we learn from transition countries? *Economics of Transition*, *20*(2), 235–269.

Machniewski, S. (2022). *Jak wojna w Ukrainie zmienia rynek pracy w Polsce?* money.pl https://www.money.pl/gospodarka/jak-wojna-w-ukrainie-zmienia-rynek-pracy-w-polsce-6776861907364416a.html

Majka, P., Rydzewska, M., & Wieleba, I. (2022). *Zatrudnianie cudzoziemców. Aspekty prawne, pracownicze i podatkowe Ze szczególnym uwzględnieniem obywateli Ukrainy*. Wolters Kluwer.

Ministerstwo Rodziny i Polityki Społecznej. (2022). *Uchodźcy na rynku pracy w Polsce*. Warszawa.

Nickell, S., & Layard, R. (1999). Labour market Institutions and economic performance. In O. Ashenfelter, & D. Card (Eds.), *Handbook of labor economics*. Vol. 3, Part C, p. 3029–3084, https://doi.org/10.1016/S1573-4463(99)30037-7.

OECD. (2023). *Active Labour Market Policies: Connecting People with Jobs*. https://www.oecd.org/employment/activation.htm

Ostoj, I. (2010). Instytucje rynku pracy jako system: Problemy projektowania i oceny. *Prace Naukowe Uniwersytetu Ekonomicznego we Wrocławiu*, *111*, 533–547

Panasiuk, J., Baryła, T., & Wiatrów, M. (2023). Projekt nowych przepisów o zatrudnianiu cudzoziemców: Ciągłość i zmiana–pomiędzy elastycznością i potrzebami rynku pracy a szeroko rozumianym bezpieczeństwem i ochroną praw cudzoziemców. *Rynek Pracy*, *184*(1), 93–106.

Przeklasa, D. (2021). Współpraca między publicznymi służbami zatrudnienia a agencjami zatrudnienia w zakresie realizacji polityki rynku pracy. *Acta Iuridica Resoviensia*, 4(35), 346–361.

Rollnik-Sadowska, E. (2019). *Efektywność instytucji publicznych–przykład powiatowych urzędów pracy w Polsce. Pojęcie, determinanty, metodyka pomiaru [Effectiveness of public institutions-example of poviat labour offices in Poland. Concept, determinants, measurement methodology]*. Oficyna Wydawnicza Politechniki Białostockiej.

Sałtykowa-Wołkowicz, M. (2023). Problemy i cechy socjalizacji uchodźców z Ukrainy w Polsce. In E. Czykwin, & I. Kochan (Eds.), *Człowiek w przestrzeni życia społecznego*, collective work (p. 59). Wydawnictwo Naukowe Chrześcijańskiej Akademii Teologicznej w Warszawie.

Stowarzyszenie Interwencji Prawnej. (2023). *Ustawa o pomocy obywatelom Ukrainy*. https://ukraina.interwencjaprawna.pl/ustawa-o-pomocy-obywatelom-ukrainy

Terczyńska, B. (2023). *Obywatele Ukrainy na podkarpackim rynku pracy. Oto najnowsze dane Wojewódzkiego Urzędu Pracy*. nowiny24.pl. https://nowiny24.pl/obywatele-ukrainy-na-podkarpackim-rynku-pracy-oto-najnowsze-dane-wojewodzkiego-urzedu-pracy/ar/c10-17455173

Urząd Marszałkowski Województwa Lubelskiego, Departament Strategii i Rozwoju. (2022), Raport o pomocy udzielonej Ukrainie przez Województwo Lubelskie. https://strategia.lubelskie.pl/rot/opracowania/raport.wsparcie.ua.pdf

8 Non-Governmental Organisations' Support for Ukrainian War Refugees on the Polish Labour Market

8.1 Activity of Non-Governmental Organisations as Social Economy Entities Supporting Migrants

The obligation to take care of refugees is vested, in principle, in the host state; however, in practice, it is often difficult to provide this group with sufficient support while relying only on public institutions. Therefore, social economy entities, including, among others, non-governmental organisations and other entities specialising in various forms of support for disfavoured people, play such a significant role in measures undertaken to support refugees (Fehsenfeld & Levinsen, 2019, pp. 422–435). Many countries recognise the solution of including social partners, as well as business sector representatives in the cooperation network of institutions representing the government and self-government administration, which provides people at the risk of exclusion with the most comprehensive support, allowing social integration and activation on the labour market (Beaman, 2012, pp. 128–161). Diversified and, at the same time, comprehensive support is especially important in crisis situations, e.g., when we deal with groups that require provision of specialist social services, or if the support has to cover a very large group of people. Both factors occurred in the case of an increased inflow of war refugees from Ukraine to Poland after February 24, 2022.

Practice shows that in many cases social economy entities are more effective in executing social tasks than officials or commercial entities. Social economy entities focus on the implementation of measures addressing the needs of the entire society and particular groups of citizens, among others, counteracting social marginalisation and exclusion, providing specific social services, establishing stable workplaces, and shaping entrepreneurship and socially responsible approaches (Valle-Mestre et al., 2022, pp. 651–665). Social mission plays a more important role in their activity than economic objectives (Weerawardena et al., 2021, pp. 762–771). Therefore, they implement projects concerning provision of very specific services or production of very specific goods by a certain community in partial or full independence from the public sector (Muñoz & Kimmitt, 2019, pp. 854–861) and on non-market conditions.

DOI: 10.4324/9781003471646-8

A key pillar of the social economy sector is made up of non-government organisations, which can implement a wide spectrum of socially important tasks. These tasks are performed with the use of different narrations than in the case of the public and commercial sectors. It can be stated that non-governmental organisations meet needs that are not, according to state and self-government authorities, primary, generate additional expenditures, engage too large organisational resources, or needs that do not fit into the political, social, or cultural mainstream (Lewis et al., 2020). Non-governmental organisations generate and produce social services that require specific resources or competences, solve specific social issues on a local scale, and create new workplaces (Hasmath et al., 2019, pp. 267–284).

Vocational activation and encouraging the spirit of entrepreneurship are important elements of social missions of many non-governmental organisations. Activity of these organisations is the most visible in the following dimensions:

- As supplementation of activities performed by other entities, e.g., public employment services, business incubators, economic activity zones, etc.
- As support in the form of providing social services on the labour market, especially for the unemployed and people searching for employment (Hope & Martelli, 2019, pp. 236–288).
- As an element of creating human capital, establishing specific workplaces in various, often flexible forms, e.g., social cooperatives, worker cooperatives, etc.

Non-governmental organisations' activities on the labour market are determined by many factors, such as:

- Being at a disposal of competent specialists with experience in provision of specific social services to the unemployed (both wage workers and co-workers running their own business activities, as well as volunteers).
- Being at a disposal of (own and foreign) funds and material resources (e.g., premises, fixed assets, and other elements of equipment, software, etc.) necessary to implement organisation's mission.
- Organisational potential and relational capital to cooperate with other labour market actors, e.g., public or commercial institutions (Zapata & Campos, 2023, pp. 1–21).
- Ability to swiftly react to processes that require intervention on the labour market, e.g., refugee crisis.
- Compatibility of the organisation's social mission with the labour market development strategy.
- Demand for activities of the organisation reported by target groups intended to be covered with support and other labour market institutions.

In the literature, the positive role of non-governmental organisations in vocational activation and employment promotion, cooperation with other labour market institutions (Feischmidt et al., 2019), as well as in other vocational aspects related to migrants (Lenner & Turner, 2019, pp. 65–95), is underlined. Furthermore, these organisations constitute an opinion-forming group with impact on new regulations concerning the labour market and create social innovations in this scope (Marino & Keizer, 2023, pp. 159–176). Unfortunately, in certain situations, negative effects of the labour market on the situation of migrants, such as imposing measures adjusted to the labour market (Ndomo & Lillie, 2023, p. 161) or accelerating migrants' adaptation measures, e.g., intensification of language courses (Arendt, 2022, pp. 169–196), undermine their trust in labour market institutions and thus in social organisations engaged in such measures. Meanwhile, these entities should be more sensitised to the social and personal situation of refugees instead of following formal regulations, and their task should involve mitigating shock experienced by many refugees taking their first steps on the labour market in the host country.

In compliance with Polish legislation, non-governmental organisations can accept from public institutions orders to implement tasks in the scope of employment promotion, mitigation of unemployment effects, and vocational activation (Act of 20 April 2004 on employment promotion…, 2004). These tasks include, among others (Sienicka & Tyrowicz, 2006, p. 6):

- Providing services in the scope of employment agency, employment agency with regard to foreign employers, vocational counselling, personal guidance, and temporary work.
- Providing extracurricular education.
- Dealing with labour market issues.
- Cooperating with public employment services and the Voluntary Labour Corps in the scope of tasks stipulated in the act.
- Implementing initiatives of labour market partners.

A. Sienicka and J. Tyrowicz analyse measures of non-governmental organisations in Poland with regard to, among others, one category of foreigners, i.e., people covered by international protection pursuant to the Act of 13 June 2003 on granting protection to foreigners within the territory of the Republic of Poland (Act of 13 June 2003 on granting protection…, 2003). These are people given refugee status or supplementary protection when the foreigner is put in their country of origin at a risk of persecution or actual risk of losing life or health. In the case of people covered by international protection, non-governmental organisations:

- Provide temporary direct aid (a shelter, a school starter kit or cleaning supplies, meeting basic material needs).
- Try to influence the Polish system of their acceptance and adaptation (consultations and monitoring of implementation of legal acts, research on refugees).

- Provide free legal aid concerning recognition of a refugee status.
- Support refugees' integration process (organisation of Polish language courses and vocational training) (Sienicka & Tyrowicz, 2012, pp. 211–228).

Activity of non-governmental organisations turned out to be a necessary supplementation to the aid offered to refugees by the government and self-governments since the outbreak of war in Ukraine on 24 February 2022. Measures of Polish non-governmental organisations addressed to migrants can include, among others: information, counselling, and material assistance; legal advice, as well as vocational counselling facilitating learning about the rules of the Polish labour market functioning. They also cover promotion of multiculturalism (ventures aimed at integration of different cultures' representatives) (Davis et al., 2012) and intervention tasks (monitoring standards related to the protection of human rights, advocacy, and giving opinions). Non-governmental organisations also implement a number of measures of educational nature addressed both to migrants (free Polish language courses) and Poles (educational measures aimed at minimising stereotypes and prejudice) (Matusz-Protasiewicz & Kwieciński, 2018, pp. 125–142). The refugee crisis from 2022 also drew attention to another dimension of assistance for migrants on the labour market – namely, providing them with healthcare, care for children, psychological support, integration through cultural activities, violence prevention, activation and development of competences and skills, vocational activation, comprehensive personalised aid (a system of mentors – assistants, advisors), legal advice for migrants, as well as seminars and conferences (Szymańska, 2022, p. 2461).

Comprehensive use of the social potential of Polish non-governmental organisations due to the refugee crisis became possible also as a result of changes in legal regulations concerning social economy. The Act on social economy of 5 August 2022 defines social economy as activity of social economy entities to the benefit of the local community in the scope of social and vocational reintegration, creation of workplaces for people at a risk of social exclusion, and providing social services performed in the form of business activity, public benefit activity, and other free activity. Furthermore, the Act stipulates the catalogue of people at a risk of social exclusion, which currently includes, among others, refugees. Refugees are defined as people who obtained refugee status in Poland or are covered with supplementary protection if their return to the country of origin puts them in danger (prison, torture, and death). The following are enumerated as social economy entities given under the aforementioned Act a possibility to undertake specific measures: cooperative entities (e.g., social cooperatives and worker cooperatives), reintegration units, i.e., social integration centres and clubs, and units acting to the benefit of people with disabilities and organising occupational therapy workshops, and vocational development centres, as well as non-governmental organisations and non-profit companies, church units, local self-government associations, and farmer's wives' associations.

New legal solutions introduced under the Act of 5 August 2022 resulted in extending possibilities of providing non-governmental organisations' support for refugees and making them more flexible. In this difficult situation, Polish community workers have proven that they can cooperate with various partners and environments, are able to unite, share tasks, and manage the crisis. Self-governments and public institutions more and more often use solutions consisting of commissioning to non-governmental organisations implementation of specific tasks related to supporting refugees as the group at a risk of social exclusion. It is clearly visible in the example of aid provided to Ukrainian refugees in Poland that non-governmental organisations operate in a systemic nature, and, if necessary, replace the state that reacts with a delay or is not able to react properly. It is also an example of bottom-up de-institutionalisation changing relations between the state and the third sector. De-institutionalisation consists of departing from large institutions that are supposed to comprehensively satisfy the needs of their wards (e.g., ensuring medical and psychological assistance, alimentation, etc.), but do not provide them with the quality of life these people could achieve while staying in home environment (Bassuk & Gerson, 2022, pp. 127–144). It concerns, among others, such basic issues as the possibility of deciding how to spend their free time, daily rhythm, menu, etc. that give a sense of self-determination. While commissioning implementation of specific social tasks to non-governmental organisations, the public administration also provides them with more freedom in personalising of the support and allows them to better adjust social services to refugees' needs.

Polish social organisations are in many cases specialised entities that know migrants' needs well. They are aware of both the need to support refugees in the new environment and the necessity to prepare the society to commune with refugees in workplaces and the local environment. Only in these two areas were non-governmental organisations faced with a number of challenges that concerned supplementing state aid for war migrants. A good example of de-institutionalisation is also given by measures such as, e.g., providing migrants by many social organisations with night shelters and a stay in homes of Polish families, and not in refugee centres as was the case before the outbreak of the war. Other examples of de-institutionalising measures were indicated by S. Grabowska and AA. Pięta-Szawara (2023, pp. 389–390), who separated several dozens of tasks most frequently entrusted to non-governmental organisations to the benefit of support for refugees from Ukraine:

- Providing asylants with a safe shelter.
- Taking care of the well-being of people accepting migrants.
- Support for people with disabilities and dysfunctions.
- Support for LGBT+ people.
- Organisation of psychological support.
- Providing legal aid.
- Voluntary organisation coordination.

- Teaching Polish language and providing educational counselling.
- Transporting refugees from military zones.
- Aid for animals.
- Support in the scope of blood donation.
- Material gifts' collections.
- Fundraisers.

An important role in stabilising the situation of migrants and refugees in the host country can also be played by non-governmental organisations representing national minorities. In the case of the refugee crisis that started in February 2022, a particular role in supporting war migrants was played by organisations representing Ukrainian minorities in Poland, among others: Association of Ukrainians in Poland, Association of Ukrainians in Podlasie, PROSVITA Foundation, Ukrainian Society, Podlasie Scientific Institute Association (Serwis Rzeczypospolitej Polskiej, 2023), Ukrainian Home Foundation, and Our Choice Foundation. These organisations undertook the following types of measures, among others:

- Engagement of volunteers speaking Ukrainian and Polish in accepting refugees at reception points, next to the Polish-Ukrainian border: interpreting conversations with officials and giving information to refugees.
- Fundraising and collections for needs of war migrants who arrived in Poland.
- Fundraising and collections for Ukraine, for the needs of victims of Russian aggression against Ukraine, for the needs of warfare and needs of Ukrainian population.
- Organisation of demonstrations and other protests expressing appeals for ceasing war, imposing sanctions, and solidarity with Ukraine.

Due to noticing the auxiliary role of various non-governmental organisations in fulfilment of state's obligations towards accepted refugees, the catalogue of social services is constantly growing, in which third sector partners can supplement or replace public institutions, labour market institutions, or even commercial entities. A lot of such forms of assistance are related to migrants' vocational activation, whereas, each measure can contribute to the improvement of their physical and mental well-being and thus, reinforce motivation to find employment. These include forms of assistance such as information activity, legal counselling, integration measures, psychological assistance, and Polish language courses. A lot of organisations that do not have the legal capacity to act as an intermediary in searching for jobs for migrants offer various types of supporting measures, e.g., workshops, artistic activities, cultural and social events, material assistance, medical assistance, language aid, classes for children or collections. In some cases, providing accommodation near to a potential employer is also helpful in finding employment. Many non-governmental organisations also undertake measures in order to prepare the society to accept foreigners and include them in the local environment, which is indirectly related to the development of a multicultural society. Often, migrants are encouraged to promote in the host country their culture, language, habits, and traditions, that is, to familiarise the environment with their identity. Many organisations support such measures undertaken by foreigners and to their benefit, which also constitutes a response to the needs of both the hosting society and refugees.

8.2 Vocational Activation and Promotion of Employment of Refugees from Ukraine in Poland – Selected Measures of Non-Governmental Organisations

At the outbreak of the refugee crisis in Poland, both public institutions as well as labour market institutions and self-governments did not have separate funds for measures supporting war migrants. The introduced statutory changes and ad hoc government decisions allowed, however, allocating funds to this end. Non-governmental organisations, which had organisational and expert potential as well as social energy to engage in such measures but did not have funds to cover related costs, found themselves in a much worse situation.

In order to meet the justified need to include non-organisational organisations in refugees' assistance, funds were separated from the state budget and allocated to this end. An example being, among others, the Departmental Activation Programme for Foreigners for the years 2022–2025, implemented by the Ministry of Family and Social Policy. An element of this programme was a contest titled "Together We Can Do More" the first edition of which covers the years 2022–2023. Approximately PLN 104 million (approx. EUR 23 million) was allocated to this contest, and the acceptance of applications was organised very quickly. It lasted from March 21, 2022, until December 31, 2023. Entities meeting the conditions specified in the Act of 24 April 2003 on activities of public interest and voluntary work (Act of 24 April 2003 on activities of public interest..., 2003), as well as labour market institutions and local self-government units, were authorised to apply in this contest. A target group of the programme were foreigners legally staying in Poland and primarily refugees from Ukraine (Announcement of the contest, 2022). Tasks and measures covered by financing within this programme have been presented in Table 8.1.

It was possible in the contest to obtain a grant at a maximal amount of PLN 1.5 million without the necessity of making their own financial contribution. Projects could be implemented until December 31, 2023. Grants for projects' implementation were obtained by 115 entities, including:

- 73 non-governmental organisations.
- 22 local self-government units.
- 10 units representing public employment services.
- 10 other units entitled to participate in the contest.

Table 8.1 Contest: Together We Can Do More – the scope of eligible tasks and measures

No.	*Priority and task*	*Eligible measures*
1	**Priority I:** Vocational activation **Task:** Integration on the labour market by vocational activation and development of entrepreneurship in foreigners searching for a job, planning to start a business activity, or already running the activity, but requiring assistance.	1 Profiling foreigner's needs and potential (expectations vs. possibilities on the labour market). 2 Organising courses, training, and other forms of education or providing assistance in finding and financing available training, courses, or other forms of education. 3 Support in necessary formalities related to the recognition of education and qualifications. 4 Professional vocational counselling and support in the process of vocational activation, also in the scope of establishing and running business activity in Poland. 5 Support in the employment agency process (executed by public employment services and other labour market institutions), as well as in contact with employers.
2	**Priority II:** Social integration and activity **Task:** Integration in the society through individual development and reinforcing activity in various areas of foreigners' social life.	1 Providing assistance of an integration assistant, drawing up a personalised path of social integration for adults, and providing support in contact with institutions and everyday life situations. 2 Providing legal, psychological, and psychotherapeutic support related to mental and physical health, among others, with regard to the experience of migration and cultural differences. 3 Providing the opportunity to learn Polish, offering courses and training in the scope of cultural orientation and in other areas of social integration. 4 Providing necessary translations and interpretations, as well as assistance in contacts with public and private institutions, e.g., opening a bank account, performing civic duties, using public transport and obtaining rights to drive vehicles, using aid offers, among others, social and housing, educational, developmental, as well as entertainment and cultural. 5 Integration support, i.e., assistance in searching for a place of residence, partial financing of the most important fees for a start, among others, rent, e.g., in the form of coupons. 6 Support of foreigners' integration in schools (e.g., assistance during classes and in contacts between carers and educational establishments, organisation of workshops and training for teachers and parents both concerning Polish culture and culture of countries of origin of foreign pupils, integration events). 7 Specialist measures for underage foreigners.

Source: Announcement of the contest (2022).

Among 115 projects selected for funding, 37 mainly concerned vocational activation, whereas others – social integration and activation. Many projects also included tasks implemented within both priorities. Activation of the acceptance of projects submitted by non-governmental organisations was the first significant measure undertaken by the Polish government after the outbreak of the refugee crisis, which was calculated for refugees' support from non-governmental organisations. Examples of ventures implemented with the support of this programme in Polish borderland regions include:

1 "Social and Vocational Integration of Refugees from Ukraine" implemented by the non-governmental organisation European Meeting Centre – Nowy Staw Foundation in the period between July 25, 2022, and May 31, 2023 (Fundacja Nowy Staw, 2022).
2 "Activity for the benefit of vocational activation and social integration of foreigners legally staying in Poland" implemented by the non-governmental organisation Caritas of Przemyśl Archdiocese in the period between June 1, 2022, and July 31, 2022 (Caritas Archidiecezji Przemyskiej, 2022b).

As we can learn from the website, European Meeting Centre – Nowy Staw Foundation (http://www.eds-fundacja.pl) is the non-governmental organisation established in 1993 in Lublin, supporting social initiatives aimed at developing a civil society, cooperation, and solidarity between nations, as well as processes of democratic changes in Belarus and Ukraine, as well as Poland's integration with the European Union. It is aimed at promoting Lublin and Lubelszczyzna as places where different cultures and nations meet. Through education addressed to representatives of all generations, the organisation supports ideas of democracy, self-government, social market economy, solidarity between nations, and cultural understanding without barriers. The project implemented by the foundation titled, "Social and Vocational Integration of Refugees from Ukraine", allowed social integration of foreigners, mainly Ukrainians living in the Lublin Voivodeship. The integration consisted of providing migrants with personalised development and reinforcing their activity in various areas of social and vocational life so that they could find themselves on the Polish labour market and become recognisable in the local community. Within this initiative, a number of measures addressed to a diverse number of recipients were conducted. These included, among others: personalised path of social integration and support in contacts with everyday life institutions, profiling foreigners' needs and potential, psychological, psychotherapeutic, and legal support, Polish language course, trips aimed at social integration, allocation of coupons for rent or other housing fees, vocational counselling, employment agency, vocational courses, as well as assistance in necessary formalities related to recognition of education and qualifications. Furthermore, project measures' participants received Polish language course completion certificates, vocational course completion certificates, and training materials, as well as used the services provided by translators and interpreters. The partner institution participating in the venture was the Active Cultural Animators Association. This project fits into a number of measures undertaken by Lublin non-governmental organisations with refugees in mind. Similar measures funded with other resources in the territory of Lublin Voivodeship were undertaken by several dozens of other organisations, among others: Homo Faber Association, the Rule of Law Institute Foundation, Friends of Children Association Regional Branch in Lublin, Food Bank, Borderland Spiritual Culture Foundation, Association for Youth Development in Lublin, Polish Red Cross District Branch in Lublin, Sempre a Frente Foundation, the Polish Scouting and Guiding Association Corps in Lublin, Saint Brother Albert Brotherhood, Voluntary Organisation Centre in Lublin, and others.

According to the information presented on the website, Caritas of Przemyśl Archdiocese (Caritas Archidiecezji Przemyskiej, 2022a) is a church charity organisation operating in the territory of the Subcarpathian Voivodeship since June 29, 1990. It deals with providing effective support to those in need and the poor in a systematic and ad hoc manner, both in spiritual and material terms. This organisation implements a lot of social projects dedicated to various disfavoured groups, financed from various sources. Since the outbreak of war in Ukraine, it has been undertaking regular measures supporting refugees in Poland and sending aid to Ukraine. In the period between June 1, 2022, and January 31, 2022, the Charity Centre of Caritas of Przemyśl Archdiocese implemented the project titled "Activity to the benefit of vocational activation and social integration of foreigners legally staying in Poland". The main objective of the project was to prepare premises for social integration and activation of foreigners and then measures related to vocational activation of refugees, among others (Caritas Archidiecezji Przemyskiej, 2022b):

- Profiling refugees' needs and potential.
- Professional vocational counselling and support in the process of vocational activation, also in the scope of establishing and running business activity in Poland.
- Providing support of an integration assistant drawing up a personalised path of social integration.
- Providing legal, psychological, and psychotherapeutic aid.
- Providing the opportunity to learn Polish, offering courses and training in the scope of cultural orientation and in other areas useful from the point of view of social integration.
- Providing necessary interpretation and translation, as well as assistance in contact with public and private institutions.
- A broad educational offer.
- Assistance in searching for a place of residence, partial financing of the most important fees for a start.

Measures undertaken by the foundation Caritas of Przemyśl Diocese fit into many similar actions implemented by Caritas branches all around Poland, among others: Caritas of Lublin Diocese and Caritas of Zamość-Lubaczów Diocese. Actions of Caritas foundation were financed with public resources as well as funds raised from private donors and funds provided by the Catholic Church congregation in Poland.

Moreover, a lot of other projects aimed at supporting refugees on the labour market were implemented in Polish borderland regions, which were funded by various public and private sources including donations. An important source of financing measures in the scope of refugees' vocational activation was the Labour Fund at the disposal of labour market institutions, as well as European Union funds, including the European Social Fund, at the disposal of, among others: regional, poviat, and local self-governments on the basis of the decision on granting funds for implementation of specific projects.

A noticeable change in the engagement of non-governmental organisations in measures supporting refugees was the intensification of networking with other partners from various sectors within large projects, smaller initiatives, as well as spontaneous actions and systemic measures implemented with the use of resources and potentials of various institutions and organisations, as well as commercial entities. Thus, complementariness of the offer and specialisation of particular partners in provision of various types of social services were used, which ensured expected comprehensiveness and synergy of measures. The table below presents selected measures undertaken in the city of Lublin, which were implemented by the self-government in cooperation with non-governmental organisations (see Table 8.2).

Measures presented in Table 8.2 are only a few of the most innovative examples of joint engagement of the City of Lublin and local non-governmental organisations in measures to the benefit of refugees. In total, in the territory of Lublin, over 40 non-governmental organisations of various profiles, as well as informal groups and citizens, were engaged in various actions supporting migrants from Ukraine. It confirms the authentic interest in the situation of refugees and a universal willingness of the society to engage in providing material support or assistance in other forms. Non-governmental organisations contributed to many measures addressed to refugees, not only powerful social energy as well as various resources and competences, but also more flexible approach to tasks, implementation of which by public entities was conditioned by many formalities, e.g., organisation of voluntary activities. On the other hand, the presented examples confirm that full social engagement can be used well only when the non-governmental organisation is treated by public institutions as a serious and equal partner and has a specific area of specialisation and own field for undertaking measures within the cooperation, e.g., assistance in searching for employment or vocational counselling. Key resources in such measures primarily include volunteers, relations with other entities, and funds.

Table 8.2 Intersectoral cooperation in the scope of providing support to refugees in Lublin

No.	*Name of the measure*	*Description of the measure*
1	Project: Friendly and safe office III Financing: The Asylum, Migration and Integration Fund	Providing refugees with broad information and counselling support by establishing information and counselling points, where with the use of modern tools and assistance of employed specialists, refugees from Ukraine received professional and comprehensive services in the scope of legal, psychological, vocational-educational, social, and health assistance. Furthermore, a website and hotline in Ukraine were activated, as well as a special online form was prepared for refugees from Ukraine in their own language. Supplementary measures: • Sightseeing trips for refugees contributing to extending their knowledge of the region and better integration with Polish society. • Thematic training concerning, among others, an active search for a job in the territory of Poland in conjunction with job fairs, starting/continuing studies, and school education in the territory of Poland with a consideration of procedures for validation of diplomas obtained at foreign universities. The project leader is Lublin Voivodeship Office in Lublin, and programme operator – European Meeting Centre – Nowy Staw Foundation. Financing: The Asylum, Migration and Integration Fund
2	Activating a website combining job offers from local companies with the demand from Ukrainian citizens	The website operates at the address: www.gospodarczy.lublin.eu/ukraina. Ukrainians can report the will to take up a job in Lublin, while at the same time specifying their competences, language skills, or experience. Whereas, employers from Lublin and Lubelszczyzna, through the agency of the website, can post their job offers. All offers are translated into Ukrainian and posted with contact data on the dedicated website. Engaged employees match information obtained from prospective employees to job offers reported by employers and support the contact between them (on the phone and via email). Job offers are also accepted by the City Labour Office in Lublin via portal: praca.gov.pl, whereas the Regional Chamber of Legal Advisors in Lublin gives legal advice. Many social organisations, including Homo Faber Association and Caritas, have been engaged in searching for jobs for refugees.

(*Continued*)

Table 8.2 (Continued)

No.	*Name of the measure*	*Description of the measure*
3	Lublin Social Committee to Aid Ukraine	A form of cooperation, which is unique on the Polish scale, exists between the City of Lublin and the following non-governmental organisations: Homo Faber Association, Borderland Spiritual Culture Foundation, and the Rule of Law Institute Foundation. The Committee operates in 21 sections dealing with, among others: providing information (hotline), legal aid, accommodation, care for children, alimentation, medical and psychological aid. In the first month of the war, 60 Lublin restaurants cooperating with the Committee provided 12.7 thousand of free meals. In consecutive months, two programmes for providing refugees and their hosts with food were activated. Approximately two thousand volunteers, including 460 translators and several dozens of employees of Lublin Municipal Office and urban cultural institutions engaged in assistance. In the period between February and June 2022, the Committee also dealt with coordination of measures in the scope of allocating accommodation in private homes. Volunteers were present at Polish State Railways' and Motor Transport Company's stations, where they were given information concerning accommodation and further aid, assisted in interpretation or organisation of next stages of journey, and distributed hot meals and drinks.

Source: Own study based on: https://strategia.lubelskie.pl/rot/opracowania/raport.wsparcie.ua.pdf; https://lublin.eu/lublin/aktualnosci/miasto-lublin-pomaga-obywatelom-ukrainy,9392,66,1.html

8.3 Experiences of Non-Governmental Organisations Supporting War Refugees from Ukraine on the Polish Labour Market – Research Results

The majority of studied non-governmental organisations from Polish borderland regions dealt with problems experienced by disfavoured people, among others, related to health condition, origin, and education even before the outbreak of war in Ukraine. Therefore, their engagement in providing support to migrants resulted from competences to provide specific social services as well as sympathising with people who suffered as a result of Russian aggression against Ukraine. One of the studied organisations is a part of the European Centre for Employee Affairs and has experience in implementation of adaptation programmes for various vocational and social groups; another organisation promotes entrepreneurship as a way to develop competences on the labour market, while another one has many years of experience in supporting, among others, war refugees from Chechnya, migrants from the

Middle East, and Belarus, as a result of which it has already developed its own model of social integration of people arriving in Poland. Thus, it can be assumed that the first wave of refugees reached borders of Lublin Voivodeship and Subcarpathian Voivodeship on February 24, 2022, studied non-governmental organisations from borderland regions had experience, albeit diverse, in these areas of social activity, which could also be combined with supporting war migrants from Ukraine on the labour market.

After the outbreak of war in Ukraine, all studied organisations intensified measures for supporting migrants coming from the eastern border. They did so within their conducted activity and in a manner proper for local needs. These organisations acquired knowledge regarding the necessary support for migrants from the local self-government, voivode, and media. Studied organisations tried to infiltrate the area of measures aimed directly at migrants to support basic aid measures in borderland reception points as well as information points located in many borderland cities and towns. It allowed joining the stream of the most necessary ad hoc aid for migrants. Simultaneously, due to cooperation with local self-governments, other non-governmental organisations, as well as public institutions and volunteers, these organisations were able to provide more specialised aid addressed to specific people, e.g., psychological support.

For studied organisations, the priority measure in the first weeks following the arrival of war migrants in Poland was to support them in the most important current affairs, such as:

- Providing accommodation.
- Providing a Ukrainian interpreter.
- Providing medical, psychological, psychotherapeutic, and legal aid to those in need.
- Providing migrants with alimentation, clothes, and cleaning supplies.
- Support in obtaining PESEL (Personal Identification Number).
- Support in applying for social aid.
- Support in ensuring education of children or help in taking care of children.

Furthermore, measures were also undertaken exceeding typical forms of support, e.g., one of the studied organisations engaged intercultural mentors to support migrants, another organisation quickly employed people fluent in Ukrainian and aware of Ukrainian reality to recognise migrants' needs and refer them to relevant institutions, while another one established systemic cooperation with other institutions to provide refugees with comprehensive support, e.g., cooperation with a poviat labour office and a poviat family support centre, which allowed combining job offers with providing care for children.

Only after providing refugees with the basic support that their situation in Poland required, the first attempts at interesting migrants with the possibility of taking up a job in Poland were made. All studied organisations were perfectly aware that this wave of refugees they were taking care of (mainly women and children) did not treat employment as priority since it was not the goal of their arrival in Poland. Despite measures aimed at motivating refugees to search for employment, studied organisations identified a number of obstacles that in many cases simply prevented them from adaptation on the labour market, at least for a short period of time. Moreover, even engagement of non-governmental organisations did not guarantee that these barriers would be successfully overcome by migrants. The barriers included:

- A language barrier.
- A lack of documents confirming education and qualifications.
- A lack of the possibility to certify competences and skills.
- A lack of the possibility to quickly validate diplomas.
- Incongruity of migrants' competences and labour market demands.
- Poor mental health and a lack of motivation to gain new skills.
- Reluctance to vocational activation resulting from the intention to quickly return to Ukraine.

The aforementioned vocational activation barriers were difficult to mitigate by non-governmental organisations in a short time, the more so since in the case of refugees, several barriers occurred simultaneously, e.g., a language barrier and a lack of motivation to gain new skills; a lack of the possibility to certify competences and reluctance to vocational activation. Another obstacle consisted of migrants' movement, which resulted in ceasing activation measures and the necessity to undertake them again in a new place and in different conditions.

Studied organisations did not observe significant changes on the Polish-Ukrainian borderland labour market after the outbreak of war in Ukraine, but they noted an increase in the demand for employees speaking Ukrainian. A noticeable change is the significantly higher visibility of the Ukrainian language in the Polish public space, which was not observed before the war (e.g., a lot of announcements and advertisements, public information, directions, and news were given in Ukrainian in the media and on social media); additionally, many public events addressed to, among others, Ukrainians were interpreted into Ukrainian. People speaking Ukrainian, including volunteers and representatives of the Ukrainian minority in Poland, were recruited by all institutions dealing with refugees, e.g., labour offices, local self-government units, schools, etc. At the same time, possibilities of working in professions that did not require communication with a customer occurred for migrants who wanted to quickly find a job, e.g., the cleaning industry, seasonal work in agriculture and processing, less paid jobs in catering, which are usually difficult to staff with Polish employees (e.g., a catering assistant, a waiter). Despite the fact that following the outbreak of war, the shortage of employees in construction and transport industries was noticeable (due to many Ukrainians returning to their country and joining the army), after some time this deficit levelled off, while the inflow of migrants did not significantly disturb balance on the labour market in borderland regions.

It was noticeable that after the situation in Ukraine settled down even a little bit, some migrants decided to return to their country since they did not cope with the Polish reality or wanted to join their families. Despite the significant engagement of volunteers and thematic specialists, studied organisations experienced failure in the case of integration of some refugees. Some war migrants, for different reasons, were not able to settle in Poland and, on the first occasion, decided to return to Ukraine. On the other hand, each studied organisation was able to quickly identify a large group of migrants they were in charge of who consciously decided to stay and settle in Poland permanently, e.g., educate children in Polish and develop competences to take up a better-paid job. Representatives of studied organisations underlined that, also before the outbreak of war, a lot of Ukrainian economic migrants lived in borderland regions; therefore, people who came after Russian invasion found themselves in the environment where Ukrainian culture had already been familiarised with and recognised. Perhaps due to their close proximity to the Ukrainian border and dynamic flows of population in recent years, it was easier for them to find themselves on the cross-border labour market than in other parts of Poland. Furthermore, many local entrepreneurs who employed Ukrainians also before the outbreak of war, in the face of the Russian aggression decided to increase employment of Ukrainian employees to support refugees. These entrepreneurs also established contacts with studied organisations and offered employment to people in their care.

At least several forms of support for migrants searching for employment offered by studied organisations can be indicated. As a rule, these measures were undertaken in cooperation with local self-government and labour market institutions. Vocational activation of migrants was, as a rule, flexibly combined with other forms of support such as accommodation (e.g., rent coupons), alimentation (e.g., alimentation coupons), or providing free healthcare and transport. Preparation for searching for a job was indirectly combined with mental, psychological, psychotherapeutic, and legal assistance for migrants and partially also care for children to provide mothers with a possibility to rest and focus on job-related issues. Only after a longer period of time, studied organisations got to know their wards well enough to offer support better adjusted to their needs, including social integration and vocational activation. Such measures included, among others: learning Polish, employment agency, vocational counselling, and vocational courses compliant with predispositions (e.g., an office worker with elements of administration, hairdressing, cosmetic courses, etc.). Some forms of support were implemented as a part of a trip (e.g., vocational training and counselling, and psychological support, i.e., psychological workshops related to coping with trauma, as well as organising free time for children). Migrants learned to fill in recruitment documents, write CVs, and write cover letters for specific positions.

Workshops were organised during which makeup standards binding in the Polish labour environment were presented to prevent applicants from image and dress code mistakes. An innovative solution proved to be establishing cooperation with an intercultural assistant in the school attended by approximately 70 children from Ukraine. Through their activities on Facebook groups, messengers, and other social media, this person was educating war migrants on how to cope in Poland, even in such cases as using the mObywatel application. A lot of Ukrainians in Poland had problems with this software, as well as with tax reports.

Non-governmental organisations' work on vocational activation of migrants was not always effective, since in the case of certain people, despite the will to stay in Poland, it was necessary to return to Ukraine, and, in the end, such migrants resigned from employment. Also, people who counted on swift ending of the war and returning to their homes did not want to take up employment in Poland. In such situations, organisations often did not have the possibilities to offer such people even a short-term employment because employers were not interested in this solution. On the other hand, people declaring a short-term stay in Poland were losing their motivation to search for even short-term employment.

Although, in general, at least at the beginning, migrants active on the labour market found employment below their education level, over time they had the opportunity to improve their qualifications and gain higher remuneration. Legislative solutions introduced under the Act of 12 March 2022, as a result of which refugees could be provided with training support covered with European funds, were very helpful. Many refugees were talented people with unique abilities and competences, e.g., in handicrafts. Such people required special support in vocational development since usually it is more difficult for them to find employment meeting the profile of their competences.

As far as the biggest long-term challenges for the Polish-Ukrainian cross-border labour market are concerned, a particular issue seems to be adjusting employment structure and human resources available in Lublin Voivodeship and Subcarpathian Voivodeship. The problem primarily remains to be the incomplete use of refugees' qualifications, since many people work in professions not corresponding to their education and aspirations. Even for people staying in Poland, as of the beginning of war, the insufficient command of Polish and reluctance to learn it continue to be barriers on the labour market.

A separate issue is the accessibility of the workforce. The majority of refugees from Ukraine are mothers with children who require taking care of, which significantly diminishes their availability for the employer and thus means worse, less paid job offers at a longer distance from their place of residence. Even temporary support for taking care of children provided by non-governmental organisations does not fully solve this issue.

Residential problems of migrants can be recognised as especially severe. It happens that migrants receive interesting job offers but do not have the possibility to take them due to the lack of accommodation near the employer or too high costs of renting flats, or reluctance of the local community to rent flats to refugees from Ukraine.

Therefore, the research conducted among non-governmental organisations shows that the actual challenge for activation of migrants on the Polish labour market comprises supporting their functioning in social and cultural dimensions to provide them with conditions for social integration.

A significantly more serious challenge seems to be preparing migrants to conduct business activity in Poland. It is more difficult since it requires developing a certain independence in a foreigner, not only as far as coping with procedures and provisions is concerned, but also a creative approach to the market, proper understanding of signals from customers, and gaining a good orientation in the industry in which such a person wishes to conduct business activity. In many cases, the problem consists of, e.g., the migrant obtaining funds for starting business activity, especially when giving a grant requires surety of another person, ensuring a proper collateral, e.g., in the form of a bill of exchange, etc. In such a situation, many fears arise regarding meeting the terms and conditions of such agreements by migrants, since it is also related to consequences for the institution that has given such a grant. Nevertheless, training in the scope of entrepreneurship is as needed as vocational training, since many migrants much prefer independence in business, including employment of other migrants, to hired labour.

Another challenge concerns long-term personal and professional plans of migrants. In this scope, for many refugees, the duration of their stay in Poland remains unknown, as they treat it as a coerced situation and not a conscious choice. Such people do not show high motivation to gain new vocational qualifications and do not search for employment in Poland. These refugees do not want to be permanently involved with the Polish labour market, and if they do take up employment, these are rather part-time and less-paid jobs, which often do not require speaking Polish. Temporariness of a stay in Poland and a lack of perspectives to get a job compliant with their qualifications constitute, in the case of often highly educated refugees (e.g., doctors, teachers, and lawyers), significant factors discouraging them from using labour market tools.

Organisations engaged in vocational activation of refugees in the years 2022–2023 also gained a lot of experience, which they can use in their further social activity related to the labour market. Primarily, the development of competences related to the intercultural communication between employers and volunteers – refugees, as well as the development of competences in the area of inter-organisational cooperation are underlined. Organisations have developed a certain sensitivity to the specific social and personal situation of refugees, have learned to understand their specific needs, and have undertaken measures that can constitute an actual support for them, not only with regard to finding employment and obtaining funds for independent maintenance in Poland but also supporting actual settlement in local environments.

Providing support to migrants has become for studied organisations the opportunity to reinforce relations with public administration units, e.g., poviat and voivodeship labour offices or local self-government units and their subordinated units. It improves the potential of such organisations to better implement their future goals. Some organisations started or intensified cooperation with enterprises, chambers of commerce, and trade organisations that offered assistance in finding jobs for migrants or providing vocational training, which was often performed under the patronage of, e.g., voivodeship labour offices.

Another competence gained by non-governmental organisations cooperating with other entities supporting refugees concerned the skill to obtain funds from, e.g., Foundation for the Development of the Education System, Batory Foundation, the Asylum, Migration, and Integration Fund, or the Polish-Ukrainian Youth Exchange Fund. Due to obtaining a grant from such sources effectively, as well as using funds from, e.g., the European Social Fund through the agency of marshal's offices or voivodeship labour offices, studied organisations could organise measures for migrants on a scale significantly exceeding their own financial potential. The ability to use external support to organise measures for migrants also greatly facilitated searching for refugees, e.g., job offers, announcements regarding accommodation, invitations to job fairs, etc. Simultaneously, due to the cooperation with poviat labour offices, organisations could apply for, among others, employment of interns who took on themselves, e.g., certain tasks related to ongoing information and organisation support for refugees in their everyday lives, which also constituted a significant reinforcement for studied organisations. Another form of cooperation with poviat labour offices consisted of delegating employees from these institutions, who provided migrants interested in taking up employment with information in-house, in associations.

Furthermore, several negative aspects of broad measures of studied organisations in the scope of helping Ukrainians should be mentioned. Namely:

- Burnout caused by, among others, mental stress related to working with a very difficult and demanding social group, that is, refugees.
- A casual nature of engagement of the majority of people supporting social organisations, i.e., in the case of volunteers, it is difficult to plan full engagement in a set number of hours, as it is in the case of employees.
- Limited possibilities of improving competences of people managing organisations and people engaged in providing support, i.e., limited funds for training, action, and experience learning, prevail.
- A lack of permanent funding for implemented measures results in limitations in the implementation of tasks in which organisations specialise, and thus, they cannot effectively use their full potential.

8.4 Conclusions

In the face of the high wave of war migrants from Ukraine coming to Poland, a lot of non-governmental organisations in Poland took upon themselves certain measures related to social integration and vocational activation of refugees. These measures were implemented spontaneously, since at the moment of the outbreak of war in Ukraine, Poland neither had a coordinated migration policy, nor legal and legislative solutions concerning the specific situation of war refugees functioned. The activity and effectiveness of the social economy sector's entities in providing assistance to Ukrainians confirmed their role in providing high-quality social services, where state support turned out to be insufficient.

While public administration units and labour market institutions, including public employment services, engaged in helping refugees had the possibility to allocate additional budgetary funds to assist war migrants (among others within vocational activation projects), the non-governmental organisations had to obtain such funds independently or establish cooperation with entities that were at a disposal of such funds, including, e.g., voivodeship and poviat labour offices. Independent fund-raising for measures supporting migrants is one of the unique features distinguishing non-governmental organisations in comparison to public institutions, which were at a disposal of budgetary funds for this purpose.

On the basis of the Act of 12 March 2022 on assistance to citizens of Ukraine in connection with armed conflict on the territory of that country, migrants obtained a number of rights to benefit from various forms of vocational development support in Poland on equal terms with the European Union citizens. Poviat and voivodeship labour offices could address at migrants the same forms of support on the labour market as in the case of Polish citizens. The same approach to migrants could also be applied by non-governmental organisations, which also had the possibility of being much more flexible in this aspect, as well as combining migrants' vocational activation measures with other supportive measures, e.g., in the scope of therapeutic support, alimentation, and accommodation, which could not have been ensured by, e.g., labour market institutions. Currently, it is difficult to indicate the number of non-governmental organisations operating in Poland, which engaged in vocational activation for refugees on the Polish labour market, since in many cases these measures were combined with other forms of support offered by these organisations in compliance with their objectives, such as, e.g., social integration.

A particular difficulty in migrants' vocational activity experienced by social organisations constituted refugees' limited interest in perspectives of employment in Poland. It was determined by, among others, such factors as belief in the temporary nature of their stay in Poland, lower personal motivation to take up gainful employment, insufficient knowledge of the employment reality in Poland, a language barrier, a lack of the possibilities to find employment compliant with their education, difficulties with validation of diplomas, housing problems, and the necessity to take care of children. The enumerated conditions determined measures that could be undertaken by non-governmental organisations to support migrants searching for employment in Poland, as well as to convince them to make an effort to gain new qualifications or skills.

Examples of projects presented herein indicate the growing specialisation of non-governmental organisations in the scope of using various forms of vocational activation and support of migrants on the labour market, among others, due to the cooperation with voivodeship and poviat labour offices, which indicate possible solutions and good practices. The development of network cooperation between non-governmental organisations and partners from other sectors, as well as the growing deinstitutionalisation, which should be connected with the public sector's growing trust in the non-governmental sector, are very visible.

Due to the short period of time following refugees' arrival in Poland, it is difficult to assess at this point long-term results of non-governmental organisations' activities in the scope of supporting migrants on the labour market. One of the results is certainly a change in the professional situation of many migrants and their becoming independent in Poland, which limits costs of their social support at further stages of their stay in the host country. Also, people who benefited from assistance provided by studied organisations and took up temporary employment gained the opportunity to improve their life circumstances and decrease dependence on social support. Moreover, advantages of the refugees' vocational activation include their socialisation, social integration, and even therapy that reduce their feeling of war-related trauma.

The research shows that non-governmental organisations, who had the opportunity to delve deeper into the essence of migrants' problems, gained in the scope of vocational activation of migrants new competences and reinforced their institutional potential to cope with this issue in the future. However, primarily due to the measures presented herein, the new social and economic problem has been captured and analysed, which will be growing in Poland until formal and permanent procedures for providing assistance to war refugees are established. Also, non-governmental organisations promoting good practices concerning support for migrants searching for employment can contribute to solving this issue; however, crucial issues such as ensuring balance on the labour market, striving to balance deficit and surplus professions, or management of additional human resources provided by migrants, belong to the tasks of labour market institutions, in implementation of which non-governmental organisations can only perform a supportive function.

Nevertheless, providing assistance to migrants entails specific risks and problems for non-governmental organisations, which should be supported in solving them by the state. Such measures should include, among others: promoting volunteer organisations, providing volunteers and non-governmental organisations' employees at a risk of burnout with psychological support, reinforcing the system of improving competences, and providing permanent funding of measures in which such organisations specialise, which should be combined with further deinstitutionalisation of the social services system in Poland.

References

Act of 24 April 2003 on Activities of Public Interest and Voluntary Work; Journal of Laws of 2020, item 1057, as amended.

Act of 13 June 2003 on Granting Protection to Foreigners within the Territory of the Republic of Poland; Journal of Laws of 2003, No. 128, item 1176.

Act of 20 April 2004 on Employment Promotion and Labour Market Institutions; Journal of Laws of 2023, item 735.

Act of 12 March 2022 on Assistance to Citizens of Ukraine in Connection with Armed Conflict on the Territory of That Country; Journal of Laws of 2022, item 583, as amended.

Announcement of the contest. (2022). https://www.gov.pl/web/rodzina/ogloszenie-konkursu-razem-mozemy-wiecej–pierwsza-edycja-programu-aktywizacyjnego-dla-cudzoziemcow-na-lata-20222024

Arendt, J. N. (2022). Labor market effects of a work-first policy for refugees. *Journal of Population Economics*, *35*(1), 169–196.

Bassuk, E. L., & Gerson, S. (2022). Deinstitutionalization and mental health services. In *Mental health care and social policy* (pp. 127–144). Routledge.

Beaman, L. A. (2012). Social networks and the dynamics of labour market outcomes: Evidence from refugees resettled in the US. *The Review of Economic Studies*, *79*(1), 128–161.

Caritas Archidiecezji Przemyskiej. (2022a). *O nas*. https://caritas.przemyska.pl/o-nas

Caritas Archidiecezji Przemyskiej. (2022b). *O projekcie*. https://caritas.przemyska.pl/uchodzcy-o-projekcie

Davis, K. A., Phyak, P., & Bui, T. T. N. (2012). Multicultural education as community engagement: Policies and planning in a transnational era. *International Journal of Multicultural Education*, *14*(3), 1–25.

Fehsenfeld, M., & Levinsen, K. (2019). Taking care of the refugees: Exploring advocacy and cross-sector collaboration in service provision for refugees. *Voluntas: International Journal of Voluntary and Nonprofit Organizations*, *30*(2), 422–435.

Feischmidt, M., Pries, L., & Cantat, C. (Eds.). (2019). *Refugee protection and civil society in Europe*. Palgrave Macmillan.

Fundacja Nowy Staw. (2022). *Integracja społeczna i zawodowa uchodźców z Ukrainy*. http://www.eds-fundacja.pl/projekty/integracjaspolecznaizawodowauchodzcowzukrainy/pl_oferta.php

Grabowska, S., & Pięta-Szawara, A. (2023). Wsparcie Polski na rzecz uchodźców z Ukrainy w obliczu wojny w 2022 r. Wybrane aspekty (Polish support for refugees from Ukraine in the face of war in 2022 – Selected aspects). *Journal of Modern Science*, *50*(1), 389–390.

Hasmath, R., Hildebrandt, T., & Hsu, J. Y. (2019). Conceptualizing government-organized non-governmental organizations. *Journal of Civil Society*, *15*(3), 267–284.

Hope, D., & Martelli, A. (2019). The transition to the knowledge economy, labor market institutions, and income inequality in advanced democracies. *World Politics*, *71*(2), 236–288.

Lenner, K., & Turner, L. (2019). Making refugees work? The politics of integrating Syrian refugees into the labor market in Jordan. *Middle East Critique*, *28*(1), 65–95.

Lewis, D., Kanji, N., & Themudo, N. S. (2020). *Non-governmental organizations and development*. Routledge.

Marino, S., & Keizer, A. (2023). Labour market regulation and the demand for migrant labour: A comparison of the adult social care sector in England and the Netherlands. *European Journal of Industrial Relations*, *29*(2), 159–176.

Matusz-Protasiewicz, P., & Kwieciński, L. (2018). Kształtowanie lokalnych polityk integracji imigrantów – Działania władz Gdańska i Wrocławia (Development of local integration policies of migrants – Case of Gdańsk and Wrocław). *Problemy Polityki Społecznej. Studia i Dyskusje*, *43*(4), 125–142.

Muñoz, P., & Kimmitt, J. (2019). Social mission as competitive advantage: A configurational analysis of the strategic conditions of social entrepreneurship. *Journal of Business Research*, *101*, 854–861.

Ndomo, Q., & Lillie, N. (2023). Resistance is useless! (and so are resilience and reworking): migrants in the Finnish labour market. *Immigrant and Asylum Seekers Labour Market Integration upon Arrival: NowHereLand*, 161.

Serwis Rzeczypospolitej Polskiej. (2023). *Ukraińcy*. https://www.gov.pl/web/mniejszosci-narodowe-i-etniczne/ukraincy

Sienicka, A., & Tyrowicz, J. (2006). *Publiczne służby zatrudnienia a organizacje pozarządowe w realizacji usług rynku pracy – Uwarunkowania prawne (Public employment services vs non-governmental organisations in the implementation of labour market services – Legal conditions)*. FISE.

Sienicka, A., & Tyrowicz, J. (2012). Social economy and CSR in Poland. In *Social responsibility, entrepreneurship and the common good: International and interdisciplinary perspectives* (pp. 211–228). Palgrave Macmillan UK.

Szymańska, J. (2022). Exodus uchodźców z Ukrainy jako wyzwanie dla Unii Europejskiej (Exodus from Ukraine: The new refugee challenge for the European Union). *Biuletyn Polskiego Instytutu Spraw Międzynarodowych*, *42*.

Valle-Mestre, L., Jiménez-Jiménez, D., & Manzanares-Martínez, D. (2022). Analysing the impact of organisation's dual mission on the development of social projects and innovation. *Journal of Organizational Change Management*, *35*(3), 651–665.

Weerawardena, J., Salunke, S., Haigh, N., & Mort, G. S. (2021). Business model innovation in social purpose organizations: Conceptualizing dual social-economic value creation. *Journal of Business Research*, *125*, 762–771.

Zapata, P., & Campos, M. J. Z. (2023). The territorial embeddedness of novel labour integration policy: Something old, something new and something borrowed. *Scandinavian Journal of Public Administration*, *27*(2), 1–21.

9 Local Labour Market Actors

Refugees and Employers on the Polish-Ukrainian Border during the Migration Crisis in 2022 Caused by the War in Ukraine

9.1 Migrants from Ukraine

As data from the United Nations High Commissioner for Refugees (UNHCR) show, Poland and other countries in the region have been heavily populated by refugees from Ukraine – between February 24, 2022, and October 31, 2023, the Polish-Ukrainian border was crossed by 29.60 million people (16.04 million from Ukraine to Poland), including 958,935 refugees from Ukraine who stayed in Poland for the duration of the war. In the same period, other countries bordering with Ukraine registered the following statistics regarding crossings of their shared border (from Ukraine): Romania 3.49 million (83,835 Ukrainians remaining in the country), Slovakia 1.77 million (109,115 Ukrainians remaining in the country), Moldova 958,230 (including 113,000 Ukrainians remaining in the country), and Hungary 3.69 million (53,370 thousand people remaining in this country). Other countries receiving more than 100,000 refugees from Ukraine include: Russia (1,275.3 thousand people), Germany (1,105.2 thousand people), Czech Republic (363,160), the United Kingdom (210,800), Spain (185,875), and Italy (167,525) (Karasapan, 2022; UNHCR, 2023).

The impact of the influx of migrants on the regional economy, labour market, and the situation facing entrepreneurs in Polish-Ukrainian cross-border areas before the outbreak of the full-scale armed conflict was assessed positively in Poland, mainly due to their potential to fill labour shortages caused by unfavourable demographics. In meso- and macroeconomic terms, regional economies and enterprises also benefited from spending by unregistered Ukrainian citizens, mostly within 50 km of the border (Cierpiał-Wolan, 2017). The existence of social relations, networks of connections, and partnerships also contributed to international student exchanges (despite significant regulatory barriers regarding the recognition of diplomas) and research cooperation between border region universities – for instance, the Poland-Belarus-Ukraine Cross-Border Cooperation Programme (Bronisz, 2017). Cross-border business cooperation pre-2021 is exemplified by business clusters that stimulate the economy on both sides of the border and the economic gravity effect within the Carpathian Euroregion. In the

DOI: 10.4324/9781003471646-9

case of the border region, the Subcarpathian Aviation Cluster plays a significant role in the global defence industry (Oleński, 2017). As this author points out, the resilience of clusters in cross-border areas is largely dependent on favourable economic and political circumstances, and this particular cluster is currently thriving due to the war in Ukraine (Oleński, 2017). The strengthening of Polish-Ukrainian relations on regional labour markets was also facilitated by visa-free travel for Ukrainian citizens and labour market shortages being filled by economic immigrants from Ukraine, especially in the construction sector or seasonally in agriculture (Igielski & Sowa, 2019). Moreover, increasing numbers of economic migrants from Ukraine were employed in the construction, industrial processing, transport, trade, and household sectors (Chmielewska et al., 2017). The research also highlights difficulties arising from misunderstandings regarding migrant diasporas differentiated according to their period of arrival in Poland (those who arrived earlier vs. the current wave of migration) or the region of origin (east or west Ukraine); on the other hand, short-term circular migration from the western part of Ukraine has occurred for many years as well as medium- and long-term migration as a method of compensating for the difficult economic situation in Ukraine after the outbreak of the current war in 2014 (Jaroszewicz & Piechal, 2016).

These processes that have occurred on the border since the outbreak of the war in eastern Ukraine in 2014 were transformed overnight when Russia launched a full-scale attack on the entire country on February 22, 2022, causing a mass exodus of war refugees. Polish municipalities located in the Polish-Ukrainian border area adopted a different role within the process of providing aid and humanitarian support to those escaping the war as the first place of safe refuge after leaving Ukraine. This chapter describes the impact of the war and refugees on local players in the Polish-Ukrainian border area, including refugees and local enterprises.

Recent literature contains discussions related to the migration crisis caused by Russian aggression on Ukraine. Until now, several studies have been conducted in Poland primarily based on qualitative methods, which often treat this issue fragmentarily (Duszczyk & Kaczmarczyk, 2022a, 2022b, 2022c; Gluszak & Trojanek, 2023; Jurek, 2022; Szaban, 2022). Almost immediately after the outbreak of war in Ukraine – i.e., in the period between March 23 and April 3, 2022 – research on the group of war refugees from Ukraine, who arrived in Poland after February 24, 2022, was conducted by A. Zymin et al. (2022). Elements of the analysis included issues such as family and origin, education and knowledge of foreign languages, residence in Poland and abroad, employment in Poland, fears, and plans. Research (Zymin et al., 2022) was conducted throughout the whole of Poland, wherever migrants were staying. The research conclusions are confirmed in consecutive research findings generated in the period between April 15 and May 15, 2022, by P. Długosz et al. (2022). The research helps characterise the stream of war refugees and presents differences between this group of migrants and economic migrants from Ukraine who arrived in Poland before the outbreak of the war. The key research conclusions are presented below:

1 The demographic structure of migrants has changed. After February 24, 2022, the vast majority of refugees (approx. 94%) were women (before the outbreak of war, the migrants were mostly men), and so there has been a change in the proportions of the migrants according to sex. The data shows that the average age of female refugees is 37, and approximately 75% of them arrived in Poland with children. However, the age structure of migrants has not changed (the most mobile group remained people aged between 26 and 46 years old), which could be because of greater incentive and increased courage to search for safety outside the borders of Ukraine or the need to protect children against the threat of the Russian army. Approximately 60% of refugees arrived in Poland with children below 18 years of age.
2 The number of more educated migrants with varied professions increased. Before the war, economic migrants from Ukraine were taking their first steps on the Polish labour market by performing physical labour (e.g., agriculture, cleaning work, taking care of children and dependent persons) or qualified work. During their stay, they improved their professional skills and qualifications, which was a requirement for promotion and better remuneration at the workplace. War migrants represent another social group. Approximately 60% have higher education, and approximately 15% have secondary school education. Before the outbreak of war, a significant percentage of war refugees (27%) worked in the service, trade, and sales sectors, whereas 17% were highly qualified specialists, and 15% worked in education.
3 The majority of refugees speak poor Polish. Economic migrants who arrived in Poland before the war usually had some basic knowledge of Polish, which made it easier to find employment. As far as war refugees are concerned, only approximately 10% of them declared a good or very good command of Polish. However, the majority intend to learn Polish, mainly on their own and at no personal expense.
4 The majority of refugees are from the northern and central regions of Ukraine, relatively few of them came from Western Ukraine, although this was the predominant source of economic migrants before the outbreak of war. The direct threat to life rather than the desire to improve one's economic situation was the motivation to emigrate (the majority of respondents assessed their financial situation before the outbreak of war as good or very good).
5 Treating Poland as the target country of stay for the period of hostilities. Before the war, for many economic migrants from Ukraine, Poland was only a transit country, and ultimately, they were planning to search for permanent employment in Western European countries. Migrants' living

conditions and welfare were assessed as significantly higher in Western European countries than in Poland, whereas the approach of refugees is different. Many made a conscious decision to stay in Poland, which is perceived as the closest country to them in terms of culture and language, where they have relatives and friends, feel safe, and have been well received. The research shows that almost 33% of refugees plan to stay in Poland longer, although almost half of the respondents had never been to Poland before the outbreak of war. However, the majority of refugees intend to return to Ukraine after the hostilities have ceased; their decision is mainly motivated by missing their families or the necessity to rebuild the country after the war damage.

6 Tendency to search for a place of residence in medium and large cities, reluctant re-allocation. The majority of refugees came from Ukrainian cities, and in Poland, they also opted for medium or large cities (3/4 of respondents) as their place of residence. Almost 70% of the refugees questioned wanted to live in cities with over 200,000 citizens. The reluctance to relocate is evidenced by the fact that 72% of them intend to stay in Poland, in regions where they currently reside, mainly in rented flats and houses (including with Polish host families), as well as in collective accommodation facilities.

7 Finding permanent employment in Poland is not a priority for refugees. While before the outbreak of war, the majority of migrants came to Poland for the sole purpose of earning money, for war refugees, this issue is not a priority. Many refugees arriving in Poland used to have good or very good living conditions in Ukraine before the war and had enough money, at least for some time, to provide for themselves in Poland without the need for employment (approx. 60% of refugees wanted to find employment in Poland and 20% declared that they were living on their own resources), whereas almost 33% of refugees staying in Poland worked remotely in Ukraine. The majority of refugees staying in Poland have obtained or intend to obtain a PESEL (personal identification) number in the near future. War migrants treat potential employment in Poland as temporary and are not as aware of the realities of the Polish labour market as the economic migrants who arrived in Poland before the outbreak of war, characterised by a strong economic motivation. For female refugees from Ukraine, a real obstacle in the way of searching for employment is childcare, as well as a lack of documented professional expertise and a poor command of Polish. Not everyone accepted the possibility of taking employment for which they were overqualified.

8 A high level of stress. The main problem facing refugees from Ukraine is their separation from their families and their fear for the safety of their loved ones who stay in Ukraine. Approximately 75% of the refugees questioned showed symptoms of trauma or high levels of stress. Over half of the refugees sought outside help to deal with problems.

The above characteristics indicate that the stream of war migrants differed from the profile of Ukrainian economic migrants active on the Polish labour market before the outbreak of war. The majority of the latter are not as well-educated as the earlier economic migrants, but they have a better command of Polish, often with experience of employment abroad, and treat their stay in Poland only in terms of potential earnings, and often also transfer a part of their remuneration to their families in Ukraine. Furthermore, essential differences also exist in terms of demographic structure and family situation, motivation to stay in Poland, ideas concerning the length of their stay, and preferences concerning employment in Poland.

During field research in the Polish-Ukrainian borderland in 2023, the authors observed some features that may embellish the social profile of war refugees depicted in the research conducted by the aforementioned teams. They noticed the following behaviours exhibited by the wave of refugees:

- Organising themselves in support groups, to provide information on their rights in Poland, accessibility of social support, etc.
- Participation in Polish courses motivated by their intention to learn more about the host country, as well as their willingness to develop social contacts along with a willingness to obtain employment in Poland.
- Focusing on achieving calm and alleviating the trauma wrought by the war, as well as lowering stress and giving their children peace of mind.
- Settling mainly in the cities perceived as offering better social conditions and in rural municipalities.
- Engagement in social life in their place of residence, in return for acceptance and provision of livelihood (e.g., engagement in cultural and charity activities, etc.).
- Postponing making decisions on their future in Poland and making it dependent on the development of the situation in Ukraine.

Undeniably, the large wave of war migrants flooding Poland required a significant mobilisation from state and government institutions, and the required scale of this engagement is evidenced by statistical data concerning arrivals from Ukraine to Poland. According to the information of the Border Guard Headquarters (Border Guard, 2023), in 2022, the total number of Ukraine citizens coming to Poland amounted to approximately 9,592,000. During the most intense period of hostilities – i.e., from February 24 to May 16, 2022 – as many as 3,000 million people from Ukraine arrived in Poland, whereas between February 24, 2022, and April 29, 2023, the Polish-Ukrainian border was crossed by as many as 11.47 million refugees from Ukraine. As underlined by Wojdat and Cywiński (2022) in their report on refugees from Ukraine in the largest Polish cities, the influx of Ukrainian citizens resulted in the size of the Polish population reaching over 40 million for the first time in history, and on April 1, 2022, it amounted to 41,451,907.

Before the outbreak of war, there were approximately one and a half million Ukrainians in Poland, whereas in the first five weeks of war, this number practically doubled. The research shows that Poland was the first choice of people escaping war in Ukraine and, at the same time, received the second largest number of refugees in the world, outranked only by Turkey. As of April 1, 2022, 79% of Ukrainians were adults and adolescents (+15 years), and 21% were children. The research conducted by Wojdat and Cywiński (2022) confirmed that war migrants primarily decided to stay longer in the largest Polish urban centres, including metropolitan areas belonging to the Union of Polish Metropolises. In March 2022, Polish cities and surrounding municipalities hosted almost 70% of all Ukrainian citizens who came to Poland after February 24 and who had lived in Poland earlier – i.e., 2,200,000 people. This meant a surge in the population of the main Polish cities. For instance, the population of Rzeszów increased by 53% (every third inhabitant was Ukrainian). The key motivations for this preference were knowledge of the location, some people living locally, or the choice was made spontaneously. As far as Lublin and Rzeszów, two key cities in the Polish-Ukrainian borderland, are concerned, it is clearly visible that a large number of refugees accumulated there, who – apart from receiving safe haven and living conditions – also expected gainful employment in Poland, even if they were overqualified for the work. In the case of Lublin, the local population grew from 338,586 (status as of December 31, 2020) to 406,982 (April 1, 2022). 17% of Lublin citizens – i.e., 68,396 people, including 16,866 children – are Ukrainian (as of April 1, 2022). Additionally, at the same moment in time, 87,048 Ukrainians resided within the Lublin Metropolitan Area and its 40 municipalities, 79% of whom were living in Lublin itself. Data concerning flows between night and day showed that 11% more Ukrainian refugees stayed in Lublin during the day than remained overnight. This trend is opposite to that in other cities and metropolitan municipalities, where 52% more Ukrainians stayed at night than remained during the day. In the case of Rzeszów, an increase was noted in the number of inhabitants from 196,638 (as of December 31, 2020) to 301,422 (April 1, 2022). 35% of Lublin inhabitants (104,784 people, including 30,802 children) are Ukrainian (as of April 1, 2022). As of April 1, 2022, Rzeszów and its 35 adjacent municipalities in the Rzeszów Metropolitan Area are inhabited by 152,203 Ukrainian adults, adolescents, and children, 69% of whom live in Rzeszów. Data concerning flows between night and day showed that 34% more Ukrainian refugees and migrants stayed in Rzeszów during the day than remained there overnight. This trend is opposite to other cities and municipalities, where 17% more Ukrainians remained overnight than stayed there during the day.

The presented data confirms that, with respect to place of residence, Ukrainian refugees prefer cities with better access to public services as well as better education opportunities for children and more opportunities for employment, even if it entails a higher cost of living. The research shows that Ukrainian refugees were not prepared to actively search for work in Poland since migration from Ukraine was not motivated by economic concerns. This means, inter alia, longer preparation to enter the Polish labour market, primarily in order to find employment consistent with education, professional qualifications, and experience, as well as command of Polish.

In the context of the acceptance of newcomers from Ukraine, it is worth mentioning a nationwide study conducted by the University of Warsaw on the social perception of refugees from Ukraine, migrants and actions taken by the government in three cycles during the first half of 2022, which reveals, inter alia, that a greater sense of threat is felt by supporters of Law and Justice (27% of respondents) (Staniszewski et al., 2022), which is also consistent with the political declarations of voters on the Polish-Ukrainian border. The research indicates that society's perception of help and its perception of the acceptance of refugees from Ukraine throughout Poland have been moving in a positive direction. The study also demonstrates that there is a consensus on the issue of assistance for Ukrainians – 69% of respondents actively helped refugees, and 91% were of the opinion that Poland should assist Ukraine during the war, with 85% positively assessing the scale of assistance so far, while only 8% disagreed with this position. However, the positive evaluation concerned selected types of action: humanitarian aid (84% of respondents), material (79%), and diplomatic (70%), while there was definitely no consent for the participation of the Polish Army in a NATO mission in Ukraine (only 17% approved).

In comparison to January 2022, a significant change with regard to migrants was noted (the percentage of respondents with a multidimensional positive perception of migrants increased from 36% to 66%). Almost a year after the start of hostilities, a vast majority of Poles (90%) believed that Poland should help Ukraine during the war with Russia. The assistance of Poland for Ukraine was very highly assessed, including for Ukrainian refugees (89% of respondents assessed it positively). The majority of Poles (53%) were in favour of accepting refugees from Ukraine until they might be able to return to their country, whereas the percentage of those who believed that Poland should be accepting refugees from Ukraine and allowing them to settle in Poland increased from 30% to 37% after April 2022. The percentage of respondents who did not notice a threat to Poland from Ukrainian refugees increased slightly (from 66% to 72%). What is equally important is that the above-mentioned study confirms a convergence of attitudes of the borderland population with the rest of the country (Staniszewski et al., 2022). This study showed that in January 2023, in general, 66% of Poles were not afraid of the influx of refugees from Ukraine, while 21% of respondents declared such fears, mainly regarding the negative impact on labour markets, the economy, the state budget, additional stimulus for inflation, nationalism, or crime (Staniszewski et al., 2022). At the same time, potential threats from Ukrainian refugees to Poland included, among others, a negative impact on the labour market, as confirmed in the aforementioned research conducted by P. Długosz et al. (2022) that identified a risk of waning compassion for, and solidarity with, the Ukrainian nation, and that tension could build between Poles and Ukrainians, sparked by a sense of injustice about the scale of social and financial support given to Ukrainians, competition on the labour market resulting in difficulties in finding employment, the suppressive effect on wages, as well as an increase in prices of residential rentals in cities fuelled by increased demand from migrants. All of the above could significantly shape the long-term perspective of Ukrainian refugees' residence in Poland.

In the context of the described literature, an important point of the research is to evaluate the impact of refugee migration forced by the war in Ukraine in 2022 on the labour market in the Polish-Ukrainian border region as well as the long-term effects.

9.1.1 Professional Experience, Skills, and Qualifications of War Refugees from the Polish-Ukrainian Border Area

The key issues determining whether the war refugees might be employed, apart from legislation and circumstances on the labour market, are the qualifications of the migrants. In the context of this issue, it is important to determine to what extent refugees who came to the border area work in accordance with their qualifications and how digitally savvy they are considering the requirements of the modern economy.

War refugees from Ukraine taking up employment in the labour market on the Polish side of the border region tend to highly rate their ability to operate computers and mobile devices, to use the Internet to obtain information and as a communication tool, as well as navigate the media and critically evaluate content and digital security. Knowledge of intellectual property protection law (subject to strong legislative pressure in the EU) was rated as average; independence was rated relatively low in terms of the ability to independently solve IT problems and very low in terms of administering website content and online services, or programming. We may therefore conclude that digital skills for the needs of non-specialised industries are sufficient to find work and perform standard digital data administration tasks. This mostly corresponds to requirements according to the structure of regional economies – see Figure 9.1.

A higher level of digital skills in all the areas above was characteristic of people with higher education, who constituted the majority in the study, but in terms of the ability to use digital solutions created for the user, people with secondary education also declared a high level of ability (sufficient for many work situations). Respondents with primary education declared a lower level of digital competency. People employed in Poland in managerial and specialist positions claimed to have excellent digital skills, as tended to be the case in the areas of content creation, security, and management of transmitted digital content. Those employed in regular trade and service jobs or blue-collar positions also confirmed a high level of ability to obtain information and operate computers and mobile devices, but smaller knowledge of the law, independence in this area, and security rules – see Table 9.1.

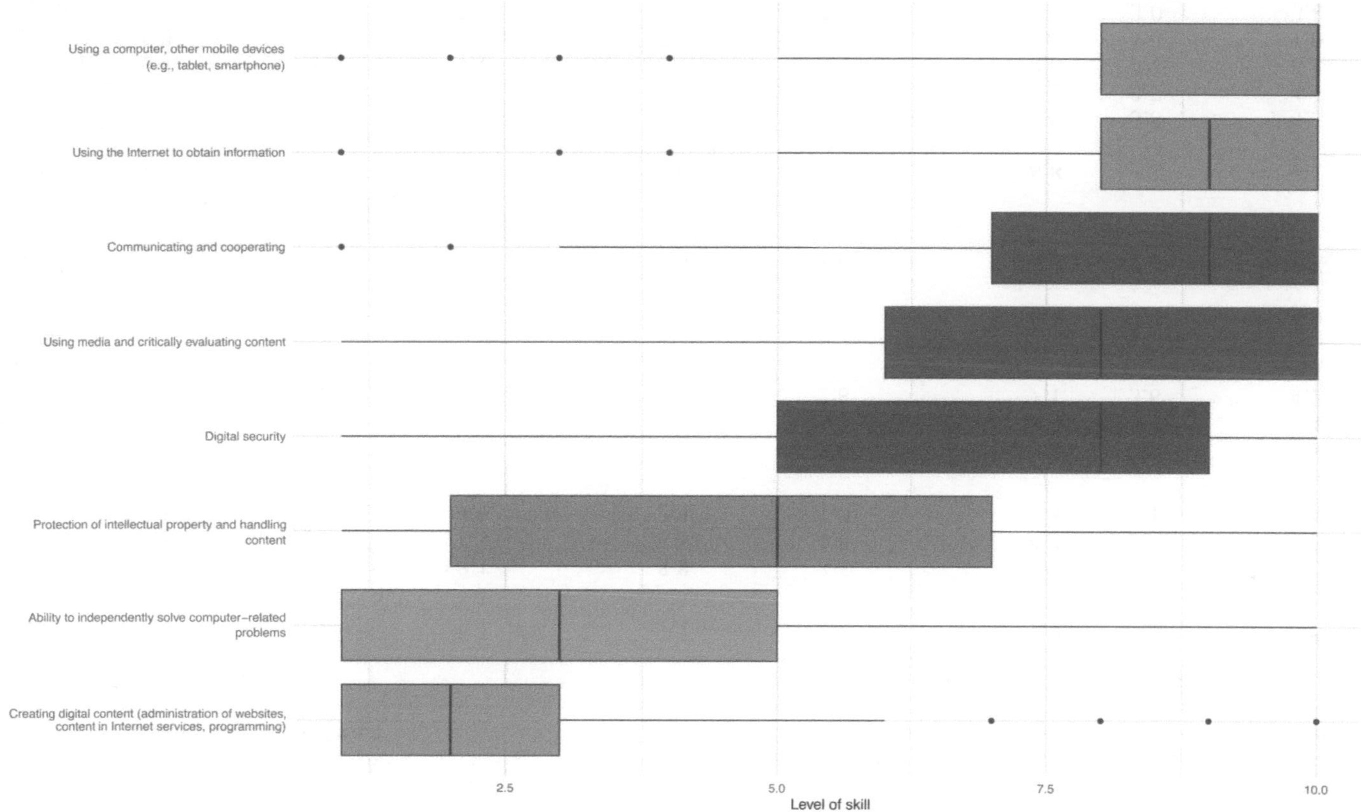

Figure 9.1 Subjective assessment of digital skills (0 – lowest rating, 10 – highest rating).

Source: Own elaboration based on research results.

Table 9.1 Level of digital competency according to education, employment position in Poland and employment sector in Ukraine

	Operating a computer and other mobile devices (e.g., tablet, smartphone)	*Obtaining information from the Internet*	*Communication and cooperation*	*Media use and critical evaluation of content*	*Creating digital content (website administration, content on websites, programming)*	*Digital security*	*Ability to independently solve computer-related problems*	*Intellectual property protection – handling content*
Average	8.5	8.4	8.1	7.5	2.7	7.0	3.6	4.6
According to education								
Higher	9.4	9.3	9.1	8.8	3.5	8.0	4.6	6.0
Secondary	7.8	7.7	7.3	6.5	1.8	6.2	2.6	3.2
Primary	5.1	4.9	4.4	3.3	1.0	3.5	1.1	1.5
According to employment position in Poland								
Managerial	10.0	10.0	10.0	10.0	8.0	10.0	7.0	7.5
Specialist	9.6	9.5	9.4	9.0	5.1	8.3	5.3	6.4
Regular trade and services worker	8.7	8.5	8.3	7.7	2.6	7.1	3.6	4.7
Skilled labourer	7.8	7.9	7.5	7.1	2.5	6.4	3.4	4.0
Unskilled labourer	7.1	7.0	6.6	5.8	1.6	5.9	2.3	2.7
According to employment sector in Ukraine								
Trade and sales	8.7	8.6	8.0	7.0	2.5	6.8	3.2	4.1
Services	8.5	8.3	8.1	7.5	2.7	6.8	3.6	4.3
Manufacturing	8.2	8.1	7.6	7.3	2.4	7.1	3.7	4.4
Public Sector	9.4	9.2	9.1	8.7	3.3	8.0	4.1	6.1
Others	6.0	8.0	9.0	7.0	1.0	8.0	1.0	1.0
Unemployed	7.5	7.6	7.2	6.3	2.1	6.2	3.0	3.8

Source: Own elaboration based on research results.

9.1.2 *Directions of Cross-Border Flows to the Polish-Ukrainian Border Area and Causes of Migration*

The largest streams of war refugees arriving on the Polish side of the border come from western Ukraine, from the Lviv and Volhynian oblasts. Individuals or small groups representing larger cities or their suburbs came from the areas occupied by the Russian army. Figure 9.2 (Main population flow – all declared destinations) presents the origin of the migrants according to their previously declared place of work. Across the entire surveyed group, these people constitute a small percentage and represent areas in north-eastern, eastern, south-eastern, and southern Ukraine, such as Kiev and its outskirts, Chernikhov, Kharkov, Sumy, Dnepropetrovsk, Donetsk, Odessa, Kherson, Mykolaiv, Zaporozhye. Although the remaining areas are not occupied (there are no Russian troops stationed there), it should be emphasised that starting from February 2022, all major conurbations have been subject to constant distant fire by missiles and drones, and warning sirens are regularly heard there.

The major Polish towns and cities where the surveyed Ukrainians work are Rzeszów, Przemyśl, Jarosław in the Subcarpathian Voivodeship, and Biała Podlaska, Chełm, and Zamość in the Lublin Voivodeship. Regarding the origin of these people (previous place of professional activity), apart from western Ukraine (especially areas bordering Poland), there is a visible diversification of origin – i.e., in the Subcarpathian Voivodeship, more people from southwestern Ukraine are employed (Lviv, Ivano-Frankivsk, Tarnoloski), whereas the Lublin Voivodeship has more migrants from the northwestern oblasts (Volhynia, Rivne – see Figure 9.3 (Main arrival destinations in host municipalities and number of surveyed refugees – border region study).

The place of origin strongly determines the reasons for decisions to migrate. This is not only due to active military operations – the proximity of the Polish border is also a factor contributing to the decision to migrate to the Polish border area. In the study, respondents were asked about the reasons for deciding to leave their country, taking into account health and safety, life situation, and security issues. The reasons for migration differ significantly in the case of one group of refugees – people from zones affected by direct military operations. In this group, 45.6% of people indicated a direct threat to health or life as the cause, 21.5% – sense of threat and uncertainty regarding the future, 19% – the economic situation after the outbreak of the conflict, and 7.6% – life situation, while only 5.1% were motivated by the opportunity to enter the EU. In other words, this means that 67.1% of refugees from war zones are exposed to a direct threat to life/health or feel a sense of threat in their place of origin (23.7 percentage points more than in the case of people outside the direct military operations zone), while another 19% feel economically insecure – see Figure 9.4.

In the case of people from unoccupied areas or those located close to the war front, two main reasons for emigration prevail: 36.2% of respondents

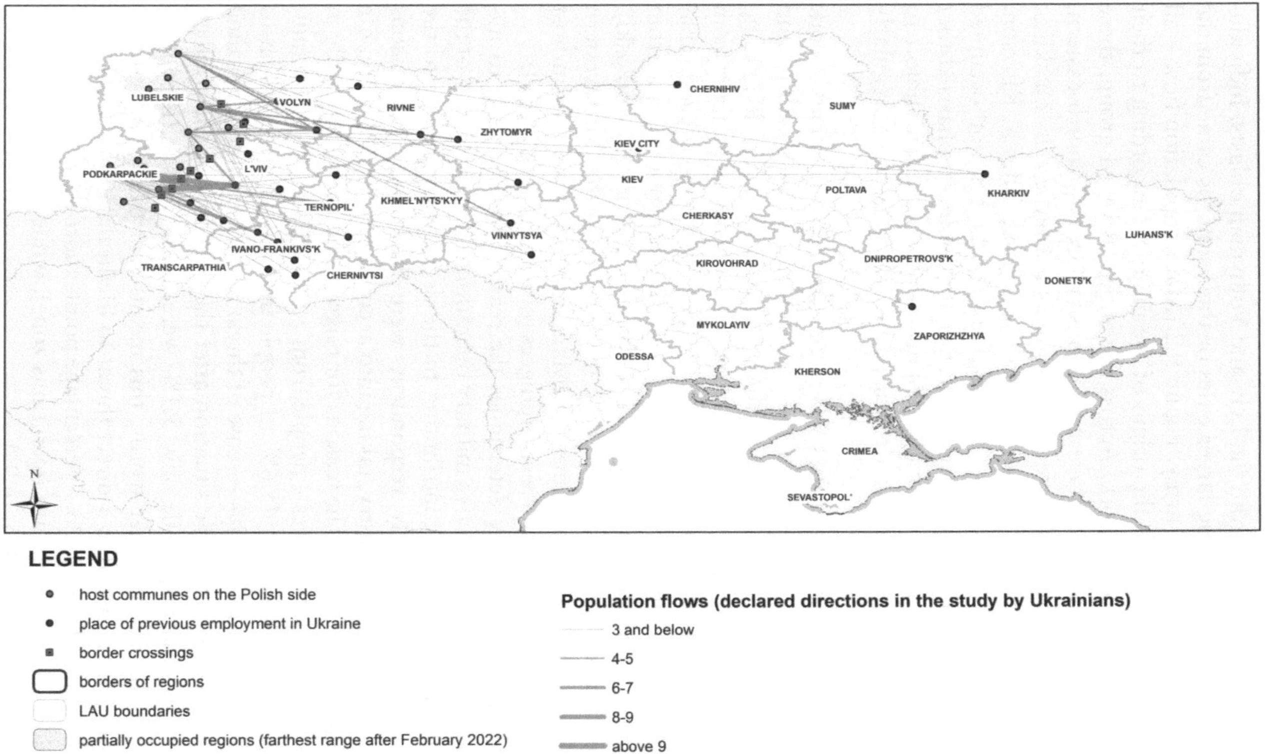

Figure 9.2 Main population flow map – all declared destinations.

Source: Own elaboration based on research results. The source of this valuable data is our own elaboration based on research results, utilising ArcGIS software from the renowned producer Esri, Inc.

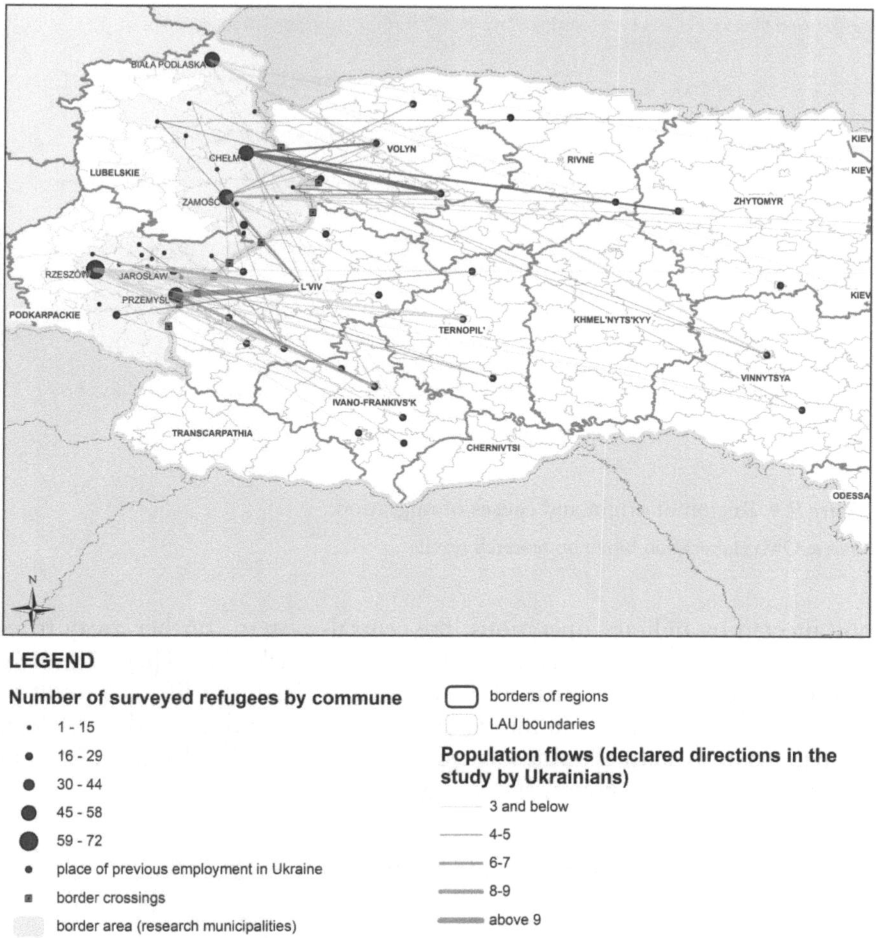

Figure 9.3 Main arrival destinations in host municipalities and number of surveyed refugees – border region study.

Source: Own elaboration based on research results. The source of this valuable data is our own elaboration based on research results, utilising ArcGIS software from the renowned producer Esri, Inc.

indicated sense of threat (indirect exposure to the area of military operations) and uncertainty regarding the future. A further 33.7% mentioned their poor economic/financial situation after the outbreak of the conflict (including, e.g., loss of employment and significant deterioration in living standards). A total of 14.3% decided to emigrate due to life circumstances (including the departure of relatives, friends, and separation) and 7.2% due to the feeling of direct threat related to military operations. Detailed data on people living in the oblasts of western Ukraine on the Ukrainian side of the border zone are similar in terms of reasons for migration to those of residents of other zones

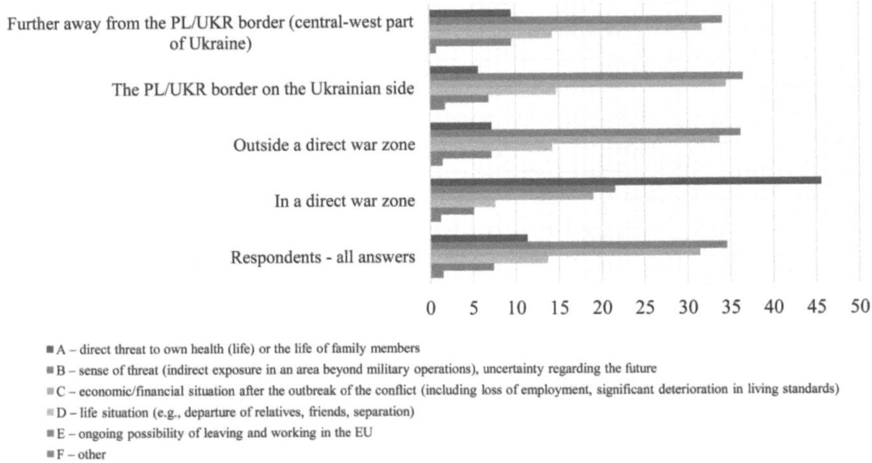

Figure 9.4 Region of origin and causes of migration.

Source: Own elaboration based on research results.

not affected by military operations: the central-western (further away from the PL/UKR border) and central-eastern areas of Ukraine. They are solely distinguished by a lower sense of direct threat to health or life as a result of military operations (5.7% in the examined border area compared to 9.5% in the regions of western Ukraine located further from the border and 15.5% in the central part of the country) – see Table 9.2.

9.1.3 Assistance with Jobseeking and Perception of Prospects in the Migration Destination

The borderland labour market offers jobs that pay less than the major national urban agglomerations. An important aim of the study was to determine what non-economic factors influenced the residence of working refugees in the Polish-Ukrainian border region. The study clearly shows that refugees from Ukraine employed in Polish border regions mostly mentioned satisfaction with their workplace – 59.9% of respondents (including 20.96% of people declaring great satisfaction) compared to 27.4% of people who are dissatisfied and 12.8% undecided. A longer period of jobseeking (two months and more) only contributed slightly to more frequent declarations of job satisfaction (see Table 9.3). What largely determined a high level of job satisfaction in Poland was compatibility between the nature of employment in Poland and Ukraine (29.3% of respondents) – in cases where the type of work matched, the percentage of people satisfied with work in Poland was 98.6% compared to 43.8% in the absence of such a match with as many as 38.4% of people declaring job dissatisfaction. The main methods of jobseeking were direct inquiries at the employer (43.6% of respondents), searching

Table 9.2 Region of origin and causes of migration

	Total number of responses	*According to reason for migration*					
		A	*B*	*C*	*D*	*E*	*F*
Respondents – all answers	795	90	275	250	109	59	12
%	***100***	***11.32***	***34.59***	***31.45***	***13.71***	***7.42***	***1.51***
Direct war zone	79	36	17	15	6	4	1
%	*100*	*45.57*	*21.52*	*18.99*	*7.59*	*5.06*	*1.27*
Outside a direct war zone	694	50	251	234	99	50	10
%	*100*	*7.20*	*36.17*	*33.72*	*14.27*	*7.20*	*1.44*
West Ukraine – PL/ UKR border zone	**510**	**29**	**186**	**176**	75	35	9
%	***100***	***5.69***	***36.47***	***34.51***	*14.71*	*6.86*	*1.76*
Central-west part of Ukraine – further away from the PL/ UKR border	126	12	43	40	18	12	1
%	*100*	*9.52*	*34.13*	*31.75*	*14.29*	*9.52*	*0.79*
Central-east part of Ukraine	58	9	22	18	6	3	0
%	*100*	*15.52*	*37.93*	*31.03*	*10.34*	*5.17*	*0.00*
Location not established	22	4	7	1	4	5	1

Source: Own elaboration based on research results.

Legend:

A – direct threat to own health/life or the lives of family members

B – sense of threat (indirect exposure in an area beyond military operations), uncertainty regarding the future

C – economic/financial situation after the outbreak of the conflict (including loss of employment, and significant deterioration in living standards)

D – life situation (e.g., departure of relatives, friends, and separation)

E – ongoing possibility of leaving and working in the EU

F – other

through friends (24.2%), or via websites (16.2%). Other methods were used by only 16% of respondents. In the case of job search methods mentioned by more than ten people, a high percentage of satisfied respondents were those who had found employment via the Labour Office (71.4%) and those who had obtained employment directly from the employer (67.1%).

A large percentage of satisfied respondents had found jobs via websites (48.3%), recommendations from friends (48.9%), and job applications (50%), while a significant percentage of people dissatisfied with their employment (36.1% and 35.7%, respectively) had obtained work via friends or job applications. According to the respondents, among the methods represented in this study, those employed through temporary employment agencies were the most dissatisfied (44.4%). A higher level of satisfaction was also declared

Table 9.3 Factors affecting job satisfaction

	Total	Declared job satisfaction in Poland*				
		Definitely yes	*Generally yes*	*Don't know*	*Generally no*	*Definitely no*
Total number of responses	501	105	195	64	132	5
%	100	20.96	38.92	12.77	26.35	1.00
According to jobseeking period (%)						
1 month	38.32	20.83	35.94	17.19	25.52	0.52
2 months	38.32	22.40	35.94	13.02	27.60	1.04
Longer	23.35	18.80	48.72	5.13	25.64	1.71
According to compatibility between work in Poland and Ukraine (%)						
No	70.66	7.06	36.72	17.80	37.01	1.41
Yes	29.34	54.42	44.22	0.68	0.68	0.00
According to method of jobseeking in Poland – 550 answers in total (%)						
Internet	16.18	10.11	38.20	25.84	25.84	0.00
Friends and acquaintances	24.18	17.29	31.58	15.04	33.83	2.26
Application	2.55	14.29	35.71	14.29	35.71	0.00
Agency for temporary work	3.27	5.56	27.78	22.22	38.89	5.56
Directly from the employer	43.64	27.50	39.58	9.17	23.33	0.42
Social media	1.09	0.00	33.33	16.67	50.00	0.00
Labour office	7.64	19.05	52.38	9.52	19.05	0.00
Others (including advertising bollards)	1.45	25.00	75.00	0.00	0.00	0.00
According to employment position in Poland (%)						
Managerial*	0.80	100.00	0.00	0.00	0.00	0.00
Specialist	6.79	47.06	41.18	8.82	2.94	0.00
Regular trade and services worker	71.86	13.06	40.83	13.33	31.39	1.39
Skilled labourer	11.38	38.60	38.60	7.02	15.79	0.00
Unskilled labourer	9.18	34.78	26.09	19.57	19.57	0.00
According to education – 536 responses in total (%)						
Higher	49.3	10.2	30.7	15.2	42.0	1.9
Secondary	39.9	29.0	50.5	10.7	9.8	0.0
Primary	4.3	69.6	26.1	4.3	0.0	0.0
Additional courses	6.5	31.4	34.3	11.4	20.0	2.9

Source: Own elaboration based on research results.

* % in a given category, Σ=100

by people holding specialist, skilled, or unskilled positions in Poland (88.2%, 77.2%, and 60.1%, respectively), while workplaces were rated the worst by ordinary trade, sales, and service workers (53.9% satisfied vs. 32.8% dissatisfied). Analysis of the respondents in terms of education leads to the conclusion that most of the higher education group were dissatisfied with their jobs

(43.9% dissatisfied compared to 40.9% of people who assessed the workplace in Poland favourably), while 79.4% and 95.7% of people with secondary and primary education, respectively, were satisfied with their workplace in Poland. The relationship described may indicate that the opportunities offered on the borderland labour market do not correspond to the needs and life aspirations of people with higher qualifications. Taking into account the respondents' job classification, these people found employment in Poland as regular trade, sales, and service workers that did not match their qualifications.

9.1.4 The Polish-Ukrainian Border Area as a Place to Settle

The willingness of refugees to settle is influenced by economic and non-economic factors that concern not only the workers themselves but also the people who accompany them to the country of emigration. The study included an analysis aimed at determining the importance of non-economic factors, in particular the possibility of finding a place to live and the conditions of settlement in a given area. This is crucial because the nature of war migration, manifested by the desire to ensure security, and the prevailing involvement of women with children, results in a greater percentage of women among working refugees (74.65% of respondents). This leads to a number of life complications, including ensuring appropriate accommodation standards, healthcare, and access to education for families.

The respondents were asked to assess their willingness to live in the Polish-Ukrainian border region. A characteristic response was a declared desire to return to Ukraine after the threat of war had ended (58.5% of the respondents). 8.6% of respondents declared that they would stay in Poland, while 14.8% expressed a wish to go to another city in Poland or Europe, but the second largest group consisted of people who were undecided as to their future place of residence (18.2%). Among people with higher education, only half declared that they wanted to return to their own country (49.2%), which may be explained by the greater mobility of this group but also indicates that the prospects for resolving social issues after the end of the war are unlikely in Ukraine. These people tended towards indecision (22.7%) regarding further decisions or a desire to stay in larger cities in Poland/Europe thanks to the opening of the European market (18.6%), and were only slightly more likely to declare a desire to stay in their current place of residence (9.5%). Returning to their own country was mentioned more by people with primary education (82.6%) and secondary education (67.3%) – see Table 9.4.

The desire to return to Ukraine was also positively correlated with number of children – in other words, the more dependent children, the more often respondents indicated a planned return to Ukraine. Even having one child resulted in an increased tendency to want to return home. In this context, it is worth noting that people without children (140 respondents) viewed themselves as extremely mobile – 29.3% indicated plans to move to another Polish/European city. 11.4% mentioned a desire to stay in their current

Table 9.4 Willingness to settle in current place of residence according to selected respondent characteristics

	Total	*Do you treat your current place of residence in Poland as your ultimate destination? (%)*			
		Don't know	*Yes*	*Planning to return to Ukraine*	*Planning to live in another town or city in Poland or Europe*
Total	501	18.16	8.58	58.48	14.77
According to education					
Higher	264	22.73	9.47	49.24	18.56
Secondary	214	14.02	7.01	67.29	11.68
Primary	23	4.35	13.04	82.61	0.00
According to number of children					
a. Childless	140	23.57	11.43	35.71	29.29
b. One child	213	17.84	7.98	60.56	13.62
c. 2–4 children	143	13.99	6.99	76.22	2.80
d. More than 4	5	0.00	0.00	100.00	0.00
According to employment sector in Ukraine					
a. Trade and sales	49	14.29	8.16	65.31	12.24
b. Services	227	20.26	12.33	52.42	14.98
c. Manufacturing	77	14.29	6.49	67.53	11.69
d. Public Sector	96	22.92	4.17	57.29	15.63
e. Others	1	0.00	0.00	100.00	0.00
f. Unemployed	51	9.80	3.92	66.67	19.61
According to length of stay in Poland					
a. Less than six months	90	18.89	12.22	53.33	15.56
b. More than six months	411	18.00	7.79	59.61	14.60
According to compatibility between work in Poland and Ukraine					
No	354	18.93	5.65	60.17	15.25
Yes	147	16.33	15.65	54.42	13.61
According to place of residence in Poland					
a. Own home	9	0.00	66.67	11.11	22.22
b. Municipal housing	4	0.00	25.00	50.00	25.00
c. Private rented accommodation	163	21.47	13.50	49.08	15.95
d. At Polish or Ukrainian friends'	220	18.64	2.73	62.27	16.36
e. Currently looking for accommodation	51	19.61	3.92	62.75	13.73
f. Other	54	9.26	11.11	75.93	3.70
According to satisfaction with place of residence					
No	138	15.22	2.17	56.52	26.09
Yes	363	19.28	11.02	59.23	10.47

(*Continued*)

Table 9.4 (Continued)

	Total	Do you treat your current place of residence in Poland as your ultimate destination? (%)			
		Don't know	*Yes*	*Planning to return to Ukraine*	*Planning to live in another town or city in Poland or Europe*
According to relations with Poland					
Polish parents	2	0.00	50.00	50.00	0.00
Polish grandparents	26	11.54	19.23	61.54	7.69
Polish great-grandparents or ancestors	132	15.91	10.61	60.61	12.88
Close family (parents, siblings, children, uncles, and aunts)	97	19.59	15.46	51.55	13.40
Distant family	195	16.92	9.74	56.92	16.41
Friends or acquaintances from Ukraine	412	19.66	9.71	56.07	14.56
Friends or acquaintances from Poland	106	12.26	16.98	47.17	23.58
Friends or acquaintances from other countries but residing in Poland	6	16.67	0.00	33.33	50.00
According to command of Polish on arrival					
None	266	16.17	6.02	61.28	16.54
Fluent	1	0.00	100.00	0.00	0.00
Weak	178	21.91	11.80	52.81	13.48
Intermediate (communication in everyday situations)	47	14.89	10.64	61.70	12.77
Advanced (fluent communication)	9	22.22	0.00	77.78	0.00
According to command of Polish now					
None	4	0.00	0.00	100.00	0.00
Fluent	1	0.00	100.00	0.00	0.00
Weak	313	17.89	5.75	61.66	14.70
Intermediate (communication in everyday situations)	170	19.41	13.53	50.59	16.47
Advanced (fluent communication)	13	15.38	7.69	76.92	0.00

Source: Own elaboration based on research results.

place of residence, while only 35.7% wished to return home, and as many as 23.6% did not indicate any specific decisions in this regard.

A longer period of employment in the border area (over six months) correlated with a greater desire to return home – 59.6% compared to 53.3% among people staying in Poland for less than six months. Although the reasons may be different (the survey questionnaire did not contain detailed questions in this regard), it should be noted that the most likely causes are homesickness as well as perceived improvement in security in areas not affected by direct military operations during the first and second half of 2022 (waiting out the danger) or directly from achieving financial satisfaction. It is also significant that the period of departure of individual waves of migrants from Ukraine was caused by various factors, mainly a wish to protect family safety during the initial phase.

Compatibility between employment positions in Poland and Ukraine has a positive impact on willingness to remain in Poland – in this group, the desire to stay in the border region was three times more popular (15.7% compared to 5.7% among those performing incompatible jobs in Poland). The inclination towards returning home among migrants working in a job for which they are overqualified was also higher (60.2% in favour of returning home, compared to 54.4% with compatible jobs).

The majority of respondents (363 people, 72.5%) declared satisfaction with their living conditions. Dissatisfaction with place of residence was the main reason for wanting to move to another place in Poland/Europe (26.1% compared to 10.5% in the group of satisfied respondents) rather than a desire to return to Ukraine, while at the same time contributing to a noticeable negative assessment of the borderland as a place of residence (only 2.2% of people dissatisfied with their place of residence declared that they would like to stay in the surveyed area). A total of 43.9% of respondents live with Polish acquaintances or Ukrainians resettled from Ukraine. 32.5% rent apartments from the free market. 10.2% are looking for an apartment. 10.8% indicated another option. Only nine respondents declared they had their own apartment, and only four rented municipal housing, which may be due to the specific nature of the borderland as an area with a predominance of single-family buildings. It also shows the weak participation of public administration units in offering refugee accommodation. People who had difficulty finding separate (independent) accommodations were more likely to declare a wish to return to their homeland. These conclusions are confirmed by the respondents themselves, who, when asked about additional actions that should be taken by administration (local governments, government), labour offices/employment agencies, and employers in order to improve employment opportunities and conditions, most often mentioned assistance in finding housing and helping to find employment. In addition, they spoke about the creation of additional work opportunities, higher/better earnings/subsidies/bonuses/subsidies, the possibility of learning and taking courses (including language courses), the organisation of childcare and medical care, and the recognition of diplomas/qualifications.

Assimilation with Poland was facilitated by having close Polish ancestors, relatives, or friends with poor or intermediate knowledge of the Polish language at the time of moving and intermediate knowledge at the end of 2022. Polish is an easy language to learn for Ukrainians, as evidenced by the pace of learning – of the people who declared complete ignorance when they arrived

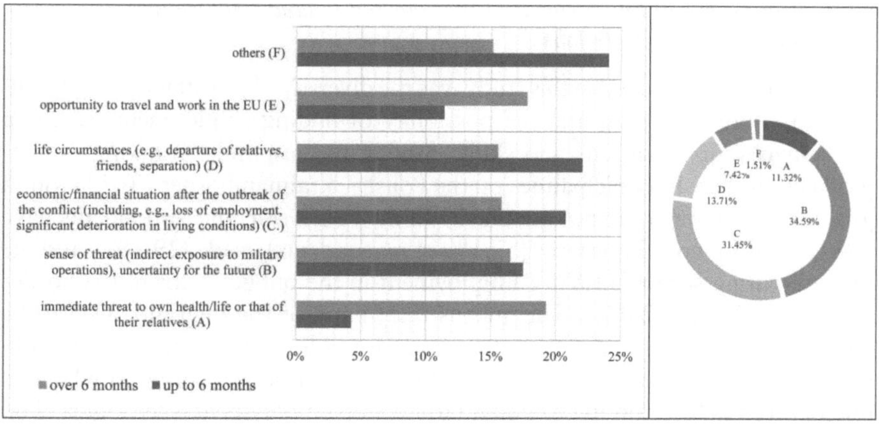

Figure 9.5 Reasons for leaving and the period of stay outside Ukraine.

Source: Own elaboration based on the results of the study.

in Poland, 98.5% after half a year declared at least a poor or intermediate command of the language (cultural and linguistic affinity). Communication in everyday situations largely contributed to declaring a wish to stay in the border area on the Polish side (see Table 9.4).

Among respondents staying in Poland for more than six months (411 people) at the end of 2022, none of these six potential reasons for leaving predominated (ranging from 15.1% to 19.3% of respondents) – threat to health, economic situation or life circumstances, or opportunity to travel – were equally cited (see Fig. 9.5). The most common cause was a direct threat to the health/life of the respondent or his or her relatives (factor A). Migration in the second half of the year (group of 90 respondents) was caused mainly by the dire economic/financial situation after the outbreak of the war (22.1% of respondents), life circumstances (including separation from loved ones, 20.8%), as well as other factors (24.0%). Migrants from this period were less likely to make decisions due to a direct threat to their own or their loved ones' lives (4.3%) or the opportunity to travel further (11.4%), while the percentage of people mentioning threats to security and uncertainty regarding the future was only slightly higher (17.5% compared to 16.5% in the group staying in Poland for more than six months), which suggests a complexity of factors influencing this uncertainty.

Other reasons for leaving given by people emigrating during the second half of 2022 include corruption in Ukraine, sluggish rate of change and lack of economic reforms, ease of leaving Poland for Canada, as well as having Polish ancestors. Other reasons indicated by emigrants from the first half of 2022 included a job offer from Poland or previous connections with this country, the evacuation of Western business enterprises and their employees, lack of prospects for a better life in Ukraine, family pressure to leave the country, as well as fear of attack on a nuclear power plant or of being drafted into the army.

9.1.5 Conditions of Employment in Ukraine and Poland – Matching Qualifications with Jobs

Another aspect examined in this study was the diversity of job offers in the Polish-Ukrainian border region and the possibility of finding employment matching the refugees' qualifications and skills. Among the respondents taking up employment in Polish municipalities on the Polish-Ukrainian border, 70.7% found jobs for which they were not qualified. On the Polish side, the respondents have been forced to work in services (57.1% of respondents), trade (29.1%), and the manufacturing sector (11.8%). Employment in the public sector in the border area was minimal (2.0%). This means that many of the migrants need to be retrained for services and trade, at the expense of less employment in the public sector, as well as the need for almost every tenth person surveyed who was unemployed before coming to Poland to take up employment – see Figure 9.6.

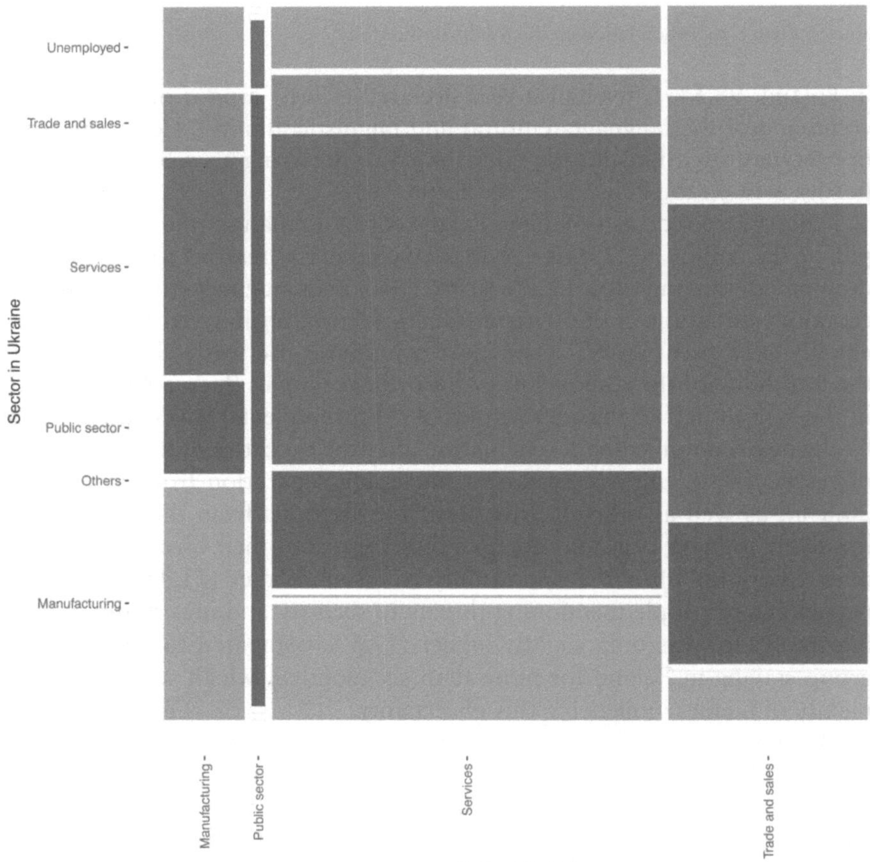

Figure 9.6 Employment sectors in Ukraine and Poland.

Source: Own elaboration based on research results.

9.1.6 *The Refugees' State of Health and Job Satisfaction*

The surveyed respondents were asked to assess their health and mental state. Most respondents assessed their health as good, especially their physical state. Across the entire study group, the average physical health assessment was 8.5 on a scale of 1–10 (where 10 is perfect), while mental health scored 7.8 points. Women declared a worse state of mental health – 7.5 points. vs. 8.6 points among the men. Moreover, relatively young people (under 45 years of age) assessed their state of health to be better and also declared a better state of mental health than people in older age groups. The state of physical health was directly related to age (worse in older people), and this group also declared worse perceived mental health – see Figure 9.7. An important determinant of health (both physical and mental) was the number of dependent children – the best health assessment was given by people without children; the greater the number of children, the worse the assessment of health, especially mental health in the case of people responsible for two or more children. Importantly, the study confirms greater diversity in the respondents' answers regarding mental health than physical health – see Table 9.5.

Important factors determining the assessment of health were how the work performed matches skills and qualifications and satisfaction with the workplace, although there was no statistically significant variability in responses in the case of declared satisfaction with the place of residence. People performing work inconsistent with their qualifications were declared to have a worse mental state (7.7 points) than people working in their given profession (8.1 points). Similarly, in the case of people dissatisfied with their workplace,

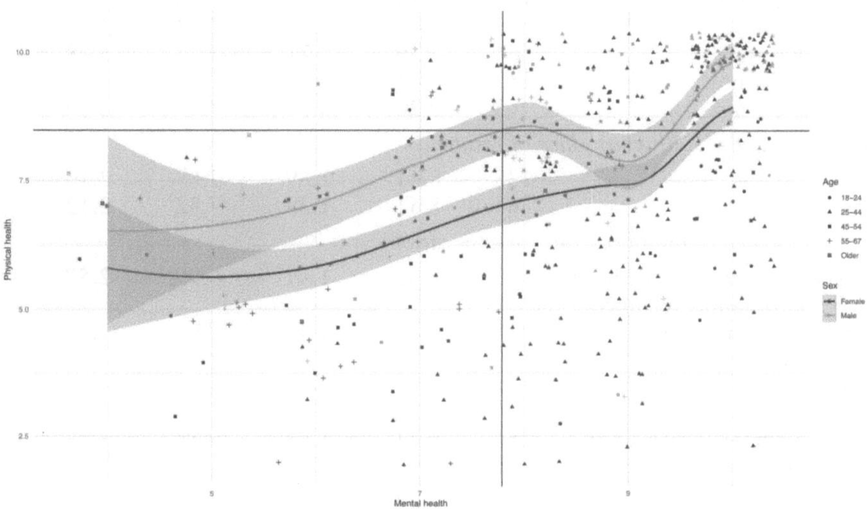

Figure 9.7 Self-assessment of health problems – physical/mental health and sex.

Source: Own elaboration based on research results.

Table 9.5 Assessment of state of health according to the characteristics of the refugees and their reasons for emigration

	Total number	*Assessment of physical health*		*Assessment of mental health*	
		Average	*Standard deviation*	*Average*	*Standard deviation*
Total	**501**	**8.48**	**1.48**	**7.79**	**2.11**
Evaluation according to sex:					
Female	374	8.44	1.49	7.51	2.17
Male	127	8.58	1.44	8.61	1.69
Evaluation according to age:					
a. 18–24	44	9.73	0.66	8.73	1.47
b. 25–44	266	9.08	1.02	8.06	2.21
c. 45–54	112	7.73	1.29	7.41	1.97
d. 55–67	72	6.94	1.37	6.86	1.97
e. Older	7	5.43	1.62	7.14	1.07
Evaluation according to number of dependent children:					
a. Childless	140	9.29	1.07	8.44	1.84
b. One child	213	8.47	1.43	7.77	2.15
c. 2–4 children	143	7.76	1.46	7.20	2.16
d. More than 4	5	6.60	1.82	6.80	1.48
Does your job match your skills and qualifications?					
No	354	8.48	1.46	7.65	2.15
Yes	147	8.47	1.51	8.12	2.00
Are you satisfied with your place of work?					
a. Definitely yes	105	8.46	1.45	7.92	2.07
b. Generally yes	195	8.41	1.51	7.82	2.06
c. Don't know	64	8.39	1.71	7.92	2.08
d. Generally no	132	8.61	1.33	7.58	2.25
e. Definitely no	5	9.20	0.84	7.40	2.30
Are you satisfied with your place of residence?					
No	138	8.41	1.69	7.69	2.10
Yes	363	8.51	1.39	7.82	2.12
Evaluation according to reasons for emigration:					
Direct threat to own life/health or that of family members	90	8.32	1.41	6.99	2.57
Sense of threat (Indirect exposure to military operations), uncertainty for the future	275	8.45	1.48	7.63	2.06
Economic/financial situation after the outbreak of the conflict (including, e.g., loss of employment, significant deterioration of living conditions)	250	8.42	1.47	8.12	1.82

(*Continued*)

Table 9.5 (Continued)

	Total number	*Assessment of physical health*		*Assessment of mental health*	
		Average	*Standard deviation*	*Average*	*Standard deviation*
Life circumstances (e.g., departure of relatives, friends, and separation)	109	8.31	1.66	7.69	2.07
Opportunity to travel and work in the EU	59	9.29	1.25	9.31	1.19
Others	12	9.42	1.00	8.42	2.84

Source: Own elaboration based on research results.

the mental health assessment was slightly lower (below 7.6 points). Such variability was not observed for physical health assessments.

In the context of health, it is important to analyse the causes of migration. Noticeably, those who had not been forced to migrate but did so in order to, for example, take advantage of the opportunity to move and work in the EU, stand out in terms of their excellent physical (9.3 points) and mental (9.3 points) state of health. Generally, when assessing physical health, differences are negligible depending on the reason for forced migration. The assessment of mental health leads to different conclusions and is clearly worse among people fleeing the country due to a threat to their own health/life or the lives of their relatives (7.0 points), or sense of threat with indirect exposure to armed conflict (7.6 points), or life circumstances that forced separation (7.7 points). These groups (although they constitute nearly 60% of all respondents) should be offered special medical and psychological care due to their particular exposure to highly stressful factors. The difficult economic/financial situation after the outbreak of the conflict had a smaller impact on the mental health of the migrants (score 8.1 points) – see Table 9.5.

The surveyed refugees were asked to assess how difficult they found it to function in everyday life (for particular groups of activities) – see Figure 9.8. The variability of the answers was significant, but having calculated the averages and the standard deviation from these averages, in all cases, the average ratings indicated the existence of a significant problem in terms of everyday activities (scores above five). According to their perception, what poses the most difficult thing is the performance of tasks requiring concentration (average score close to nine), and here the diversity of opinions was also the smallest. Refugees find it relatively more difficult to engage in social activities outside the home (an average score of eight) but experience slightly fewer problems with sleep and getting up in the morning (average score: seven). It should be emphasised, however, that the refugees considered all categories included in the study as difficult. Although the respondents

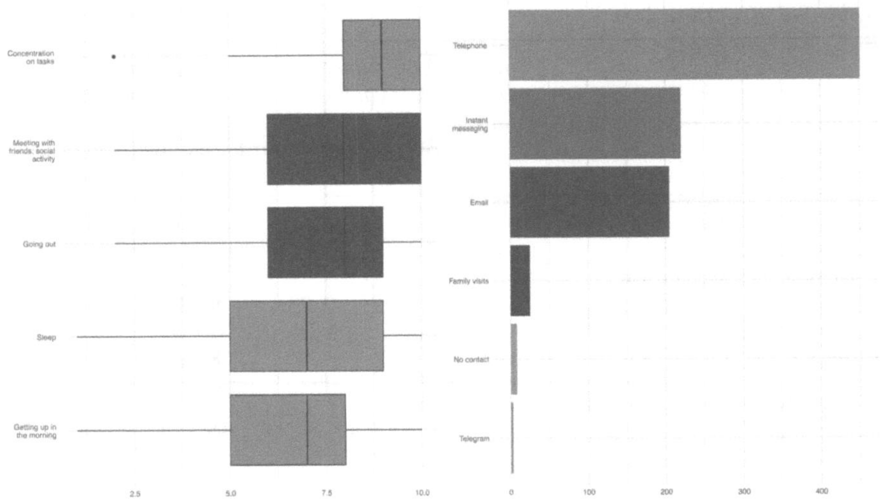

Figure 9.8 Difficulties experienced by refugees in everyday life and ways of contacting family.

Source: Own elaboration based on research results.

assessed their mental health as good, the difficulties they described in everyday functioning indicate trauma related to war and separation. This is an important tip for decision-makers who wish to employ war migrants or offer them assistance. In the context of social activity and contact with loved ones, respondents rarely had the opportunity to visit or meet their family; the prevailing forms of contact are distance relations, mainly via telephone, and, to a lesser extent, via instant messaging or e-mail. It is therefore important to take action to enable real contact – operators providing travel packages for refugees.

9.2 Employers on the Labour Market

After the outbreak of a full-scale conflict in Ukraine in 2022, a number of institutions and citizens became involved in helping migrants, and businesses also offered help, including enterprises operating in the border area. The impact of refugee migration on markets and business depends on many external factors, especially the course of the war and Polish government policy. The factors that may potentially increase the flow of migrants include the escalation of the conflict, its prolongation, and the effects of the economic crisis in Ukraine. Lack of action aimed at creating conditions for permanent residence will lead to a drain of more ambitious people to other countries/regions, despite attempts made by employers to manage a more diverse workforce (Deloitte, 2022). At the same time, filling vacancies represents significant potential for the Polish economy (Poland has one of the lowest unemployment rates in the EU and has very unfavourable demographics) and economies of other European countries, as well as for demand on the domestic market, which may be stimulated due to the sheer scale of refugees settling.

Business also felt the negative impact of the war in terms of realising contracts and completing commissions. Data from the Polish Economic Institute show that 24% of companies in Poland felt that the war had severely impacted their operations. 36% mentioned a moderate impact, and 40% felt that the effect was weak. The war caused a sharp increase in the prices of industrial supply and investment goods (excluding means of transport), products, or services offered by businesses, operating costs, operation risk, as well as supply chain disruptions. Research has revealed that four main areas remained relatively unaffected: changes in employment due to the outflow or inflow of employees from Ukraine, withdrawal from some sales markets, deterioration of cooperation with foreign contractors, and increase in payment backlogs (Dębkowska et al., 2023, p. 4). PIE researchers concluded that all industrial processing enterprises (section C), micro- and medium-sized construction enterprises, small commercial enterprises, large transport firms, accommodation and catering businesses, medium-sized financial and insurance companies, and all businesses dealing with professional, scientific, and technical commodities and services were severely affected by the war (Dębkowska et al., 2023, p. 5).

Despite the above-mentioned difficulties, the business sector in Poland organised financial and material support for war refugees as well as assistance with telecommunications, logistics, and human resources, jobs for refugees, support for employees' families (including childcare and education), integration, support for the tourism sector, mainly in terms of accommodation and volunteering. Difficulties reported in cooperation between local governments, non-governmental organisations, and businesses include cases of attempts to achieve hidden business goals under the guise of ethical action, unrealistic expectations, excessive bureaucratisation, political tensions, lack of previous cooperation resulting in difficulties in working together, as well as refusal to support aid action. Despite this, business involvement is clearly assessed positively (Jarosz & Klaus, 2023). In the context of the involvement of institutions and the impact of the war on regional entrepreneurship, this chapter aims to determine how the crisis involving the wave of refugees from Ukraine influenced the development of entrepreneurship in the Polish-Ukrainian border region. In this case, the analysis included an evaluation by entrepreneurs from this area of the impact of refugees on entrepreneurship and the economic situation in the Polish-Ukrainian border region, comprehensively covering issues of demand and employment conditions for Ukrainian workers, their skills and adaptation to the needs of employers, as well as action undertaken activities to help employees from Ukraine and how their enterprises have been affected. Detailed study results are presented in the sections below.

9.2.1 *The Demand for Work from Ukrainian Employees and Matching the Skills and Qualifications of Refugees to the Employers' Requirements*

The regions of eastern Poland are characterised by a significant outflow of young people to larger urban agglomerations, often in other regions of the country or abroad – according to data from the Local Data Bank (Statistics Poland), in 2022, the net foreign and domestic migration for groups of young residents in the Lublin Voivodeship indicated the following: 260 people of pre-working age (net migration coefficient: –7.1) and 4,089 people of working age (–34.8). In the Subcarpathian Voivodeship, the statistics are as follows: 413 people of pre-working age (ten, six), and 2,465 people of working age (–19.9). Therefore, the exodus of young residents from these areas is clear. At the same time, in the case of the Lublin Voivodeship, people of post-working age are also leaving the area (the net migration rate in 2022 was –3.1), but such a constant trend has not been observed in the Subcarpathian Voivodeship.

The structure of the economy in the studied regions creates fewer opportunities for employment in specialised or high-tech services than in many other regions of the country since it is characterised by a low level of automation and, consequently, strong dependence on the availability of human capital along with lower average wages and lower costs of living. The structure of enterprises included in the study according to economic sectors reflects the described circumstances – a significant representation of construction, trade, and service companies, especially ones related to transport, shipping, tourism, and catering. Total employment in the surveyed enterprises employing workers from Ukraine amounted to 1.5 thousand workers, of whom 10% were migrants from Ukraine, but the percentage differed by sector, ranging from 2.3% to 40%. The vast majority of regional firms mentioned staff shortages. 35 out of 55 companies declared their willingness to employ new workers, most of them in lower-level positions (32 out of 35 companies declared that they wish to employ additional staff). This indicates a significant deficit of workers with lower qualifications, which, despite the migration crisis of 2022, has not been covered – see Table 9.6.

The skills and qualifications of workers were deemed to be largely mismatched with the job positions undertaken. In most of the surveyed companies, the level of matching varied – only in the case of 29.1% did the skills and qualifications of employees meet the needs of their employers. This implies, inter alia, the need for more extensive training on the job, incurring additional costs, and lower efficiency during the initial period of employment. Looking at the cross-section of individual sectors, the match was the poorest in the manufacturing sector, where people tended not to be employed in accordance with their qualifications, and the best in the public sector (due to regulations governing employment in education). The best match within the

Table 9.6 Employment volume and labour demand throughout the companies studied in the Lublin and Subcarpathian Voivodeships by economic sector

Enterprises according to PKD classification	*Enterprises researched*	*Employment in the enterprises researched*			*Plans to employ new workers**		*Companies planning to employ workers by position*	
		Total employment	*Ukrainian employees*		*Not planned*	*Planned*	*Low level*	*High level*
	number	*number*	*number*	*%*	*number*	*number*	*number*	*number*
Section 10 - Food production	2	34	6	17.65	0	2	2	0
Section 18 - Printing and reproduction	1	14	1	7.14	1	0	0	0
Section 23 - Manufacturing of products from non-metallic mineral raw materials	1	522	21	4.02	0	1	1	0
Section 33 - Repair, maintenance, and installation of machinery and equipment	1	9	3	33.33	1	0	0	0
Section 41 - Construction work	1	34	3	8.82	0	1	1	0
Section 43 - Specialised construction work	10	58	23	39.66	5	5	5	0
Section 45 - Wholesale and retail of motor vehicles; repair of motor vehicles	2	10	4	40.00	2	0	0	0
Section 46 - Wholesale trade excluding motor vehicles	3	31	7	22.58	1	2	2	0
Section 47 - Retail trade, excluding motor vehicles	11	64	22	34.38	3	7	7	0

(*Continued*)

Table 9.6 (Continued)

Enterprises according to PKD classification	*Enterprises researched*	*Employment in the enterprises researched*			*Plans to employ new workers*[*]		*Companies planning to employ workers by position*	
		Total employment	*Ukrainian employees*		*Not planned*	*Planned*	*Low level*	*High level*
	number	*number*	*number*	*%*	*number*	*number*	*number*	*number*
Section 49 - Land and pipeline transport	3	80	10	12.50	1	2	2	0
Section 52 - Warehousing and services for transport	1	60	5	8.33	0	1	1	1
Section 53 - Postal and courier services	3	37	7	18.92	0	3	3	0
Section 55 - Accommodation	3	68	10	14.71	0	3	3	0
Section 56 - Food and catering	6	32	9	28.13	3	3	3	0
Section 62 - Programming and IT consultation	1	18	2	11.11	0	1	0	1
Section 85 - Education	3	384	9	2.34	0	3	1	2
Section 88 - Social services excluding accommodation	1	37	5	13.51	1	0	0	0
Section 96 - other individual service activities	2	10	4	40.00	1	1	1	0
All sectors - in total	**55**	**1502**	**151**	**10.05**	**19**	**35**	**32**	**4**

Source: Own elaboration.

* 1 enterprise did not answer

Table 9.7 Matching the skills and qualifications of employees from Ukraine and planned additional employment by sector and company size

Sector/company size	*Number of enterprises*	*Employment compliant with skills and qualifications (%)*			*Companies planning to employ workers by position*		
		a. Yes	*b. No*	*c. Various*	*Low level*	*High lever*	*Not planned*
Trade and sales	13	15.4	23.1	61.5	8	0	4
micro-enterprises	13	15.4	23.1	61.5	8	0	4
Manufacturing	3	0	33.3	66.7	3	0	0
micro-enterprises	1	0	100	0	1	0	0
small enterprises	1	0	0	100	1	0	0
large enterprises	1	0	0	100	1	0	0
Services	36	33.3	13.9	52.8	20	0	15
micro-enterprises	20	30	10	60	8	2	12
small enterprises	15	40	20	40	11	1	3
large enterprises	1	0	0	100	1	1	0
Public Sector	3	66.7	0	33.3	1	2	0
small enterprises	1	100	0	0	0	1	0
large enterprises	2	50	0	50	1	1	0
All sectors – in total	**55**	**29.1**	**16.4**	**54.5**	**32**	**4**	**19**

Source: Own elaboration.

private sector was noted in services (33.3% compliance), while in the case of sales and trade, only 15.4% of the enterprises employed qualified employees. Statistics show that the small companies (employing between ten and 49 workers) had the best match – see Table 9.7 and Figure 9.9.

Workers from Ukraine tend to be employed in professions not requiring special qualifications or confirmation of skills and qualifications (as is typical in the case of migration), as well as in technical positions in companies facing regional staff shortages (significant number of vacancies). In retail, vacancies were mainly sales positions (ten out of 55). In the service sector, Ukrainians

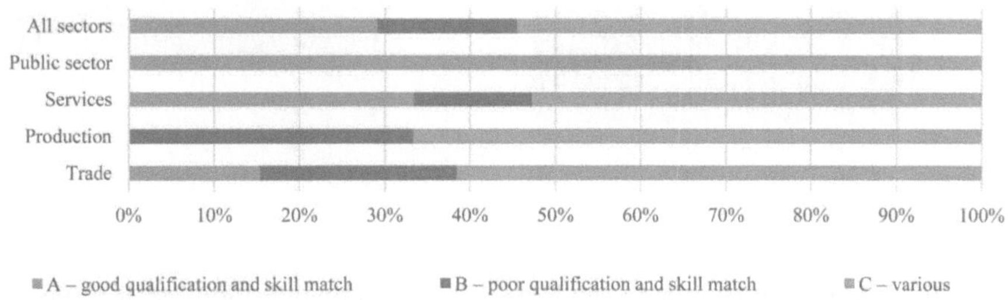

Figure 9.9 Matching the skills and qualifications of employees from Ukraine by regional economic sectors.

Source: Own elaboration.

were employed in the following positions: kitchen help (five mentions, combined with other tasks), cook (three), driver or courier (five), cleaner (four), construction/finishing industry (four), plumbers/installers (four), warehouse workers (three), mechanics/car mechanics (three), and hairdresser (two). In the case of the public sector, the surveyed institutions employed teaching assistants or class tutors (three).

Because the matching of employee skills and qualifications to job requirements is rated as poor, meaning additional costs for employers, it is important to encourage workers to stay with the company long-term. The surveyed enterprises were more likely to mention lower employee turnover when their skills and qualifications were matched to their job positions – this suggests a synergy of factors beneficial for such companies. Enterprises that pursued a less restrictive policy in terms of matching employee qualifications must expect a much higher staff turnover and lower job commitment, which results in higher costs and outlays related to training, HR, and payroll services, for example. The reason for employment despite the mismatch of employee qualifications is the reality of severe staff shortages in current circumstances – 38 out of 43 companies that responded to the questionnaire mentioned difficulties in finding employees at lower levels, while two businesses indicated shortages of potential employees at higher levels – see Figure 9.10. Generally, in this region, an "employees market" prevails, with accompanying significant shortages of human resources.

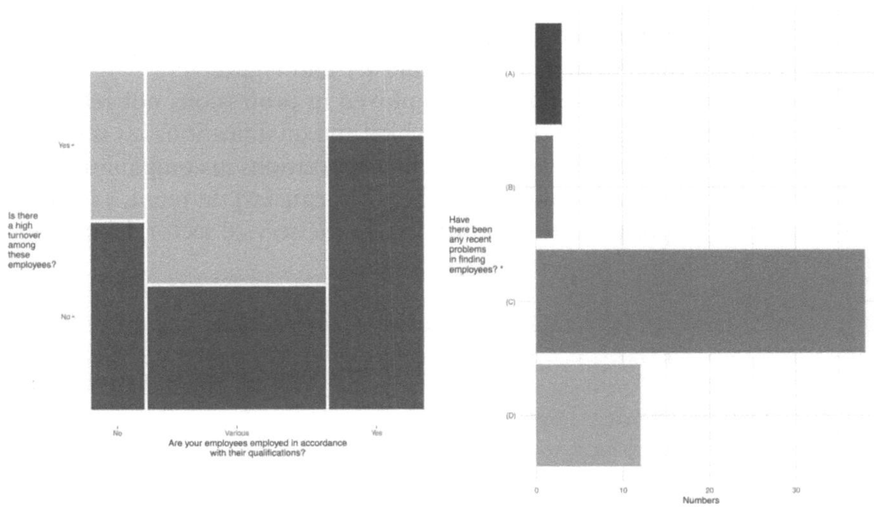

Figure 9.10 Matching Ukrainian employees' skills and qualifications, staff turnover, and difficulties in filling vacancies by position.

Source: Own elaboration.

* (A) hard to say, (B) yes, higher-level employees, (C) yes, lower-level employees, (D) not applicable

9.2.2 *Inclusion of Ukrainian Employees in Companies, Methods of Finding Employees, Conditions, and Motivation for Employment*

Of the surveyed companies, only five had taken any steps to adapt employees to Polish circumstances (50, i.e., 90.9%, had not taken such action). Such programmes were run by enterprises employing ten or more people and included integration (information or integration meetings) and material support (donations, financial assistance, material assistance, and collection of gifts). It should be mentioned that the action described was undertaken from the very start of the full-scale war (February 2022) by the local government sector and NGOs. In the context of integration, it is worth mentioning the cultural and linguistic similarity between Polish and Ukrainian societies, which influences the mutual perception of these nations (significant spatial proximity and cultural affinity).

Companies find employees from Ukraine mainly through digital media or recommendations from friends, including previous or current employees. For this purpose, Internet services (35 out of 55 companies), company websites (34 companies), and social media (20 companies) are used. Nearly half of the surveyed companies (27) rely on recommendations from friends. Only one in five companies works with labour market institutions established for this purpose, such as the Labour Office (11 companies). Seven companies indicated that they have established relationships with employment agencies. Other methods included candidates recommended by current employees (seven companies), advertisements on notice boards, internal recruitment, and other unspecified methods. The widespread use of electronic media, on the one hand, enables wider access to job offers, but on the other hand, it may constitute a barrier for digitally challenged people, including those in dire economic circumstances or the elderly – see Figure 9.11.

Despite the previously indicated cultural similarity, difficulty communicating in work situations is the main factor hindering cooperation with employees from Ukraine. In this context, the fact that the war migrants came from various parts of Ukraine should be noted: eastern – Russian-speaking and western – Ukrainian-speaking. One ought to also mention that some bridges do exist – Poles over 50 years of age have at least basic knowledge of the Russian language, which was commonly taught in schools during Poland's membership of the Eastern Bloc. However, the conclusions of the study indicate its limited usefulness in work situations.

Furthermore, employers from the Polish-Ukrainian border region indicated short-term employment periods mentioned by migrants before starting work, as well as mismatched or insufficient skills and qualifications, as factors hindering cooperation. The reluctance to commit to long-term employment, on the one hand, testifies to the honesty of the migrants and, on the other hand, a fear of being tied up by a contract that might per cent their assumed return to their homeland. This was a significant factor for 23 of the 55 companies, which may reflect the largely short-term nature of this

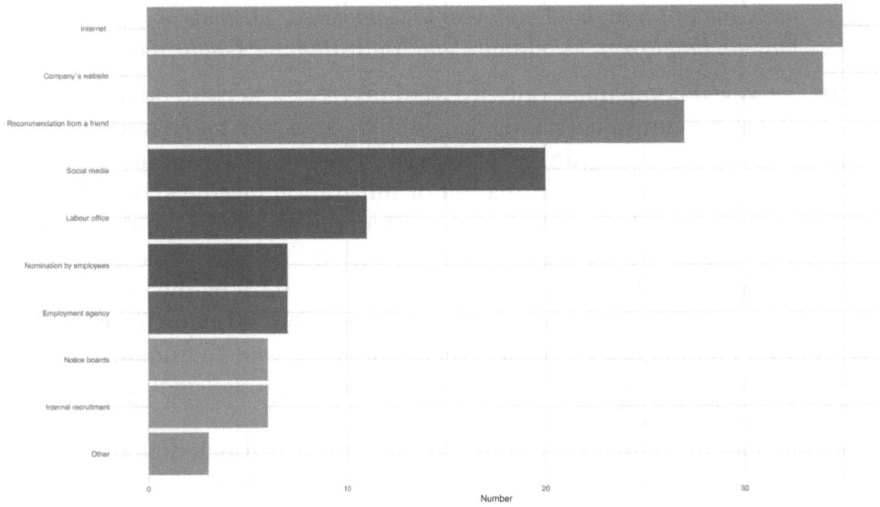

Figure 9.11 Jobseeking methods used by employees from Ukraine.

Source: Own elaboration.

wave of migration. Moreover, for a significant group of employers, significant difficulties were related to excessive financial expectations, withdrawal of candidates at later stages of recruitment, no-shows at scheduled interviews, and resignations after obtaining better job offers. Some enterprises also mentioned a lack of candidates – see Figure 9.12. In this context, it is worth mentioning the significant heterogeneity of the region's economy, both in terms of industry and spatial arrangement. This also justifies the uneven spatial distribution of migrants from Ukraine, who tend to concentrate in larger urban centres (see Section 9.1).

In the context of maintaining good working relations, the greatest difficulty is also (as in the case of the recruitment process) the language barrier – 47 out of 55 companies. In addition, economic difficulties for employed migrants were often mentioned, related to financing their stay in Poland, finding an apartment near the place of employment and organising childcare. In this case, systemic solutions to integrate these people and offer social protection could eliminate the difficulties indicated by the enterprises. However, it should be noted that the largest wave of war migrants occurred in February/March 2023 (during winter), which is a period when providing accommodation to people in need is a form of mandatory social support. Moreover, in this context, one ought to note the single-family character of buildings in smaller towns with little possibility of organising accommodation, as well as shortfalls in the availability of municipal and social housing. From the companies' perspective, relevant organisational factors included lack of commitment to long-term employment, lack of soft, hard, and digital skills, lack of social skills, and associated lack of integration with other employees in the company. Employers also mentioned

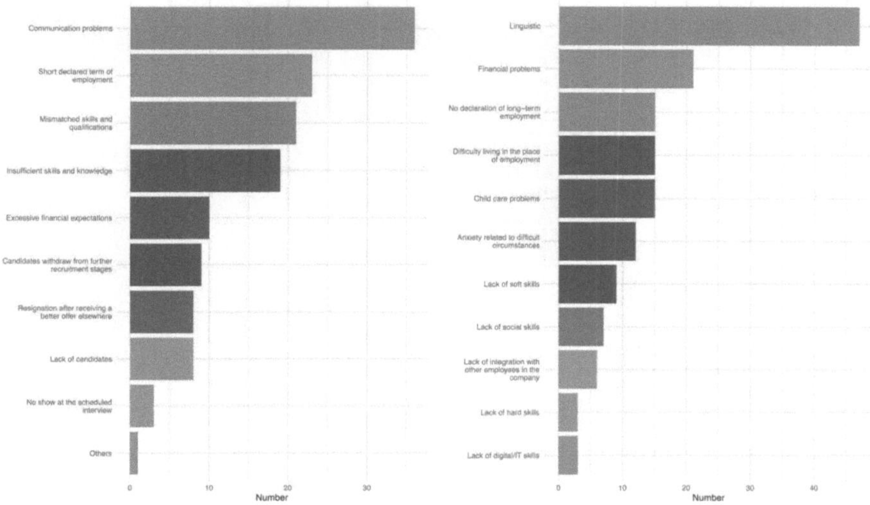

Figure 9.12 Difficulties in hiring and maintaining cooperation with employees from Ukraine.

Source: Own elaboration.

common adaptation problems resulting from the of refugees' poor mental state and anxiety associated with separation from loved ones, trauma, and difficult life circumstances – see Figure 9.12.

Companies have taken a number of steps to minimise difficulties related to staff shortages. In order to optimise employee recruitment, they commonly offer current employees overtime, employ workers from Ukraine and offer higher salaries. Every fifth company is open to recruiting employees of retirement age as well as retirees. Frequently used methods of acquiring employees include cooperation with employment agencies and vocational schools in the region. Several surveyed companies decided on other solutions, including employing foreigners (other than Ukrainians), automating selected processes, limiting numbers of orders/contracts, cooperating with other employers (job sharing), or employer branding – see Figure 9.13. In relation to refugees/employees from Ukraine, mainly financial incentives apply: bonuses (42 out of 55 surveyed companies) or, to a lesser extent, an increase in remuneration (18 companies). Every fifth company offers flexible working hours or provides a work laptop/telephone. Non-financial perks are offered by a much narrower selection of firms, such as integration events, sports and medical packages, employee programmes (work-life balance), and tickets for cultural/sports events. In several cases, they offered free additional medical care, co-financing of children's holidays, additional insurance, or career path planning (two cases). Among the surveyed group, only three companies did not offer additional incentives to employees from Ukraine – see Figure 9.14.

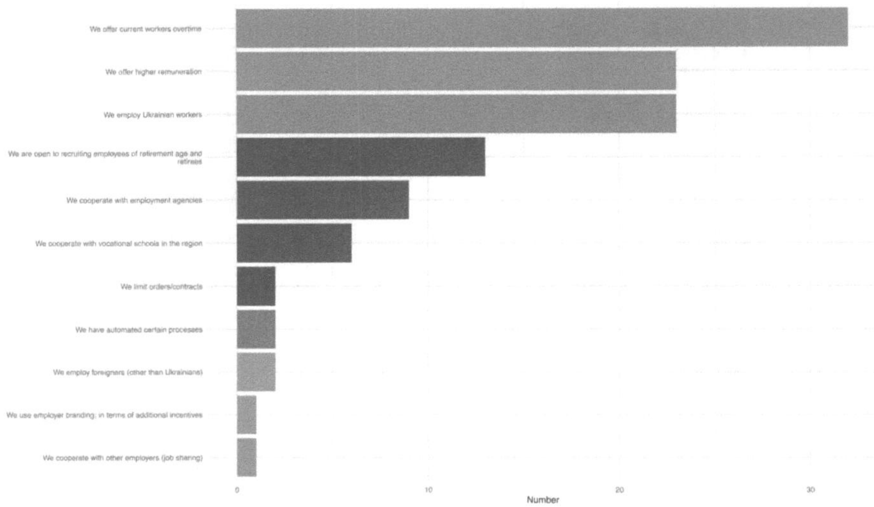

Figure 9.13 Methods of assisting recruitment of employees from Ukraine.

As the full-scale armed conflict continues in 2022, Ukrainian employees and employers prefer increasingly long terms of employment. Two periods were analysed: the first half of the year (March–June 2022) and the final period of 2022. During the latter period, short-term forms of employment (less than three months) were practically abandoned – most contracts of this

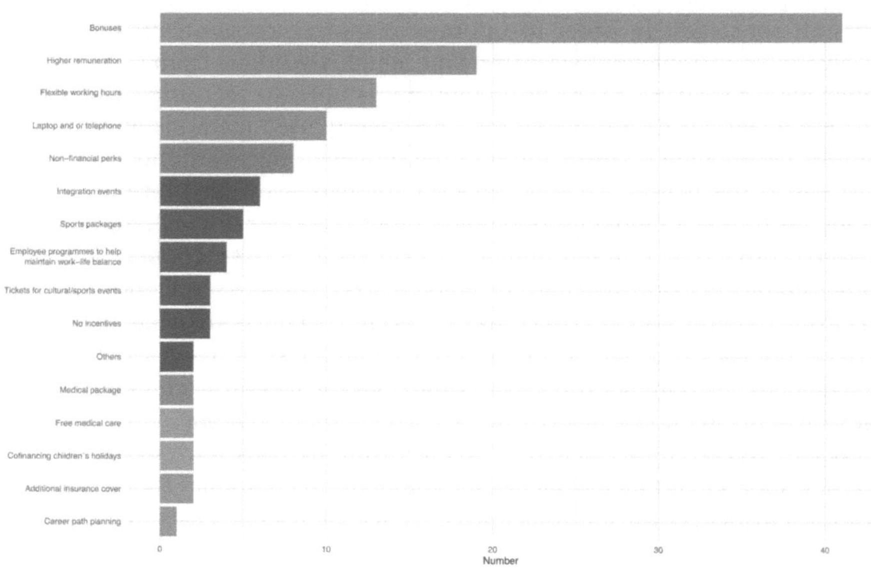

Figure 9.14 Incentives offered to employees from Ukraine.

Source: Own elaboration.

type were concluded in the first half of 2022 (43.6% of companies concluded such contracts in the first period). At the same time, the number of companies concluding contracts with refugees for 6–12 months increased significantly (by 16.4 percentage points from 21.8% to 38.2%) as was the case for contracts exceeding 12 months (by 12.7 percentage points) – see Table 9.8. The reasons may lie both in a change in the attitude of migrants who, in the face of the prolonged state of war in their homeland, have decided to stay longer in Poland or their satisfaction with their working conditions, as well as the positive verification of their work and attitude by employers from the region, manifested in the extension of work contracts. This area would require additional research.

The reason why the employment of Ukrainian employees is taking such a foothold may also be concluded from the employers' declarations regarding the types of contracts signed – fewer contracts of mandate contracts based on civil law in favour of full-time employment based on an employment contract (up by 10.9 percentage points). The increase in employment contracts for an indefinite period in the case of subsequent contracts signed with an employee should be related to the provisions of Polish labour law (Act of 26 June 1974 – Labour Code Act). An employment contract has consequences, including the obligation to pay national insurance and pension contributions, and it ensures certain benefits, such as sick pay.

Only 12 enterprises indicated their desire to help people in difficult situations as the reason for employing Ukrainians. The most important reasons for employment were mostly of a market or organisational nature – the necessity to find employees and the lack of qualified employees on the labour market. Half of the employers mentioned four main reasons: the high level of motivation of employees from Ukraine, their reliability, low non-salary expectations, and lack of other employees on the market. According to the companies, wage factors had a greater impact on war migrants than non-wage factors. As secondary motives, the companies indicated issues related to the high quality or efficiency of employees, lower wages/labour costs of workers from Ukraine, and the desire to help people in difficult situations. Only in three cases were Ukrainians employed because of their stronger skills and qualifications or their better fit with the company's needs. Employers' responses regarding the motivation to cooperate with employees from Ukraine are presented in Figure 9.15.

9.2.3 *The Impact of Ukrainian Workers on the Labour Market and Entrepreneurship in the Polish-Ukrainian Border Region*

The surveyed enterprises positively assess the impact of employing employees from Ukraine – beneficial for the company (37 companies, 67.3%) or definitely beneficial (six companies, 10.9%). Only 12 companies (21.8%) assessed that the employment of war immigrants had no impact on the

Table 9.8 The period of employment declared by Ukrainian employees and the type of employment contract – from the first months of the full-scale conflict to the current period

			Sector				*Total*
			Trade and sales	*Manufacturing*	*Services*	*Public Sector*	
Number of companies			**13**	**3**	**36**	**3**	**55**
How long is the typical term of employment declared by Ukrainian workers?	In the first half of the year (March–June)	3 months or less	46.2	100.0	38.9	33.3	43.6
		3–6 months	38.5	0.0	36.1	33.3	34.5
		6–12 months	15.4	0.0	25.0	33.3	21.8
	at the end of 2022	3 months or less	7.7	0.0	0.0	0.0	1.8
		3–6 months	61.5	66.7	44.4	0.0	47.3
		6–12 months	23.1	33.3	38.9	100.0	38.2
		12 months or more	7.7	0.0	16.7	0.0	12.7
What type of labour contract does the company/organisation sign with employees from Ukraine?	First contract	Employment contract – trial period	7.7	33.3	8.3	33.3	10.9
		Employment contract – fixed term	0.0	0.0	5.6	66.7	7.3
		Contract of mandate	92.3	66.7	86.1	0.0	81.8
	Subsequent contract	Employment contract – fixed term	0.0	0.0	16.7	33.3	12.7
		Employment contract – indefinite period	7.7	33.3	13.9	66.7	16.4
		Contract of mandate	92.3	66.7	69.4	0.0	70.9

Source: Own elaboration.

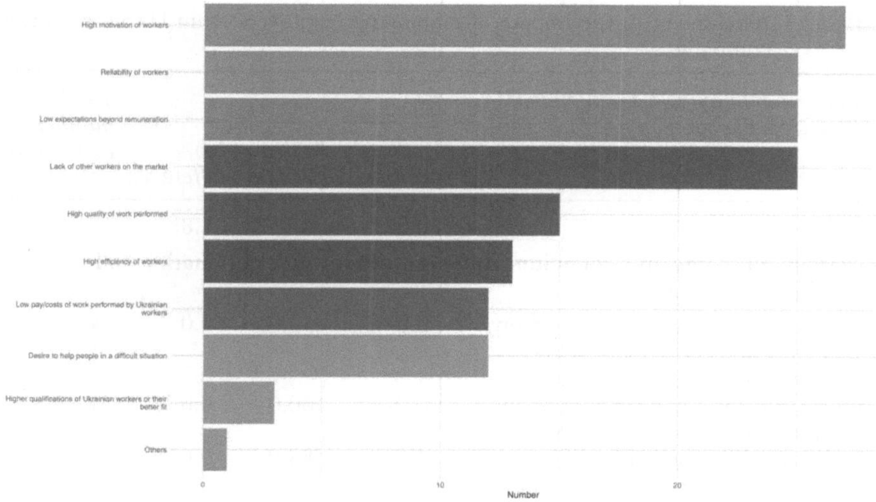

Figure 9.15 Motivations for employing Ukrainians.

Source: Own elaboration.

company (including two out of three public companies), and no company assessed this impact negatively – see Table 9.9.

The main advantages of employing Ukrainians were indicated by the surveyed companies as follows: diligence and performance of assigned work, longer/more stable cooperation, and positive impact on turnover. In addition, the following were less frequently cited: conscientiousness, availability, willingness to work, cost-effectiveness, and level (quality) of work performed. Employers also mentioned the advantages of making the company more stable, the possibility of extending working time, filling staff shortages, taking on new or larger orders, lower salary expectations, and, in two cases, even the possibility of remaining on the market and continuing to do business. An obvious obstacle was the language barrier, which caused communication problems (including completing the necessary documents). Other difficulties included excessive alcohol consumption, mainly on days off, and the consequences of reduced effectiveness at work or intoxication, as well as short periods of employment combined with relatively long periods of work training, problems with respecting procedures and the need to adapt to Polish regulations and labour standards, cultural differences and poor integration with the team, leaving after being paid and difficulty in searching for employment.

Evaluation of the impact of employing Ukrainians on the company depended on the level of advancement of, or planning for, the introduction of work automation, the declared average period of employment, as well as the types of work contracts offered. A higher percentage of positive and definitely positive assessments were given in the case of companies that do not plan to implement automation to downsize employment, which at the same

Table 9.9 Assessment of the impact of employing employees from Ukraine on the company

Impact of employing Ukrainian war refugees on the company	%			*Total number of companies*
	Definitely positive	*Rather positive*	*No difference*	
Total	10.9	67.3	21.8	55
Regarding the company's commitment to activities towards automation and employment downsizing				
Automation has a huge impact on my company and is currently being implemented	0.0	50.0	50.0	4
Automation has a huge impact on my company and we plan to implement it	0.0	100.0	0.0	1
Automation is on our radar of interest, but we do not plan to implement it yet	11.1	88.9	0.0	9
Our company is not interested in automation	12.2	63.4	24.4	41
According to period of employment with the company				
3 months or less	0.0	100.0	0.0	1
3–6 months	3.8	69.2	26.9	26
6–12 months	9.5	66.7	23.8	21
12 months or more	42.9	57.1	0.0	7
According to type of employment contract signed with Ukrainian employees (subsequent contracts)				
Employment contract – fixed term	11.1	22.2	66.7	9
Employment contract – indefinite period	42.9	57.1	0.0	7
Contract of mandate	5.1	79.5	15.4	39

Source: Own elaboration.

time constituted the majority of companies covered by the study (74.5%). The reason for a generally positive assessment of the impact of Ukrainian employees on the company lies in the fact that most of these companies belong to the service sector, which is based to a greater extent on human work. Among the companies that do not plan to implement automation in the near future (nine companies, 16.4% of the surveyed companies) or may possibly plan to do so, all companies assessed the impact of refugees on the company positively. Positive evaluations were more often given by labour-intensive companies, which may indicate a greater potential for stimulating the economies of peripheral regions. In a broader context, there is a suspicion that these positive effects on business may apply to regions with a low level of automation, based on unskilled work or with lower productivity, although conclusions in this area should be confirmed by additional in-depth research. The impact of war migrants on companies was also proportionally related to longer periods of employment (over 12 months), fixed-term employment contracts or (and usually short-term) contracts of mandate.

9.3 Conclusions

The Polish-Ukrainian border region, a peripheral area of the European Union, is in a phase of strong economic growth stimulated largely by the intervention policy of the state and the European Union to enhance the internal cohesion of the group and stimulate underdeveloped regions. This economic growth, despite a low level of entrepreneurship, has been accompanied by a strong decline in unemployment – these regions are experiencing labour shortages, especially for lower-level employees. Research conducted in Poland (including the authors' own work discussed here) indicates that Poles are willing to help refugees if their residence is temporary, but are largely against their permanent settlement.

The main goal of this chapter is to explore the extent to which local people and enterprises have been involved in helping refugees from Ukraine, the impact of mass forced migration on the region, and the situation faced by local businesses on the Polish-Ukrainian border (their perception of the situation). For this purpose, a questionnaire (survey) was conducted among all these groups. The results are presented in modules regarding individual local actors – Section 9.1 and Section 9.2 about refugees and entrepreneurs, respectively – from the Polish-Ukrainian border area.

In the context of the research question regarding how migration caused by the war in Ukraine in 2022 influenced the labour market on the Polish-Ukrainian border (How did migration forced by the war in Ukraine in 2022 affect the labour market on the Polish-Ukrainian border?), the impact of the migration of Ukrainian refugees on the labour market and entrepreneurship in the Polish-Ukrainian border region was assessed positively, mainly due to the alleviation of labour shortages and enhanced business opportunities for some sectors (including tourism, gastronomy, sales, and trade). Consideration of the detailed research questions allows us to pinpoint the key factors determining decisions to settle in the border region. One of the main questions to answer here was to what extent the possibility of finding housing is a positive factor attracting refugees from Ukraine on the Polish-Ukrainian border (How do refugees assess the living and working conditions on the Polish side of Polish-Ukrainian border area?). The findings show that this factor is not crucial for people settling in the border area. Taking into account the ownership structure (mainly private property) and the low intensity of housing development (mainly single-family houses in areas with a low level of urbanisation typical of the region), the possibility of finding an apartment in the Polish-Ukrainian border region should be evaluated as relatively worse than in the case of other regions and, above all, large cities in Poland. In the context of the research question about other important non-economic factors that influenced the refugees' stay in the Polish-Ukrainian border region (What are the specifics of the Polish-Ukrainian borderland, with particular emphasis on the economy and cross-border flows, including the labour market?), it should be noted that this decision was largely determined by the proximity of the border with Ukraine, which offers the opportunity to maintain contact with relatives and the country of origin. As the results show, the largest waves of refugees from Ukraine arriving on the Polish side of the Polish-Ukrainian border come from the oblasts of western Ukraine directly bordering Poland: Lviv and Volhynia. The remaining respondents usually represent larger Ukrainian towns and cities affected by constant military operations at a distance and aimed at civilian targets, as well as Kiev and suburbs, Chernikhiv, Kharkov, Sumy, Dnipropetrovsk, Donetsk, Odessa, Kherson, Mykolaiv, and Zaporozhye, located in temporarily occupied or directly attacked areas. 45.6% of respondents from the latter group mentioned a direct threat to their health or life as the reason for leaving the country. 21.5% indicated a sense of threat, and another 19% indicated a lack of economic security. Refugees living in other parts of the country were less likely to declare direct risk of loss of health or life (5.7% in the examined border area compared to 9.5% in the regions of western Ukraine located further from the border and 15.5% in central regions). The major destinations in Poland where the surveyed Ukrainians work are in the Subcarpathian Voivodeship: Rzeszów, Przemyśl, Jarosław, as well as in the Lublin Voivodeship: Biała Podlaska, Chełm, and Zamość.

The nature of war migration, manifested by increased mobility of women with children as well as a desire to ensure security, results in a greater percentage of women among working refugees (74.65% of respondents), which in turn affects the need to provide them with appropriate opportunities to settle. Due to the fact that 58.5% of the surveyed people declared a wish to return to Ukraine after the end of the war, it was mostly a case of offering temporary shelter for an indefinite period of danger. The temporary nature of residence in the border region is confirmed by the fact that only 8.6% of respondents declare that they want to stay in this place, while 18.2% are undecided and 14.8% would like to move to another city in Poland or Europe. Returning home was mentioned more by people with primary education (82.6%) and secondary education (67.3%). Moreover, the more dependent children they have, the more often the respondents indicated a planned return to Ukraine, while those without children (140 respondents) declared themselves to be highly mobile. Longer periods of employment in the border area (over six months) contributed to a greater willingness to return home (59.6% compared to 53.3% among people staying in Poland for less than six months). Likewise, a job position in Poland that matches the profession performed in Ukraine is favourable in this respect. In the context of how residence in the host country is perceived, it is also relevant that declared dissatisfaction with the place of residence corresponded with a desire to move to another place in Poland/Europe rather than return to Ukraine. Most respondents did not live in independent accommodation (only 1/3 of the respondents) – as many as 43.9% of the respondents live with Polish friends or people resettled from Ukraine, while the remaining people are looking for an apartment (10.2%) or have another form of accommodation (10.8%).

Regarding the question about matching qualifications to work done in Poland and computer literacy (How much computer literacy do refugees have and do they work in accordance with their qualifications?), the study highlights the mismatch between the quality of the job positions offered and the qualifications of refugees, which does not allow them to use their full potential. The surveyed refugees declared that they have higher education and a good level of digital/IT skills, especially in using computers or the Internet, which should be considered sufficient for non-specialised industries (standard digital data administration). When considering the needs of this particular regional economy, higher education is often not required, which makes it difficult for refugees to find satisfactory employment on the Polish side of the border. This was also confirmed by the refugees interviewed. Therefore, the study indicates that the qualifications and education of Ukrainian employees tend not to be well-matched with the realities of the regional economy, which is largely based on the production sector, human services, catering services, and tourism.

An important aspect included in this study but not in others regarding how refugees function on the labour market, their potential and ability to work, was the question: How do refugees perceive their mental and physical health? The respondents' answers were not uniform in this regard. Most respondents assessed their state of health as good, especially their physical health (average assessment: 8.5 points on a scale of 1–10, while the average assessment of mental health was 7.8 points). Women declared a worse state of mental health – 7.5 points vs. 8.6 points among the men. Health seemed to be significantly benefited by a job position matched to skills and qualifications, satisfaction with the workplace, and was also influenced by the extent to which migration was forced or voluntary. The assessment of mental health was clearly worse among people who had encountered highly stressful situations: those fleeing the country due to a threat to their own health/life or that of their relatives (7.0 points), due to a sense of threat with indirect exposure to armed conflict (7.6 points), or life circumstances forcing separation (7.7 points). According to the surveyed refugees, the place of residence had no impact on their feelings about their health. Adaptation problems may be evidenced by difficulties in performing tasks requiring concentration, social activity, and leaving the house, and slightly less discomfort related to sleep and getting up in the morning. Although the surveyed refugees assess their mental health well, the significant difficulties in everyday functioning described by most of them confirm trauma associated with war and separation, which should be an indication to take action to improve their health or take preventive measures on the Polish side. In this case, the municipalities of eastern Poland have poorer availability of such services, which suggests the need for more support in this area.

Referring to the question about refugees assessing the conditions offered by the Polish-Ukrainian border region (How do refugees assess the living and working conditions in the Polish-Ukrainian border area?), refugees from

Ukraine employed in the surveyed municipalities mostly say they are content and happy with their workplace – 59.9% of respondents. Due to lower average wages in the eastern part of Poland, questions about other non-salary and non-economic factors that encourage refugees to stay in the studied peripheral region become crucial. A factor that largely determined the high level of job satisfaction in Poland was the compatibility of the nature of employment in Poland and Ukraine, although such a match was mentioned by only 29.3% of respondents. Refugees employed in Poland as specialists, skilled and unskilled workers declared a higher level of satisfaction. Among those employed on the Polish side of the Polish-Ukrainian border, 70.7% have jobs that are incompatible with their skills and qualifications. The mismatch between employment opportunities and refugees' qualifications is evidenced by the fact that those with higher education are largely dissatisfied with their jobs and declared that they did not match their aspirations – these people found jobs in Poland as regular trade and service workers, which did not suit their skills and qualifications. Refugees with lower skills and qualifications were more likely to declare job satisfaction (79.4% with secondary education, 95.7% with primary education).

In the context of assessing living conditions in the region, individuals expressing difficulty in finding separate (independent) housing more frequently declared a desire to return to their homeland. Finding independent housing in the conditions of a border region characterised by extensive development and a significant private sector involvement in housing construction proved to be a crucial area identified by working refugees from Ukraine as requiring support from administration and institutions. The second-most-mentioned area among their priorities was institutional assistance in finding suitable employment. They also emphasised the importance of childcare organisation during hours suitable for parental work and the availability of medical assistance. Working refugees from Ukraine demonstrated significantly proactive attitudes – when asked about their needs regarding local governments and employers, they most often mentioned assistance in finding housing and helping to find employment, and to a lesser extent, creating opportunities for additional work, higher/better earnings/subsidies/bonuses/subsidies, opportunities for education and taking courses (including language courses), organising childcare and medical care, and nostrification of diplomas/recognition of skills and qualifications. Assimilation with Poland was facilitated by having close ancestors, relatives, or friends from this country with poor or intermediate knowledge of the Polish language at the time of moving and intermediate knowledge at the end of 2022. However, refugees mentioned significant progress in their knowledge of Polish between February–September 2022.

With regard to the research question about the impact of the influx of Ukrainian refugees on the development of entrepreneurship and labour market in the Polish-Ukrainian border region and the assessment given by employers from the region (Questions: How do refugees affect the labour market on the Polish-Ukrainian border and to what extent does the migration crisis related to the influx of refugees from Ukraine have a positive impact on business development in the Polish-Ukrainian border region and how do businesses assess this?), the results of the study clearly indicate that employers perceive the employment of Ukrainians as a factor stimulating the development of their enterprises, and the scale of employing migrants leads to the conclusion that this factor has a positive impact on entrepreneurship in the region and partially eliminates entrenched regional difficulties in recruiting employees. This is especially visible in entities where automation is not relevant – labour-intensive sectors such as trade or services. Considering the state of the economy in the Polish-Ukrainian border region as well as trends related mainly to the social situation, this is a clearly favourable fit. The motivations for employment were dictated by the market and to ease the organisational difficulties felt by companies – mainly resulting from a lack of qualified employees on the market. Employers also emphasised the positives: the high level of motivation among Ukrainian employees, their reliability, and low non-wage expectations.

Apart from the supply of employees in the quantitative sense, it should be noted that what hinders the full use of this potential is the qualitative mismatch between the skills and qualifications of Ukrainian employees and the requirements of the job positions offered. Employers' declarations confirm that staff shortages make it necessary to employ workers despite the mismatch between skills and the requirements of the job positions offered, which means that companies have to incur additional costs during the initial period of employment. In the region, jobs were offered in occupations that did not require high qualifications or confirmation of skills or in technical positions where there were shortages. As a result, there was a common mismatch between job positions and employee aspirations, which in turn translated into higher employee turnover (unfavourable for employers). Similar conclusions were reached by an analysis carried out in the same period in the Lower Silesian Voivodeship, which clearly shows that as many as 78% of employees from Ukraine were employed as manual workers without qualifications; no one was employed in intellectual work requiring high qualifications, with only 4.3% working as lower-skilled white-collar workers and another 2.1% as qualified white-collar workers (Dolnośląski Wojewódzki Urząd Pracy w Wałbrzychu, 2022). It should be emphasised, however, that qualified employees from Ukraine from professions regulated by legislation on acquiring the right to perform a profession may have difficulty confirming their qualifications on the EU labour market due to legislative differences or a lack of appropriate documents (the case of people fleeing from hostilities) – such a situation has been observed in the case of employing workers in the public sector. The limited opportunity to profit from cross-border cooperation in the case of labour markets in the Polish-Ukrainian border area is permanent in nature and believed to be caused by the location of Ukraine outside the EU (lack of facilitations in cross-border cooperation within the Schengen area and the customs union), the depreciation of the Ukrainian currency in relation to the Euro and Polish zloty and the decline in its purchasing power at the beginning of the war, or the existence of the shadow economy (Himstedt, 2017). However, these trends seem to have been shifting over the last two years (due to shortages or increases in the cost of living in Ukraine), as indicated by trade balances in the border area.

The study shows that companies actively look for employees via electronic media and, to a lesser extent, use traditional methods, which naturally do not give digitally excluded people access to job offers. This includes people in a difficult economic situation or the elderly. Among the significant employment obstacles, employers pointed out difficulties in communicating with employees from Ukraine in work situations, the short-term employment initially preferred by migrants, as well as the mismatch or lack of skills and qualifications. The involvement of the public system may be effective in eliminating economic difficulties related to financing migrants' lives in Poland, finding an apartment near the place of employment and organising childcare. So, the most important factors inhibiting professional engagement and entrepreneurship among migrants indicated in the study coincide with the results of research on the entrepreneurship of women war migrants from Ukraine (Hello entrepreneurship, 2022), which additionally emphasised issues related to their mental state, concerns, fear, and loneliness about their relatives remaining in Ukraine.

An important factor that enabled quick adaptation to the influx of migrants was the previous experience of entrepreneurs employing Ukrainians on regional labour markets (especially since 2014) and the good practices and relations with local migrant diasporas developed in this area. Moreover, the proximity of the border is naturally conducive to cooperation with Ukrainian partners, and fosters economic activity on both sides, as reflected in the results of cross-border trade, which are important for Poland's balance of payments. The pay conditions offered in the cross-border area are weaker than the national average and the refugees' far greater interest in remuneration rather than non-wage factors leads one to assume that other factors determine the attractiveness of offers on the border labour market. Considering the length of employment periods for which contracts are signed, declarations in this regard, and the destinations of the refugees, it can be assumed that one of the key factors is the proximity of the border with a guarantee of security from military operations or previously existing relations with this area. The results of the conducted study align in this aspect with the findings of research conducted in other areas of Poland. For example, research conducted in Krakow (Pędziwiatr et al., 2022), which is one of the largest hubs accepting refugees in Poland, indicates that they would like to return quickly to their homeland after the end of the war, despite the protective measures and access to the labour market that they were offered based on national regulations, or the importance of family and loved ones who had already come to Poland in search of employment.

References

Act of 26 June 1974 – Labour Code Act; Journal of Laws of 1974, No. 24, item 141, as amended.

Border Guard (Poland). *Zarząd Graniczny KGSG*. https://www.strazgraniczna.pl/pl/granica/statystyki-sg/2206,Statystyki-SG.html. Accessed in 2023.

Bronisz, U. (2017). Higher education as a factor of Polish-Ukrainian cross-border cooperation. *Challenges in the development of the Polish-Ukrainian borderland*. Norbertinum.

Chmielewska, I., Dobroczek, G., & Panuciak, A. (2017). *Obywatele Ukrainy pracujący w Polsce – raport z badania*. Departament Statystyki NBP. https://nbp.pl/wp-content/uploads/2022/11/obywatele-Ukrainy-pracujacy-w-Polsce-raport-2017.pdf. Accessed in 2023.

Cierpiał-Wolan, M. (2017). Wpływ dynamicznych przemieszczeń ludności na rozwój społeczno-gospodarczy polsko-ukraińskich obszarów transgranicznych. In *Wyzwania rozwojowe pogranicza polsko-ukraińskiego*. Norberinum.

Dębkowska, K., Kłosiewicz-Górecka, U., Szymańska, A., Wejt-Knyżewska, A., & Zybertowicz, K. (2023). *Wpływ wojny w Ukrainie na działalność polskich firm*. Polski Instytut Ekonomiczny. https://pie.net.pl/wp-content/uploads/2023/02/Wplyw-wojny-na-PL-firmy.pdf. Accessed in 2023.

Deloitte. (2022). *Refugees from Ukraine in Poland. Challenges and potential for integration*. Monitor Deloitte. https://www2.deloitte.com/content/dam/Deloitte/pl/Documents/Reports/pl_ENG_Report_Refugees_from_Ukraine_in_Poland.pdf. Accessed in 2023.

Długosz, P., Kryvachuk, L., & Izdebska-Długosz, D. (2022). *Problemy ukraińskich uchodźców przebywających w Polsce*.

Długosz, P., Kryvachuk, L., & Izdebska-Długosz, D. (2022). *Uchodźcy wojenni z Ukrainy – życie w Polsce i plany na przyszłość*. Wydawnictwo Academicon.

Dolnośląski Wojewódzki Urząd Pracy w Wałbrzychu. (2022). *Obywatele Ukrainy na dolnośląskim rynku pracy – problemy, wyzwania, perspektywy. Raport końcowy*. https://wupdolnoslaski.praca.gov.pl/documents/91541/10909303/2211_Obywatele%20Ukrainy%20na%20dolno%C5%9Bl%C4%85skim%20rynku%20pracy.pdf/42358b43-dd73-4f24-92f2-c3b9c2aa1763. Accessed in 2023.

Duszczyk, M., & Kaczmarczyk, P. (2022a). The war in Ukraine and migration to Poland: Outlook and challenges. *Intereconomics*, *57*(3), 164–170.

Duszczyk, M., & Kaczmarczyk, P. (2022b). War and migration: The recent influx from Ukraine into Poland and possible scenarios for the future. *Cmr Spotlight*, *39*(4), 1–13.

Duszczyk, M., & Kaczmarczyk, P. (2022c). Poland and war refugees from Ukraine – Beyond pure aid. In *Cesifo forum*. München: Ifo Institut-Leibniz-Institut Für Wirtschaftsforschung An Der Universität München.

Gluszak, M., & Trojanek, R. (2023). War in Ukraine, Refugee Crisis, and Housing Market in Poland. *Refugee Crisis, and Housing Market in Poland*.

Hello entrepreneurship. (2022). *Czynniki hamujące oraz wspierające przedsiębiorczość migrantek z Ukrainy, które przyjechały do Polski po eskalacji wojny 24 lutego 2022 roku. Raport*. Fundacja Kronenberga & Citi Handlowy. https://www.ashoka.org/pl-pl/story/raport-o-przedsiebiorczosci-kobiet-ktore-przyjechaly-do-polski-po-eskalacji-wojny-w-ukrainie. Accessed in 2023.

Himstedt, K. (2017). Labor market on the Polish-Ukrainian borderland as an economic and social aspect. *Rynek – Społeczeństwo – Kultura*, *4*(25), 114–119. https://dspace.uni.lodz.pl/bitstream/handle/11089/39306/rsk4-2017-himstedt.pdf?sequence=1&isAllowed=y. Accessed in 2023.

Igielski, K., & Sowa, B. (2019). Migracja obywateli Ukrainy do Polski i jej konsekwencje dla Polskiego rynku pracy. *Rynek – Społeczeństwo – Kultura*, *2*(33), 44–47.

Jarosz, S., & Klaus, W. (2023). *Polska Szkoła pomagania. Przyjęcie osób uchodźczych z Ukrainy w Polsce w 2022 roku.* Warszawa. https://konsorcjum.org.pl/wp-content/uploads/2023/04/Polska-Szkola-Pomagania-raport-1.pdf. Accessed in 2023.

Jaroszewicz, M., & Piechal, T. (2016). Ukrainian migration to Poland after the "Revolution of Dignity": Old trends or new exodus? In D. Drbohlav, & M. Jaroszewicz (Eds.), *Ukrainian Migration in times of crisis: Forced and labour mobility* (pp. 87–88). Charles University Faculty of Science.

Jurek, K. (2022). Polish labour market for refugees from Ukraine. *Kultura Bezpieczeństwa. Nauka – Praktyka – Refleksje*, 42, 8–17.

Karasapan, O. (2022). *Ukrainian Refugees: Challenges in a Welcoming Europe. Commentary*. The Brookings Institution. https://www.brookings.edu/articles/ukrainian-refugees-challenges-in-a-welcoming-europe/. Accessed in 2023.

Oleński, J. (2017). *Klastry transgraniczne jako stymulatory rozwoju i współpracy w warunkach otwartej gospodarki rynkowej*. Norbertinum.

Pędziwiatr, K., Brzozowski, J., & Nahorniuk, O. (2022). *Refugees from Ukraine in Kraków*. Centre for Advanced Studies of Population and Religion Cracow University of Economics. https://owim.uek.krakow.pl/wp-content/uploads/user-files/reports/refugeereport1.pdf. Accessed in 2023.

Staniszewski, R., et al. (2022). *Social perception of refugees from Ukraine, migrants and measures undertaken by the government of Mateusz Morawiecki – Report on public opinion survey*. Wydział Nauk Politycznych i Studiów Międzynarodowych, Uniwersytet Warszawski. https://doi.org/10.13140/RG.2.2.17930.34243

Szaban, D. (2022). Ukrainian migrants on the Polish labour market. Hrm selected issues. *Journal of Eastern Europe Research in Business and Economics, 2022*. https://doi.org/10.5171/2022.813170

UNHCR. (2023). *Operational Data Portal. Ukraine Refugee Situation*. https://data.unhcr.org/en/situations/ukraine. Accessed in 2023.

Wojdat, M., & Cywiński, P. (2022). *Urban Hospitality: Great Growth, Challenges and Opportunities. Report on Refugees from Ukraine in the Largest Polish Cities*. Centrum Badań i Analiz. Unia Metropolii Polskich. https://ec.europa.eu/migrant-integration/system/files/2022-04/Ump_Ukraina_RAPORT_final_2.pdf. Accessed in 2023.

Zymin, A., Kowalski, M., Karasińska, A., Lytvynenko, O., Dąbrowska, E., Bryzek, S., Gliński, P., & Koszykowska, D. (2022). *Special Report. Refugees from Ukraine in Poland*. Platforma Migracyjna EWL, Fundacja na Rzecz Wspierania Migrantów na Rynku Pracy "EWL" i Studium Europy Wschodniej Uniwersytetu Warszawskiego. https://ec.europa.eu/migrant-integration/system/files/2022-04/Raport%20Specjalny%20Uchod%C5%BAcy%20z%20Ukrainy%20w%20Polsce.pdf. Accessed in 2023.

10 Summary

The war between Russia and Ukraine has had significant economic implications, both regionally and globally. The conflict has led to a massive shock to the global economy, particularly to the energy and food markets, squeezing supply and pushing up prices to unprecedented levels. Currently, economies must function in conditions of turbulence. This fact is confirmed primarily by today's global socio-economic and geopolitical reality, which is characterised by extremely negative and disturbing events, primarily related to Russia's attack on Ukraine, ongoing since February 24, 2022 – furthermore, a war provoked at a time when the world had not yet fully dealt with the COVID-19 pandemic. Multiple crises have forced countries and regions to overcome challenges of a very diverse nature. Discussions rage about pandemic, war, climate, food, and geopolitical crises – including debt, demographics, global order (world balance of power), globalisation, neoliberalism, global elites, immigration, and the cost of living crisis recently revealed as a result of global inflation (Mączyńska, 2023). This list is not exhaustive. It could be extended to include other areas, such as turmoil in the labour markets, the ongoing crisis of social trust, democracy, and others. Adam Tooze, a professor at Columbia University specialising in the study of economic crises, describes the current situation in the world as a "polycrisis", emphasising that even a single crisis is difficult enough to analyse and find ways out (Tooze & Fertik, 2014). However, when combined with other crises, it generates infinitely greater chaos through a synergy of effects. The British publisher of the Collins English Dictionary announced the word permacrisis as the word of the year (Assadourian, 2023). 2023 is a year of increasing inflation, political instability, increased immigration, and other calamities.

The main aim of the study has been signalled in the introduction: a multidimensional assessment of the situation of the war refugees in the Polish labour market after Russia attacked Ukraine in 2022, including recommendations for changes in the long-term labour market policy considering the expected rise in migration. In this context, one might ask whether, and to what extent, the location factor affects the situation of regions located on the border with a country at war? How are border regions able to cope with

DOI: 10.4324/9781003471646-10

extreme situations? How does refugee migration change the labour market on the Polish-Ukrainian border? The authors of the book attempted to answer this question by presenting research findings from various economic perspectives (regional, local, and cross-border), as well as in relation to various regional actors. Our main area of interest is war refugees arriving in Poland, rather than economic migrants. "Refugee" is a term used in legislation. It was defined in the 1951 Convention relating to the Status of Refugees. A refugee has a well-founded fear of imminent danger and cannot return home or is afraid of returning (Baszczak et al., 2023).

This monograph presents an integrative approach from the point of view of academic disciplines and the international Polish-Ukrainian composition of the research team. Finding partners to cooperate on an interdisciplinary basis is a challenge facing contemporary projects. Based on the results of our research, we present the opinion that the Polish-Ukrainian border region faces numerous challenges in the context of the polycrisis in the following areas: regional development, migration policy, institutional development, and strengthening relations in the cross-border area. Accordingly, in the first part, we summarise our conclusions referring to the theoretical aspects presented in Chapter 2, and then we present implications for the institutions of labour markets and local governments, as well as limitations and directions for future research.

10.1 Challenges for Researchers in the Light of Research on the Polish-Ukrainian Border

The questions formulated by contemporary economists as well as researchers dealing with regional analysis, in light of the sometimes groundbreaking findings of studies on regions over the previous centuries, present analogous dilemmas, while issues related to regional development present fundamental similarities. Unfortunately, categorical answers to issues such as the sources of regional differentiation, the degree of innovation, different anti-fragility, or institutional development remain thin on the ground. On the contrary, every progress, regardless of its nature, whether technological or otherwise, implies the emergence of new questions and the complexity of the problems to be solved.

In the context of these developments, significant turning points include events such as the conflict between Russia and Ukraine, as well as its ramifications. The dynamics of socio-economic and geopolitical processes mean that established beliefs are subject to criticism, dominant certainties are overturned, and valued worldviews are subject to revision. New factors influencing regional development, such as dynamic migration processes, security problems, or diversified resilience, significantly determine the dynamics of regional progress. Taking into account available economic statistics, including GDP as a measure of economic growth only, the situation of border regions has changed quite significantly. The influencing factor is the overlap between crises related to the pandemic and the war in Ukraine. GDP growth in Polish border regions is lower than the national average, which results in a larger development gap, and the economy of the Lublin and Subcarpathian regions (the Polish-Ukrainian border region analysed here) is characterised by lower productivity according to gross value added per one employee. The most important macroeconomic traits in terms of regions of analysis (NUTS2) include (Statistics Poland):

- Global production is growing more slowly in these regions than in the country as a whole: in the years 2015–2019 in the Lublin Voivodeship by 24.96% (PLN 155,095 million in 2019, i.e., 3.31% of national production), in the Subcarpathian Voivodeship by 28.58% (PLN 172,767 million in 2019, i.e., 3.68% of national production). During this period, the increase in national global production amounted to 29.37% (PLN 4,691,699 million in 2019).
- A stronger impact of the COVID-19 pandemic on the dynamics and volume of global production (issues of economic adaptation), which exacerbated the disparity in the growth rate of global production in the analysed regions compared to the country as a whole. The slowdown in the growth rate in 2019–2020 was stronger in the Subcarpathian Voivodeship (a decrease of 1.56%), with an increase in the Lublin Voivodeship by 0.73% and a decrease in the entire country by 0.08%. At the same time, the GDP of the Subcarpathian Voivodeship responded more strongly to the stagnation caused by COVID-19 (y/y dynamics decreased in 2020 to 99.8% of the previous year's level) and generated a stronger rebound after the crisis than the country's average (y/y dynamics of 113.67% in 2021). In the Lublin Voivodeship, changes in GDP dynamics were synchronous with respect to the country.
- Regional GDP (at current prices) of the surveyed regions in 2021 at 3.70–3.86% of the national GDP: in the Lublin Voivodeship PLN 97,523 million (GDP per capita equal to PLN 47,611, i.e., 68.7% of the national average), in the Subcarpathian Voivodeship PLN 101,498 million (GDP per capita equal to PLN 48,544, i.e., 70.1% of the average in Poland). The growth dynamics of GDP per capita in 2019–2021 amounted to an average annual rate of 8.09% in Poland, 8.36% in the Lublin Voivodeship, and 7.72% in the Subcarpathian Voivodeship.
- Productivity of regional economies expressed in gross value added at current prices per employee is 77.0% of the national value in the Lublin Voivodeship and 80.1% in the Subcarpathian Voivodeship.
- A low level of entrepreneurship: in 2022, 1,752 businesses per 10,000 residents of working age in the Lublin Voivodeship (77.76% of the national average), and 1,642 businesses per 10,000 residents in this age group in the Subcarpathian Voivodeship (72.88% of the national average), compared to 2,253 businesses/10,000 people of working age nationwide.

The structure of work permits for foreigners differs from the national one (the most common sections are the same but in different proportions). In the Lublin Voivodeship, the most permits in 2021 were issued for section H (5,156: 39.7%), followed by F (4,050: 31.2%), while in the Subcarpathian Voivodeship, there were three main industries: F (2,831: 33.1%), N (2,608: 30.5%), and H (1,530: 17.9%). It should be emphasised that the labour markets in the border regions are less diversified and more focused on work in male-dominated professions (transport and warehousing – H, construction – F) than the national average. This situation, according to the study, does not encourage people to look for a job in this region. Finding niches in the labour market could attract other groups of migrants who are looking for employment in new innovative services. The challenge is to examine what areas of the economies of border regions could develop in the current climate of polycrisis. Currently, the Polish-Ukrainian border region is being transformed into a military, medical, and logistics hub, which, in cooperation with other important industries, could succeed in attracting human capital. Additionally, parallel action should be taken in terms of the economy and quality of life, which must be improved. Therefore, migrants ought to be relocated according to the profile of regional economies and of the migrants themselves.

Regardless of industry, on the Polish side of the Ukrainian border, wages are lower or significantly lower than Poland's average. Average net earnings in 2020 amounted to EUR 1,012 per month in the Lublin Voivodeship (EUR 12,140 per year, 89.3% of the national average), and EUR 978 per month (EUR 11,732 per year, 86.3% of the national average) in the Subcarpathian Voivodeship, compared to the average national salary of EUR 12,589 per year. Remuneration disparities compared to the national average are visible in every section of the economy but are the widest in the case of specialised services, especially two industries related to professional, scientific, and technical activities (section M, only 40.96–48.24% of the national average) and information and communication (section J, only 49.35–57.66% of the national average) – see Table 10.1. This means that salaries offered by employers in the border area are clearly less attractive compared to other regions of the country. The impact of spending by unregistered Ukrainian citizens, which stimulates regional economies and the development of entrepreneurship in border areas, is strongest within 50 km of the border (Cierpiał-Wolan, 2017). What needs to be examined in the context of the existing crisis, or even polycrisis, is the role played by cross-border clusters and the relations between businesses, including the Subcarpathian Aviation Cluster, in supporting the effect of economic gravity within the Carpathian Euroregion and especially for the global defence industry (Oleński, 2016).

Regional development is confronted by new challenges that must become a permanent part of the research area when building development models for regions with relatively weaker economic results than the national average and with different needs when it comes to improving competitiveness. Maintaining consistent resilience in the face of deepening crisis will not come

Table 10.1 Average annual wages by industry* in 2020 by economic sector

	Average annual wages by industry in 2020 (EUR** per employee)*											
	B	C	D	E	F	G	H	I	J	L	M	N
Poland	20662	11815	19040	12382	6780	8854	9115	6383	17187	9227	10084	10933
Lublin	16373	10233	15294	10832	5621	6894	6654	4748	9911	8865	4131	7991
Subcarpathian	17581	10762	17822	11417	5866	7278	6610	4991	8482	8166	4865	8014
% of national average (Poland = 100.00)												
Lublin	79.24	86.61	80.32	87.48	82.90	77.86	73.00	74.38	**57.66**	96.09	**40.96**	73.09
Subcarpathian	85.09	91.09	93.60	92.21	86.52	82.20	72.52	78.19	**49.35**	88.51	**48.24**	73,30

Source: Own elaboration based on Statistics Poland, Local Data Bank.

* selected industries: B – Mining and quarrying, C – Industrial processing, D – Production and supply of electricity, gas, steam, hot water and air for air conditioning systems, E – Water supply: sewage and waste management and activities related to recultivation, F – Construction, G – Wholesale and retail trade; repair of motor vehicles, including motorcycles, H – Transport and warehousing, I – Accommodation and catering services, J – Information and communication, L – Real estate services, M – Professional, scientific, and technical activities, N – Administration services and support.

** according to the average exchange rate of the National Bank of Poland on 31/12/2020: PLN/EUR = 4.6148 automatically from the market. Solidarity with border regions is needed to maintain their socio-economic development, which is primarily related to the quality of life and security of the people living there when faced with illegal migration. An important element of policy is the reconstruction of social capital – cooperation between Polish and Ukrainian businesses and the lack of trust that also arises when employing workers. These regional challenges and needs will intensify in the years to come, and so it is necessary to take action to provide flexible support for local governments in border areas.

Remuneration disproportions compared to the national average are visible in every section of the economy, most significantly in the case of specialised services, and in particular two industries related to professional, scientific, and technical activities (section M according to the Polish system of classifying businesses, only 40.96–48.24% of the national average) and information and communication (section J, only 49.35–57.66% of the national average) (Statistics Poland). This means that the salaries offered by employers in the border area are significantly less attractive when compared to other regions of the country. Furthermore, research on the competitiveness of the Polish-Ukrainian border area, including Ukrainian regions, in EU terms based on a three-factor competitiveness model that measures the state of the economy, knowledge, and creativity, as well as labour market efficiency, proves the substandard competitiveness of all administrative units of the Polish-Ukrainian border on both sides of the border and most regions of Poland (with the exception of the Masovian and Greater Poland Voivodeships) and Ukraine (except Kyiv), mainly for reasons related to the level of economic development. Regions of so-called new EU Member States as well as Greece, the southern regions of Italy, Spain, and Portugal have similar characteristics (Jakubowski et al., 2017) and are considered peripheral in terms of Europe as a whole (Domański, 2002). The authors also point to difficulties in identifying the reasons why these regions may potentially have a competitive advantage (Jakubowski et al., 2017). The issue of building competitiveness in regions that expect, first and foremost, equal opportunities in terms of socio-economic development is relatively often discussed in the literature (Smętkowski, 2015; Smętkowski et al., 2017). The challenge for regionalists is to explore the possibility of dual-track support that includes competitiveness and compensatory support for development gaps. This research vision needs to overlap with geopolitical scenarios that should build a strong region capable of development and open to investors. The role of investments already commenced – for example, Via Carpatia – is also important. However, due to political changes in Poland, their financing may be at risk. The involvement of regional governments, as well as poviats and municipalities, to some extent, in operational support for Ukraine's military potential – offered, inter alia, at Rzeszów Jesionka airport and in many other locations in the Subcarpathian and Lublin Voivodeships – may indicate new areas of specialisation for these regions and can be used to help reconstruct Ukraine. Such action may have a positive impact on the regional development of these areas, especially in terms of the labour market. A key venture would be, in cooperation with the Ukrainian side, to update the development strategy for the Lublin and Subcarpathian Voivodeships as well as poviat and municipal local governments, which might take into account future channels of support for the reconstruction process of Ukraine after the war with Russia.

In close relation to the aforementioned issue, the conclusion of our research is that neighbouring regions influence each other considerably, which means that in a situation of war crisis, the attractiveness of Polish regions bordering Ukraine is reduced. According to in-depth interviews, the Polish border region is also perceived as less attractive than the central regions. The low level of urbanisation (41% for the Subcarpathian Voivodeship and 46% for the Lublin Voivodeship, according to www. gus.gov.pl in 2021) and the fact that most job vacancies are in the SME sector mean that war refugees from Ukraine do not consider that this region offers good prospects for earning money. Nevertheless, it should also be noted that it is perceived positively as a place of temporary residence. Due to uncertainty regarding how long Ukrainian citizens intend to stay in Poland, when planning economic development, it is necessary to account for the following variants: the current situation will continue or more migrants will arrive.

The factors negatively influencing this assessment also include the peripheral location and close proximity to areas where local and regional cross-border cooperation is extremely limited by infrastructural factors (few border crossings and poor road infrastructure) and does not favour regional development. Border region residents mention the lack of sufficient municipal and social housing for refugees, growth in the commercial housing rental market, and the deficit of apartments for rent, as well as hikes in housing prices. Changes in housing policy must include refugees among the social groups that need support in this respect. Municipalities should have housing resources that they can use in crisis situations, or there should be mechanisms in place so that groups at risk of social exclusion – for instance, the homeless or war refugees – may rent cheap housing. Our study confirms the impact of living conditions on willingness to stay in a given place. In a borderland situation, housing issues are particularly difficult due to the structure of housing. Difficulties in finding independent accommodation have led to migrants declaring a desire to return to their homeland. Housing policy is an important factor influencing people's willingness to stay in a given place. Preferences in this regard can be used to attract specific groups of employees with skills the labour market needs (demographics). Also, the development structure of the borderland hinders relocating people to this area, which in turn makes it difficult for them to settle there. In the context of a potential increase in migration, housing policy should also be designed and implemented with migrants in mind (social/intervention housing).

One ought to mention that until the conflict escalated, tourism, as an area of cross-border cooperation, was developing relatively well in this region. This is confirmed by the following data on the financial value of projects run between 2014 and 2020, which are not yet complete, but the forecast total is EUR 175.8 million (Buchko, 2020). It was predicted that growth in tourist services per se may increase the number of arriving tourists from abroad, and this rise may result in an inflow of capital, lead to the creation of new jobs, enable the improvement of infrastructure, and ensure more intercultural communication (Buchko, 2020). The noticeable strong asymmetry in cross-border movement during the war reduced Polish citizens' interest in travelling to Ukraine due to the threat associated with military operations. Tourist arrivals at the Polish frontline border also dropped. After the end of the hostilities, efforts should be made to balance Polish-Ukrainian cross-border flow and, in particular, rebuild trade between the border regions of both countries, as well as support the development of cross-border tourism in order to revitalise the entire borderland. The factors inhibiting the development of the Polish-Ukrainian region under study include those of a geopolitical nature, such as the ongoing war in Ukraine since 2014, which escalated after February 2022, which is not conducive to building cross-border ties despite the enormous humanitarian aid given to Ukraine until the end of 2023. There is also the problem of threats of possible incidental attacks resulting from the location near the front. Investors also face numerous problems, such as unprepared land for investment, lack of legal assistance, etc.

The disparity (major asymmetry described in Chapter 4) in the socio-economic development in the border regions is not only due to differences in GDP per capita but primarily in the quality of life experienced by the inhabitants of Ukrainian regions and, currently, also frontline Polish regions. The development of the Lublelskie and Subcarpathian Voivodeships is largely determined by the economic situation on the Ukrainian side. The poorer socio-economic development of the regions bordering Ukraine is related not only to their peripheral location but also to the socio-economic situation of the neighbouring regions. There is also a close relationship between the development of these regions and the historical path of development (path dependence) (Loewen, 2018; Martin & Sunley, 2010). The threats related to the ongoing war make this region less attractive from an economic and security perspective. These regions are further blighted by the lowest rates of urbanisation across Poland's border regions, which is not perceived as an advantage by war refugees from Ukraine. How refugees from Ukraine perceive a given place is a fairly complex issue, since it is seen through the prism of housing availability, infrastructure, cost of living, personal contacts, previous experiences, etc., but above all through the "imagination" of these places. Therefore, for most refugees, border regions and small towns are less attractive due to associations with their own country. Large cities offer better access to public services such as education, health, and transport, which can be important for refugees. In March 2022, 70% of refugees arriving in Poland were located in cities (Wojdat & Cywiński, 2022), while in the case of Poland only in the Silesian Voivodeship does the proportion of urban residents exceed 70% (in 2022, according to the Central Statistical Office, this was 75.9%), whereas in the Lublin and Subcarpathian

Voivodeships this figure stands at a mere 46.2% and 41.1%, respectively (BDL Central Statistical Office).

The structure of the Polish-Ukrainian border region economies is characterised by a low level of automation as well as specialisations that require significant involvement on the part of employees. The vast majority of regional businesses claim staff shortages, but this applies to what are considered to be male-dominated professions (technical) in Polish society. There is a mismatch between refugees' skills, on the one hand, and staffing needs and shortages, on the other hand. No significant, up-to-date studies have been conducted in this particular area, especially in the context of the border area, which is a widely discussed issue in the case of internal EU regions (Åslund & Engdahl, 2018; Böhm & Opioła, 2019).

The idea of a better life in a big city, a dream shared by many refugees from Ukraine, works to the detriment of small and medium-sized cities. On a macroeconomic scale (EWL Migration Platform and EWL Foundation, 2023), social factors had the greatest impact on refugees' decision to move from Poland to Germany – for example, friends and family in Germany (43%). Material issues also played an important role – more attractive social benefits (42%), the possibility of saving more money (38%), and job offers with higher remuneration (27%). In turn, 26% of respondents decided to leave Poland due to better development prospects for their children in Germany. For only 16% of Ukrainian citizens, the main reason for further migration was the issue of greater security in Germany than in Poland.

Ukrainian diasporas in Poland have noticeably developed and grown in strength, a phenomenon that manifests features of internal differentiation, especially the current refugee wave from Eastern Ukraine (Jaroszewicz & Piechal, 2016). Our research shows that people from Western Ukraine (including Ukrainian-speaking people) are more willing to come to the border area. Potentially stronger historical differences between the migrant and indigenous peoples are, however, hampered by cultural proximity. It follows from this that efforts should be made to minimise tension and limit the escalation of potential animosities in the border regions. This area is noticeably more sensitive to conflict-related issues. Ukrainian war migration to Poland was characterised by (Długosz et al., 2022; Duszczyk & Kaczmarczyk, 2022; Gluszak & Trojanek, 2023; Jurek, 2022; Szaban, 2022; Zymin et al., 2022) as follows:

1 The demographic structure of migrants has changed.
2 The number of more educated migrants with varied professions increased.
3 The majority of refugees speak poor Polish.
4 The majority of refugees are from the northern and central regions of Ukraine, and relatively few of them came from Western Ukraine.
5 Treating Poland as the target country of stay for the period of hostilities.
6 Tendency to search for a place of residence in medium and large cities, a low tendency for re-allocation.
7 Finding permanent employment in Poland is not a priority for refugees.

Our research unquestionably confirms points 2, 3, 4, 5, 6, and 7 with regard to border regions:

2 Educational profile and qualifications require recognition.
3 Language command was weak at the beginning; the ability to learn the language was quick; however, in relation to previous periodic economic migrations (recurrent), the language command was poorer.
4 In the border region, refugees come from the west (to a lesser extent, the centre) and want to maintain relations with their families on the western side.
5 Strong indecision in the borderland as to whether to stay even until the end of the war (migrants consider leaving for other cities in Poland or the EU). However, most declare a willingness to return to Ukraine.
6 They definitely choose cities/towns but are considering relocation further west.
7 At the same time, performing work consistent with skills and experience enhances job satisfaction.

The nature of this migration is completely different from previous ones throughout the country, which largely confirms that the specificity of border regions is also related to their attractiveness to migrants. With regard to border regions, the migrants have specific traits that translate into separate recommendations:

- Organise support for potential reallocation.
- Assist with jobseeking in support positions in the public sector and services for people with higher qualifications, opening channels of information about market requirements.
- Organise language training in the first period as a response to communication difficulties mentioned by employers.
- Since there is a greater tendency to stay in the border area despite the worse wage conditions offered in the region due to non-financial motivations, provide support to guard against the effects of separation.
- In the border area, expect migrants to stay in Poland only/mainly temporarily.
- Because they are less willing to abandon the border region and secure better economic conditions elsewhere, greater social support (including monitoring their financial situation) should be considered for refugees from Ukraine remaining in the border area.

Research shows that directions of development in border regions are linked with new challenges in the context of emerging migration flows and the problem of illegal migration. These challenges can certainly involve policy in the following areas: real estate, pro-family, social, cultural, etc. This issue has implications for the theory of regional development, placing particular emphasis on the sustainable development of border regions while taking into account quality of life. This specific issue also includes proposals for instruments for regions with a separate economy, different regional statistics, and variations in the competence of regional and local authorities. For the domestic labour market, Ukrainian citizens constitute an important group, providing workers in sectors with structural shortages consistent with the skills and experience of those arriving in Poland. It is necessary to update regional development plans (as well as for the country's economic development) due to the shortage of employees in key sectors (e.g., construction and transport), as well as to take into account migration in local labour markets. It is also worth emphasising that Ukrainian citizens constitute the largest group of people working in Poland to apply for work permits (in 2021, they constituted 64.5% of foreigners obtaining a work permit in Poland). Their impact on the Polish labour market grew in the years 2014–2019, when there was a 12-fold increase in the number of permits issued. This group was dominated by young men (approx. 2/3), less educated, speaking Polish, and performing mainly manual work. In the period after the annexation of Crimea, the number of qualified technical workers and specialists gradually increased. The unemployment rate in 2022 in the largest host regions (WP, MZ, DS, SL, MA, and PM) after the return of significant numbers to Ukraine was within the natural unemployment rate (2.9–4.6%).

Poles and Ukrainians perceive problems related to the development of the Polish-Ukrainian border differently. For Ukraine, it is important that refugees and migrants return and bring with them new skills, experience, and financial resources. This is one of the conditions for rebuilding Ukraine and putting it back on the road to development. Relationships established during seasonal work made it easier for war refugees in 2022 to adapt. In Ukraine, a network of agencies has grown that help find people willing to work on a temporary or permanent basis (Kindler & Szulecka, 2022). Poland's location in the EU guarantees assistance, shelter, and temporary solutions to many problems of a humanitarian, financial, and military nature. The Polish perspective on this location is associated with threats, uncertainty, lack of cross-border cooperation, restrictions on tourist traffic, low border crossing capacity, etc. Insufficient cross-border cooperation between local governments on the Polish-Ukrainian border meant that the neighbouring communities were insufficiently prepared for cooperation in a crisis situation (e.g., insufficient knowledge of the language, legal regulations, etc.). Cross-border cooperation needs to be ramped up at the local government level, as well as between other social partners in order to take the experience of the refugee crisis and strengthen cooperation in areas important for both countries – for example, eliminating differences in educational and vocational training systems, increasing knowledge of the Polish and Ukrainian languages, cooperation in the field of crisis management, etc. These activities are particularly important in terms of starting the negotiation process and helping Ukraine become a candidate for joining the European Union. Therefore, the question arises about a further framework for cooperation that would benefit both parties. Undoubtedly, only regional policy instruments will be able to alleviate the growing problems.

Research on refugees from Ukraine who came to Poland has demonstrated that the regions of inflow are also the regions of outflow. The two-way nature of migration is highly relevant when it comes to monitoring the unstable situation on the labour and housing markets, as well as issues connected with social assistance, children joining Polish schools, healthcare, etc. Refugees' quality of life should be monitored, and, depending on their needs, there should be flexible options on how to respond to crisis situations. The literature (Błędowski & Krajewski, 2011; Janicki, 2015; Prytula et al., 2023) tends to think of border areas as regions of outflow, and therefore the current situation changes this standpoint quite significantly. In six EU countries, the number of Ukrainian citizens under temporary protection has decreased: in the Czech Republic (by almost 50,000 people), France (by almost 5,000), Sweden (by over 2,000), and Poland (by over 350,000) (EWL Migration Platform and EWL Foundation, 2023).

Research conducted in Poland as well as our study indicate that Ukrainian citizens in exile have a proactive attitude, which applies not only to work but also to cultural, social, and charitable activities. Refugees are particularly important for border regions to be able to fill labour shortages because these regions suffer from negative net migration as well as a lower degree of urbanisation than other regions in Poland. Employers employ Ukrainians as a means of growing their enterprises on a scale that allows us to conclude that this factor has a positive impact on entrepreneurship in the region and partially eliminates persistent difficulties in recruiting workers. Organisational incentives (housing and childcare) and relocation assistance may help stimulate entrepreneurship and economies in peripheral areas, but regions of low urbanisation are unattractive for refugees besides their proximity to the homeland.

Refugees (mostly women) found employment in professions that did not require special qualifications or confirmation of skills and experience, as well as in technical positions where there were labour shortages. They adapted to the local labour market and sought temporary shelter for the indefinite duration of the military threat. Refugees in the border region are often employed in jobs that do not match their needs or qualifications. When planning employment assistance, developments in the internal situation in Ukraine should be taken into account and monitored. The continuation of the conflict will result in an extension of the blockade on male workers crossing the border. The various possible endings of the conflict or events that are difficult to predict at the moment may significantly change the situation regarding the movement of labour across the Ukrainian border to Poland. Therefore, we need to be prepared for situations of crisis.

The conducted research shows that non-agricultural sectors are particularly attractive to migrants from Ukraine. The analysed border area is characterised by a relatively high proportion of employment in agriculture compared with Poland in general (e.g., 19.6% in the Lublin Voivodeship: https://gospodarka.lubelskie.pl/pl/struktura-zatrudczenia-1029), and so this is another factor limiting the attractiveness of job offers for migrants since migrants prefer jobs in non-agricultural sectors. In 2021, the following number of work permits were issued in the following employment sectors: F – 76,283 people, C – 74,433, H – 71,018, N – 69,303 (Public Employment Services Portal, Ministry of Family and Social Policy; https://psz.praca.gov.pl). The conclusion of this analysis is the need to build amenities for investors (the role of local governments in preparing infrastructure, marketing, and allocating land for investments in local spatial development plans).

Most refugees reported good physical health (8.5 on a scale from 1–10). Mental health was rated worse, especially among women (7.5), compared to 8.6 among men. The study was based on an analysis of personal self-assessment rather than medical or psychological tests. Assessment of state of health was directly proportional to the match between jobs and qualifications as well as job satisfaction. People forced to migrate coped with separation worse; mental health was rated the worst by those forced to emigrate due to safety threats or separation from their loved ones. The trauma of war and separation had a strong negative impact on the ability to focus and concentrate (intellectual work), willingness to socialise and leave the house, as well as the ability to sleep and get up in the morning. These criteria objectively indicate the difficulties felt by refugees in terms of functioning on a daily basis. There is a strong need for psychological support for all age groups and, if possible, to monitor the situation, especially since these are families that are experiencing traumatic separation.

Additionally, the dynamics and scope of labour migration from Ukraine to the EU in 2014–2021 were analysed. Key factors that influence the scope and destination chosen by citizens of non-EU countries are identified. While the working-age population is declining, migrants are filling vacancies and expanding the workforce. Modern migration policy should provide for more proactive measures and become more inclusive, which means that it is extremely important to identify what war refugees and economic migrants from Ukraine need in order to pursue their professional, scientific, and cultural ambitions, as well as to learn about the culture, religion, norms, and customs of Poland as well as how to write in Polish. The role of researchers is to examine the integration process and learn about expectations in order to significantly boost the attractiveness of Polish regions.

The period of COVID-19 restrictions largely influenced short-term stays in Poland related to local border traffic. Border regions that depended on everyday cross-border relations – for example, Ukrainians purchasing construction materials in the border zone or Poles buying fuel in Ukraine – have suffered. Within 50 km of the border, people used to shop for basic provisions. Due to the pandemic, war, and border controls, these activities have been curtailed. Border regions should be treated as connected vessels that benefit from mutual relations, differences in the economic level, price differences, cultural differences, etc. In the face of the war crisis in Ukraine, which looks as if it will be long-term, this disrupts natural cross-border movement and may develop in ways that are difficult to predict. That is why it is so important to support projects to build greater resilience in areas of small cross-border traffic too, and economic support limiting the impact of crisis should cover the entire relational system of the formal/informal economy in the border zone.

The Polish-Ukrainian border area is an area of untapped opportunities for scientific collaboration, including cooperation between universities and student exchange. The idea of building awareness among young people about the existence of a multicultural border university with a special programme for young Ukrainian adults may be an opportunity for young people from less wealthy families who cannot afford to cover living costs in other cities in Poland. Cultural and linguistic proximity is an advantage that makes it far easier to achieve this goal than, for example, opening a joint university, Collegium Polonicum, on the Polish-German border. Young people choosing to study in urban centres of the Subcarpathian Voivodeship (Przemyśl and Rzeszów) perceive the quality of education in Poland to be superior to their country of origin (Długosz, 2018), thus demonstrating a positive attitude towards education in Poland. The aim should be for various regional actors to cooperate in order to develop strategies to attract young people from Ukraine to Poland, as well as to help marketing campaigns run by labour market institutions that will yield tangible benefits for the development of these regions.

10.2 Conclusions for Stakeholders

The previously mentioned polycrisis and civilisational crisis both confirm the enormous complexity of the current situation and, therefore, the need to look for solutions that are flexible and transcend the current measures of institutional operation and organisation of assistance for migrants in Poland. The current situation requires us to show a special kind of solidarity with regions in crisis and not cling to existing solutions. They should constantly evolve towards being more agile. Many economists around the world are currently raising the issue of the crisis of civilisation. This is a situation in which old socio-economic models, rules, and recipes fail and become irrelevant, while new ones are lacking or are only just taking shape (Mączyńska, 2022). Unfortunately, the issue of "civilisational expansiveness" is still relevant. According to Kleer (2021), no civilisation, regardless of type or character, has ever been free from attempts to conquer societies belonging to the same or different civilisations. Suffice it to say that the current war in Ukraine is the tenth act of Russian aggression against other countries since 1992. Following this line of reasoning, the cooperation of local governments with labour market institutions in the face of the refugee crisis went significantly beyond what is defined by current legal provisions. Therefore, the conclusion of our research is that the legal provisions regarding the role of labour market institutions and local government units in Poland (counties and communes) should be amended to foster better coordination of cooperation in the process of helping refugees join the Polish labour market and, in the future, other groups of migrants. Further in the text, conclusions are formulated for local governments, labour market institutions, and then for entrepreneurs.

Data from the Polish Border Guard show that in 2022, 13.7 million foreigners crossed the Polish state border, of whom 8.7 million were refugees from Ukraine crossing the border after the outbreak of war with Russia. A significant number – 3.7 million people – entered Poland via border crossings in the Lublin Voivodeship (Kawałko, 2023). At the same time, almost 11.7 million foreigners left Poland, of whom 6.8 million were Ukrainian citizens, including over 2.9 million refugees returning to their own country through the border crossings in the Lublin Voivodeship. The main recipients of aid given during the peak period of migration from Ukraine were private individuals – 67.1% of all NGOs operating in Poland offered help (Bojanowski et al., 2023). In total, social economy entities offered assistance to approximately 8.0 million recipients (however, the same person could have been multiple recipients of various types of aid). However, not only private individuals were helped but also the Ukrainian equivalent of non-profit organisations, Ukrainian hospitals, orphanages, local and professional governments, and assistance was given to animals living in the conflict area, which also suffered greatly as a result of the warfare. On average, one non-profit organisation assisted 447 recipients, but in half of the cases, there were no more than 21 beneficiaries. Organisations offering assistance in Poland alone counted 5.2 million recipients; those operating in both countries had 2.6 million recipients, while Ukraine-based operations helped 0.1 million recipients (Bojanowski et al., 2023).

Institutions that played a particularly active role on the labour market and were considered in the study included local governments, poviat labour offices, voivodeship labour offices, and non-governmental organisations. The synergetic endeavours of these institutions helped control the rather difficult situation at the border. It is also worth emphasising the role of churches, schools, and all Polish residents who showed great empathy towards the situation. The first to come into contact with refugees were local governments located in border municipalities. Local governments played a significant role in helping refugees. They were the ones who offered hot meals, transport, accommodation, medical, and social assistance on the first front line while people were fleeing Ukraine. It did not take long for non-governmental organisations to join their ranks. It should be emphasised that cooperation between local governments and other local partners, such as non-governmental organisations, has proven to be extremely effective in offering comprehensive support for refugees, thanks to the simplification of certain procedures for outsourcing public tasks to NGOs. Basically, each municipality organised assistance with its available resources in a different way. Office workers, young people, and various institutions took part. Very often, local government representatives would emphasise that they mainly helped organise further transport or offer meals. A national policy for solving the problems of war migrants and political refugees should be developed in collaboration with various stakeholders, providing those who meet the required criteria with support so they may lead independent lives in Poland and integrate into Polish society.

Often those who came to the border region were from areas not affected by the hostilities. In the surveys, local governments in the border area mentioned a variety of different experiences when it came to cooperating with municipalities in Ukraine. This is due to the fact that in the Lviv region, especially its western part, nationalist sentiments run high, in the opinion of respondents. Respondents from Przemyśl mentioned that they cooperate closely with patriotic organisations from the borderland region and scouts, and in this spirit of cooperation, they do encounter some difficulties and come across Bandera flags. There are many repatriates from the east in the border areas. In the first weeks of the war, most refugees – from Kharkiv and Kyiv – reached Przemyśl, while inhabitants of western Ukraine did not arrive in significant numbers. The Jarosław district, which is also close to the border, has partners, but only in Transcarpathian areas (people of Hungarian origin). This frays relationships and explains the lack of prior cooperation. However, this was not an obstacle to providing aid in the war crisis. Active assistance from local governments is also to be a permanent feature throughout 2023.

The wave of war migration from Ukraine resulted in legislative changes regarding this specific target group (Act of 12 March 2022). Poland does not have a comprehensive migration policy that also regulates the issue of bringing refugees onto the labour market. There are no specific labour market instruments specifically for refugees and no specific details regarding sources of financing such programmes. The current global geopolitical situation should be an incentive to work on developing a comprehensive migration policy for Poland, taking into account various aspects of hosting refugees, including their integration with society and the labour market. Such action should primarily draw from the experience gained from the 2022–2023 refugee crisis and the positive experiences of other countries such as Germany, where employment offices are the main means of bringing refugees onto the job market and civic patrons mentor the refugees, and the USA, where private and public institutions cooperated towards the rapid inclusion of refugees in labour market (Deloitte, 2022). The recommendations of the European Commission should also be followed (e.g., the EC communication of 14 June 2022 containing guidelines on access to the labour market, vocational education and training, and adult education in the case of people fleeing the Russian war of aggression against Ukraine). Polish migration policy should be formed in accordance with territorial factors – in cooperation with countries neighbouring Poland.

Labour market institutions were not organisationally prepared to work with refugees and were unaware of the specifics of war migration (women with children, elderly people, and disabled people), which made it difficult to tailor support to the real needs of the refugees. There was also a lack of understanding of the specific situation of refugees after arriving in Poland (their hierarchy of needs). The research shows that knowledge and experience gleaned from the 2022–2023 refugee crisis should be used to provide labour market institutions with appropriate know-how regarding how to work with refugees in terms of regional and local labour markets, and this includes the following:

- Establish independent research institutions that offer advice on various at-risk areas of the economy, including migration. The experience of other countries shows that such institutes are highly effective at developing guidelines for regional development.
- Monitor the situation on the labour market, especially in the face of a shortage of workers and limited support from the Polish budget, in order to bring refugees into the job market, especially in industries that suffer from a labour shortage, for example by creating conditions for the professional reorientation of refugees.
- Treat war refugees as a separate target group in terms of joining the labour market.
- Specify the scope of tasks that should be performed by labour market institutions towards refugees and define the relations and dependencies between them, as well as establish a targeted, multi-level method of coordinating these activities from the national, regional, and down to the local level.
- Prepare internal procedures for action to be taken by individual labour market institutions in response to a similar crisis in the future, or other crisis scenarios, e.g., climate refugees.
- Track the professional careers of refugees in Poland in order to learn more about the kind of work performed by migrants.

Ukrainian refugees' needs have evolved since February 2022. Initially, psychological help turned out to be necessary, which helped refugees to make further decisions regarding whether they wanted to continue their journey or stay where they were, etc. The conducted research shows that career advisors and employment agents representing district labour offices were psychologically and professionally unprepared to work with war refugees (communication skills, empathy, ability to overcome the language barrier and build trust with refugees) so that they might devise their own action plans; nor did they sufficiently take into account factors such as short planned stays in Poland, poor mental condition and post-traumatic stress, lack of motivation to seek jobs, etc. It is necessary to develop a range of training and other forms of professional development to build a body of public employees prepared to work with refugees, including career advisors and employment agents. From the point of view of existing needs, it is important to help people who work with refugees and create a motivational system for them to undertake such difficult work. Such teams could be established on an ad hoc basis, but it is important that they are ready and able.

Labour market institutions involved in supporting refugees generally worked within the scope provided for by law, but in practice the need arose to provide refugees with comprehensive support such as child care for working refugees, organising PESEL numbers – Polish personal ID numbers – for them with the help of the local government, or psychological help provided by an NGO. This required cooperation with many other public institutions (e.g., local governments), commercial businesses, and social organisations (NGOs), as well as private individuals (volunteers), none of which was yet sufficiently regulated by law. The research shows that it is necessary to formally regulate and specify transparent principles of cooperation and partnership between various actors who should be involved in providing comprehensive support to refugees on the labour market, and in particular the principles of cooperation of public employment services with businesses and social organisations, as well as informal groups (e.g., volunteers), including the rules for financing the programmes run by such partners to help refugees join the labour market.

Undoubtedly, one of the key elements necessary for local governments to work more effectively is the issue of information flow, data collection, and analysis. The possibilities offered by modern technologies, in particular personal communication devices, provide better solutions for communication flow between the city and citizens and the collection of feedback. Help for refugees was based intuitively on tasks coordinated by labour market institutions, especially voivodeship labour offices and poviat labour offices. Nevertheless, complete knowledge about all refugee support instruments offered by various labour market actors throughout Poland was lacking, as was full information flow. It is necessary to analyse the cooperation between various labour market institutions during the 2022–2023 refugee crisis and develop a nationwide system for coordinating action and information flow on all refugee support instruments offered by various labour market actors.

During the refugee crisis, a number of tools were developed to help refugees, which provided them with effective assistance – for instance, launching a network of information points, individual action plans, creating a diversified range of job opportunities (short- and long-term), mapping potential employment opportunities for refugees, informing employers about the benefits related to employing Ukrainians, etc. Many innovative projects were implemented, including ones co-financed by the EU, which tested innovative support tools or combined various existing forms of support in an innovative way. Polish legislation defining labour market instruments and forms of support for jobseekers should be analysed, and instruments that were used during the refugee crisis ought to be permanently included, along with other instruments such as those recommended by the European Commission, to ensure a better response to the needs of specific target groups in labour market – for example, war refugees.

Bringing refugees into the labour market also resulted in positive, large-scale organisational changes in Polish public employment services, i.e., mutual learning, enhanced organisational agility, less resistance to change, greater openness to innovations on the labour market, as well as the development of a network of cooperation with many public, social, and business. The organisational changes that have occurred in Polish public employment services as a response to the refugee crisis should be appreciated and promoted positively as good practices, thereby improving the ability of labour market institutions to respond to crises and disruptions in the labour market. The refugee crisis has revealed that labour market institutions still prefer individual contact with clients and independent searches for job offers for the unemployed, while research has shown that most refugees look for work online on social media. Employees of labour market institutions should develop digital skills to communicate with the unemployed via electronic media to make their work more effective by, for example, focusing on profiled support for refugees, while publishing as much information as possible via electronic media.

The refugee crisis revealed that labour market institutions themselves reached out to employers with employment offers for refugees because, currently, few employers look for employees via such institutions. A much more popular method is to use websites such as www.pracuj.pl. So, it was necessary to re-establish relationships with many businesses about which labour market institutions had no current information. Public employment services should strive to strengthen relations with employers on the local labour market and simplify the process of submitting offers to district labour offices. It is very important to provide employers with information about the professional profile of job-seeking refugees and non-financial motivators that are important to them (e.g., child care). The aim should be to increase the number of job vacancies for refugees submitted by employers to district labour offices, which could then be combined with offering refugees the support they need on the labour market – courses and training – which would relieve the employer of the financial burden of upgrading refugees' know-how.

Along with the action taken to assist refugees on the labour market, the Ukrainian language is also becoming more and more present in the public space – bilingual signs, translations of important notices for refugees, etc. A significant problem in bringing refugees into the workforce turned out to be the shortage of translators and Ukrainian language teachers, as most of the refugees did not know Polish. While potentially monitoring the directions of refugee inflow, databases should include people who can help labour market institutions in formal and informal communication with refugees in their own language. Organisations operating in Poland that bring together members of national minorities from the migrants' countries of origin can play a supporting role, as was the case with organisations representing the Ukrainian minority in Poland. NGOs managed to effectively promote employment, thus alleviating the potential harm of unemployment, and the social services they offered significantly assisted labour market institutions and local governments, contributing at the same time to the further deinstitutionalisation of social services.

Non-governmental organisations have such a flexible formal and legal status that they were able to combine activities related to the employment of migrants with other support – for instance, therapeutic assistance, nutrition, or accommodation – that labour market institutions could not offer. This created a greater synergy of assistance than if labour market institutions or local governments had acted alone. Due to the expected increase in the number of refugees in Poland in the coming years (as well as in other European societies), it is necessary to consider permanently involving social economy entities and NGOs in selected tasks such as the provision of selected social services in which they specialised during the refugee crisis after February 24, 2022.

It is also reasonable to consider changes to the procedures for selecting social economy entities to carry out specific outsourced work to extend their period of involvement in the provision of such services, and not only in order to obtain co-financing for a project that usually does not exceed three years. Based on positive examples of deinstitutionalising the system of providing social services for refugees, non-governmental organisations may be increasingly involved in, for example, vocational training, language learning, intercultural education, etc. Providing NGOs with permanent sources of financing for selected outsourced work will help them specialise further in this field and maximise their potential. It will also be beneficial to form a network with other partners representing various sectors involved in helping refugees find jobs in Poland (e.g., at the regional level), who may then swap experiences and learn together how to leverage their potential to best assist war refugees. Provincial labour offices might coordinate such a network.

Moreover, in order to collate all the information that is available about organisations providing various types of support for refugees and to consolidate data about their experience and potential, it will be necessary to create a database, which should be updated on an ongoing basis. NGOs offered social services for war migrants, based on their limited experience in this field gained before the outbreak of the war in Ukraine, and relying on volunteers. There was a lack of competent specialists who had been properly prepared to work with refugees. In order to maximise the institutional and human potential of NGOs to offer social services for refugees, employees, and volunteers should receive training and other forms of professional development. Action to prevent burnout among the volunteers and employees of these organisations should also be taken, and the government and local government administration should create a system of support.

Before the outbreak of the war in Ukraine, and even now, Poland did not have a comprehensive migration policy that also included how to bring refugees into the labour market in collaboration with partners from various sectors (public, commercial, and social), which in fact turned out to be the most effective solution in terms of providing comprehensive job support for refugees. The expected further influx of refugees to Poland and other countries in the region should prompt urgent action to develop a comprehensive Polish migration policy, taking into account the cooperation of a network – nationally, regionally, and locally – of partners representing the public, commercial, and social sectors while also assigning them appropriate roles. For example, social service organisations might help refugees achieve professional and social independence in the host country and strengthen their integration with the local environment.

Non-governmental organisations and other social economy entities did not have sufficient knowledge about the nature of the refugee crisis in Poland after the outbreak of the war in Ukraine; nor were they sufficiently aware of the situation on the labour market in Polish border regions. This made it difficult to tailor support to the actual needs of the refugees. Knowledge and experience from the 2022–2023 refugee crisis should be used to provide social services with appropriate know-how regarding how to work with refugees regionally and locally, taking into account the needs of the job market, for example, by taking the following steps:

- Informing them in advance about a possible increase in refugee arrivals to Poland.
- Monitoring the situation on the labour market, especially by using the potential of refugees interested in gaining employment, and informing third-party organisations able to help refugees fill job vacancies and reorient them professionally.

The changes taking place in Ukraine challenge the government to develop a comprehensive, modern programme to promote Polish culture – both traditional and contemporary. Such action is even more relevant because the positive attitude of Ukrainian society towards Poland and geographical proximity do not translate into good cultural awareness, especially in more distant regions (Rogoża & Nieczypor, 2023).

A number of good practices have been identified in Polish border regions regarding how NGOs might assist refugees and cooperate with partners from other sectors in order to, for example, organise reception points at the border with Ukraine, combine various forms of assistance offered to the same refugee by various social services such as the Lublin Social Committee to Aid Ukraine, launch a website matching job offers from local companies with supply from Ukrainian citizens, and to involve representatives of the Ukrainian national minority in Poland in action to support refugees. We recommend systematising good practices for helping refugees in order to assist other non-governmental organisations throughout Poland. An important task undertaken by NGOs during the refugee crisis was to provide education on cultural differences, accustoming refugees to life in Poland and Polish society to refugees. One example of this was the involvement of intercultural mentors to support refugees. This kind of action has become an important part of the process of integrating refugees and helping them lead an independent life in Poland. It is recommended that local governments take interest in intercultural education among urban or municipal communities in order to more effectively integrate migrants, as well as to counteract any manifestations of misunderstanding, hostility, or cultural conflict.

In the period immediately preceding the attack, in 2021, mainly male migrants worked in Poland. The situation changed dramatically in the first few weeks after the outbreak of the war – the mass flow of Ukrainians was two-way: men returned to Ukraine to their families and the army, while women, children, and elderly people began to arrive in Poland *en masse* looking for safety, which completely transformed the supply of foreign workers. Potential jobseekers should be monitored based on their country of origin and reasons for migration, and the flow of information between national and regional institutions should be improved. When analysing regional job markets, the major foreign groups should be taken into account. The forms of information flow should be more flexible (recording stays and job requirements).

Entrepreneurs constituted a separate group of respondents in this study, which revealed some important conclusions for their further operation. Data from the Polish Economic Institute show that 24% of companies in Poland felt that the war had severely impacted their operations. 36% felt a moderate and 40% a weak impact (Dębkowska et al., 2023), in particular all industrial processing enterprises, micro- and medium-sized construction companies, small commercial enterprises, large transport firms, accommodation, and catering businesses, medium-sized financial and insurance companies, as well as all professional, scientific, and technical enterprises. The impact of the war initially manifested in the loss of male economic migrants, who had strongly contributed to the Polish labour market after 2014. This dependence (international connection) was felt by approximately 60% of the companies surveyed by the PIE. An important recommendation in this context is to study dependencies and relationships regarding changes in the labour market. It is important to consider various scenarios of how the situation in Ukraine might play out in order to protect the national (Polish) labour market against harmful labour shortages (particularly in male-dominated professions).

Regional employers rate the match between the qualifications of war refugees and the needs of their companies as low. The mismatch is also confirmed by working refugees from Ukraine. Employers point out the need to incur additional costs for job training. At the same time, the refugees' inability to decide how long they will stay in Poland increases uncertainty regarding the employment of refugees. Employment costs are also reflected in the initial poorer work efficiency of employees – for instance, due to lack of knowledge of the Polish language. The attitude of employers depends to a large extent on the flexibility of their approach towards the refugees, whose work should be treated as a temporary supplement, especially in the border area.

Employers observed that mismatch between refugees' qualifications and the work performed resulted in higher turnover. To a large extent, the decision to employ them was made due to severe staff shortages. Employment was connected with market forces, arising from actual needs and difficulties in finding employees. The analysed Polish-Ukrainian region is generally a so-called "employees" market' featuring significant shortages of human resources. In order to maximise performance, the implication for entrepreneurs is to strive to match jobs with the needs of the refugees. This is also reflected in the costs of hiring and training employees. Employers should take into account the unspecified needs of refugees looking for work in Poland and their job instability and be prepared to train employees to meet their own needs.

Companies tended to look for employees through their own channels, while only five of them used the services of the employment office. In order for labour market institutions to better match qualifications and monitor the general situation, a recommendation may be to extend cooperation with labour market institutions (including PUP – the Polish government-run employment office) beyond searching for suitable employees, to areas such as training – for instance, language training before starting work (or in the first period).

Employers argue that financial incentives are the main concern for refugees/employees from Ukraine; bonuses or, to a lesser extent, an increase in remuneration are what count. Non-wage factors were applied less frequently. Wage factors have a greater impact on attracting refugees to work and maintaining employment than non-wage factors.

Companies generally did not run programmes to acclimatise employees – only five of them (over 10%) took measures to adapt employees to the Polish labour market. On the other hand, the migrants do not intend to stay in Poland for a long time. The issue of employment is also not improved by the asymmetric spatial distribution of migrants, who manifest a desire to concentrate in selected cities. Additionally, obtaining accommodation near the workplace or arranging childcare is problematic. Considering war migrants' social needs, border areas with a poor level of urbanisation and access to services are less attractive than highly urbanised regions. Managing the refugee migration process from an administrative, organisational, and regulatory perspective also requires (apart from the demand for labour and the type of vacancies on offer) spatial analysis and consideration of social and living issues.

Employers consider the main advantages of cooperation with refugees to be as follows: diligence in performance of assigned work, longer/more stable cooperation, and positive impact on turnover. However, some obstacles include the language barrier, excessive alcohol consumption mainly on days off and, consequently, intoxication or reduced effectiveness at work, short terms of employment with a relatively long period of training on the job. A positive assessment was more frequently given by labour-intensive businesses. Such companies noticed a positive impact on war migrants if they stayed with the company longer. Polish employers value the work of refugees and speak overwhelmingly positively in this regard. However, they emphasise the associated instability, which may impede strategic business planning.

10.3 Limitations and Directions for Future Research

All researchers who undertake to study a specific economic problem from a cross-border perspective face a particularly difficult task since they encounter many limitations, rooted in a lack of statistical coherence, and obstacles in the way of constructing comparative analyses. The difficulties are compounded by issues related to the particular situation in which Ukraine finds itself and its current problems, which have spread to nearby regions. Border regions and enterprises on either side of the border operate in separate and specific political, social, and cultural frameworks. Therefore, the quality of government operation is fundamental when it comes to assessing the situation, determining efficient infrastructure, institutions, and rationalisation of socio-economic policy, conducive to sustainably developing the economy and improving working conditions and quality of life (Mączyńska, 2022). Research difficulties are also related to the regions' openness to research, which has caused many problems during the ongoing war since February 2022. Therefore, this study is confined to the impact of war refugees on the labour market on the Polish side. Some topics that are very important, yet currently impractical to research, have been omitted regarding the effects of the outflow of labour from Ukraine, the resilience of individual regions, the issue of company relocation, etc. The Central Economic Information Centre indicates that there are 24,100 companies operating in Poland with Ukrainian capital – as much as 25% of all companies with foreign capital (Dębkowska et al., 2023). Businesses with German (10%), Belarusian (4%), Dutch (4%), or Chinese (4%) capital are less numerous. The crisis of the Ukrainian economy is associated with attacks by the aggressor and the escape of Ukrainian people and enterprises that do not see the possibility of developing in such circumstances (Olechnicka & Kniazevych, 2023). It is also worth mentioning that the migration of refugees from Ukraine is one element of migration from this country. At the same time, there is an influx of economic migrants, mainly women, who, forced by their difficult financial situation since the outbreak of the war, perform various jobs in Poland in order to send regular remittances to their families who remained in Ukraine (Prytula & Łaźniewska, 2023). This situation creates the basis for new discussions around the new challenges facing the studied Polish-Ukrainian border region. One may ask how the outlined situation affects the regional development of the border region on the Polish side. What problems are associated with the methodology of examining these regions as border regions? What features of this region generate new implications for the concept of regional development?

The theory of regional development incorporates various trends, methods, and instruments for explaining socio-economic reality. The selection of research methods and their application are the basis of a long-standing dispute in the literature about measuring the "wrong things" – i.e., economic growth rather than socio-economic development. This raises the question of searching for other ways of measuring economic development. This problem was also encountered by the authors of a study who used GDP per capita to compare, for example, the competitiveness of border regions on the Polish-Ukrainian border. It is essentially the only statistic that is so widely available at a regional level as well as comparable in international contexts. In relation to the study of cross-border processes, such as the process of the flow of refugees from Ukraine, there is the issue of the availability of open-access data that might complement the material collected through surveys. The basic challenge that arises in terms of statistical material for conducting cross-border comparative studies enabling a broader analysis of the situation is the issue of collecting data, for example, at border crossings, and making them available on official websites in a systematic way. Such statistical material, presented more broadly in terms of subject matter, could be valuable for conducting regional development policy, developing the labour market, as well as a sustainable migration policy. At the same time, one might mention the apparent lack of interest in gathering data and poor dissemination of this information for the purposes of shaping migration policy. This is a challenge comparable to the modern achievements of the digital economy, but it is absolutely achievable. However, it can certainly be assumed that this future world will not be free from economic crises, despite the expected progress in economists recognising and understanding their essence and causes (Mączyńska, 2022).

The presented considerations do not exhaust the subject matter nor represent the entirety of the extensive knowledge on the problem under consideration. There are many identified problems left to be investigated. In parallel, apart from this monograph, its authors have written numerous articles, which supplement the presented area of consideration but focus more on aspects of the analysis of statistical material. At the time of completing this work, the war in Ukraine has been ongoing for two years, and its effects are increasingly affecting the economies of neighbouring countries.

References

Åslund, O., & Engdahl, M. (2018). Open borders, transport links, and local labor markets. *International Migration Review*, *53*(3), 706–735. https://doi.org/10.1177/0197918318789067

Assadourian, E. (2023). From Polycrisis to Permacri- Sis, Resilience. https://www.resilience.org/stories

Baszczak, Ł, Wincewicz, A., & Zyzik, R. (2023). *Polacy i ukraińcy – Wyzwania integracji uchodźców*. Polski Instytut Ekonomiczny. https://pie.net.pl/wp-content/uploads/2023/05/Wyzwania-integracji-.pdf

Błędowski, P., & Krajewski, P. (2011). *Migracje a rynek pracy w województwie lubelskim: Rekomendacje opracowane w ramach projektu: Praca zbiorowa*. Instytut Nauk Społeczno-Ekonomicznych.

Böhm, H., & Opioła, W. (2019). Czech-Polish cross-border (non) cooperation in the field of the labor market: Why does it seem to be un-de-bordered? *Sustainability (Switzerland)*, 11(10), 2855. https://doi.org/10.3390/su11102855

Bojanowski, T., Celiński, P., Iwańczyk, P., Kułakowski, M., Szewczak, M., Rybikowski, K., & Wieczorek, K. (2023). *Raport o pomocy polskich organizacji pozarządowych dla Ukrainy*. Warszawa.

Buchko, Z. (2020). Cross-border Ukrainian–Polish cooperation in the sphere of tourism. *Economic and Regional Studies/Studia Ekonomiczne i Regionalne*, *13*(3), 271–283. https://doi.org/10.2478/ers-2020-0020

Cierpiał-Wolan, M. (2017). Wpływ dynamicznych przemieszczeń ludności na rozwój społeczno-gospodarczy polsko-ukraińskich obszarów transgranicznych. In *Wyzwania rozwojowe pogranicza polsko-ukraińskiego*. Norberinum.

Dębkowska, K., Kłosiewicz-Górecka, U., Szymańska, A., & Wejt-Knyżewska, A. (2023). *Wpływ wojny w Ukrainie na działalność polskich firm*. Polski Instytut Ekonomiczny.

Deloitte (2022) *Uchodźcy na rynku pracy w Polsce*. chrome-extension://efaidnbmnnnibpcajpcglclefindmkaj/https://www2.deloitte.com/content/dam/Deloitte/pl/Documents/Reports/pl_Uchodzcy_Na_Rynku_Pracy.pdf

Długosz, P. (2018). Integracja ukraińskich studentów podejmujących naukę w Polsce. *Studia Migracyjne-Przegląd Polonijny*, *2*, 67–92.

Długosz, P., Kryvachuk, L., & Izdebska-Długosz, D. (2022). *Problemy ukraińskich uchodźców przebywających w Polsce*.

Domański, (2002), *O ruchliwościspołecznej w Polsce*. Warszawa

Duszczyk, M., & Kaczmarczyk, P. (2022). Paweł. War and migration: The recent influx from Ukraine into Poland and possible scenarios for the future. *CMR Spotlight*, 4(39).

EWL Migration Platform and EWL Foundation (2023) https://ewl.com.pl/en/report-from-poland-to-germany-new-trends-in-ukrainian-refugee-migration/ (23.04.24)

Gluszak, M., & Trojanek, R. (2023). War in Ukraine, Refugee Crisis, and Housing Market in Poland. *Refugee Crisis, and Housing Market in Poland*.

Jakubowski, A., Bronisz, U., & Miszczuk, A. (2017). Polityka spójności oraz Europejski Instrument Sąsiedztwa i Partnerstwa jako narzędzia wsparcia współpracy transgranicznej na wewnętrznych i zewnętrznych granicach Unii Europejskiej. *Roczniki Nauk Społecznych*, *45*(3), 73–89.

Janicki, W. (2015). Migracje kompensacyjne jako czynnik wzrostu obszarów peryferyjnych. Rola ukrytego kapitału ludzkiego. Wydawnictwo UMCS.

Jaroszewicz, M., & Małynowska, O. (2018). *Najnowsza migracja z Ukrainy do Polski: (Nie)stały fenomen?* Fundacja Batorego.

Jaroszewicz, M., & Piechal, T. (2016). Ukrainian migration to Poland after the 'Revolution of Dignity': old trends or new exodus? In Drbohlav D. & Jaroszewicz M. (Eds.), *Ukrainian migration in times of crisis: Forced and labour mobility* (s. 87–88). Charles University Faculty of Science.

Jurek, K. (2022). Polish labour market for refugees from Ukraine. *Kultura Bezpieczeństwa. Nauka – Praktyka – Refleksje*, 42, 8–17.

Kawałko, B. (2023) *II RAPORT o Pomocy udzielonej Ukrainie przez województwo lubelskie*. Lublin.

Khrystyna, P., Łaźniewska, E., Maksymenko, A., Kalat, Y., & Demedyuk, O. (2023). Increasing local community resilience in the EU-Ukraine cross-border area. *Studia Regionalne i Lokalne*, 2.

Kindler, M., & Szulecka, M. (2022). Messy arrangements? A social networks perspective on migrant labor brokerage: The case of Ukrainian migration to Poland. *Polish Sociological Review*, *4*, 457–484.

Kleer, J. (2021). *Ekonomiczne i społeczne skutki przesileń cywilizacyjnych*. INE PAN.

Loewen, B. (2018). *Towards Territorial Cohesion? Path Dependence and Path Innovation of Regional Policy in Central and Eastern Europe*.

Mączyńska, E. (2022). Cywilizacyjne Przesilenie i Społeczny, Gospodarczy (Nie)Ład. *Biuletyn PTE*, *97*.

Mączyńska, E. (2023). Zarządzanie w cyfrowej erze samotności. *Biuletyn PTE*, 1(100).

Martin, R., & Sunley, P. (2010). The place of path dependence in an evolutionary perspective. *The Handbook of Evolutionary Economic Geography*, *438*(4), 62–93. https://doi.org/10.1093/jeg/lbl012

Olechnicka, A., & Kniazevych, A. (2023). *Relokacja firm high-tech w wyniku wojny. Perspektywa ukraińsko-polska*. https://www.euroreg.uw.edu.pl/dane/web_euroreg_seminary_files/2306/olechnicka_seminarium_euroreg_12.10.23_presentation.pdf

Oleński, J. (2016). Typology of transborder economies and the need of transborder statistics in globalized world. *Transborder Economics. International Journal on Transborder Eco-Nomics, Politics and Statistics*, *1*.

Platforma Migracyjna, E. W. L., & Fundacja, E. W. L. (2023). Z Polski do Niemiec. *Nowe trendy ukraińskiej migracji uchodźczej*. Warszawa.

Prytula, K., & Łaźniewska, E. (2023). Modern trends and challenges of the development of adjacent border regions of Ukraine and Poland. *Efektivna Ekonomika*, (5). https://doi.org/10.32702/2307-2105.2023.5.8

Prytula K., Łaźniewska E., & Efektivna E. (2023). Modern trends and challenges of the development of adjacent border regions of Ukraine and Poland, nr 5, s.1–18. DOI:10.32702/2307-2105.2023.5.8

Rogoża, J., & Nieczypor, K. (2023). *Do Polski Przez Polski Fenomen Popularności Języka Polskiego Na Ukrainie*. Centre For Eastern Studies. https://www.osw.waw.pl/sites/default/files/Raport-OSW_Do-Polski-przez-polski_net_1.pdf

Smętkowski, M. (2015). Zróżnicowanie i dynamika rozwoju regionów Europy Środkowo-Wschodniej w okresie prosperity i kryzysu. *Prace Komisji Geografii Przemysłu Polskiego Towarzystwa Geograficznego*, *29*(2), 37–52.

Smętkowski, M., Olechnicka, A., & Płoszaj, A. (2017). Współpraca Naukowa Jako Element Potencjału Innowacyjnego Regionów Europejskich. *Studia Regionalne i Lokalne*, *67*(1), 5–25. https://doi.org/10.7366/1509499516701

Szaban, D. (2022). Ukrainian migrants on the Polish labour market: HRM selected issues. *Journal of Eastern Europe Research in Business and Economics*, *2022*. https://doi.org/10.5171/2022.813170

Tooze, A., & Fertik, T. (2014). The world economy and the great war. *Geschichte Und Gesellschaft*, *40*(2), 214–238. https://doi.org/10.13109/gege.2014.40.2.214

Wojdat, M., & Cywiński, P. (2022). *Urban Hospitality: Great Growth, Challenges and Opportunities. Report on Refugees from Ukraine in the Largest Polish Cities*. Centrum Badań i Analiz. Unia Metropolii Polskich. https://ec.europa.eu/migrant-integration/system/files/2022-04/Ump_Ukraina_RAPORT_final_2.pdf

Zymin, A., Kowalski, M., Karasińska, A., Lytvynenko, O., Dąbrowska, E., Bryzek, S., Gliński, P., & Koszykowska, D. (2022). *Special Report. Refugees from Ukraine in Poland*. Platforma Migracyjna EWL, Fundacja na Rzecz Wspierania Migrantów na Rynku Pracy „EWL" i Studium Europy Wschodniej Uniwersytetu Warszawskiego. https://ec.europa.eu/migrant-integration/system/files/2022-04/Raport%20Specjalny%20Uchod%C5%BAcy%20z%20Ukrainy%20w%20Polsce.pdf

Index

Note: Page references in *italics* denote figures and in **bold** tables.